3 36
Cop

FAMILY CHILD CARE
2015 Tax Workbook & Organizer

Being a Family Child Care Professional

Family child care is a special profession for those who love young children. As a professional family child care provider, you must balance the skills required to care for children with those required to operate your business. Here are some tips that will keep your family child care business as healthy and successful as possible:

- Learn the child care regulations for your area, and follow them.

- Join your local family child care association.

- Sign up with your local child care resource and referral agency.

- Join the Child and Adult Care Food Program (CACFP).

- Find good professional advisers (such as a tax professional, insurance agent, and lawyer).

- Participate in training to acquire and improve your professional skills.

Additional Resources

Redleaf Press (www.redleafpress.org; 800-423-8309) publishes resources for family child care professionals. Redleaf Press offers the following publications to support your business:

- Starting a family child care business:
  Family Child Care Business Planning Guide

- Promoting your business:
  Family Child Care Marketing Guide, 2nd edition

- Creating contracts and policies:
  Family Child Care Contracts and Policies, 3rd edition
  Sharing in the Caring: Agreement Packet for Parents and Providers
  The Redleaf Complete Forms Kit for Family Child Care Professionals

- Keeping accurate records and filing your taxes:
  Family Child Care Record-Keeping Guide, 9th edition
  The Redleaf Calendar-Keeper: A Record-Keeping System for Family Child Care Professionals
  Family Child Care Tax Workbook and Organizer
  Family Child Care Tax Companion

- Reducing business risks:
  Family Child Care Legal and Insurance Guide

- Managing your money and planning for retirement:
  Family Child Care Money Management and Retirement Guide

FAMILY CHILD CARE

2015 Tax Workbook & Organizer

TOM COPELAND, JD

Redleaf Press®
www.redleafpress.org
800-423-8309

Tom Copeland is a licensed attorney and has conducted tax workshops for family child care providers since 1982. In 2014, his website (www.tomcopelandblog.com) was chosen as one of the top 50 money management blogs in the country by Direct Capital, a national financing company. In 1998, he won the Child Care Advocate of the Year award from the Minnesota Licensed Family Child Care Association. In 2003, he received the Friend of the National Association for Family Child Care (NAFCC) award from NAFCC. In 2004, Tom received the Advocate of the Year award from NAFCC. Tom is the author of *Family Child Care Business Planning Guide*, *Family Child Care Contracts and Policies*, *Family Child Care Legal and Insurance Guide* (with Mari Millard), *Family Child Care Marketing Guide*, *Family Child Care Money Management and Retirement Guide*, *Family Child Care Record-Keeping Guide*, and *Family Child Care Tax Companion*. These publications are available from Redleaf Press. Tom Copeland can be reached by e-mail at tomcopeland@live.com, by phone at 651-280-5991, or through his website at www.tomcopelandblog.com.

Published by Redleaf Press
10 Yorkton Court
St. Paul, MN 55117
www.redleafpress.org

Cover design by Jim Handrigan
Cover photograph © iStockphoto.com/DNY59
Typeset in Times
Printed in the United States of America
ISBN 978-1-60554-444-1

DISCLAIMER
This publication is designed to provide accurate information about filing federal tax returns for family child care providers. Tax laws, however, are in a constant state of change, and errors and omissions may occur in this text. We are selling this publication with the understanding that neither Redleaf Press nor the author is engaged in rendering legal, accounting, or other professional services. If you require expert legal or tax assistance, obtain the services of a qualified professional. Because each tax return has unique circumstances, neither the author nor Redleaf Press guarantees that following the instructions in this publication will ensure that your tax return is accurate or will enable you to find all the errors on your tax return. In addition, this book addresses only tax issues related to family child care. This publication is to be used for filling out 2015 tax forms only. For information on how to fill out tax forms after 2015, please consult later editions of this publication.

Contents

Acknowledgments

Thanks to the many tax preparers who helped answer my questions for this edition and for previous editions. Any errors in this book are my responsibility.

Thanks to David Heath and Alyssa Lochner for their editorial and production help.

Readers may contact Tom Copeland directly by e-mail at tomcopeland@live.com, by phone at 651-280-5991, or through his website at www.tomcopelandblog.com.

Highlights of the New Tax Laws

- There has been a significant change in how the IRS defines a repair and a home improvement. It has expanded the definition of a repair to possibly include items such as windows, doors, fence, patio, driveway, wood/tile floors, and some remodeling. The result is that many providers will be able to deduct in one year thousands of dollars worth of these items, rather than depreciating them. See page 74.

- Providers may deduct in one year items that cost less than $2,500 as long as the proper tax statement is attached to their tax return. See page 74.

- Only a very few providers should use the Simplified Method to claim house-related expenses. For details, see chapter 2.

- The standard meal allowance rates for 2015 are $1.31 breakfast, $2.47 for lunch and supper, and $0.73 for snacks. The rates are higher for Alaska and Hawaii. For details, see chapter 4.

- The standard mileage rate for 2015 is $0.575 per business mile. For details, see page 130.

- The income eligibility limits for the Earned Income Credit have increased to $44,651 (for married couples filing jointly with one child) and $39,131 (if single with one child). For details, see page 139.

- The income limits to qualify for the IRS Saver's Credit has increased to $61,000 (adjusted gross income) for couples filing jointly; $45,750 for heads of household; and $30,500 for individuals or married people filing separately. For details, see page 141.

Introduction

The purpose of the *Family Child Care Tax Workbook and Organizer* is to guide you as you prepare your federal tax forms for your family child care business. Since this book covers only the federal income tax rules and forms, you may also need to complete additional forms for your state and local tax returns. Because the tax laws can change every year, the *Tax Workbook and Organizer* is updated each year to reflect the latest changes in the tax rules and forms. For this reason, it's important to use only the current year's edition of this book.

Note: Family child care providers who operate as a partnership or corporation should not use this book to file their taxes because they must use different tax forms. Providers who are set up as a single-person limited liability company (LLC) will use all the forms as described in this book.

Getting Help

The *Family Child Care Tax Workbook and Organizer* is designed to enable you to fill out important tax forms for your business. The following resources are available if you need further help:

Getting Help from the IRS

- Call the IRS Business and Specialty Tax Line at 800-829-4933 with your questions. This number is for business-related questions. Tax help is also available at IRS offices nationwide.

- Visit the IRS website (www.irs.gov) to download tax forms, publications, and instructions or to search for answers to your questions.

- You can call 800-829-3676 to order a free copy of any IRS publication or form. Many post offices and libraries also carry the more common IRS forms and instructions.

- If you are running out of time, you can get a six-month extension (to October 15) to file your taxes. You must still pay the taxes you owe by April 15 or pay interest on the amount you owe.

- For a list of IRS resources, revenue rulings, court cases, and publications relevant to family child care providers, see appendix B.

Getting Help from a Tax Professional

- If you need help finding a tax professional, visit my website (www.tomcopelandblog .com) for a tax preparer directory.

Finding IRS Publications and Other Resources

- For copies of all the relevant IRS publications, tax forms, revenue rulings, court cases, and other materials, visit my website at www.tomcopelandblog.com.

Notes on This Edition

New Record-Keeping and Tax Tips is a regular feature that includes IRS updates and new information to help you keep your records, file your tax return, and deal with the IRS. This year's tips cover the following topics:

- the truth about claiming business deductions
- how to determine the "primary purpose" of a car trip
- what are the tax consequences of selling items at a garage sale?
- are donations deductible?
- the costs and benefits of hiring an employee
- how to record your cleaning hours
- don't show your love by spending
- are there personal records you should keep?
- if licensing rules require it—deduct it!
- why are you buying things for your business?
- "I gave a discount to a parent. can I deduct it?"
- the truth about end-of-the-year parent receipts
- "I've got some money saved for retirement: now where do I put it?"
- the newest IRA: MyRA
- time to invest in your 2016 IRA!

IRS Child Care Provider Audit Technique Guide

The IRS **Child Care Provider Audit Technique Guide** is one of a series of audit guides that the IRS produced to help auditors better understand specific businesses. I refer to this guide several times in this book. I have posted a copy of the guide on my website, www.tomcopelandblog.com, along with a more detailed commentary about the guide.

How to Find a Tax Professional

Many family child care providers use tax professionals to help prepare their tax returns; however, many tax preparers aren't familiar with how the IRS Tax Code affects family child care businesses. You need to find out if the tax preparer you are considering is aware of the unique tax rules for your business. (The *Record-Keeping Guide* contains more information about hiring and working with a tax preparer.) Here are some ways that you can find a qualified tax preparer:

- Ask other family child care providers or the members of your family child care association for the names of their tax preparers.

- Find out if there are any community resources you can use. For example, some communities have taxpayer assistance services for low-income people. Contact your local United Way for more information about these programs.

- There are three national tax preparer organizations that offer state listings of their members: the National Association of Enrolled Agents (www.naea.org or 202-822-6232), the National Association of Tax Professionals (www.natptax.com or 800-558-3402), and the National Society of Accountants (www.nsacct.org or 800-966-6679). You can also look in the phone book to find the local chapter of any of these organizations.

Using Tax Preparation Software

An increasing number of family child care providers are using tax preparation software to do their own taxes. The two leading tax preparation software programs are H&R Block at Home and TurboTax. Both programs are available on disk or can be used online and offer special instructions for family child care providers. These programs can be helpful in doing math calculations (such as depreciation) and completing your tax forms; they may also help catch some of your mistakes. They also have drawbacks—specifically, tax software *will not* do the following:

- Identify the items you can deduct for your business. The software will merely list the category (for example, Supplies); it will be up to you to figure out what you can claim on that line.

- Explain how to deduct items that are used both for business and personal purposes. You will need to figure out how to claim not only the supplies that you use exclusively for your business but also the supplies that you use for both business and personal purposes. Here's an example: Let's say that you spent $120 on arts and crafts supplies that were used only by the children in your care and $600 on household cleaning supplies that were used by both your business and your family. In this case, you can deduct the full amount of the arts and crafts supplies but not of the cleaning supplies. You must multiply that $600 by your Time-Space percentage and add that amount to the $120 for arts and crafts supplies. The total is the number that you enter on **Schedule C**, line 22. If you don't know that you can't claim either $720 or the Time-Space percentage of $720 for your supplies, then you shouldn't be using a tax software program.

- Alert you to all the special rules that apply to your business. For example, it won't remind you that the reimbursements you received from the Food Program for your own children are not taxable income.

- Ask you detailed questions to make sure that you are reporting the highest Time-Space percentage and business deductions that you are allowed to claim.

Using Tax Software

- Enter your business expenses (advertising, supplies) *after* applying your Time-Space percentage or actual business-use percentage.

- Be sure to keep records of how you calculated your business-use percentage (if you will not be using your Time-Space percentage).

- Read chapter 3 for a clear explanation of depreciation rules and how to use them. Unless you know a lot about depreciation, it is easy to make a mistake claiming depreciation expenses.

- Before filing your return, compare **Form 8829**, **Form 4562**, and **Schedule C** with the numbers you entered into the Tax Workbook and the Tax Organizer to see if all your deductions are properly reported. Sometimes it's easy to lose track of a deduction that you enter into a software program.

Using TurboTax

I reviewed the 2014 Home & Business version of TurboTax (https://turbotax.intuit.com). The 2015 version was not available by the time this book went to press. In addition to the drawbacks cited above, there are some additional things to watch for.

Except for house expenses and items you are depreciating, TurboTax will assume that any expense you enter is used 100% for your business. Since you will have many items that are used by your business and your family, you will need to multiply them by your Time-Space percentage before entering them into the software. This means you will have to know how to calculate your Time-Space percentage on your own.

Food Expenses

TurboTax tells you to enter your food expenses under Meals and Entertainment Expenses. You are given two choices: Meals and Entertainment: 50% Limit or 100% Limit. Always choose 100% Limit for food served to child care children.

Home Office Deductions

TurboTax has a series of screens to fill out to determine how much you can deduct of your house expenses. There are several screens that can cause confusion.

On the screen "Do You Have a Home Office?" it asks, "Do you use part of this home exclusively for this business or does it meet one of these exceptions?" Answer "yes," because child care is one of the exceptions.

On the screen that says "Home Office Summary" you must click "Edit" to enter your Time-Space percentage information.

The screen "Enter the Square Footage of Your Home and Home Office" asks you to enter the "total hours used for daycare during the year." But the explanatory box only talks about hours you are caring for children. It does not tell you to include all the hours you spend on business activities in your home when child care children are not present (cleaning, activity preparation, meal preparation, record keeping, and so on).

This is a major omission because most providers work hundreds of hours a year on such activities. Unless you know to add all these additional hours on this screen, your Time-Space percentage will be much smaller than it should be, and you will pay more in taxes than you owe.

The screen "Business Conducted in Home Office" directs you to "enter the percentage of time (your name) spends conducting business in the home office." You should enter 100% here. What they are asking is not how many hours you spend on business activities in your home (your Time Percent), but rather how much of your business is conducted in your home, versus somewhere else.

Then the screen asks if you "use this home office on a regular basis for this business?" Answer "yes" to this question.

HEALTH INSURANCE PREMIUMS

TurboTax tells you "deduct up to 100% of the premiums for you, your spouse, and your dependents if your business shows a net profit."

This is misleading. It doesn't tell you that you are not entitled to claim this deduction unless you are not eligible to purchase health insurance through an employer. Therefore, if your husband's employer health insurance plan will cover you, you cannot use this deduction, even if you don't purchase the insurance through your husband's employer.

SAFE HARBOR/SIMPLIFIED HOUSE DEDUCTION METHOD

House expenses represent a significant business deduction for you. They include property tax, mortgage interest, house insurance, utilities, house repairs, and house depreciation.

TurboTax gives you three choices in how to claim your house expenses on a screen entitled "How Do You Want to Enter Your Home Office Expenses?"

1. "I'll enter my actual expenses with the Office Expense Expert."

2. "I'll enter my actual expenses spreadsheet-style."

3. "I'll take the simplified deduction."

Almost every family child care provider should choose the first option. You can easily compare which option will give you the higher house deductions. Enter your expenses under the first option and see how this will impact your taxes. Then go back to this screen and choose the simplified deduction, and you will immediately see that you will be entitled to claim fewer deductions.

The simplified deduction option allows all home-based businesses to multiply $5 by the number of square feet they use in their home for their business, up to a maximum of 300 square feet. This means the maximum house expenses you can claim under this option is $1,500 ($5 x 300 = $1,500). Because nearly every child care provider will have higher actual house expenses than this, it doesn't make sense to use this option.

But, more importantly, you don't want to choose the simplified deduction option because TurboTax has failed to include a special rule that applies only to family child care providers! This rule says that providers must first multiply the $5 by their Time percentage. So if your Time percentage was 40%, your maximum house deduction would be $600 (40% x $5 x 300 = $600). Clearly, $600 is not going to be more than your actual house expenses.

The fact that TurboTax has left out this limitation for family child care providers is a big problem. Because of this, I don't know how you could use this software if you wanted to use this rule.

DEPRECIATION

Calculating your depreciation deductions is always a complicated task. Here are some tips to making this process easier if you use TurboTax:

As a general rule, items you purchased that cost more than $500 should be depreciated. This means you will be claiming the deduction over a number of years, not all in one year. When you start entering information about an item you will see this screen: "Describe This Asset."

Unfortunately, the screen will not tell you over how many years you can depreciate these items and you may be confused about which one to choose. I've listed the options below and added the number of years they are to be depreciated.

- Computer, Video, Photo, and Telephone Equipment: These items will be depreciated over five years. Include copier, scanner and other office equipment here.

- Tools, Machinery, Equipment, Furniture: These items will be depreciated over seven years. Include appliances, children's equipment, and all other items not attached to your home or land.

- Real Estate: This is where you enter home improvements and your home. These items will be depreciated over 39 years.

- Intangibles, Other Property: This is where you put land improvements (fence, patio, driveway) that are depreciated over 15 years.

If you select the Tools, Machinery, Equipment, Furniture option, the next screen gives you the following options:

- office furniture, fixtures, and appliances

- general purpose tools, machinery, and equipment

- construction machinery and tolls

- trailers and trailer-mounted containers

Choose "office furniture, fixtures, and appliances." These items will be depreciated over seven years.

When you select the Real Estate option, the next screen will give you the following options:

- nonresidential real estate

- qualified retail improvements

- qualified restaurant property

- qualified leasehold improvements

Choose "nonresidential real estate" for both home improvements and your home.

When you get to the screen "Tell Us about This Asset" it will give you the following three choices:

1. I traded in an old asset to acquire this one

2. I purchased this asset new

3. The item was sold, retired stolen, destroyed . . .

What do you do if you purchased a used item? There is no place to choose this. Therefore, enter every item you purchased as "new."

For items you owned before you went into business and are now depreciating, enter the value of the items at the time you first started using them in your business, as if you purchased them new at that time.

Using H&R Block at Home

I reviewed the free edition of H&R Block at Home (www.hrblock.com/online-tax -preparation/free-edition.html). There are also more expensive versions: deluxe and premium. In addition to the drawbacks cited above, here are some additional things to watch for:

- Like TurboTax, H&R Block's explanation for claiming depreciation is hard to follow. When you depreciate an item, a screen will ask for your business-use percentage. The software makes it extremely difficult to use your Time-Space percentage because you can't see what your percentage is until you have filled out all your tax forms and are ready to file your taxes. Only then can you see your percentage entered onto **Form 8829**. So you must enter all other information for your taxes and then go back to the depreciation section to enter your Time-Space percentage.

- When the screen appears that says Vehicles and Depreciable Assets, this is the section in which to enter all items you are depreciating, including your home. There is no special section to cover home depreciation, so you might otherwise miss this. You also enter your car expenses here, even though you may be using the standard mileage rate method.

- When depreciating your home, identify it as nonresidential real estate not as a component of nonresidential real estate.

- The screen Basic Depreciation Information asks you to choose between Depreciation and a Home Office. If you click on a Home Office, the software will assume that the item you are depreciating is used 100% for your business. If you are depreciating a home improvement (a new furnace or new roof, for example) that is used for both business and personal use, choose Depreciation.

- The Method screen gives you the choice of ADS MACRS, Straight Line, 5 Years, or Force the Use of a Specific Amount. If you choose the first, it will use the straight-line depreciation rules rather than allowing you to use accelerated rules. I haven't been able to figure out how to get the software to use accelerated rules. If you deselect Force the Use of a Specific Amount, you can enter the correct depreciation amount if you can calculate it on your own.

Unlike the software, a tax professional familiar with the special rules for your business should be able to help you with all of the above issues. Because of these and other weaknesses (software programs can contain errors), I don't recommend that you use tax preparation software unless you already have a good understanding of all the tax rules for family child care businesses. (If you do use tax software, be sure to read the *Record-Keeping Guide* to identify all the allowable deductions for your business and the current *Tax Workbook and Organizer* to make sure that you are following the latest tax rules.)

How to Use This Book

Although filling out tax forms isn't a pleasant task, it's an essential part of operating a family child care business. Many family child care providers don't claim all the business deductions they're entitled to because they're unaware of the tax rules and don't think the deductions are worth the time it takes to learn the tax rules. As a result, providers end up paying more taxes than they need to. Taking advantage of all the legal business deductions that you're entitled to, however, ends up lowering your tax bill.

Because a family child care business requires you to use your home for business purposes, the tax rules for your business are unlike those that apply to most other small businesses. A professional tax adviser might not be familiar with all the details of the tax laws as they apply to your business, which is why you need to take an active role in learning the tax rules and what they mean for your business.

This book is designed to guide you through all aspects of preparing your taxes and filling out your federal tax forms for the current year. (In most states, you will also have to pay state income taxes, but there are no special state tax forms to file if you are a family child care provider.) The *Family Child Care Record-Keeping Guide* provides additional tax preparation information about how to keep good records and how to determine which expenses are deductible.

Careful, accurate business records are an essential part of preparing your taxes; when family child care providers get into trouble with the IRS, it's usually because they can't separate their deductible business expenses from their nondeductible personal expenses. These personal and business expenses are usually closely intertwined, and the IRS requires you to have written evidence for all your business deductions.

This book provides you with two different approaches to preparing your taxes—the Tax Organizer and the Tax Workbook—as well as copies of the common tax forms that most providers need to file for their business.

The Tax Organizer

The Tax Organizer is a set of worksheets on which you can gather, calculate, and organize all the information you need to fill out your tax forms. The Tax Organizer doesn't include a lot of explanation of the tax laws, but if you don't have any unusual tax issues, it can be a great way to gather all your data, thus making it much easier to complete your tax forms. There are many ways you might use this section of the book. You might complete the Tax Organizer (referring to the Tax Workbook if you need more information about a particular topic) and then transfer the information directly to your tax forms. You might complete the Tax Organizer and then give the information to a professional tax preparer. Or if you just need information on a particular tax form or topic (such as depreciation or the Food Program), you might skip the Tax Organizer completely and just use the Tax Workbook.

The Tax Organizer worksheets help you record and organize all your business income and expenses. Once you fill in the information, the Tax Organizer provides specific directions about where to enter each line on your tax forms. After you complete the Tax Organizer, tear it out of this book and save it with your other tax records. Since the tax laws and forms are always changing, this Tax Organizer applies only to the year 2015; don't use it for any other year.

The Tax Workbook

The second section of this book is the Tax Workbook, which is designed to guide you line by line through the key tax forms you need to file for your business. For each form, it's important to read the instructions carefully and take the time to understand the rules. Most of the tax issues covered in this book are discussed in more detail in the *Family Child Care Record-Keeping Guide*. If any of your tax-preparation questions aren't addressed in this book, you can refer to the *Record-Keeping Guide* or my website (www.tomcopelandblog.com), or you can contact the IRS (www.irs.gov) for more information (also see appendix B).

Tax Forms

The final section of this book (Part V) includes copies of forms **W-10**, **1040**, **1040 Schedule C**, **1040 Schedule SE**, **4562**, and **8829**. It's best to tear out these forms, copy them, and then do your rough work on the copies so you can make adjustments as you go along. Once you have your final numbers, write them on a clean copy before submitting your forms to the IRS.

You may also need forms for special situations. For example, if you're making estimated tax payments, you'll need to file **Form 1040-ES Estimated Tax for Individuals**. If you want to change your tax return for an earlier year, you'll need to file **Form 1040X Amended U.S. Individual Income Tax Return**. In addition, if you hire employees, you must file a series of tax forms throughout the year. Copies of those tax forms are available at www.irs.gov.

Complete Your Tax Forms in the Correct Order

Since some tax forms must be filled out before others can be completed, it's important to fill out your tax forms in the proper order. For example, **Form 8829**, **Form 4562**, and **Schedule C** are closely linked; you can't complete **Schedule C** before you've completed **Form 4562**. You need to fill out Part I of **Form 8829** before you can complete most of **Form 4562** and **Schedule C**. And you need to complete most of **Schedule C** before you can finish **Form 8829**. Here's the best way to proceed:

1. Start by filling out Part I of **Form 8829** (lines 1–7) and determining your Time-Space percentage (see chapters 2 and 1, respectively).

2. Complete **Form 4562** (see chapter 3); enter the amount on line 22 of **Form 4562** on line 13 of **Schedule C**.

3. Complete lines 1–29 of **Schedule C** (see chapter 5), and enter the amount on line 29 of **Schedule C** on line 8 of **Form 8829**.

4. Finish filling out **Form 8829**; enter the amount on line 35 of **Form 8829** on line 30 of **Schedule C**.

5. Finish filling out **Schedule C** and any other tax forms that you need to complete, such as your **Form 1040** and your state tax forms.

Here's a flowchart that shows the proper order for filling out your tax forms:

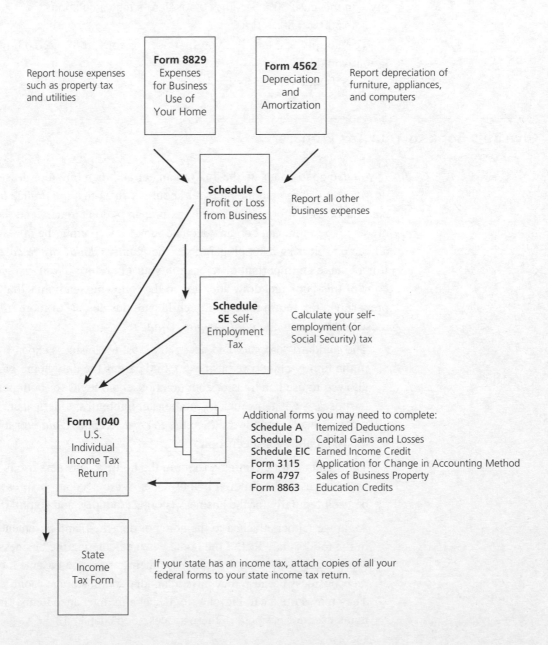

About the Math in This Book

The calculations in this book use exact amounts so you can track how to do the calculations; however, the IRS allows you to round numbers to the nearest dollar, and we recommend that you do so on your tax forms. Here's a reminder of how to round numbers correctly: If the cents portion of an amount is $0.49 or less, round down to the nearest dollar (for example, round $3.39 down to $3.00). If the cents portion of an amount is $0.50 or more, round up to the nearest dollar (for example, round $3.68 up to $4.00).

In this book we also do a lot of multiplying by percentages. Here's a reminder of how to do this: Let's say that you want to multiply $500 by 30%. To multiply by a percentage, you need to move the decimal point two places to the left before you multiply—in this case 30% becomes 0.30. Here's the calculation:

$500 × 0.30 = $150

To multiply $500 by 3%, you first need to convert 3% to 0.03. In this case, the calculation would be

$500 × 0.03 = $15

Give This Book to Your Tax Preparer

If you decide to complete the Tax Organizer and then hire a professional tax preparer to do your return, remind the preparer about tax rules that are unique to the family child care business. Unfortunately, some tax preparers don't understand the nature of this business and therefore can't do an adequate job of interpreting the tax law in your favor. (For advice on selecting a tax preparer, see the *Family Child Care Record-Keeping Guide*.) It may make an important difference in your tax return if you give your tax preparer a copy of this book and draw attention to the following ten points that are the foundation of preparing a tax return for a family child care business. (For more information on any of these points, see the *Record-Keeping Guide*.)

- The standard "ordinary and necessary" test for business expenses casts a wide net in the family child care business. Child care is the only home-based business that is allowed to use hundreds of common household items for both personal and business purposes. Such items include toothpaste, lightbulbs, toilet paper, garbage bags, a lawn mower, sheets, and towels. (See the *Record-Keeping Guide* for a list of more than a thousand allowable deductions.)

- The standard for claiming a room in the home as business use is regular use, not exclusive use. The children in a provider's care need not be present in a room for it to be used regularly for the business (storage, laundry, and so on). (See chapter 1.)

- A garage (either attached to the home or detached) and basement should be included in the total square feet of the home when calculating the business use of the home. Most family child care providers use their garage and basement on a regular basis for their business because they have a laundry room, storage room, or furnace area there. They may store a car, bicycles, tools, lawn maintenance items, firewood, or other items used for business in these spaces. (See chapter 1.)

- Providers can claim a higher business-use percentage of their home if they have one or more rooms that are used exclusively in their business. The tax preparer should add the Space percentage of this exclusive-use area to the Time-Space percentage of the rest of the home to determine the total business-use percentage of the home. (See chapter 1.)

- When counting the number of hours the home is used for business, include the number of hours that the children in the provider's care are present as well as the number of hours that the provider spends on business activities when the children are not present. These hours include the time the provider spends cleaning, preparing activities, interviewing parents, keeping records, and preparing meals. (See chapter 1.)

- Reimbursements from the Child and Adult Care Food Program (CACFP) are taxable income to the provider. Reimbursements for the provider's own child (if the provider is income-eligible) are not taxable income. Providers are entitled to deduct all the food that they serve to the children in their care, even if their food expenses are greater than their Food Program reimbursements. (See chapter 4.)

- Providers who are not licensed or registered under their state law are still entitled to claim their home expenses as business use if they have applied for a license or are exempt from local regulations. (See page 6.)

- All providers are better off financially if they claim depreciation on their home as a business expense. When a provider sells her home, she will have to pay a tax on any depreciation that she claims (or was entitled to claim) after May 6, 1997. She will owe this tax even if she hasn't claimed any home depreciation as a business deduction. (See chapter 12.)

- Providers who use their home for business can avoid paying taxes on the profit on the sale of the home if they have owned the home and lived in it for at least two of the last five years before the sale. (See chapter 12 and the *Record-Keeping Guide*.)

- Providers are entitled to claim depreciation on any property that is used in their business, including the home or home improvements; a computer, TV, VCR, DVD player, washer, dryer, refrigerator, sofa, or bed; and many other types of property. Many tax preparers have avoided calculating these depreciation deductions because of the small amounts involved; however, tax preparers should take another look at claiming depreciation, since IRS Revenue Procedure 2011–14 states that all previously unclaimed depreciation can now be deducted in the current year. This can mean hundreds of dollars in deductions for providers who have been in business for a number of years. (See chapter 10.)

If You File Electronically

If you will be filing your tax return electronically (or if your tax preparer will be doing so), be sure to keep paper copies of all your backup documentation, such as your depreciation schedules, the calculations for your Time-Space percentage, and your mileage records. The electronic documents can get lost, and you will need paper copies to provide evidence that your numbers are accurate if you are ever audited.

A Few Other Issues before We Get Started

What If You Aren't Licensed or Certified?

For tax purposes, you don't need to have a business name, be registered with your state or Chamber of Commerce, or even meet the requirements of your local regulations in order to be considered a business. Your child care business begins when you are ready to care for children and are advertising that you are ready to accept children. At this point you can begin claiming all "ordinary and necessary" expenses for your business. You don't have to be licensed or actually caring for children in order to be considered a business and start claiming your expenses.

Suppose that you're paid to care for children but don't meet the requirements of your local regulations. You may still deduct many expenses as business deductions, as long as you report your income. You can deduct all direct expenses, such as car expenses, depreciation on personal property (such as furniture and appliances), office expenses, equipment rental, repairs, supplies, education, food, and other miscellaneous home expenses. You may deduct these expenses even if you are caring for more children than your local regulations allow. Although we don't recommend operating outside of your local regulations, you should be aware of the tax advantages of deducting these expenses from your business income on **Schedule C**.

The only expenses that you aren't entitled to deduct if you don't meet your local requirements are your home utilities, mortgage interest, home repairs, homeowners insurance, home depreciation, and real estate taxes. (These expenses appear on **Form 8829**. If you aren't entitled to claim expenses on **Form 8829**, you can still deduct all your mortgage interest and real estate taxes by itemizing on **Schedule A**.)

If your local regulations are voluntary, or if you are exempt from them, you may claim all the same business deductions as a licensed or certified provider. For example, your state rules may require that child care providers be licensed only if they care for more than four children. If you care for three children, you would be exempt from the licensing rules and thus would be able to deduct the same business expenses as a licensed provider.

Do You Need an Employer Identification Number?

If parents want to claim the child care tax credit, they will ask you for your Social Security or employer identification number (EIN). Because of privacy concerns, I strongly recommend that you get an EIN for your business. Using an EIN can reduce the chances that your Social Security number will get into the wrong hands and cause you problems with identity theft. If you hire an employee or set up a Keogh retirement plan, you are required to have an EIN. You can get an EIN by filing **Form SS-4** (go to www.tomcopelandblog.com and click on "2015 IRS Tax Forms" to download the form) or by calling the IRS Business and Specialty Tax Line at 800-829-4933.

Another easy way to get your EIN is by going online. The application process is quicker, with fewer questions, and a simpler format to follow. Go to www.irs.gov and enter "EIN" in the search box. Once you fill out the application online, you will instantly get your EIN. You'll be asked, Why is the sole proprietor requesting an EIN? This question includes the following choices for answers: started a new business, hired employee(s), banking purposes, changed type of organization, or purchased active business. Always answer, "Started a new business," to this question, unless you are hiring employees. This may seem like a strange answer if you've been in business for a long time, but the instructions say to choose an answer that is closest to your situation.

If you have an EIN, you should use it instead of your Social Security number on forms **Schedule C** and **Schedule SE**. On all other forms, including **Form 1040** and **Form 1040-ES**, you should use your Social Security number.

About Parent Payments and Form W-10

If the parents of children in your care want to claim the child care tax credit, they will ask you to fill out **Form W-10**. **Form W-10** is easy to complete: simply enter your name, address, and Social Security or employer identification number, and sign the form. If you have an employer identification number, you must use it, rather than your Social Security number, on this form.

If you don't fill out **Form W-10** when a parent asks you to do so, you face a penalty of $50, even if you don't file tax returns or meet state regulations. Since the parents are responsible for giving you this form, you don't have to track them down and give it to them if they don't ask for it. Don't, however, refuse to sign **Form W-10** in the hope of hiding some of your income from the IRS. Not signing this form is one of the things that can trigger an IRS audit of your tax return.

Parents don't file **Form W-10** with their tax return. Instead, they keep it for their records. When they file **Form 2441**, they take the information from **Form W-10** and record each provider's name, address, and employer identification number, and the amount paid to each provider. The IRS uses this information to check whether or not the providers listed filed tax returns and reported all their income.

In the past, some parents overstated the number of their dependent children, and some providers understated the amount of their income. The IRS is trying to reduce such false reporting by requiring parents to list the Social Security or employer identification number of each provider. Still, some parents may report child care expenses on their **Form 2441** that are higher than what they paid you. This can happen, for example, when parents use two providers but report all of their child care expenses under one provider because they don't have the other provider's Social Security or employer identification number.

To protect yourself, you need to keep careful records of how much each parent paid you during the year. You should also get a signed receipt from each parent that indicates how much they paid you that year and keep the receipt with your tax records.

Providing Receipts for Parent Payments

There are three types of receipts that you can use, as shown in the examples below.

1. One type of receipt is **Form W-10**, which shows the amount paid and the parent's signature. Keep a copy of all the **Form W-10**s that you fill out. You can also fill out copies of **Form W-10** and give them to parents in January each year. (See the example below.) Parents find this helpful, and it's a professional touch that many will appreciate. There's a blank copy of **Form W-10** in the back of this book that you can use.

2. Another option is to use a standard book of sales receipts that you can buy in a stationery or office supply store. (See the example below.)

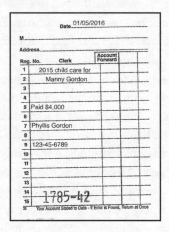

3. You can also use the receipts in the *Family Child Care Business Receipt Book,* which are designed especially for family child care providers. (See the example below.)

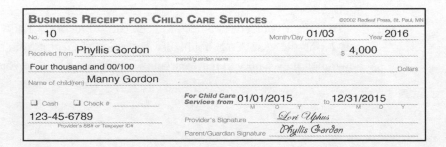

New Record-Keeping and Tax Tips

These tips are exclusive to this edition of the *Tax Workbook and Organizer.* They highlight the tax changes and issues that have been identified over the past year.

The Truth about Claiming Business Deductions

Have you ever heard these from your tax preparer or another family child care provider?

"You can't deduct that because you use it for personal purposes."

"You can't deduct that because you owned it before your business began."

"You can't deduct your house expenses because you are not licensed."

"You can't deduct food expenses because you are on the Food Program."

I have. I've even heard them from IRS agents. They are all false.

The **IRS Child Care Provider Audit Technique Guide** is a publication used to train IRS auditors on how to audit family child care providers. It contains a lot of clarifying information that will help us find out what the truth is for the above statements.

"You Can't Deduct That Because You Use It for Personal Purposes."

The **Child Care Provider Audit Technique Guide** says, "It is important to stress the fact that having a personal usage element present does not disqualify the property from being a deductible IRC Section 162 expense." IRC Section 162 allows businesses to deduct "all ordinary and necessary expenses" for their business.

Ordinary and necessary means: common, accepted, helpful, and appropriate. The **Child Care Provider Audit Technique Guide** lists allowed expenses such as soap, kitchen equipment, furniture, appliances, piano, VCR, DVD player, television, office supplies, and cleaning supplies. Clearly, these items are used for personal purposes.

"You Can't Deduct That Because You Owned It Before Your Business Began."

The **Child Care Provider Audit Technique Guide** says, "For many providers, when they start their business many items which were personal use only are used in the business. They are entitled to depreciate the business use portion of those assets. . . .The fact that the asset was only used for personal purposes prior to being placed in service does not disqualify it from being converted to use in the business."

"You Can't Deduct Your House Expenses Because You Are Not Licensed."

To claim house expenses, Internal Revenue Tax Code **Section 280A(c)(4)(B)** says, "The provider must have applied for, been granted, or be exempt from having a license, certification, registration, or approval as a day care center or as a family or group day care home under state law."

This language is repeated in the **Child Care Provider Audit Technique Guide** and in IRS **Publication 587 Business Use of Your Home**. So, if you applied for a license in 2015 and didn't get your license until 2016, you can still deduct your house expenses on your 2015 tax return.

"You Can't Deduct Food Expenses Because You Are on the Food Program."

In 2003 the IRS issued a ruling (IRS Rev. Proc. 2003-22) that established the standard meal allowance rate. It says, "The [standard meal allowance rates] apply regardless of whether a family day care provider is reimbursed for food costs, in whole or in part, under the CACFP, or under any other program, for a particular meal or snack."

Summary

The **Child Care Provider Audit Technique Guide** is not the final word on these statements, as new Tax Court decisions or other IRS documents may offer new clarifications. However, you can use the guide in conversations with your tax preparer or auditor to make a persuasive case in your defense.

Therefore, if you hear someone make one of the above statements, or any other statement you are not sure is correct, ask the person, "Where does it say that?" If the person can't back up what they are saying with some written IRS document, you should not accept their position.

For copies of all IRS documents, court cases, and other materials, see the IRS Audits/ Documents section of my website (www.tomcopelandblog.com).

How to Determine the "Primary Purpose" of a Car Trip

Family child care providers can deduct expenses associated with their car based on the number of business miles they drive. You can count the miles of a trip as business as long as the "primary purpose" of the trip is for your business.

A trip is primarily for business purposes if more than half of the reason for the trip is business. Taking day care children on field trips or transporting them to or from your home can clearly be counted as a business trip. Trips to the bank to deposit parent fees, to the library to get children's books, or to training workshops also count as business trips.

What about these trips?

1. **You drive to the gas station to get gas.** You can count this trip only if more than half the miles your drove your car were for business purposes. This would be highly unlikely unless you have a second car that you use primarily for your business.

2. **You drive to the grocery store to buy business and personal food.** If you spent more money on business food than personal food, you can count this trip. Many providers almost always buy more business food than personal food. Even so, don't try to

claim every trip to the grocery store as a business trip. The IRS will never allow this. Instead, if you normally buy 75% of food for your business, count 75% of your trips.

3. **You drive to school to drop off two day care children and two of your own.** This example is tricky. If the primary reason to go to school is to drop off the day care children, then count the trip. If the primary reason is to drop off your own children, don't count the trip. If you weren't in business and would drop off your own children, don't count these trips.

Claiming Business Trips

Once you have determined whether or not your trip is a business trip, add up all the miles for your business trips. You have two ways to claim car expenses. You can use the standard mileage method or the actual expenses method.

If you choose the standard mileage method, multiply your business miles by $.575 (2015 standard mileage rate). In addition, you can claim parking expenses, tolls, and the business portion of your car loan interest and any personal property tax on your car.

If you use the actual expenses method, you can claim the business portion of all expenses associated with your car: gas, oil, repairs, insurance, parking, tolls, membership in AAA, car wash, depreciation, and so on.

The business portion of your car expenses is determined by dividing the number of business miles by the total number of miles your drove your car. For example, if you drove 3,000 business miles and 10,000 total miles, your business use is 30%. You could then deduct 30% of your car loan interest and personal property tax if you use the standard mileage rate, or 30% of all your vehicle expenses if you use the actual expenses method.

If you have more than one vehicle, you can choose either method for each vehicle.

What Are the Tax Consequences of Selling Items at a Garage Sale?

Family child care providers often hold garage and yard sales. They sell their old toys, clothing, and a variety of used household items. They do so because they are going out of business or just want to unload some of the stuff they have accumulated over the years.

What are the tax consequences of selling your stuff?

Items You Never Used in Your Business

As a general rule, if you sell it at a loss, there is no tax consequence. If you sell it at a gain, report the gain on **Schedule D** and then on **Form 1040**.

In the vast majority of cases, you are selling items at a garage sale for a lot less than what you paid for them. Therefore, pocket the cash and don't report anything to the IRS. If you bought a sleeping bag on sale for $100 and managed to sell it for $125, report the $25 gain on **Schedule D**. You'll pay a little in taxes.

Items You Used in Your Business

The general rule is that items sold at a loss are not deductible because you already got a tax benefit by deducting them. Items sold at a gain are reported as taxable income.

Items used 100% for your business: If you sold it at a gain, report the gain on IRS **Form 4797** and carry it over to **Schedule D** and then **Form 1040**. You'll pay a small amount in taxes. If you sold it at a loss, you cannot claim a business loss. See exception below.*

For example, let's say you bought ten toys for a total of $300 and deducted them several years ago. If you sell them for $320, report $20 as a gain on **Form 4797**. If you sold them for $100, don't report any loss. That's because you already got the tax benefit of deducting the items.

Items Used for Your Business and Your Family

Determine if there is a gain or loss on the business portion.

For example, let's say you bought several children's chairs for $500 and your Time-Space percentage was 40%. The business deduction you claimed was therefore $200 ($500 x 40%). If you sold them for $100, the business portion of the loss is $40 ($100 x 40%). However, you can't both claim a deduction and a loss, so don't report the loss. If you sold them for $600, however, then the business gain is $40 ($600 x 40% = $240 – $200 = $40). Report the gain on **Form 4797**.

Summary

In almost every case, you will be selling items at a garage or yard sale at a loss. In that case, you won't be able to deduct anything as a business expense. You can keep the money you received and you don't have to report it as income.

If you are out of business when you sell your stuff at a loss there is also nothing to report on your taxes. If you sold them at a gain, report the gain on **Schedule D**.

*Exception: It's possible you could claim a business loss if you bought items used in your business and have not fully depreciated them. In this case you must take into account the depreciation when determining if you have a gain or a loss. This involves a complicated calculation (see chapter 11). Because the calculation is so complicated, many providers don't bother with trying to deduct a small loss.

So, you can enjoy the garage and yard sale and keep your cash without having to worry about the IRS!

Are Donations Deductible?

Family child care providers are generous people. Is there a tax benefit for being generous? More specifically, can you deduct as a business expense money or items you donate to your local hospital, softball team, high school, Salvation Army, church, and so on?

It depends.

If giving money or items promotes your business, you can deduct it as a business expense. In other words, if you make a donation and receive something in return, you can deduct the donation as a business expense.

For example, if you donate $100 to your local girls' softball team and they put your business name in a small display ad in their program, you can deduct the $100 as an advertising expense. On the other hand, if you give $100 and receive nothing in exchange, you can't deduct it as a business expense.

You can deduct the donation of money or items on your personal tax return (**Schedule A**) to a qualified charitable contribution. Typically, churches, Salvation Army, non-profit hospitals, and so on would qualify as charitable organizations.

If you donate your time to help sell tickets to softball games or volunteer at your local hospital, you cannot deduct the value of your time as either a business expense or charitable contribution.

Note: if you are incorporated as a C corporation, you may be able to deduct your donation of money or items as a business expense.

The Costs and Benefits of Hiring an Employee

Most family child care providers who hire employees do so primarily because they can expand their program and care for more children. But there are a number of costs and benefits that should be considered before taking this step. First, let's look at the benefits:

- An additional adult can result in an increased quality of care.

- It's helpful to have another adult you can talk to.

- You're able to help someone who needs a job.

- An employee allows for increased flexibility, which gives you more control over your schedule.

There is also a downside when you hire an employee.

- You must pay a number of federal and state payroll taxes.

- You must purchase workers' compensation insurance and file a series of tax forms.

- Because you are responsible for virtually anything your employee does, you must take the time to properly hire, supervise, and possibly fire the employee.

Will Hiring an Employee Actually Increase Your Profit?

The answer depends on how many more children you enroll after hiring an employee. To take a close look at this, providers should examine the additional costs of hiring an employee as compared to the additional income on enrolling more children.

Let's look at an example: Lainie Provider decides to hire an employee at the federal minimum wage of $7.25 per hour (your state minimum wage may be higher). Here are her additional weekly costs:

- Wages: $7.25 per hour x 40 hours per week (overtime is due for more than 40 hours of work in a week) = $290

- Payroll taxes (7.65% Social Security/Medicare tax + .6% federal unemployment tax) = $24

- State unemployment tax: varies

- Workers' compensation insurance: varies

- Other employee costs (training, supplies, food, benefits, etc.): varies

- **Total weekly employee costs: $314+**

To offset this additional expense, Lainie will have to enroll two additional children at $157+ per week. This doesn't include the possible additional costs of toys and supplies needed for two more children.

I've created a tool called the Hiring an Employee Worksheet (http://www.redleafpress. org/Family-Child-Care-Money-Management-and-Retirement-Guide-P338.aspx) that you can use to plug in your numbers and quickly see how much you will need to charge to break even. As a general rule, you won't increase your profit until you care for more than two additional children after hiring a full-time employee.

Consider What Can Happen If Your Enrollment Drops

Let's say under your state's licensing rules you can care for no more than 10 children, but with an employee you can care for up to 14 children. You decide to hire an employee and you enroll two additional children under your state licensing rules. If one child leaves your program, you can't reduce your employee hours, so you are likely to start losing money. To avoid this, you would have to ask another child to leave to bring you down to the proper ratio and then lay off your employee because you wouldn't need her anymore.

Therefore, from a strictly financial point of view, I would suggest that you not hire a full-time employee unless you are confident that you can enroll (and keep enrolled) at least three additional full-time children.

For some providers, the non-financial benefits may outweigh the financial risks. I know of providers who are very successful and have several employees. I know of other providers who didn't realize the actual costs of hiring employees and found out later that their employee earned more than they did.

Plan ahead before making this decision.

How to Record Your Cleaning Hours

Family child care providers spend a lot of time cleaning their home. You clean each morning before the children arrive and clean each evening after the children leave. You probably also clean during some nights and on most weekends. Keeping careful track of all of these hours will help you significantly reduce your taxes.

This is because each additional hour you spend cleaning your home will raise your Time-Space percentage, which will raise your business deductions, which will then lower your taxes. In fact, time spent on any business activity when children are not present in your home (planning, record keeping, meal preparation, and so on) also will increase your Time-Space percentage.

Because cleaning hours usually represent the most time you spend on business activities when children are not present, I want to explain in more detail the proper way to document these hours.

An Example

Let's say you care for children from 6:00 a.m. to 5:00 p.m., Monday through Friday. Each morning you get ready for the children and clean from 5:30 a.m. to 6:00 a.m. Each evening you clean up after the children leave from 5:00 p.m. to 5:30 p.m.

How should you record these hours to be able to count them on your tax return and withstand the scrutiny of an IRS audit?

If you don't write down the hours you spent cleaning and simply add five hours a week to your Time percentage calculation, you run the risk of the IRS not accepting these hours without further proof.

The IRS may also not accept your short written statement that you worked "five hours per week cleaning."

The Proper Way to Record Cleaning Hours

Write down enough details to show exactly what you were doing while cleaning. Put down the time of day you do your cleaning so the IRS can see that it's not being done when children are present. You want the IRS to see why it takes you half an hour in the morning to clean.

For example, you might record: "Cleaning, Monday, 5:30–6:00 a.m. Sweep front hallway and front steps; vacuum living room, dining room, and playroom; mop kitchen floor; clean kitchen countertops; take out toys from basement storage and put in playroom; fill dishwasher; do a load of laundry; wipe off tables and chairs in playroom; and clean downstairs bathroom (scrub toilet, mop floor, clean sink, wipe down surfaces and mirror, put out new towels from dryer)."

If your write down this level of detail, you shouldn't be challenged on the hours you claim. The more details you can record, the better.

I strongly recommend that providers complete at least two months of careful record keeping. Show all the business activities you do. If you conduct the same cleaning activities Monday through Friday, you only need to record this detail once. Then, for these two months, you would record "5:30–6:00 a.m. cleaning" and "5:30–6:00 p.m. cleaning" for Monday through Friday on a calendar. Be sure to track any cleaning hours you do in the evenings and on weekends.

Exceptions to Your Normal Routine

There may be times when you have special circumstances that result in extra time cleaning. This could be doing spring cleaning, cleaning out the basement or garage, or cleaning up after a special event. When this happens, keep records of these hours and add them to your total hours of cleaning.

For example, if you averaged 40 hours of cleaning for two months and 20 hours of extra cleaning for the year, your total cleaning hours would be 500 hours (40 hours a month x 12 months = 480 hours + 20 hours = 500 hours).

Personal Cleaning

You can't count all of the time you spend cleaning your home in your Time-Space percentage calculation. Some of the cleaning time is for your own family. Therefore, for at least two months you should also record how much time you spend—and when—on personal cleaning.

For example, if you worked two hours on Saturday morning cleaning, you might record it as follows: "Saturday, 7:00–9:00 a.m.: Clean downstairs and upstairs bathrooms (scrub toilet, mop floor, clean sink, wipe down surfaces and mirror, put out new towels from dryer); make bed, vacuum floor and pick up in master bedroom; clean kitchen (do a load of dishes, clean out refrigerator, clean off and wipe down countertops, mop floor, put away dishware, clean sink); vacuum living room, playroom, and dining room; take out garbage and recycling; sweep front steps and deck. One hour personal cleaning and one hour business cleaning."

Conclusion

I can't stress enough how important it is to record this level of detail when tracking your cleaning hours. For example, every one and a half hours of cleaning work you do in a week will increase your Time percentage by one percent. That's a lot when applied to all of your house expenses (property tax, mortgage interest, house insurance, utilities, house repairs, and house depreciation).

For users of the Minute Menu Kids Pro software, I've posted an instructional video on how to record the hours you are working when children are not present. Visit: http://tinyurl.com/pzp8jj7.

Don't Show Your Love by Spending

It's natural to love the children in your program and to want to show your love in every way you can. The only problem with this natural desire is that too many providers make the mistake of thinking that expressing their love means spending more money on the children.

But showing your love *doesn't* mean spending more.

Some providers keep buying more toys every year until their closets, basement, and garage are all overflowing. Many providers have turned their habit of buying children's items that they don't really need into a "hobby."

Certainly, toys are an important part of helping children learn. However, providing a hundred toys won't help children learn much more than far fewer toys, and it may even be counterproductive.

The parents of the children in your care won't expect you to spend a lot of money on their children. In fact, if you do, they may feel uncomfortable and worry that they won't be able to keep up with you.

Here are some responses from providers who responded to a survey I conducted as part of the research for my book *Family Child Care Money Management and Retirement Guide*:

- "Learn to set a budget and don't let your heart take over and buy too many things just because you love the kids. You have to set limits on holidays and birthdays. It's really important to put the cash away for emergencies before you get into a situation where you have no extra money to spare."

- "Stop making so many purchases for your business. You really don't need another book or toy. Use the resources you have. You don't need one of each kind of whatever it is you want."

- "Stop spending money on your business—it's too easy to 'nickel and dime' away your cash for new things that you don't really need. I have updated my equipment and environment with quality items—but it's the little stuff that really adds up without adding much to my business."

- "Stop buying so much stuff for your day care. Most providers I know continually buy junk because it's on sale or a good deal at a garage sale. Then they have too much stuff, and complain that they can't get organized."

- "Save, save, and spend only what you need to. Reduce, re-purpose, reuse, trade. You do have to be creative, but kids don't need expensive toys to be happy and keep learning."

Wise words.

Are There Personal Records You Should Keep?

Most family child care providers are well aware of the need to keep business records. Such records include receipts for items used in your business, children's attendance records, records of the hours worked in your home, records of the meals and snacks served to the day care children, mileage records, and so on.

You might think, "Isn't this enough? Don't tell me I need to keep more records!" I wish I could say that keeping your business records is all you need to do. But it isn't.

Why You Need to Keep Personal Records

When you are a family child care provider, it can sometimes be difficult to sort out the business from the personal.

- When you go to a grocery store or Walmart or Target—is this a business or personal trip?

- When you buy cleaning supplies for your home—are these business or personal expenses?

- When you clean your home—is this a business or personal activity?

This becomes important if you are audited by the IRS.

Let's say you are being audited and the IRS agent asks for your mileage records. You show him your records for your business trips (receipts, cancelled checks, credit/debit card statements, calendar notations). They include 40 trips to the ABC Grocery Store, 15 trips to Walmart, and 30 trips to Target.

The IRS agent says, "I'm not going to allow you to claim every trip you made to these destinations, because some of them had to be for personal purposes. Did you make other trips to these destinations that you didn't claim as a business trip?" You say, "Yes, I did make other trips that I didn't claim." The IRS agent responds, "Prove it."

If you can't prove you made some personal trips to these destinations, the IRS is likely to disallow some of your business trips. Therefore, you need to save records of personal trips you made in your car. Such records can include: receipts for items that you didn't deduct, debit/credit care statements, or cancelled checks.

The same goes for the purchase of cleaning supplies and the tracking of your cleaning hours.

Some providers deduct half the cost of cleaning supplies, but only save every other receipt. This will be a problem in an audit because the IRS won't allow you to deduct 100% of cleaning supply receipts unless you can show personal receipts. If your records show you spent five hours a week cleaning your home for your business, the IRS won't accept all of these hours unless you can show you spent some personal hours cleaning as well.

If you use the Minute Menu Kids Pro software, you don't need to enter your mileage for personal trips, but you should keep records as described above. You don't need to enter expenses for personal items, but you should keep these receipts. You should enter personal cleaning hours at the same time you enter business cleaning hours.

Conclusion

Save all your receipts, business and personal! In my opinion, it's easier to do this than to try to determine which purchase is business and which one is personal.

Here's an example: If you bought a birthday toy for your own child, you probably were not thinking it was a business expense. But if your child lets the day care children play with the toy, you can deduct part of the cost.

I know I'm asking you to keep more records, but it's worth it! At the end of the year you might realize you can deduct more than you first thought. And in the event of an IRS audit, you will have everything you need to defend yourself.

If Licensing Rules Require It—Deduct It!

What do an egress window, a gun safe, a dog fence, and a yard fence have in common? They are all items that many state child care licensing rules require family child care providers to install to keep children safe. And because of this, 100% of the cost of such items may be deducted for your business.

Sometimes tax preparers resist allowing providers to deduct such items because they believe they are personal expenses. (What other home-based business could deduct a gun safe?) But providers can deduct all "ordinary and necessary" business expenses under the IRS **Tax Code Section 162(a)**. Ordinary and necessary means useful, helpful, appropriate, or common in that particular business. Importantly, necessary doesn't mean absolutely necessary or indispensable. So, a provider who buys a gun safe because her licensor tells her she must can consider it an ordinary and necessary expense for her business.

When your licensor tells you to purchase something to comply with your state's child care licensing rules, ask her to put it in writing and then add the note to your tax records. Keep a copy of your state licensing rules on file as well. Additionally, I recommend deducting 100% of the cost of items that you are required to purchase to comply with child care rules. Such items can also include smoke detectors, fire extinguishers, fireplace screens, child locks, and so on.

If an item costs less than $500, deduct it on **Schedule C**. If an item costs more than $500, you can use Section 179 rule (**Form 4562,** Part I) and deduct it in one year.

Under new IRS rules, it's not yet clear to me how to treat an egress window. Under the old rules, you would treat it as a home improvement and depreciate it over 39 years. Under the new rules, it seems that you can treat it as a repair/improvement and deduct it in one year. But I haven't seen specific enough directions to feel comfortable recommend doing this. When I get further information, I'll write about it.

What about your phone? The IRS adopted a rule many years ago denying a deduction for the first phone line into your home. The first phone line can be a landline or cell phone number. It makes sense that providers should be able to deduct a phone line required for their business, but they can't. If you have more than one phone line, you can determine which one is the first phone line (non-deductible), and deduct the business portion of a second or third phone line (use your Time-Space percentage or an actual business use percentage).

Why Are You Buying Things for Your Business?

At tax time, it's reassuring to see how much you can deduct as a business expense for all of the items you purchased last year. The more things you purchased last year, the lower your taxes will be. In fact, for every $100 you spend on items for your business, you'll be able to reduce your taxes by about 30%–40% (depending on your family's overall income).

But focusing too much on trying to lower your taxes is not always a good idea. **Your main goal should not be trying pay as little tax as possible.** Your main goal should be to set short- and long-term financial priorities for your family and then take steps to meet them.

What are your financial goals for 2016, for 2020, for your retirement? What is important to you? You want to be spending money on things that are consistent with your financial goals and your values. Taxes are secondary.

Two Providers

I remember one provider, Lisa from Texas, whom I helped many years ago when she was audited by the IRS. She was a single mother with two young children. Her gross income for her family child care business was about $12,000. One of the items she bought was a $1,200 central vacuum cleaning system.

She clearly could not afford to buy the system. Was having a clean home really so important that she needed to spend 10% of her income? I don't think so. But she hadn't thought about what was truly important to her. She hadn't tried to set any financial goals. If she had, I don't think she would have purchased it.

Another provider, Pat from Minnesota, once said to me that before she buys anything for her business she asks herself, "Will this improve my business, will it entice parents to come to my program, or will it not matter?" If it didn't matter, she wouldn't buy it. Then she told me that "mostly it doesn't matter." This thinking helps her keep expenses down.

When You File Separately

When you file separately, you and your spouse each file your own **Form 1040**. You would still complete the same business tax forms and transfer your profit onto your own **Form 1040**. You would be solely responsible for paying any tax you owe. This means you should be paying in estimated taxes quarterly, using **Form 1040ES**.

Your spouse would be responsible for filing his own **Form 1040** and paying any taxes he might owe.

Why Buy for Your Business?

You don't want to buy something for your business that costs $100 if you get back only $30 to $40 on your taxes. If it's important to buy an item for your business, do so. But don't buy something to get a tax break! And don't buy something unless you need it. Even better, save your money to meet specific financial goals.

So, when you get finished with your last year's tax return, look ahead and set some financial goals for 2016. If you don't set goals, you are unlikely to meet them.

"I Gave a Discount to a Parent. Can I Deduct It?"

The short answer is "no." Family child care providers sometimes offer discounts or scholarships to parents to help them afford their child care services. For example:

- A provider gives a parent a $100 discount on her services because the parent lost her job.

- A provider gives a parent a $300 scholarship by forgiving the amount the low-income parent was supposed to pay her as a co-pay.

- A provider gives a parent a reduced fee of $50 for the first week of care as an incentive for the parent to enroll in her program.

- A parent leaves a provider owing her $700. The provider decides not to try to collect from the parent.

In all of these situations the provider cannot deduct the amounts involved as a business expense. Instead, the provider will report less income on her taxes, and pay less in taxes as a result. Report as income only money that you receive. Do not deduct money that was owed to you and not paid, or amounts that you offered to reduce your rates as a discount or scholarship.

Note: In general, to deduct a "bad debt," you must have previously included the amount in your income. So, if you entered into your records that a parent paid you $200 when, in fact, she paid you only $100, you could then report the unpaid $100 as a "bad debt." But the better way to go is to only report as income money you actually receive.

The Truth about End-of-the-Year Parent Receipts

Every January I get many questions from family child care providers on the same topic.

"Do I have to give the parents in my program an end-of-year receipt?"

"Am I responsible for giving parents my Social Security number, even if they left owing me money?

"Do I have to complete IRS Form W-10 and give one to each parent in my program?"

The answer to all of these questions is "no."

There seems to be a lot of confusion around this issue, so let's clear things up. Most parents who pay a child care provider are entitled to claim a federal child care tax credit using IRS **Form 2441 Child and Dependent Care Expenses**. This form requires the parent to list the name, address, identification number of the child care provider, and amount paid to the provider.

The instructions to **Form 2441** tell parents they can use IRS **Form W-10 Dependent Care Provider's Identification and Certification** to collect the identification number of the caregiver. It's a parent's responsibility to give this form to the child care provider. It's not your responsibility to give this form to the parent. Few, if any, parents are giving their family child care provider **Form W-10**!

According to the law, family child care providers are not required to give parents their identification number and are not required to give parents an end-of-year receipt. If the parent left your program in 2015, you are not required to track them down to give them this information. **But if you are on good terms with the parents in your program, I do recommend that you give parents an end-of-year receipt, along with your identification number.**

Ask the parent to sign a copy and keep it in your records. This can help protect you if you are audited and are asked to provide evidence of what the parent paid you for the year. Many providers give end-of-year receipts to parents, but most don't keep a copy signed by the parent. You can use the **Form W-10** as your end-of-year receipt. Although the form doesn't provide a space indicating how much the parent paid, you can write the amount across the top of the form and have the parent sign a copy of the form that you keep in your records.

Form W-10 is included in the Minute Menu Kids Pro software program as well as in my *Family Child Care 2015 Tax Workbook and Organizer*. Redleaf Press also publishes their *Family Child Care Business Receipt Book*. You can also create your own receipt: "Received by [your name] for child care services for the care of [name of child] for 2015. Provider identification number [number]. Signed: [parent] [your name] Dated: [date]"

If a parent left owing you money, I would recommend telling the parent that you will give them your identification number only once they have paid you in full. The only time you face a consequence is if the parent gives you a copy of **Form W-10** and you fail to fill it out. If this happens, you will face a $50 penalty. But since 99% of parents don't know they are supposed to do this, I wouldn't worry about it.

Don't give parents your Social Security number. Instead, get an employer identification number (EIN) and use it instead of your Social Security number with parents.

"I've Got Some Money Saved for Retirement: Now Where Do I Put It?"

Most family child care providers are not comfortable with choosing investments for their retirement.

Unless you are spending a lot of time researching various investment options, it can be daunting to decide what to do with your money. If you are someone who doesn't know much about investing, this section offers my simple explanation for what to do to get started. Later you can learn more and make changes to your investments.

When investing for retirement you want to minimize your risk and maximize your return. To do this, you need to have a proper balance of two major kinds of investments—fixed income investments and equities.

Fixed income investments are like IOUs; they include bonds, money market funds, and certificates of deposit (CDs). A company or government entity promises to pay you back your investment at a certain date in the future with a fixed rate of return. The interest you earn on fixed income investments is relatively low, but they also have a relatively low risk.

Equities are investments in which you assume some ownership of an asset, such as a company in which you buy shares. These investments include stocks and real estate. Equities have a potential high return and a potential high risk.

You want some of each type of investment. You don't want to put all of your money into fixed income assets because your return will be too low to beat inflation. You don't want to put all your money into equities because their value may decline abruptly just at the point when you want to start withdrawing money to live on. So, what is the best mix of these two types of investments?

Here are two simple options:

OPTION #1

60% in the Vanguard Total Stock Market Index Investor Shares Fund
40% in the Vanguard Total Bond Market Index Investor Shares Fund

OPTION #2

45% in the Vanguard Total Stock Market Index Investor Shares Fund
25% in the Vanguard Total Bond Market Index Investor Shares Fund
10% in the Vanguard REIT Index Investor Shares Fund
20% in the Vanguard Total International Stock Index Fund

Here's why I selected these options: to get the broadest possible exposure to the stock market, invest in a total stock market fund that invests in a representative sample of all companies. You are spreading the risk of equities by buying into the entire stock market.

To get the broadest possible exposure to bonds, invest in a total bond market fund that buys the various types of bonds (short term, long term).

Invest in index funds, because index funds have the lowest management fees. According to a 2004 study by Standard & Poor's (an investment research and rating firm), the annual costs of a fund is the most important factor in determining the performance of a fund. The basic conclusions of this 2004 study have yet to be challenged.

Your choice about how much of your money to put into fixed income and equities can be influenced by your age, your willingness to take risks, your health, and other personal circumstances. My suggestions above are a starting point. See my article "Where Should I Invest My Money for Retirement?" on http://tomcopelandblog.com for a detailed discussion of where to invest and why you should invest in index funds.

Note: I chose to use the Vanguard company in my options because it is the biggest investment company offering the most choices for index funds. Here are three other companies that offer many index funds. I've listed the names of their funds that are the same as Option #1 above:

- Fidelity: Spartan Total Market Index Fund and Fidelity U.S. Bond Market Index

- Charles Schwab: Schwab Total Stock Market Index and Schwab Total Bond Market Fund

- T. Rowe Price: Total Equity Market Index and U.S. Bond Index

Summary

Don't know much about investing? Choose Option #1. If you are a little more knowledgeable about investing and want to diversify more, choose Option #2. Caution: Don't invest in something if you don't understand it. My Option #1 is very basic, but if you don't understand it, don't do it. Begin to educate yourself about investing for retirement so you can make informed decisions later.

The Newest IRA: myRA

It's an unfortunate fact that many family child care providers are not saving enough money for their retirement, even though Individual Retirement Accounts (IRA) have been around for a long time. Although there are significant tax advantages to contributing to an IRA, many people still do not participate. Why?

They put other spending priorities first; they don't understand the value of establishing an IRA; or they don't know how to go about setting one up.

The myRA is the government's attempt to make it easy and cost-free for many providers to set up an IRA. There are no fees to establish or maintain a myRA and there is no risk you will lose money! The myRA has a low $25 minimum contribution requirement.

Anyone can set up a myRA for themselves without having to participate through an employer plan. Previously, family child care providers could only contribute through their spouse's employer. This means you can set up a recurring or one-time contribution to your myRA from your checking or savings account. This is a big step forward in making the IRA accessible to more people. The myRA is intended to encourage low- to middle-income people to start contributing to an IRA.

Here's how it works.

You are eligible to contribute to a myRA if your income and your spouse's gross income is less than $191,000. If you are single, you must earn less than $129,000.

The myRA will be invested in a Roth IRA and will earn interest at the same rate as investments in the U.S. government securities fund now available to federal employees. This fund has had an average annual return of 3.19% over the last ten years.

You can contribute as little as $25 to get started and add to it with as little as $5. You and your spouse can contribute a maximum of $5,500 per year (or $6,500 if you or your spouse is age 50 or older). Once the account reaches $15,000 you will have to roll it over to a private Roth IRA.

A Roth IRA works differently than other IRAs. Money you contribute to a Roth IRA doesn't reduce your taxable income (unlike all other IRAs). It earns interest tax-free. When you take money out of your Roth IRA after age 59 1/2, you won't owe taxes on your contributions or the interest it earned.

The myRA is not tied to any job, so if you quit child care and take another job, the account stays with you.

It costs nothing to set up a myRA. You can decide how much to set aside on a regular basis each month or only make contributions when you want.

How can you open a myRA? Go to www.myra.gov for more information or call 855-406-6972.

This new retirement saving option is good news for everyone. I hope it will encourage more providers to take advantage. With no fees, it's a no-brainer!

Although the interest earned on a myRA is currently relatively low, it's a great place to start if you haven't already established an IRA.

Time to Invest in Your 2016 IRA!

Many family child care providers wait until they file their 2015 tax return before making a contribution to their 2015 IRA. Here's a simple way to boost your retirement savings. Contribute to your IRA at the beginning of the year. This will generate substantially higher returns than if you wait until after the year is over.

The reason is that money invested in January will take full advantage of the power of compound interest. Money you invest at the beginning of 2016 will earn interest throughout the year. Over the long run, money invested months early in the year will make a big difference in your retirement. Let's look at some examples.

Providers Kim and Teresa are the same age. They invest $5,000 each year in their IRA and earn the same rate of interest (5%) each year. Kim invests her $5,000 each January, while Teresa waits until April of the following year to invest her $5,000. This means Kim's month is earning interest for 15 extra months (January 2016–April 2017) each year.

After 30 years Kim has $16,000 more in her IRA and after 40 years she has $34,000 more.

If they both earned 9% (the historic long-term return of the stock market), Kim would have $75,000 more than Teresa after 30 years and $193,000 over 40 years.

What if Kim invested her money on January 1, 2016 for her 2015 IRA and Teresa invested on April 15? Even the 3.5 month difference still adds up to $30,000 more in Kim's pocket after 30 years and $45,000 over 40 years (at 9% a year).

Under all of these scenarios, that's a lot of money!

It's Not Too Late

If you are in your 50s, it's not to late to boost your retirement savings. If you are age 55 and you contribute $2,400 on January 1 each year for 10 years (earning 7% a year), you will have $273,000 at age 65. Not bad.

So, when is the best time to start saving money for your retirement? Answer: Today! When is the next best time? Answer: Tomorrow! Now is the time to contribute towards your 2016 IRA.

2016 Webinars with Tom Copeland

You can now listen to a monthly webinar on family child care business topics from your home computer. These webinars are created in cooperation with National Association for Family Child Care (NAFFC). Participants of the webinar will see a PowerPoint presentation and receive a series of handouts for each session. Participants can ask questions live. The schedule for 2016 follows:

- January 12th: Eight Things Every Provider Should Know About Organizing Their Paperwork
- January 19th: What's New? Tax Changes You Should Know for Your 2015 Tax Return
- February 9th: The Top Five Tax Deductions Every Family Child Care Provider Should Know
- February 16th: Your Most Important Tax Number: The Time-Space Percentage
- March 8th: Worried About an IRS Audit? Preparing for the Possibilities
- April 12th: The Facts, Not Fiction: The Financial Impact of Being on the Food Program and How to Claim Food Expenses
- May 17th: Accounting Made Easy: How to Effectively Use the New KidKare Software (formerly Minute Menu Kids Pro)
- June 14th: Don't Let Your Income Manage You, Manage Your Income
- August 9th: Communicating with Clients: The Importance of Strong Contracts & Policies
- September 13th: Dealing with Difficulties: Enforcing Your Contract and Policies
- October 11th: Internet Marketing: Six Tricks to Make Your Business Shine
- November 15th: Expect the Unexpected: How to Use Insurance to Protect Yourself From Real Life Scenarios

Each webinar costs $25 and discounts are available when you enroll in three or more webinars. For details, visit the NAFCC website at www.nafcc.org/training.

Retirement Plan Limits for 2015

Here are the contribution limits for various individual retirement account (IRA) plans for 2015:

- Traditional IRA and Roth IRA: $5,500, plus an additional $1,000 if you are age 50 or over
- SIMPLE IRA: $12,500 of your net profit, plus an additional $2,500 if you are age 50 or over (Note: you must have established a SIMPLE IRA by October 1, 2015 to make a 2015 contribution.)
- SEP IRA: 18.58% of your net profit

The deadline for your contribution is April 15, 2016.

Saver's Credit Limits for 2015

The Retirement Savings Contribution Credit (Saver's Credit) allows providers to claim a tax credit for making a contribution to a qualified IRA—in addition to claiming a tax deduction for the IRA contribution.

The income eligibility limits for the Saver's Credit for 2015 are higher than in 2014. That is, you qualify for this credit if your adjusted gross income is $61,000 or less (married filing jointly), $45,750 or less (head of household), or $30,500 (single or married filing separately). The tax credit is calculated based on contributions to any qualified IRA up to $2,000 per person per year. This includes contributions to a traditional IRA, Roth IRA, SIMPLE IRA, SEP IRA, and 401(k) or 403(b) plan by you or your spouse. The amount of the tax credit is 10%, 20%, or 50% of the contribution, based on your family's adjusted gross income.

The credit is claimed on IRS **Form 8880 Credit for Qualified Retirement Savings Contributions** and carried forward to IRS **Form 1040**, line 50. If you made a contribution to an IRA from 2012 to 2014 and were income eligible for this credit in those tax years but did not take advantage of the credit, you can file an amended tax return to claim the credit.

For a comprehensive discussion of retirement plans and how to save more money, see the *Family Child Care Money Management and Retirement Guide*, available from Redleaf Press (www.redleafpress.org).

PART I

The Tax Organizer

The Tax Organizer

The Tax Organizer is a series of worksheets that help you organize all the income and expenses for your family child care business and show you where to enter the information on your tax forms. After you complete the Tax Organizer, cut it out and save it with your other tax records for the current tax season. Because the tax laws change constantly, do not use this Tax Organizer for any year other than 2015.

If you plan to give this Tax Organizer to your tax preparer, show it to the preparer before you start recording information. Some tax preparers have their own tax organizer that they will ask you to use, but ask your tax preparer if you can use this one instead. This Tax Organizer can help your tax preparer better understand the deductions that you're entitled to claim for your child care business and can save her a lot of time as she completes your tax return. Before you give your completed Tax Organizer to your tax preparer, be sure to make a copy for your records.

Once your tax return is complete, review the deductions in your Tax Organizer and make sure that they've all been entered on your tax forms. If it appears that any of the deductions you listed aren't included, ask the tax preparer why.

There are several record-keeping books that can help you record and organize your tax records, including the following:

> *Redleaf Calendar-Keeper*
> *Inventory-Keeper*
> *Mileage-Keeper*

If you use these products to track your income and expenses throughout the year, you will be able to complete this Tax Organizer much more quickly (and your tax return will be more accurate). Each part of the Tax Organizer explains how to get the information from these other tools and enter it in the Tax Organizer.

Let's start with some identifying information:

Name _____

Address _____

_____

Social Security or employer ID number _____

Your Income

In the chart below, list all the child care income you received from both parent fees and county or state subsidy programs for parents. If necessary, continue on another sheet of paper.

Name of Parent	Income from Parents Jan 1–Dec 31	Income from Subsidy Programs Jan 1–Dec 31
_____	_____	_____
_____	_____	_____
_____	_____	_____
_____	_____	_____
_____	_____	_____
_____	_____	_____
_____	_____	_____
_____	_____	_____
_____	_____	_____
_____	_____	_____

Totals   **(A)** _____   **(B)** _____

Total parent fees **(A + B)**   _____

Plus government grants   + _____

Enter on **Schedule C**, line 1   = _____

Food Program reimbursements
received Jan 1–Dec 31   _____

Less Food Program reimbursements
for your own children (total **[C]**
from page 43 of this Tax Organizer)   – _____

Other income   = _____

Enter the total "other income" on **Schedule C**, line 6.

Your Time Percentage

Your Time percentage is the ratio of hours spent on business activities in your home during this tax year to the total hours in a year. There are two ways to calculate this ratio, depending on whether the care you provide for children is on a regular or irregular schedule throughout the year. In either case, you need to have written records of the hours you worked.

A. If You Cared for Children on a Regular Schedule throughout the Year

Complete this section if the hours you cared for children were fairly consistent from week to week during this tax year. If the hours weren't consistent, go to section B on page 33.

HOURS CARING FOR CHILDREN ON A REGULAR BASIS

	_____	Time the first child regularly arrived at your home
	_____	Time the last child regularly left your home
	_____	(A) Number of hours in a day the children were present, from the time the first child regularly arrived until the last child regularly left
x	_____	Number of days you worked per week
=	_____	Hours you worked in a week
x	_____	52 weeks
=	_____	(B) Tentative hours caring for children

You cannot count time spent on vacations, holidays, illnesses, or other days your business was closed. Below, record these days for the entire year and subtract this total from the tentative hours caring for children:

	_____	Vacations
+	_____	Holidays
+	_____	Illnesses
+	_____	Other
		(describe: _____)
=	_____	Total days closed
x	_____	(A) Hours worked in a typical day
=	_____	(C) Total hours closed
	_____	(B) Tentative hours caring for children
–	_____	(C) Total hours closed
=	_____	(D) Total hours caring for children on a regular basis

ADDITIONAL HOURS CARING FOR CHILDREN

	Average # Hours		# Times per Year		
Children arriving early or staying late	_____	x	_____	=	_____
Children staying overnight	_____	x	_____	= +	_____
Occasional care on weekends	_____	x	_____	= +	_____
Other (describe: _____)	_____	x	_____	= +	_____
Total additional hours caring for children				(E) =	_____

BUSINESS HOURS IN THE HOME WHEN CHILDREN WERE NOT PRESENT

Activity Worked	Average # Hours		# Weeks in Business		Hours
Business phone calls	_____	x	_____	=	_____
Cleaning	_____	x	_____	=	+ _____
E-mail/Internet activity	_____	x	_____	=	+ _____
Family child care association activities	_____	x	_____	=	+ _____
Food Program paperwork	_____	x	_____	=	+ _____
Meal preparation	_____	x	_____	=	+ _____
Parent interviews	_____	x	_____	=	+ _____
Planning/preparing activities	_____	x	_____	=	+ _____
Record keeping	_____	x	_____	=	+ _____
Other (identify: _____)	_____	x	_____	=	+ _____
Other (identify: _____)	_____	x	_____	=	+ _____
Total business hours when children were not present				**(F)** =	_____

SUMMARY OF BUSINESS HOURS

Total hours caring for children on a regular basis   **(D)** = _____
Total additional hours caring for children   **(E)** + _____
Total business hours when children were not present   **(F)** + _____
Total business hours   **(G)** = _____
Enter the Total business hours **(G)** amount on **Form 8829**, line 4.

If you were not in business as of January 1 of last year, cross out the amount on **Form 8829**, line 5 (8,760 hours) and enter the number of hours in the year from the day you started your business until December 31 of last year.

IF YOU USE THE *REDLEAF CALENDAR-KEEPER*
The total number of hours you worked should be recorded on the year-to-date total line in the box in the upper-right corner of the December calendar page. Enter this amount in **(G)** above or directly on **Form 8829**, line 4.

B. If You Cared for Children on an Irregular Schedule

If your hours of business were not on a regular schedule throughout the year, you will have to carefully track your hours worked for each month. Calculate the number of hours you cared for children each day, from the moment the first child arrived until the last child left. Don't count any days that your business was closed because of vacations, holidays, or illnesses. Next, calculate your business hours when children were not present by filling out the table Business Hours in the Home When Children Were Not Present on page 32.

	# Hours Caring for Children
January	_____
February	+ _____
March	+ _____
April	+ _____
May	+ _____
June	+ _____
July	+ _____
August	+ _____
September	+ _____
October	+ _____
November	+ _____
December	+ _____

Total hours caring for children: (H) = _____

SUMMARY OF BUSINESS HOURS

Total hours caring for children	(H)	_____
Total business hours when children were not present	(F) +	_____
Total business hours	(I) =	_____

Enter the Total business hours (I) amount on **Form 8829**, line 4.

IF YOU USE THE *REDLEAF CALENDAR-KEEPER*

Follow the same directions as listed above to report your total number of business hours.

Your Space Percentage

List all the rooms in your home (including the basement and garage). Enter the square footage of each room in the column that best applies to how that space is used.

Room	Used 100% for Business	Used Regularly for Business	Not Used Regularly for Business
_____	_____	_____	_____
_____	_____	_____	_____
_____	_____	_____	_____
_____	_____	_____	_____
_____	_____	_____	_____
_____	_____	_____	_____
_____	_____	_____	_____
_____	_____	_____	_____
_____	_____	_____	_____
_____	_____	_____	_____
_____	_____	_____	_____
_____	_____	_____	_____

Total square feet   _____   _____   _____
                          (J)   (K)   (L)

Total square footage of your home: (J + K + L = M)   (M) = _____

Your Time-Space Percentage

1) If you have no entries in column (**J**):

Enter the amount from line (**K**) on **Form 8829**, line 1.

Enter the amount from line (**M**) on **Form 8829**, line 2.

2) If you have any entries in column (**J**), you have one or more rooms that are used *exclusively* for your business. Calculate your Time-Space percentage for these rooms as follows:

Enter the amount on line (**J**) _____

Enter the amount on line (**M**) _____

Divide (**J**) by (**M**) = _____% (**N**) Space percentage for exclusive-use rooms

Enter the amount on line (**K**) _____

Enter the amount on line (**M**) _____

Divide (**K**) by (**M**) = _____% (**O**) Space percentage for regularly used rooms

Enter the amount from line (**G**) or (**I**) = _____ (**P**)

Enter the total number of hours in the year from **Form 8829**, line 5* _____ (**Q**)

Divide (**P**) by (**Q**) = _____ (**R**) Time percentage for regularly used rooms

Multiply:

    (**O**) _____

x (**R**) _____

=   _____ (**S**) Time-Space percentage for regularly used rooms

Add:

    (**N**) _____

+ (**S**) _____

=   _____ (**T**) Final Time-Space percentage

Enter the Final Time-Space percentage (**T**) amount on **Form 8829**, line 7.

Do not fill in lines 1–6. Attach a copy of these calculations to **Form 8829**.

---

*If you weren't in business as of January 1 of last year, enter the number of hours in the year from the day you started your business until December 31 of last year.

Your Business Expenses

Start by entering your business expenses in the categories below, then transfer the amounts to the indicated lines on **Schedule C**. (See the *Record-Keeping Guide* for a list of more than one thousand deductions.)

Advertising	_____	Enter on **Schedule C**, line 8
Liability insurance	_____	Enter on **Schedule C**, line 15
Legal and professional services (for your business)	_____	Enter on **Schedule C**, line 17
Business taxes and licenses (payroll taxes and child care licenses)	_____	Enter on **Schedule C**, line 23
Business travel expenses (vehicle expenses go on line 9)	_____	Enter on **Schedule C**, line 24a
Business meals and entertainment	_____	Enter on **Schedule C**, line 24b
Wages (paid to both family and nonfamily employees)	_____	Enter on **Schedule C**, line 26

Your expenses may be 100% deductible or partly deductible, based on either the Time-Space percentage or the actual business-use percentage:

- **100% business use**: Items that are never used for personal purposes after business hours. Do not claim something as 100% business use unless it meets this qualification.

- **Time-Space percentage**: Items that are used for both business and personal purposes. To calculate your Time-Space percentage, see pages 31–35.

- **Actual business-use percentage**: Items that are used extensively but not exclusively for business purposes. Calculate the percentage of time that the item is actually used in your business (each item will usually have a different business-use percentage). You must have written records to show how you arrived at each business-use percentage. Most providers reserve this method for more expensive items that they use considerably more than items in their Time-Space percentage.

For each business category that follows, enter your expenses:

Credit Card Interest

100% business use			$ _____
Time-Space percentage	$_____ x _____% =		+ $ _____
Actual business-use percentage	$_____ x _____% =		+ $ _____
Enter the total on **Schedule C**, line 16b			= $ _____

Office Expenses

100% business use $ _____

Time-Space percentage $_____ x _____% =   + $ _____

Actual business-use percentage $_____ x _____% =   + $ _____

Enter the total on **Schedule C**, line 18   = $ _____

Rent of Items

100% business use $ _____

Time-Space percentage $_____ x _____% =   + $ _____

Actual business-use percentage $_____ x _____% =   + $ _____

Enter the total on **Schedule C**, line 20b   = $ _____

Repairs and Maintenance on Business Property
(doesn't include home repairs)

100% business use $ _____

Time-Space percentage $_____ x _____% =   + $ _____

Actual business-use percentage $_____ x _____% =   + $ _____

Enter the total on **Schedule C**, line 21   = $ _____

Supplies
(includes children's supplies and kitchen supplies)

100% business use $ _____

Time-Space percentage $_____ x _____% =   + $ _____

Actual business-use percentage $_____ x _____% =   + $ _____

Enter the total on **Schedule C**, line 22   = $ _____

Toys

100% business use $ _____

Time-Space percentage $_____ x _____% =   + $ _____

Actual business-use percentage $_____ x _____% =   + $ _____

Enter the total on one of the blank lines on **Schedule C**, Part V   = $ _____

Household Items
(includes yard expenses, safety items, tools)

100% business use $ _____

Time-Space percentage $_____ x _____% =   + $ _____

Actual business-use percentage $_____ x _____% =   + $ _____

Enter the total on one of the blank lines on **Schedule C**, Part V   = $ _____

Cleaning Supplies

100% business use $ _____

Time-Space percentage $_____ x _____% =   + $ _____

Actual business-use percentage $_____ x _____% =   + $ _____

Enter the total on one of the blank lines on **Schedule C**, Part V   = $ _____

Activity Expenses

(includes field trips, birthday parties, special activities)

100% business use $ _____

Time-Space percentage $_____ x _____% = + $ _____

Actual business-use percentage $_____ x _____% = + $ _____

Enter the total on one of the blank lines on **Schedule C**, Part V = $ _____

Other Expenses

(items not included in any of the above expense categories)

100% business use $ _____

Time-Space percentage $_____ x _____% = + $ _____

Actual business-use percentage $_____ x _____% = + $ _____

Enter the total on one of the blank lines on **Schedule C**, Part V = $ _____

IF YOU USE THE *REDLEAF CALENDAR-KEEPER*

There are two places where you can find the totals of your **Schedule C** deductions. One is the year-to-date total at the bottom of the monthly expense report for December. The second is the list of direct business expenses on the income tax worksheet. Take the totals that best represent your deductions, and enter them in the appropriate expense category in the Tax Organizer.

Your Vehicle Expenses

To calculate the miles that you drove on trips for which the primary purpose was business, enter information from your written records, such as the *Redleaf Calendar-Keeper,* the *Mileage-Keeper,* receipts, and canceled checks on the lines below. If you used more than one vehicle for your business last year, photocopy this part of the Tax Organizer and fill out one worksheet for each vehicle you used.

Odometer Readings

Make and model of vehicle _____

Year first used in your business _____

Purchase price of vehicle _____

Odometer reading December 31 of last year _____

Odometer reading January 1 of last year – _____

Total miles vehicle was driven last year **(A)** _____

Business Mileage

Add up your business mileage and then multiply it by the standard mileage rate.

Business miles January 1–December 31 ____   x   0.575   = _____

Total mileage deduction   = _____ **(C)**

Business-Use Percentage of Vehicle

Total business miles last year   _____ **(B)**

Divided by total miles vehicle was driven last year   ÷ _____ **(A)**

Business-use percentage of vehicle   = _____ **(D)**

Other Vehicle Expenses

Parking/tolls/ferry   _____

Vehicle loan interest   + _____

Vehicle property tax (if applicable)   + _____

Total other vehicle expenses   = _____

Multiplied by business-use percentage of vehicle   x _____ **(D)**

Business-use percentage of other vehicle expenses   = _____ **(E)**

Standard Mileage Rate Method

Mileage deduction   _____ **(C)**

Total business-use percentage of other vehicle expenses   + _____ **(E)**

Total business deduction (standard mileage rate method)   = _____

Enter the Total business deduction on **Schedule C**, line 9

Actual Vehicle Expenses Method

To use this method, you must have recorded all your vehicle expenses so that you can add them up at the end of the year.

Gas   _____

Oil/lube/filter   + _____

Tune-up/repairs/tires   + _____

Lease payment   + _____

Wash/wax   + _____

Supplies   + _____

Vehicle insurance   + _____

Other   + _____

Total actual vehicle expenses   = _____

Multiplied by business-use percentage of vehicle   x _____ **(D)**

Business deduction for actual vehicle expenses   = _____ **(F)**

Vehicle Depreciation

Fair market value of vehicle when first used for business   _____

Business-use percentage of vehicle   x _____ **(D)**

                                                            = _____

Depreciation percentage (from tables on page 109)   x _____ %*

Depreciation deduction   _____ **(G)**

Actual Business-Use Deduction

Business deduction for actual vehicle expenses   _____ **(F)**

Extra business endorsement on vehicle insurance (if any)   + _____

Depreciation deduction   + _____ **(G)**

Business-use percentage of other vehicle expenses   + _____ **(E)**

Total business deduction (actual vehicle expenses method)   = _____

Enter the Total business deduction on **Schedule C**, line 9

Compare your total business deduction under the standard mileage rate method and the actual vehicle expenses method. If you began your business last year or used the standard mileage rate method for this vehicle in earlier years, you may choose to use the total from either method. If you used the actual vehicle expenses method for this vehicle in earlier years, you must continue using this method. (For more information, see chapter 5.)

IF YOU USE THE *REDLEAF CALENDAR-KEEPER*

Refer to the year-to-date total mileage at the bottom of the December expense report. If you tracked your actual vehicle expense in one of the monthly expense columns, enter the year total from December on the appropriate lines above.

IF YOU USE THE *MILEAGE-KEEPER*

Enter the amounts recorded for mileage and actual vehicle expenses from pages 34–35 (if you use the standard mileage rate method) or pages 44–45 (if you use the actual vehicle expenses method) on the appropriate lines above.

---

*See chapter 3 for limitations on the depreciation deduction each year. Also, if you purchased a vehicle last year, see the Section 179 rules in chapter 3.

Your Food Expenses

You have two choices when calculating your food expenses. You can use the standard meal allowance rate or the actual cost of food. The standard meal allowance rate was established by the IRS so that providers could claim their food expenses without having to keep food receipts. (For a complete discussion of how to report Food Program reimbursements and food expenses on **Schedule C**, see chapter 4. For a detailed discussion of how to track food costs, see the *Record-Keeping Guide*.) Here's a summary of these two methods:

USING THE STANDARD MEAL ALLOWANCE RATE

You must keep the following records throughout the year: each child's name, dates and hours of attendance, and number of meals served. If you were on the Food Program during the year, save your monthly claim forms, which contain this information. Track nonreimbursed meals on your copy of the claim form or someplace else. Use the meal form to track nonreimbursed meals for last year (or all meals if you weren't on the Food Program). Use the year-end meal tally to total your reimbursed and nonreimbursed meals for last year.

USING THE ACTUAL COST OF FOOD

There are many ways to calculate your actual food costs. One way to do this is to buy and store your business food separately from buying and storing food for your personal use. Probably the simplest and most accurate method is to estimate the average cost per child per meal and multiply that number by the number of meals and snacks served. To calculate the average cost, track the ingredients that you served for four typical menus for breakfast, lunch, supper, and snacks. Estimate the cost of the food for each menu, and divide that number by the number of children served. (For more information about how to calculate the actual cost of food, see the *Record-Keeping Guide*.)

IF YOU USE THE *REDLEAF CALENDAR-KEEPER*

If you tracked your food expenses each month, your yearly total will be on page 83 of your December expense report. You may also have entered your food expenses on the income tax worksheet as direct business expenses on page 85. If you haven't estimated your business food expenses, you may want to fill out the meal form and year-end meal tally in this book to get a more accurate deduction rather than using the totals on your *Redleaf Calendar-Keeper*.

Calculating Food Program Reimbursements for Your Own Children

If you received Food Program reimbursements for your own children this year, subtract this amount before reporting your reimbursements as taxable income on **Schedule C**. To calculate the reimbursements for your own children, you'll need to calculate the first and the second half of the year separately, because the reimbursement rates go up on July 1 every year.

Begin by filling out the two worksheets below, taking the information requested from the meal counts on your monthly claim forms.

Worksheet 1:
Food Program Reimbursements
for Your Own Children, Jan–June 2015

Number of Meals	Breakfasts	Lunches	Snacks	Dinners
January	_____	_____	_____	_____
February	_____	_____	_____	_____
March	_____	_____	_____	_____
April	_____	_____	_____	_____
May	_____	_____	_____	_____
June	_____	_____	_____	_____
Total meals	_____	_____	_____	_____

Total meals
times CACFP Tier 1

reimbursement rate	x $ 1.31	x $2.47	x $0.73	x $2.47
	(Alaska: $2.09)	(Alaska: $4.00)	(Alaska: $1.19)	(Alaska: $4.00)
	(Hawaii: $1.33)	(Hawaii: $2.88)	(Hawaii: $0.86)	(Hawaii: $2.88)

CACFP
reimbursements for

your own children =	_____	_____	_____	_____
	(1)	(2)	(3)	(4)

Add reimbursement totals 1–4 to get the total
reimbursements for your own children, Jan–June   = _____ **(A)**

Worksheet 2:
Food Program Reimbursements
for Your Own Children, July–Dec 2015

Number of Meals	Breakfasts	Lunches	Snacks	Dinners
July	_____	_____	_____	_____
August	_____	_____	_____	_____
September	_____	_____	_____	_____
October	_____	_____	_____	_____
November	_____	_____	_____	_____
December	_____	_____	_____	_____
Total meals	_____	_____	_____	_____

Total meals
times CACFP Tier 1
reimbursement rate

	Breakfasts	Lunches	Snacks	Dinners
	x $1.32	x $2.48	x $0.74	x $2.48
	(Alaska: $2.11)	(Alaska: $4.02)	(Alaska: $1.20)	(Alaska: $4.02)
	(Hawaii: $1.54)	(Hawaii: $2.90)	(Hawaii: $0.86)	(Hawaii: $2.90)

CACFP
reimbursements for
your own children =

(1)	(2)	(3)	(4)
_____	_____	_____	_____

Add reimbursement totals 1–4 to get the total
reimbursements for your own children, July–Dec   = _____ **(B)**

Once you have calculated amounts **(A)** and **(B)**, add them together to get the total **(C)**:

Reimbursements for your own children, Jan–June   _____**(A)**
Reimbursements for your own children, Jul–Dec   + _____**(B)**
Total reimbursements for your own children   = _____**(C)**
        Enter the total reimbursements for your own children **(C)** amount on page 30
        of this Tax Organizer.

MEAL FORM Week of _____ 2015

The form consists of two meal-tracking tables (left and right), each with columns:

Child	Mon	Tue	Wed	Thu	Fri	Sat	Sun	Totals

Each day cell contains the entries:
- Bkst
- Lun
- Din
- Sn1
- Sn2
- Sn3

Each Totals cell contains:
- B
- L
- D
- S

Place a check mark (✓) next to each meal or snack you serve. Do not count meals served to your own children. If you are on the Food Program, use this form to track your nonreimbursed meals only. Add the reimbursed meals from your monthly claim forms and the nonreimbursed meals from this form together, and put the totals on the year-end meal tally. If you are not on the Food Program, use this form to track all your meals, and put the totals on the year-end meal tally.

Make copies of this form for each week of the year. If you have six or fewer children in your program, you can use one form for two weeks. You can download this form at the Redleaf Press website. Go to www.redleafpress.org, and find the page for the *Redleaf Calendar-Keeper 2015*. There will be a link to this form.

Weekly Totals

| Breakfasts | _____ | Dinners | _____ |
| Lunches | _____ | Snacks | _____ |

YEAR-END MEAL TALLY

If you are not on the Food Program, enter all meals and snacks in the column labeled "Number Not Reimbursed by Food Program."

	Breakfasts		Lunches		Dinners		Snacks	
	Number Reimbursed by Food Program	Number Not Reimbursed by Food Program	Number Reimbursed by Food Program	Number Not Reimbursed by Food Program	Number Reimbursed by Food Program	Number Not Reimbursed by Food Program	Number Reimbursed by Food Program	Number Not Reimbursed by Food Program
January								
February								
March								
April								
May								
June								
July								
August								
September								
October								
November								
December								
TOTAL								

2015 Standard Meal Allowance Rate*

Number of Breakfasts	_____	X	$1.31	= $ _____
Number of Lunches	_____	X	$2.47	= $ _____
Number of Dinners	_____	X	$2.47	= $ _____
Number of Snacks	_____	X	$0.73	= $ _____
		Total Food Deductions		$ _____ †

Do not report any meals served to your own children (even if they are reimbursed by the Food Program).

* The IRS standard meal allowance rate for 2015 used in these calculations is based on the Tier I rate as of January 1, 2015. This rate is used for all meals and snacks served throughout 2015, even though the Tier I rate goes up every July. All providers, whether on Tier I or Tier II (and all providers not on the Food Program), will use the rates listed.

† Enter this amount on Form 1040 Schedule C, Part V. Be sure to enter any reimbursements from the Food Program (with the exception of reimbursements for your own children) as income on Form 1040 Schedule C, line 6.

Your Home Expenses

Casualty losses   _____ Enter on **Form 8829**, line 9, col. b

Mortgage interest paid last year   _____ Enter on **Form 8829**, line 10, col. b

Real estate taxes paid last year   _____ Enter on **Form 8829**, line 11, col. b

Homeowners/renters insurance   _____ Enter on **Form 8829**, line 17, col. b

Home repairs and maintenance   _____ Enter on **Form 8829**, line 19, col. b

Other assessments   _____ Enter on **Form 8829**, line 21, col. b

Utilities

Gas   _____

Oil   _____

Electricity   _____

Water   _____

Sewer   _____

Garbage   _____

Cable TV   _____

Total utilities   _____ Enter on **Form 8829**, line 20, col. b

Apartment or home rent   _____ Enter on **Form 8829**, line 18, col. b

You can never claim monthly costs associated with the first phone line in your home. If you have a second phone line in your home, you may claim part of its monthly costs based on your business-use percentage. Calculate your business-use percentage by tracking your business and personal use for at least two months. Divide your business hours by the total (business and personal) hours of use.

Cost of second phone line   _____

Actual business-use percentage   x _____ %

     = _____ Enter on **Form 8829**, line 20, col. a

IF YOU USE THE *REDLEAF CALENDAR-KEEPER*

Enter the amounts in the Total column (not the FCC Business Expense column) from the house expenses worksheet.

Your Depreciation

Enter all the depreciable items you bought last year on the worksheet. (Use the depreciation tables in chapter 3 to fill in the Table % column in the depreciation worksheet.) Enter your depreciation deductions on **Form 4562**. For depreciable items that you bought before last year and after you went into business, fill out copies of this page. Enter depreciation for each year on **Form 4562**. Enter the first year of depreciation as described in chapter 3. After the first year, enter depreciation (except home and home/land improvements) on **Form 4562**, line 17.

Your Home Depreciation
(including home and land improvements)

Purchase price of your home   _____

Value of land (at time of purchase)   − _____

Value of any improvements
to your home or land that you
completed *before* your business began (see below)   + _____ **(A)**

Your home's adjusted value   = _____
      Enter your home's adjusted value on **Form 8829**, line 36

Improvements Completed before Your Business Began

Description of Project	Month/Year Completed	Cost of Project
_____	_____	_____
_____	_____	+ _____
_____	_____	+ _____
_____	_____	+ _____
_____	_____	+ _____
_____	_____	+ _____
Total cost of all projects		= _____ **(A)**

IF YOU USE THE *INVENTORY-KEEPER*
Use the numbers from page 53.

Depreciation Worksheet

Depreciation Category[1]	Date Put into Service	Cost or Other Basis[2]	Method/ Convention	Business-Use %[3]	Business Basis[4]	Table %	Depreciation Deduction	Section 179 Deduction
Computers/printers								
Furniture/appliances								
Home improvements								
Land improvements								

[1] See chapter 3 for a definition of what items belong in each depreciation category.

[2] Enter the original cost or the fair market value of the item when it was first used for business last year, whichever is lower.

[3] Enter one of the following percentages: 100% business use, Time-Space percentage, or actual business-use percentage. See chapter 5 for a definition of each option.

[4] Multiply the amount in the Cost or Other Basis column by the percentage in the Business-Use % column.

Your Employee Payroll Tax Record

Your Employee Payroll Tax Record

Employee Name	Date Paid	Gross Amt. Pd.	Social Sec./ Medicare Withheld[1]	Fed. Inc. Tax Withheld	State Inc. Tax Withheld	Total Deductions[2]
_____	_____	_____	_____	_____	_____	_____
_____	_____	_____	_____	_____	_____	_____
_____	_____	_____	_____	_____	_____	_____
_____	_____	_____	_____	_____	_____	_____
_____	_____	_____	_____	_____	_____	_____
_____	_____	_____	_____	_____	_____	_____
_____	_____	_____	_____	_____	_____	_____
_____	_____	_____	_____	_____	_____	_____
_____	_____	_____	_____	_____	_____	_____
Totals Enter on:		**Schedule C, line 26**	**Schedule C, line 23**	**Schedule C, line 23**	**Schedule C, line 23**	

[1] 6.2% Social Security + 1.45% Medicare = 7.65%

[2] Social Security/Medicare Amount Withheld + Federal Income Tax Withheld + State Income Tax Withheld

PART II

The Tax Workbook

CHAPTER 1

Calculating Your
Time-Space Percentage

Before you start filling out your tax forms, calculate your Time-Space percentage for this tax year. This percentage is one of the most important numbers that you will use for your taxes because it determines how much of your key expenses you will be able to deduct as business expenses. For example, the Time-Space percentage is used in calculating home expenses on **Form 8829**, personal property depreciation expenses on **Form 4562**, and shared household supplies and other expenses on **Schedule C**. The specific deductions that are based on the Time-Space percentage include these:

- casualty losses
- mortgage interest
- real estate taxes
- homeowners insurance
- home repairs and maintenance
- utilities

- rent of a house or apartment
- home depreciation
- personal property depreciation
- home improvements
- land improvements
- household supplies and toys

Since the total of these costs is usually a significant amount, it's important to calculate your Time-Space percentage correctly. The Tax Organizer includes worksheets that you can use to calculate your Time-Space percentage quickly; this chapter provides a more detailed description of that process.

Computing your Time-Space percentage is a three-step process. First you calculate your Time percentage, then you calculate your Space percentage, and then you multiply the two together. The formula that you will use looks like this:

$$\frac{\text{\# hours your home is used for business}}{\text{Total \# hours in a year}} \quad \text{x} \quad \frac{\text{\# square feet of your home used regularly for business}}{\text{Total \# square feet in your home}} \quad = \quad \text{Time-Space percentage}$$

Step One: Calculate Your Time Percentage

The Time percentage is how much time your home is used for your business. You calculate it by using the following formula:

$$\frac{\text{\# hours your home is used for business}}{\text{Total \# hours in a year}} \quad = \quad \text{Time percentage}$$

You can include the following activities in calculating how many hours your home is used for your business:

- caring for children
- cleaning the home for your business
- cooking for the children in your care
- planning and preparing activities for your business
- keeping business records, including paperwork for the Child and Adult Care Food Program (CACFP)
- conducting interviews with parents
- talking to parents on the telephone about your business
- locating resources and information on the Internet
- any other business-related activities that you do in your home

In calculating your Time percentage, you may not count time that you spend outside your home on activities such as shopping or transporting children to school. For those activities, you are not using your home for business purposes.

Maximize Your Claim

Many family child care providers don't include all their working hours in calculating their Time percentage and therefore do not take full advantage of the law. Although there is no maximum Time percentage, it is important to track your working hours so that you have evidence to back up your claim. Also, you must recalculate your Time percentage each year, because the number of hours you work usually isn't exactly the same from year to year. Here are some tips for recording your business hours:

HOURS SPENT CARING FOR CHILDREN

Throughout the year, keep records that show how much time you spend caring for the children in your business. Keep attendance records, or save a copy of a document that describes your normal working day, such as a parent contract or a flyer advertising your business.

> EXAMPLE
>
> This year you cared for children from 7:00 a.m. to 5:00 p.m., five days a week, and took one week of vacation. In this case, you spent 2,550 hours caring for children (10 hours a day x 5 days a week x 51 weeks = 2,550 hours).

To come up with this number, count all the hours when children are in your care from the time the first child arrives to the time the last child leaves. If you usually work from 7:00 a.m. to 5:00 p.m., but a child regularly arrives early or stays late, note this on a calendar or in your record book and count the additional time. If a child stays overnight occasionally, count all the hours that the child is in your house. If you regularly care for children overnight, your Time percentage could be very high. In this case, it is extremely important to keep exact records of when children are present.

If you take a vacation, don't count this time as business hours. You probably should not count the hours for paid holidays, either, although there are no IRS guidelines on this point.

HOURS WORKING WHEN CHILDREN ARE NOT PRESENT

In addition to counting all the hours you spend caring for children, you should also include all the hours that your home is used for business purposes when the children in your care are not present. This includes time spent cleaning, cooking, planning activities, keeping records, interviewing, making phone calls, and doing other activities related to your business. Don't count hours spent on general home repairs or maintenance activities, such as cutting the lawn, repairing fixtures, or putting up storm windows.

You may not count the same hours twice. For example, if you clean the house during the day while the children sleep, you cannot count the cleaning hours because you are already counting this time as caring for children. You may only count these hours if the children you care for are not present. For example, if between 7:00 a.m. and 8:00 a.m. you are preparing breakfast for the children in your care and your spouse is cleaning your home, you can only count one hour toward your Time percentage. If your spouse did the cleaning the night before while you were not conducting business activities, then you can count the time spent doing both tasks.

Keep records showing that you spent these hours on business activities and not on personal activities. If you spend one hour cleaning after the children leave, count this hour as business time. If you are cleaning your house in general, count only the time that is associated with the mess created by your business. Mark on a calendar when you do these business activities, or make up a weekly schedule that you regularly follow.

EXAMPLE

In addition to the 2,550 hours you spent actually caring for children, you spent 60 hours a month (720 hours a year) on business activities such as cleaning, preparing meals, planning activities, record keeping, meeting parents, and making business phone calls. You add this to your total business hours for the year and get 3,270 hours, which gives you a Time percentage of 37% (3,270 divided by 8,760 hours [24 hours a day x 365 days = 8,760 hours]).

Step Two: Calculate Your Space Percentage

The Space percentage is how much space you use in your home on a regular basis for your business. You calculate it by using the following formula:

$$\frac{\text{\# square feet of your home used regularly for business}}{\text{Total \# square feet in your home}} = \text{Space percentage}$$

For a room to be counted as child care space, it must be used on a *regular* basis for your business. Regular means consistent, customary use. Using a room only occasionally for business is not regular use. A room doesn't have to be used every day to be considered regularly used, but using it once every two weeks probably isn't regular use. If the children in your care sleep in your bedroom for an hour a day, count the bedroom as being regularly used for the business. However, using the bedroom for sick children once a month would not be regular use.

If there are any rooms in your home that you use exclusively for your business, refer to the section titled Exclusive-Use Rooms (in this chapter) before you calculate your Space percentage.

In the total square footage of your home, include every area of your home, including your basement, porch, deck, carport, detached garage, basement, and other structures on your land, such as a barn. Do not include the following spaces: lawn, garden area, driveway, sidewalk, sandbox, or outdoor play space.

IRS Child Care Provider Audit Technique Guide on the Space Percentage

The guide explicitly states that providers should count both their basements and garages as part of the total square feet of their home. A Tax Court case (see the *Uphus and Walker v. Commissioner* case in appendix B) has also ruled that providers can claim their laundry room, storage room, and garage as regularly used in the business, even if the children in care never use the rooms.

This means that when you count your basement in the total square footage of your home, you may be able to count areas such as the following as regularly used by your business: the furnace and water heater area (if used regularly to heat the home and water used by the business), the laundry room (if used regularly to wash children's clothes, bedding, and blankets), and the storage areas (if used regularly to store toys, holiday decorations, or home maintenance equipment used in the business).

The inclusion of basements and garages into the Space percentage calculation can have different consequences for providers. For providers who use these areas on a regular basis for their business and have other rooms that are not regularly used in their business this is good news because it will increase their Space percentage. For providers who have exclusive-use rooms and did not previously count these areas, this is bad news because it will decrease their Space percentage. For providers who use all of their rooms on a regular basis for their business as well as their basement and garage, this will not make any difference. In my experience working with thousands of child care providers, I have found that it is very common for providers to use all the rooms of their home on a regular basis for their business. If this applies to you, don't hesitate to claim 100% Space percentage.

Let's look at an example of a Space percentage calculation:

	Used regularly for business?	Count as business space	Don't count as business space
Living room	Yes	300 sq ft	
Dining room	Yes	200 sq ft	
Kitchen	Yes	150 sq ft	
Entryway or stairs	Yes	150 sq ft	
Second-floor hallway	Yes	75 sq ft	
Master bedroom	Yes	200 sq ft	
Child's bedroom	Yes	150 sq ft	
Child's bedroom	No		250 sq ft
Bathroom	Yes	100 sq ft	
Basement playroom	Yes	275 sq ft	
Basement furnace/ laundry area	Yes	50 sq ft	
Basement storage area	Yes/No	150 sq ft	250 sq ft
Garage/carport	Yes	200 sq ft	
Total		2,000 sq ft	500 sq ft

$$\frac{\text{\# square feet of your home used regularly for business}}{\text{Total \# square feet in your home}} = \frac{2,000}{2,500} = 80\% \text{ Space percentage}$$

Step Three: Calculate Your Time-Space Percentage

To find your Time-Space percentage, multiply your Time percentage by your Space percentage. In our example:

37% Time x 80% Space = 30% Time-Space percentage

Here's the Time-Space percentage formula again:

| # hours your home is used for business / Total # hours in a year | x | # square feet of your home used regularly for business / Total # square feet in your home | = | Time-Space percentage |

Use your 2015 Time-Space percentage only for the expenses you are claiming in 2015. *Remember that you will have to recalculate your Time-Space percentage each year and apply the new percentage to your expenses.*

If you discover that in previous years you have not been counting all the business space in your home or all your business hours, you may want to file **Form 1040X** (see chapter 9) to amend your previous tax returns and collect refunds from the IRS.

Exclusive-Use Rooms

If you use one or more of the rooms in your home exclusively for your business, you will need to calculate your Space percentage a bit differently. For example, an exclusive-use room might be a separate playroom that is used only by the children in your care. Exclusive use means 100% business use—it means that you don't use the room for any personal purposes at all, at any time. You can walk through the area during your personal time to get to another room or to go outside, but if you use the room for personal use at all, it is no longer used exclusively for business.

Let's say that in the example on the previous page the basement playroom is an exclusive-use room that is used 100% for the child care business. This room will serve as an example of how to calculate the Space percentage if you have an exclusive-use room:

1. Divide the square feet of the exclusive-use room by the total square feet of the home: 275 ÷ 2,500 = 11%

2. Divide the square feet of the rooms used regularly for business by the total square feet of the home: 1,725 ÷ 2,500 = 69%

3. Multiply the Space percentage of the shared rooms by the Time percentage: 69% x 37% = 26%

4. Add the percentages that resulted from Step 1 and Step 3: 11% + 26% = 37% Time-Space percentage

Notice that this Time-Space percentage is significantly greater than the 30% that we calculated previously for this example. If you use any rooms exclusively for your business, you should use this formula and claim the higher Time-Space percentage.

If you use some rooms exclusively for business, try not to set aside any other rooms exclusively for personal use, if you can avoid it. If you use one room exclusively for business and all your other rooms regularly for business, you will have a higher Time-Space percentage than if you use one room exclusively for business and all your other rooms exclusively for personal use.

You don't need to have a physical barrier around an area that is used exclusively for business. If a room has an area used exclusively for business but is otherwise a personal area, measure the two parts of the room and claim the exclusive-use rule for the exclusive area.

Because of the significant impact that an exclusive-use room can have on your Time-Space percentage, an IRS auditor is likely to look closely at the measurements of these rooms. If you claim any exclusive-use rooms, draw a simple diagram of your home showing which areas you used exclusively for your business, and keep this diagram with your records. This is important because your use of the rooms or the square footage of the rooms may change (if you remodel, for example). Save any copies of your house plans, blueprints, or other documents that can verify the square footage of your home.

Actual Business-Use Percentage

An actual business-use percentage is an alternative to the Time-Space percentage for items that you regularly use for business. It results in a much higher rate than your Time-Space percentage. You determine an item's actual business-use percentage by dividing the number of hours you use it for business by the total number of hours you use it for all purposes. If you use this method, you must document your business use in writing and be prepared to back up your number if the IRS challenges it.

Here's an example: You bought a swing set this year for $1,000; your Time-Space percentage is 25%. Using your Time-Space percentage, you could only depreciate $250 ($1,000 x 25%) of this expense this year. (See chapter 3 for an explanation of depreciation.) You determine that the children in your care use the swing set 10 hours a week (2 hours/day x 5 days), while your own children only use it 7 hours a week (1 hour/day x 7 days). In this case, your business-use percentage would be 59% (10 hours of business use ÷ 17 hours of total use), and you would be able to depreciate $590 ($1,000 x 59%). Since this item represents a large expense, and 59% is significantly greater than 25%, you should definitely use your business-use percentage in this case.

If you use a business-use percentage, you must keep records to support your calculation. If the IRS challenges it, it will be up to you to prove that your figure is accurate. This doesn't mean that you have to keep a log every day to show the business use, but you may need several weeks or months of logs to show a pattern. The higher your business-use percentage, the more evidence the IRS may request to justify your number.

You may use a business-use percentage for a few items and your Time-Space percentage for everything else. You can use either method for any items you are depreciating.

For more information about the tax issues discussed in this chapter, refer to the related topics in the other chapters of this book and the Redleaf Press *Family Child Care Record-Keeping Guide*.

CHAPTER 2

Claiming Your Home Expenses:
Form 8829

This chapter explains how to fill out **Form 8829 Expenses for Business Use of Your Home**. The following expenses are listed on this form:

- casualty losses
- mortgage interest
- real estate taxes
- homeowners insurance
- home repairs and maintenance
- utilities
- rent
- home depreciation

The goal of **Form 8829** is to determine how much of your home expenses you can claim as a business deduction. There are limits on this amount; for example, you cannot claim a loss from your business because of home expenses (other than real estate taxes and mortgage interest). You can carry forward any home expenses that aren't allowable this year and claim them in a later year. (If you live on a military base and pay no home-related expenses, you don't need to fill out **Form 8829**.)

To finish **Form 8829**, you will have to complete **Schedule C** through line 29 (see chapter 5). It's a good idea to read this chapter first so you'll know what to do when you reach that point on **Form 8829**. You may want to begin **Form 8829** while the Time-Space percentage calculation is fresh in your mind, then switch to other forms needed to complete **Schedule C** and return to **Form 8829** when you're done with **Schedule C**.

New Simplified Method
Starting in 2013 you may use a new IRS Simplified Method to claim up to $1,500 of your house expenses without receipts on **Schedule C**, line 30. If you choose to use this new rule you will not fill out IRS **Form 8829** and you will not be able to deduct house depreciation, utilities, property tax, mortgage interest, house insurance, or house repairs. You will be able to claim 100% of your property tax and mortgage interest on **Schedule A Itemized Deductions**. The vast majority of providers should not use this Simplified Method. See chapter 5 for an explanation.

How to Fill Out Form 8829

This section explains how to fill out **Form 8829** for your business by taking you through the form line by line and referring to the filled-out example at the end of this chapter. Before you start filling out **Form 8829**, you should also skim the section titled Special Cases for **Form 8829** on page 69 to see if any of the situations described there apply to your business in this tax year.

Part I: Part of Your Home Used for Business

Line 1: Enter the number of square feet of your home that you use regularly for your business. Ignore the phrase "area used exclusively for business" on this line. Every other kind of business is only allowed to count the space that is used exclusively for business, but family child care providers are exempt from this regulation (see IRS **Publication 587 Business Use of Your Home**).

Line 2: Enter the total square footage of your home. Some providers use the number of rooms in their home on lines 1 and 2 instead of the square feet of those rooms. This might lower your business use of your home by a greater margin than if you were counting square feet.

Line 3: Divide line 1 by line 2 to get your Space percentage. If you used 2,200 square feet of your 2,200-square-foot home regularly for your business, you would enter 100% on this line (2,200 ÷ 2,200 = 100%).

Line 4: Enter the number of hours that you used your home for business purposes in this tax year. Be sure to include both the hours that children were present and the hours that you spent on business activities when they weren't present.

Line 5: This line shows the total number of hours in a year (365 days x 24 hours = 8,760 hours). If you didn't operate your business every day of the year, cross this number out and enter the total number of hours that your home was available for business use. To find this number, multiply the number of days you were in business by 24 hours. Include Saturdays, Sundays, and holidays between working days. Here's an example: You began your business on April 1 of last year and were still in business at the end of the year. Since there are 275 days between April 1 and December 31, on line 5 you would enter 6,600 hours (275 days x 24 hours).

Line 6: Divide line 4 by line 5. If you worked 3,514 hours last year, and you were in business the entire year, your Time percentage would be 40% (3,514 ÷ 8,760).

Line 7: Multiply line 6 by line 3. If your Space percentage was 100% and your Time percentage was 40%, your Time-Space percentage would be 40% (100% x 40%). This percentage will affect your other tax forms, so be sure to double-check your math. An error will mean mistakes on all your tax forms. Be sure to save the records that show how you calculated your numbers for Part I. The Time-Space percentage is a favorite area for IRS audits, so it's important to have good, clear documentation.

If You Weren't in Business the Entire Year
Recall that the total number of hours your home was available for business use was calculated on line 5 of Part I. When you enter your home expenses in Part II, you can only list the expenses that you incurred when your home was available for business use; the dates of your expenses must match the dates you used for that calculation.

If you based that calculation on the 275 days between April 1 and December 31 of last year, you can only enter expenses that you incurred between April and December. You cannot include the March utility bill that you paid in April, but you can include the January bill for December's utilities.

You will also need to enter a prorated amount of your home expenses for the year, such as property tax and homeowners insurance. In our example, you would enter 75% of these yearly expenses (275 days ÷ 365 days = 75%).

Let's look at an example to see how being in business for less than the full year will affect **Form 8829** and **Schedule A**. Last year you began your business on April 1, and your Time-Space percentage between April 1 and December 31 was 40%. Your mortgage interest for the year was $5,000, and your property tax was $2,000. Since you were in business for only 75% of the year, multiply these expenses by this percentage:

Mortgage interest	$5,000 x 75% = $3,750
Property tax	$2,000 x 75% = $1,500

Next, multiply the results by your Time-Space percentage (40%):

Mortgage interest	$3,750 x 40% = $1,500
Property tax	$1,500 x 40% = $600

These numbers represent the amount that you can deduct on **Form 8829**. If you itemize your tax return, enter the remaining amounts on **Schedule A**:

Mortgage interest	$5,000 – $1,500 = $3,500
Property tax	$2,000 – $600 = $1,400

Remember, the amount that you claim for mortgage interest and property tax on **Form 8829** and **Schedule A** should equal (and never exceed) 100%.

Part II: Figure Your Allowable Deduction

Before you fill out this part of **Form 8829**, go to **Schedule C** and complete lines 1–29 (see chapter 5). Then return to this point and continue.

Line 8: Enter the amount from **Schedule C**, line 29. If you sold any items that you used in your business during the last year (see chapter 11), add the net gain or loss from these items on this line. If you sold your home last year, don't include the net gain or loss from the sale on this line.

If there is a negative number on line 8, your mortgage interest and real estate taxes (lines 10 and 11) will be the only home expenses that you can claim this year. Complete the rest of this form anyway, because you may be able to carry over any excess expenses to next year.

The next several lines of **Form 8829** include two columns. The following numbers are an example of how you might fill out lines 9–35. For this example, assume that the provider was in business for the entire year.

Time-Space percentage	40%
Net income from line 29 of **Schedule C**	$3,500
Casualty losses	$0
Mortgage interest	$2,000
Real estate taxes	$1,500
Home insurance	$900
Child care homeowners insurance endorsement	$400

Repairs and maintenance	$800
Utilities	$1,000

Col. (a): Under column (a) you will enter only your *direct* expenses—expenses that were incurred 100% for your business or for which you are using an actual business-use percentage instead of a Time-Space percentage. Continue reading for a description of each line in this column.

Col. (b): Under column (b) you will enter your *indirect* expenses—expenses that were incurred partly for your business and partly for your personal use. Continue reading for a description of each line in this column.

Line 9: Hurricanes and fires have certainly made people aware of the terrible damage that can be caused by a natural disaster. A casualty loss is defined as the damage, destruction, or loss of property resulting from an identifiable event that is sudden, unexpected, or unusual, such as an earthquake, tornado, flood, storm, fire, vandalism, theft, or car accident.

You must file an insurance claim in a timely manner in order to deduct a sudden or unexpected loss. If your insurance fully covers your losses, then you can't claim them as losses for tax purposes. If your insurance doesn't fully cover them (for example, if you have to pay a deductible or are underinsured), then you may be able to claim some business deductions that will reduce your taxes at the end of the year.

You are entitled to deduct any casualty losses of items used in your business (not covered by insurance), including your home, furniture, appliances, and business equipment. Expenses that result from a casualty loss or theft may also be deductible. These expenses include medical treatment, cleanup, minor repairs, temporary housing, a rental car, replacing spoiled food, and boarding up your home or sandbagging your property in anticipation of a flood.

If a natural disaster forces you to shut down your business temporarily, you cannot deduct your loss of income as a business expense. You will simply report less income on your tax return and therefore pay less in taxes.

If an item is completely destroyed, the business loss is the purchase price of the item minus the depreciation you have claimed on it or were entitled to claim on it. For example, let's say that you have a Time-Space percentage of 40% and are uninsured. You buy a swing set for $1,000 and depreciate it for two years, and then it is destroyed in a fire. In this case, your business loss would be $245 ($1,000 x 40% = $400 – $155 [two years of depreciation deductions] = $245).

If you received an insurance payment of $200 for this loss, the business portion of that payment would be $80 ($200 x 40% Time-Space), and your business loss would be $165 ($245 – $80). If you received a payment of $1,000 for this loss, you would have a business gain of $155 ($245 – $400 [$1,000 x 40% Time-Space = $400] = – $155), which you would report on **Form 4797**.

If an item that you use in your business is damaged but not destroyed, use the lower of the adjusted value of the property (the original cost minus the depreciation claimed) or the difference between the fair market value of the item immediately before and immediately after the casualty. In other words, in the above example the adjusted value of the swing set was $245. If the business portion of the swing set's value before damage was $300 and its value after the damage was $100, the difference would be $200 ($300 – $100 = $200). You would compare the $200 to the adjusted value ($245) and use the lower number ($200) as your business loss.

Calculate your business loss (or gain) on a separate piece of paper and enter the total on line 9, column (a). Notice that the expenses entered on this line are taken out on line

34 and transferred to **Form 4684**. From that form, the business losses (or gains) are transferred to **Form 4797** and then to **Form 1040**, where they are deducted. This means that you will not actually claim your business losses as an expense on **Form 8829**. (Personal losses are calculated on **Form 4684** and then transferred from there to **Schedule A**.)

Although casualty losses can't create a loss on **Form 8829** (see the IRS instructions for **Form 8829**), you can carry the excess amount forward to next year. If you suffer a loss in an event that leads to your community being declared a federal disaster area, see the instructions to **Form 4684**. If you buy new property to replace the damaged or destroyed property, begin depreciating the new property under the rules described in chapter 3.

An Insurance Note

Many homeowners insurance policies only cover up to $2,000 worth of property used in a family child care business. Examine your policy to find out if your business property is properly covered. If it's not, you should purchase additional business property insurance. Business liability insurance usually will not cover the loss of business property. See the *Family Child Care Legal and Insurance Guide* for detailed information about how to protect your home and business through insurance.

To help prepare for a natural disaster, you should conduct an inventory of all the property in your home. Use the *Family Child Care Inventory-Keeper* to help you identify and track all your property and estimate its fair market value. Take photographs of all of the rooms in your home, and store the photographs and your inventory records in a safe-deposit box.

Line 10: Enter your total deductible mortgage interest in column (b), including any interest paid on a contract-for-deed mortgage. Don't include interest on a mortgage loan that didn't benefit your home (such as a second mortgage used to pay off your credit cards or buy a car). Claim the rest of your mortgage interest on **Schedule A**.

Note: Before 2014 you might have been able to deduct the cost of the premiums for mortgage insurance. But as of 2014 this deduction is gone.

Refinancing Points

The points, or mortgage closing fees, paid on a home loan are treated as prepaid interest. You can deduct on line 10, column (b), the business portion of points paid on a loan to buy, build, remodel, or improve a home in the same year. (Deduct the personal portion of the points on **Schedule A** as personal interest.) You must deduct any points paid to refinance a loan over the term of the loan.

If you refinance with the same lender, add the remaining points of the old loan to the points of the new loan and spread the total over the life of the new loan. For example, let's say that you're paying $200 a year in points for a twenty-year loan. Six years into the loan, you refinance with the same lender and get a new twenty-year loan, and the points for the new loan amount to $3,000. Add the remaining points of the old loan ($4,000 − $1,200 = $2,800) to the new points ($3,000) and spread the total ($5,800) over twenty years, at $290 a year. Put $290 on line 10, column (b) each year for the next twenty years (where it will be multiplied by your Time-Space percentage to calculate business use).

If you refinance with another lender, you can deduct all the remaining points from the old loan on line 10, column (b) in the year you refinance.

Line 11: Enter your total real estate taxes in column (b). You will be able to deduct only part of this amount on **Form 8829**, but you will be able to claim the remaining amount of your real estate taxes on **Schedule A**, line 6.

Line 12: Enter the total of lines 9, 10, and 11. (In the example at the end of this chapter, $0 + $2,000 + $1,500 = $3,500.)

Line 13: Enter the total of line 12, column (b), multiplied by line 7. (In the example, $3,500 x 40% = $1,400.)

Line 14: Enter the total of line 12, column (a), and line 13. (In the example, $0 + $1,400 = $1,400.)

Line 15: Enter the total of line 8 minus line 14. (In the example, $3,500 – $1,400 = $2,100.)

The amount on line 15 ($2,100) is the most that you can claim on **Form 8829** for the remaining home expenses. You *must* claim the business amount of your mortgage interest and real estate taxes on this form; you can claim the rest of these expenses as itemized deductions on **Schedule A**. Use your Time-Space percentage to determine your business deduction. Here's the calculation, building on the previous example, using a 40% Time-Space percentage:

	Total Expense	Form 8829 Expense 40%	Schedule A Expense 60%
Mortgage interest	$2,000	$800	$1,200
Property tax	$1,500	$600	$900

You may wish to claim all of your mortgage interest and real estate taxes on **Schedule A** rather than dividing them between **Schedule A** and **Form 8829**; however, this is both against the law and not in your best interests. Unlike your personal income, your business income is subject to Social Security and Medicare taxes as well as income tax. For this reason, a business deduction will reduce your taxes more than a personal deduction will.

Don't make the error of claiming your Time-Space percentage of these expenses on **Form 8829** and then claiming 100% of the same expenses on **Schedule A**. You are never allowed to claim more than 100% of any deduction. In addition, if your state offers a property tax rebate, you must calculate the amount of your rebate based on your personal-use percentage of the property tax, not the business- and personal-use percentage of the property tax. For example, if a family child care provider has a Time-Space percentage of 40%, then her personal use of the home is 60%, and she is entitled to use only 60% of her property tax to calculate her rebate.

Remember that only mortgage interest and real estate taxes can create a loss on **Form 8829**. What happens if they do? Building on the previous example, if the business share of the mortgage interest and real estate taxes was greater than $3,500, that amount could be claimed as a loss for the business. If the mortgage interest was $6,000 and real estate taxes were $4,000, the amount on line 12 would be $10,000. Multiply this by 40% (line 7), and line 13 would be $4,000 ($10,000 x 40%). Line 14 would also be $4,000. Since $4,000 is more than $3,500 (line 8), 0 would be entered on line 15.

No other expenses could be claimed on **Form 8829**. Line 34 would be $4,000, and this amount transfers to **Schedule C**, line 30, where it would create a $500 loss on that form. The other expenses on this form would be put on Part IV and carried over to **Form 8829** in the next year.

Line 16: If the amount of home mortgage interest that you deduct on **Schedule A** is limited (see the IRS instructions for **Schedule A**), enter any excess mortgage interest that qualifies as a direct or indirect expense. (Most family child care providers don't have excess mortgage interest.)

Line 17: Enter your homeowners insurance in column (b). If you purchased a special policy just for your business or bought a business endorsement for your homeowners insurance policy, enter this amount in column (a). You can no longer deduct any premiums for mortgage insurance.

Line 18: If you rent your home, enter your total rent payments in column (b). As a renter, you may claim the Time-Space percentage of your monthly rent and any utilities you pay, plus a portion of any home improvements you make and any losses due to the theft of personal property used in your business.

Line 19: Enter your home repair and maintenance expenses in column (b). (See chapter 3 for a discussion of the difference between a repair and a home improvement.) Repairs (painting, wallpapering, fixing a broken window, or mending a leak) keep your home in good working order. Repairs to an exclusive-use room are 100% deductible; enter these expenses in column (a).

Line 20: Enter your total utility expenses (gas, electricity, water, sewage, garbage, and cable TV) in column (b), even if you rent your home. Monthly fees for telephone service are not deductible. If your phone service includes charges on a cost-per-minute basis, however, you can deduct the cost of your local business calls. Enter the cost of local business calls on line 20, column (a).

Actual Business-Use Percentage of Utilities Costs

Because of the significant cost of heating oil, gas, and electricity, you may benefit from using your actual business-use percentage of utility expenses. The actual business-use percentage of utilities costs for heating a home during the day for ten or more hours, Monday through Friday, is probably significantly more than the cost calculated by using a typical 30%–40% Time-Space percentage, especially since you can turn the heat down in the evening.

How can you determine the actual business-use percentage of your utility expenses? If you have only been in business for a short time, look at your energy usage before and after your business began. You might also call your local utility company to see if it can determine your energy usage during daytime hours.

If you decide to use a method other than your Time-Space percentage to calculate your utility expenses, be sure to keep careful records of your calculations and save them. Enter the actual business-use amount of your utilities on line 20, column (a).

Line 21: If you have other house expenses not claimed elsewhere, claim them here.

Line 22: Enter the total of lines 16–21. (In the example, $0 + $900 + $0 + $800 + $1,000 + $0 = $2,700.)

Line 23: Enter the total of line 22, column (b), multiplied by line 7. (In the example, $2,700 x 40% = $1,080.)

Line 24: If you had any home operating expenses in 2014 that you were unable to deduct that year because of the home expense limitation, enter that amount here.

Line 25: Enter the total of line 22, column (a), and lines 23–24. (In the example, $400 + $1,080 + $0 = $1,480.)

Line 26: Compare the amounts on line 15 and line 25, and enter whichever is the least. (In the example, $2,100 is the larger of the two, so $1,480 is entered.)

Line 27: Enter the amount of line 15 minus line 26. (In the example, $2,100 – $1,480 = $620.) In the example, this is the upper limit of the home depreciation expenses that can be claimed.

Line 28: Enter any excess casualty losses.

Line 29: Enter your home depreciation total from line 41. (The same example will be used in the next section to illustrate how to depreciate a home.) In the example, $934 is entered ($11 will be added later for a home improvement; see the instructions for line 41 on page 68).

Line 30: Enter any excess casualty losses and depreciation that you carried over from 2014.

Line 31: Enter the total of your home depreciation, excess casualty losses, and carryover of excess casualty losses and home depreciation from 2014. In the example, $934 is entered.

Line 32: Compare the amounts on line 27 and line 31, and enter whichever is the least. (In the example, $620 is entered because it is less than $934.)

Line 33: Enter the total of lines 14, 26, and 32. (In the example, $1,400 + $1,480 + $620 = $3,500.)

Line 34: If you had any casualty loss from line 14 or 32, enter that amount here. The example does not have anything to record.

Line 35: Enter the amount of line 33 minus line 34. (In our example, $3,500 – $0 = $3,500.)

On line 35 is the allowable expenses for the business use of your home that you can claim on **Schedule C**. Enter this amount on **Schedule C**, line 30.

Using an Actual Business-Use Percentage

Although in most cases you will apply the Time-Space percentage from line 7 to all your indirect home expenses on **Form 8829**, in some cases you can use an actual business-use percentage instead. (See the section titled Actual Business-Use Percentage at the end of chapter 1 for a discussion.)

If a home expense is partly for your business and partly for personal use, you would normally enter it in column (b) and use the Time-Space percentage from line 7 to calculate the allowable business portion of the expense.

You aren't required to use the Time-Space percentage if you can show that one or more of your home expenses should be allocated in a different way. This is most common in the case of repairs to a room that is used heavily, but not exclusively, for your business. (If the room was used exclusively for business, you would enter 100% of the cost of the repair in column [a].)

Let's say that your Time-Space percentage is 37%, and you incurred a $200 repair to fix the radiator in a room that you use 80% of the time for your business. In this case you can claim 80% of the cost of this repair, or $160. To do this, simply enter the amount that you calculate according to the business-use percentage in column (a), and enter nothing in column (b). In this example, you would list $160 in column (a). All the amounts that you list in column (a) are deducted 100% as business expenses.

Part III: Depreciation of Your Home

If you first began using your home for your business last year, you must fill out **Form 4562**, line 19i (see chapter 3). Next, fill out lines 36–41 of **Form 8829**. If you used your home for your business before last year, don't enter any information about home depreciation on **Form 4562**; just fill out lines 36–41 of **Form 8829**, as described below.

Line 36: Enter your home's adjusted basis or its fair market value, whichever is the least. In the example, this amount is $103,800. Your home's adjusted basis is the sum of the purchase price of your home plus the value of any home improvements before you began using your home for your business (for more information, see chapter 3).

Line 37: Enter the value of the land at the time you purchased your home ($10,000 in the example). This amount should be included in the purchase price of your home on line 36; however, land can't be claimed as a business expense.

Line 38: Enter the amount of line 36 minus line 37. This is the basis of your home ($93,800 in the example). This number doesn't change from year to year. You'll enter the same numbers on lines 36–38 of **Form 8829** each year that you own this home.

Line 39: Enter the amount of line 38 multiplied by line 7 ($37,520 in the example). This is the business basis of your home.

Line 40: If you first began using your home for business before 1987, consult IRS **Publication 534 Depreciating Property Placed in Service Before 1987** to determine what rules were in effect when you began using your home for business. If you first used your home for business after 1986 but before May 13, 1993, enter 3.175% on this line. If you first used your home for business after May 12, 1993, but before last year, enter 2.564% on this line.

If you first began using your home for business last year, enter the percentage from the chart below, based on the first month you used your home for business:

January	2.461%	July	1.177%
February	2.247%	August	0.963%
March	2.033%	September	0.749%
April	1.819%	October	0.535%
May	1.605%	November	0.321%
June	1.391%	December	0.107%

In the example, the business began in January, so 2.461% is entered on this line. For years 2 through 39, 2.564% will be used for our depreciation calculations (for information about home depreciation, see chapter 3).

Line 41: Enter the amount of line 39 multiplied by line 40. This is the amount of home depreciation you can claim. In the example, this amount is $923. After $11 is added for a home improvement, the total ($934) is entered on line 29. (See the example form at the end of this chapter.)

Part IV: Carryover of Unallowed Expenses

Line 42: Subtract line 26 from line 25. A positive number here represents excess operating expenses that can't be deducted this tax season but can be carried forward and deducted next tax season. If you have a carryover here, put a copy of your **Form 8829** in your files for next tax season so you won't forget to claim it.

Line 43: Subtract line 32 from line 31 ($934 − $620 = $314). A positive number here represents excess casualty losses and home depreciation that can't be deducted this tax season but can be carried forward and deducted next tax season. If you have a carryover here, put a copy of your **Form 8829** in your files for next tax season so you won't forget to claim it.

If you go out of business in a tax year and don't operate your business the following year, you won't be able to claim any carryover expenses. If you go back into business in a later year, however, you will be able to claim your carryover expenses at that time.

What You Can't Claim on Form 8829

You can't claim the following kinds of expenses on **Form 8829**:

- **Property assessments**
  Property assessments (sidewalks, sewer, other improvements to your land made by your local government) are usually included with your property tax bill. Subtract them from your property tax before you enter your property tax on line 11. The cost of a property assessment can be depreciated as a land improvement. For an explanation of how to depreciate these expenses, see page 97.

- **Monthly mortgage payments**
  Don't put your monthly mortgage payments on **Form 8829**. These payments consist of interest and payments toward the principal of your loan. Your monthly principal payments have nothing to do with how much you can deduct as a business expense. Your mortgage interest is claimed on line 10, column (b), of **Form 8829**. The principal is accounted for when you depreciate your home. Your home depreciation is based on the purchase price of your home, which you claim on line 29 of **Form 8829**.

- **Home expenses if you aren't a sole proprietor**
  If you have formed a partnership or a corporation and are working out of your home, you can't claim your home expenses on **Form 8829** because a partnership or a corporation can't file **Form 8829**; it is for individuals only. If you have established a single-person limited liability company (LLC), however, you are entitled to claim all home expenses on **Form 8829**.

Special Cases for Form 8829

If You Have Any Exclusive-Use Rooms

You can claim a higher Time-Space percentage on **Form 8829** if you use one or more rooms in your home exclusively for business. The following example shows you how to calculate the Time-Space percentage in this situation:

- Polly Jones's home totals 2,000 square feet.

- She has one 300-square-foot room that she uses exclusively for her business.

- She uses the other 1,700 square feet regularly for her business.

- Polly works 2,628 hours during the year in the 1,700-square-foot area.

Because Polly has a room that she uses exclusively for her business, she can't complete Part I of **Form 8829**. Instead she will have to write "see attached" across Part I of the form and attach a separate sheet of paper that shows her Time-Space calculation.

Supporting Statement for Form 8829, Part I

Name: Polly Jones
Social Security #146-28-3333
Total square footage of home: 2,000
Square footage of room used exclusively for business: 300
Remaining 1,700 square feet are used regularly for child care
Hours 1,700-square-foot area is used for child care: 2,628

$300 \div 2,000$ = 15% actual business-use percentage of exclusive-use area
$1,700 \div 2,000$ = 85% Space percentage for business use of remainder of home
$2,628 \div 8,760$ = 30% Time percentage for business use of remainder of home
$85\% \times 30\%$ = 25.5% Time-Space percentage for business use of
                      remainder of home
$15\% + 25.5\%$ = 40.5% Time-Space percentage for business use of entire home

---

Here's what her attachment would say:

CLAIMING AN EXCLUSIVE-USE ROOM WITH A TAX SOFTWARE PROGRAM

If you use a tax software program to do your taxes, it can be difficult to claim a 100% exclusive-use room. Most software programs won't allow you to enter a Time-Space percentage on line 7 of **Form 8829** unless you have filled out lines 1 through 6, and when you have a 100% exclusive-use room, you can't fill out lines 1 through 6. Here's how to overcome this problem:

1. Complete the calculation of your Time-Space percentage on your supporting statement for **Form 8829**. Let's assume that your Time-Space percentage is 40%.

2. Enter the total number of square feet in your home on lines 1 and 2. Your Space percentage on line 3 will then be 100%.

3. Enter on line 4 the number of hours that you would need in order to arrive at 40%. Do this by multiplying line 5 (8,760 hours) by 40%. Your total on line 4 will now be 3,504. Enter 40% on line 6.

4. Your computer will now properly calculate line 7 at 40%. Fill out the rest of **Form 8829**. Indicate on your supporting statement that you have adjusted lines 1 through 6 to reach the correct total on line 7. Your supporting statement will show that you properly calculated line 7. If you are uncomfortable leaving incorrect numbers on lines 1 through 6, you can use correction fluid to white out these numbers before sending in your tax return.

If You Provide Child Care Outside Your Home

It's a growing trend for child care providers to operate at a location other than their own home. If you only provide child care in a building that's separate from your home, you can claim 100% of the expenses associated with that space, such as rent, utilities, furniture, and supplies. But if you operate out of another building, or two separate locations, you won't be eligible to file **Form 8829**. Instead, you will show your expenses for the other building on **Form 4562** and **Schedule C**, as follows:

ENTER ON **FORM 4562**

- depreciation (line 19i)

ENTER ON **SCHEDULE C**

- insurance (line 15)
- mortgage interest (line 16a)
- rent (line 20b)
- repairs and maintenance (line 21)
- property taxes (line 23)
- utilities (line 25)

Since you can only claim one location for your business, you won't be able to claim a Time-Space percentage for your home expenses if you're using both your home and a building separate from your home for your business. This is true even if you're still using your home for business activities such as keeping records and planning lessons. You can claim part of the cost of the business equipment that you use in your home such as your computer, printer, file cabinet, and desk. Follow the depreciation rules described in chapter 3, and use your actual business-use percentage.

You won't be eligible to claim travel to and from your home and your place of business as business trips; this travel will be considered commuting to work. You can still count a trip for business purposes as business mileage if you are departing from and returning to your place of business.

If you provide child care at a location other than your home, you won't be eligible to use the IRS standard meal allowance rate in calculating your food expenses (see chapter 4). In addition, you may not be eligible to participate in the Food Program (check with your sponsor). Also, check your state regulations, which may prohibit you from providing child care in a home that you do not live in.

If You Receive a Military Housing Allowance

The IRS **Child Care Provider Audit Technique Guide** clarifies how to treat housing allowances if you are a family child care provider living in military housing.

If you live in on-base housing, you can't claim any home expenses except for those you pay out of your own pocket. Since you have no property tax or mortgage interest expenses, you can't deduct these expenses. If you spend your own money on a home repair, fence, or improvement, you can deduct the business portion of this expense on **Form 8829** or **Form 4562**.

If you live in off-base housing, you're entitled to claim the Time-Space percentage of your property tax and mortgage interest on **Form 8829** and the personal portion of these expenses on **Schedule A**. (You can do this even if your housing allowance covers these expenses.)

The **Child Care Provider Audit Technique Guide** offers a detailed formula to determine how much of your other home expenses not covered by your housing allowance (such as utilities, home depreciation, homeowners insurance, and home repairs) you can deduct as a business expense. Enter the allowable portion of these expenses on **Form 8829**, line 21, column (a). (For more information about how to claim these expenses, see the *Record-Keeping Guide*.)

If You Went Out of Business

If you went out of business last year, you can't claim a full year's worth of home depreciation. Instead you can claim a prorated percentage of the full year's depreciation based on how many months you used your home for your business. Count the month that you stop using your home for business as a half month (this is according to the Mid-Month Convention rule; see chapter 3).

For example, let's say that you went out of business in November of last year. The business basis of your home is $17,550 and you have been in business for three years. Normally, your depreciation deduction would be $449.98 ($17,550 x 2.564% [the percentage of depreciation for a 39-year-old property]); however, in this case your deduction would be $449.98 x (10.5 months ÷ 12 months), or $393.73.

If Your Spouse Also Claims a Home Office Deduction

If your spouse is self-employed and also claims a deduction for home office expenses, you must file **Form 8829** and **Schedule C** for your business, and your spouse must file his own **Form 8829** and **Schedule C** for his business. Since the space that he claims for his business cannot also be claimed as space for your child care business, your Space percentage will be less than 100%.

If your spouse uses 10% of the home exclusively for his business, then he can claim 10% of the home expenses (such as utilities, real estate taxes, and mortgage interest). If you regularly use the rest of the home for your child care business, your Space percentage will be 90%. If your Time percentage is 35%, your Time-Space percentage will be 31.5% (90% x 35%), and you will claim 31.5% of the home expenses on your **Form 8829**.

If your spouse doesn't use any rooms exclusively for his business, then he won't file **Form 8829** because he won't be entitled to claim any home expenses (although he can still claim other business expenses on his **Schedule C**).

If you both use the same office for your business, he is using it nonexclusively, and you are using it regularly, you can claim the office space in your Time-Space calculation. Under these circumstances, you might have a Space percentage of 100% even if your husband runs his business in the home.

If You Made Home Improvements

If you made a home improvement before your business began, include the cost of the improvement in the cost of your home when you depreciate it in Part III of **Form 8829**.

If you made a home improvement after your business began but before 2015, calculate the depreciation deduction (see chapter 3), and include that amount on **Form 8829**, line 40. Write "see attached" next to this line, and attach a supporting statement showing how you calculated your home improvement deduction.

Here's an example:

Supporting Statement for Form 8829, Part III

Name: Polly Jones
Social Security #146-28-3333
Total square footage of home: 2,000
$580 access window installed in basement in 2014
x 75% business use
$435
x 2.564% depreciation amount for 39-year-old property
$11.15 enter on line 41

If you made a home improvement in 2015, first fill out **Form 4562**, line 19i (see chapter 3). Transfer the depreciation deduction from **Form 4562**, column (g), line 19i, to **Form 8829**, line 41. Don't include this amount in the depreciation deduction carried forward from **Form 4562**, line 22, to **Schedule C**, line 13. You can't claim an expense twice.

If You Moved

If you moved during the last year and continued to provide child care in your new home, you must file two copies of **Form 8829**, one for each home. You will need to calculate a separate Time-Space percentage for each home. On both forms, cross out the number printed on line 5 (8,760), and enter the number of hours you occupied the home during the last year. For example, if you moved on May 1, enter 2,904 hours (January–April = 121 days x 24 hours) on line 5 for the first house and 5,880 hours (May–December = 245 days x 24 hours) on line 5 for the second house. List your expenses for each home on the appropriate form. Add together lines 35 on both forms, and enter the total on **Schedule C**, line 30.

To determine what Time-Space percentage to use on shared items you are claiming on **Schedule C** (toys, household items, activity expenses, cleaning supplies, and so on), use the average of the two Time-Space percentages for each home. To account for the different number of months that each house was used for your business, use the following formula: multiply your Time-Space percentage for each house by the number of months the business was in each home. Add the two totals together and divide by 12. This is the Time-Space percentage to use for all shared expenses on **Schedule C**. For example, your Time-Space percentage was 35% for your first home (used January–April), and it was 25% for the second home (May–December): 35% x 4 months = 140%; 25% x 8 months = 200%; 140% + 200% = 340%, divided by 12 months = 28%.

For more information about the tax issues discussed in this chapter, refer to the related topics in the other chapters of this book and the Redleaf Press *Family Child Care Record-Keeping Guide*.

Form **8829**	**Expenses for Business Use of Your Home**	OMB No. 1545-0074
Department of the Treasury Internal Revenue Service (99)	▶ File only with Schedule C (Form 1040). Use a separate Form 8829 for each home you used for business during the year. ▶ Information about Form 8829 and its separate instructions is at *www.irs.gov/form8829*.	20**15** Attachment Sequence No. **176**

Name(s) of proprietor(s)   Your social security number

Part I   Part of Your Home Used for Business

1	Area used regularly and exclusively for business, regularly for daycare, or for storage of inventory or product samples (see instructions)	**1**	2,200
2	Total area of home	**2**	2,200
3	Divide line 1 by line 2. Enter the result as a percentage	**3**	100 %

For daycare facilities not used exclusively for business, go to line 4. All others, go to line 7.

4	Multiply days used for daycare during year by hours used per day	**4**	3514 hr.	
5	Total hours available for use during the year (365 days x 24 hours) (see instructions)	**5**	8,760 hr.	
6	Divide line 4 by line 5. Enter the result as a decimal amount . . .	**6**	· 40	
7	Business percentage. For daycare facilities not used exclusively for business, multiply line 6 by line 3 (enter the result as a percentage). All others, enter the amount from line 3 . . . . . ▶	**7**		40 %

Part II   Figure Your Allowable Deduction

		(a) Direct expenses	(b) Indirect expenses		
8	Enter the amount from Schedule C, line 29, **plus** any gain derived from the business use of your home, **minus** any loss from the trade or business not derived from the business use of your home (see instructions)			**8**	$3,500
	See instructions for columns **(a)** and **(b)** before completing lines 9–21.				
9	Casualty losses (see instructions). **9**				
10	Deductible mortgage interest (see instructions) **10**		$2,000		
11	Real estate taxes (see instructions) **11**		$1,500		
12	Add lines 9, 10, and 11 . . . . **12**		$3,500		
13	Multiply line 12, column (b) by line 7 . . . . **13**		$1,400		
14	Add line 12, column (a) and line 13			**14**	$1,400
15	Subtract line 14 from line 8. If zero or less, enter -0-			**15**	$2,100
16	Excess mortgage interest (see instructions) . **16**				
17	Insurance **17**	$400	$900		
18	Rent **18**				
19	Repairs and maintenance **19**		$800		
20	Utilities **20**		$1,000		
21	Other expenses (see instructions). **21**				
22	Add lines 16 through 21 . . . . **22**	$400	$2,700		
23	Multiply line 22, column (b) by line 7 . . . . . **23**		$1,080		
24	Carryover of prior year operating expenses (see instructions) . . **24**				
25	Add line 22, column (a), line 23, and line 24			**25**	$1,480
26	Allowable operating expenses. Enter the **smaller** of line 15 or line 25			**26**	$1,480
27	Limit on excess casualty losses and depreciation. Subtract line 26 from line 15			**27**	$620
28	Excess casualty losses (see instructions) **28**				
29	Depreciation of your home from line 41 below **29**		$934		
30	Carryover of prior year excess casualty losses and depreciation (see instructions) **30**				
31	Add lines 28 through 30			**31**	$934
32	Allowable excess casualty losses and depreciation. Enter the **smaller** of line 27 or line 31 . .			**32**	$620
33	Add lines 14, 26, and 32.			**33**	$3,500
34	Casualty loss portion, if any, from lines 14 and 32. Carry amount to **Form 4684** (see instructions)			**34**	
35	**Allowable expenses for business use of your home.** Subtract line 34 from line 33. Enter here and on Schedule C, line 30. If your home was used for more than one business, see instructions ▶			**35**	$3,500

Part III   Depreciation of Your Home

36	Enter the **smaller** of your home's adjusted basis or its fair market value (see instructions) . .	**36**	$103,800
37	Value of land included on line 36	**37**	$10,000
38	Basis of building. Subtract line 37 from line 36	**38**	$93,800
39	Business basis of building. Multiply line 38 by line 7.	**39**	$37,520
40	Depreciation percentage (see instructions).	**40**	2.461 %
41	Depreciation allowable (see instructions). Multiply line 39 by line 40. Enter here and on line 29 above	**41**	$934

Part IV   Carryover of Unallowed Expenses to 2016

42	Operating expenses. Subtract line 26 from line 25. If less than zero, enter -0-	**42**	
43	Excess casualty losses and depreciation. Subtract line 32 from line 31. If less than zero, enter -0-	**43**	$314

For Paperwork Reduction Act Notice, see your tax return instructions.   Cat. No. 13232M   Form **8829** (2015)

CHAPTER 3

Calculating Your Depreciation:
Form 4562

Major Change in Depreciation Rules

In 2013 the IRS made a sweeping change in how to deduct items costing more than $100. Under the old rules, items costing more than $100 and lasting longer than one year had to be depreciated on **Form 4562**. Such items included computers, furniture, appliances, play equipment, fences, and home improvements. The new rule, Treasury Regulation Section 1.263(a), covers four areas: repair versus home improvement, materials and supplies, $500/$2,500 safe harbor, and small taxpayer safe harbor.

Repair versus Home Improvement

The rule expands what can be treated as a repair and offers the clearest explanation yet of the difference between a repair and a home improvement. A repair may be deducted in one year (regardless of the cost) while a home improvement must be depreciated over 39 years. Repairs deal with normal wear and tear and routine maintenance. They are expenses that do not materially add to the value of a home or prolong its life; they simply keep it in good operating condition. Examples of repairs include: painting, wallpapering, fixing a broken window, and mending leaks. Under the new rule, it appears that the replacemement of about 20% of the windows or doors in your home would be considered a repair. In addition, replacing roof shingles (rather than the entire roof) and installing a wood or tile floor in one or two rooms of your home would also be considered a repair.

A home improvement is something that results in the betterment of the property, restores the property, or adapts the property to a new or different use. If you replace a significant or substantial portion of a major component of your home (walls, plumbing, electrical, heating, and so on), you must depreciate such items over 39 years. Examples of home improvements include building a new addition, remodeling your bathroom or your kitchen, adding a deck or garage, installing new wood or tile floors throughout your home, or replacing a substantial portion of your home's windows. It's not clear what a "substantial portion" means. Replacing 20% of your windows or doors would not be substantial (and thus can be treated as a repair), but replacing 60% of them would probably be considered a home improvement. If you remodel your bathroom and spend money on new towel racks and paint, you must lump together these normal repair expenses with the bathroom improvement project and depreciate the entire amount over 39 years.

This new clarification of what is a repair and what is a home improvement is complicated, and I advise you to consult with your tax professional before applying the rule to your situation.

Material and Supplies

The new rule allows you to deduct up to $200 of the cost of any item for your business not attached to your home or land in one year, rather than depreciating it.

$500/$2,500 Safe Harbor

The new rule allows you to deduct up to $2,500 of the cost of any item for your business not attached to your home or land in one year, rather than depreciating it. The original rule allowed you to deduct up to $500, but a late IRS notice raised this number to $2,500! If a receipt says, "Chairs $3,600," you must depreciate them. But if the receipt says "1 table at $2,000 and 4 chairs at $400 each" you may deduct the business portion of them in one year. If an item costs $3,000 you may not deduct $2,500 of it in one year.

To use this rule you must elect it by filing a statement with your tax return. Here's the statement you should use:

"Section 1.263(a)-1(f) De Minimis Safe Harbor Election

Your name, address, and EIN or Social Security number

For the year ending December 31, 2015 I am electing the de minimis safe harbor under Treas. Reg. Section 1.263(a)-1(f) for my business expenses of less than $2,500."

You must file such a statement each year you use this $2,500 rule. You can use the $500 rule on your 2015 tax return. The updated $2,500 rule goes into effect for your 2016 tax return. However, the IRS has said that if you use the $2,500 rule on your 2015 tax return, you will not be challenged on this point if you are audited.

Small Taxpayer Safe Harbor

The new rule allows some providers to deduct in one year the cost of a certain amount of home repairs and home improvements. This includes remodeling, adding a new deck, or buying a fence, patio, or driveway. The amount that can be deducted in one year is the lesser amount of $10,000 or 2% of the unadjusted basis of your home (the purchase price of your home minus the value of the land at the time you bought it, plus the value of any home improvements you made before and after your business began). For example, if you purchased your home for $300,000, you could deduct up to $6,000 of improvements in one year ($300,000 x 2% = $6,000, which is less than $10,000). If you purchased your home for $500,000 or more, you can deduct up to $10,000 of improvements. Let's look at two examples.

EXAMPLE #1

Bernice installed a new deck for $4,500 and made no home repairs. Her Time-Space percentage is 40%. Her home's unadjusted basis is $250,000. Because $4,500 is less than $5,000 ($250,000 x 2% = $5,000), she can use this rule. She could deduct $1,800 for the deck in one year ($4,500 x 40% = $1,800).

EXAMPLE #2

Bernice installed the same deck but also spent $2,000 on house repairs. She can't use this rule because the $6,500 of repairs and improvements ($4,500 + $2,000) is higher than $5,000. She can deduct $800 of the repairs ($2,000 x 40% = $800) in one year, but she must depreciate the deck over 39 years.

To use this rule you must elect it by filing a statement with your tax return. Here's the statement you should use:

"Section 1.263(a)-3(h) Safe Harbor Election for Small Taxpayers

Your name, address, and EIN or Social Security number

For the year ending December 31, 2015 I am electing the safe harbor election for small taxpayers under Treas. Reg. Section 1.263(a)-3(g) for the following: [list your improvements]."

You must file such a statement each year you use this small taxpayer safe harbor rule.

Notes

You can only use these new rules for the 2014 tax forms and subsequent years. If you started depreciating a home improvement over 39 years on your 2014 tax return and realize that you could have deducted it in one year, you can amend your tax return. You cannot go back earlier than 2014 to amend your return or use IRS **Form 3115** to recapture this depreciation (see chapter 10). You can use these rules even if you rent your home. Once you elect either the $2,500 rule or small taxpayer safe harbor rule you cannot later amend your tax return to change it.

Review

This new rule creates the opportunity for many providers to deduct many large house-related expenses in one year and avoid complicated depreciation rules explained later in this chapter. Here's summary of what the rule says:

ITEMS NOT ATTACHED TO YOUR HOME OR LAND (FURNITURE, APPLIANCES, EQUIPMENT)

Costing less than $200: Deduct in one year

Costing $2,500 or less: Deduct in one year if you file the statement above with your tax return

Under the new, expanded definition of house repairs (can now potentially include roof shingles, wood/tile floors, windows, and doors), regardless of the cost: Deduct in one year

ITEMS ATTACHED TO YOUR HOME (FENCE, PATIO, DRIVEWAY, DECK; INCLUDING REPAIRS)

Costing less than the lesser of $10,000 or 2% of the unadjusted basis of your home: Deduct in one year if you file a statement with your tax return

Because these new rules represent a significant change to the tax law, and they can be subject to different interpretations, I recommend you discuss them with your tax preparer.

This chapter explains how to fill out **Form 4562 Depreciation and Amortization**. Many child care providers feel that depreciation is the most complex tax concept that they have to deal with, so I will try to keep it as simple as possible. Basically, depreciation is a way to spread the deductible cost of an item over several years by deducting a certain percentage of the total amount each year. (When dealing with depreciation, remember that the deductible portion of any expense depends on how the item is used; for more information, see chapter 5.)

Here are the general rules about when you must depreciate an item:

- If an item costs less than $2,500, you can claim it as a business expense in the year you purchased it as long as you attach a statement to your tax return electing this rule (see page 252). You may deduct all or part of the cost of the item, as described in chapter 1.

- If an item costs more than $2,500 but doesn't last until the end of the year, you can claim it as a business expense in the year you bought it. For example, if you bought a stroller for $2,550 in May of last year, but it broke and you threw it away in November of that same year, you can deduct it, rather than depreciating it over several years.

- If an item costs more than $2,500 and lasts longer than one year, you may have to depreciate it. There are two exceptions to this rule: home repairs and the Section 179 rule (see page 84). As we saw on page 74, there is now an expanded definition of what can be considered a home repair.

- If you buy an item before your business begins and later start using it in your business, the following rules apply (see the section titled Start-Up Costs):

  - If the item was subject to depreciation when you bought it (that is, it cost more than $2,500), then you'll have to depreciate it when you start using it for business, even if it is worth less than $2,500 at that time.

  - If the item wasn't subject to depreciation when you bought it and you bought it in anticipation of starting your business (for example, a smoke detector, a fire extinguisher, or toys), you can claim it when you file your tax return (you can claim up to $5,000 for these kinds of items).

  - If you bought an item costing less than $2,500 without consideration for starting your business (for example, food storage containers, or household items), you must depreciate it.

- If you began depreciating an item last year, you must continue depreciating this item according to the depreciation rules for that year, even if the rules change in later years.

The IRS divides depreciable items into categories and sets a depreciation period for the items in each category—in other words, it tells you over how many years you must spread the cost for items in each category. The depreciation method and the length of the depreciation period determine the percentage of the total amount that you can deduct each year. The depreciation tables at the end of this chapter show the percentages that will be used this year.

Here are the categories of items that you must depreciate and the number of years that the IRS says you must depreciate them. Every item that you depreciate must fall into one of these categories:

Category	Number of Years of Depreciation
Personal computers/office equipment	5
Other personal property	7
Home improvements	39
Land improvements	15
Home	39
Vehicle	5

The years of depreciation rules for 2015 (as shown on page 77) are the same as those for 2014. This chapter describes how to apply those depreciation rules and fill out **Form 4562**. In many cases, home depreciation will be shown on **Form 8829**. Bear in mind that before you fill out **Form 4562**, you should complete Part I of **Form 8829**, since you will need your Time-Space percentage calculation from **Form 8829** to determine your depreciation deductions on **Form 4562**.

> **IRS Child Care Provider Audit Technique Guide on Depreciation**
> The guide lists a number of items that are commonly depreciated in the family child care business, including computers, office equipment, kitchen equipment, playground equipment, furniture, appliances, DVD players, televisions, and pianos. The guide clearly states that providers may depreciate items that were purchased before their business began that were originally exclusively personal use and then later put into business use. The guide states, "The fact that the asset was only used for personal purposes prior to being placed in service does not disqualify it from being converted to use in the business."

The Benefits of Depreciation

Because the depreciation rules are complicated and involve extra work, many providers and some tax preparers don't claim depreciation. They assume that the financial benefits of depreciation aren't worth the time it takes to calculate them. Let's see if that's true.

Let's say that you began your business in January of last year and that your home was filled with items that you started using in your business then, such as your washer, dryer, refrigerator, stove, microwave, stereo, television, VCR, DVD player, sofa, beds, tables, and other furniture. If all these household items were worth $10,000 (a conservative figure) when your business began and your Time-Space percentage is 40%, you would probably be able to claim about $4,000 in depreciation ($10,000 x 40% = $4,000) over the next seven years, or about $571 each year ($4,000 ÷ 7 years = $571).

If you began your business before 2015 and haven't been depreciating your home, home or land improvements, and household items, you may be entitled to recapture this previously unclaimed depreciation on **Form 3115**, which could result in hundreds or even thousands of dollars of deductions this year (see chapter 10 for more information).

Taking a Household Inventory

Are you claiming *all* of your allowable depreciation deductions? To find out, conduct an inventory of the items in your home that are used regularly in your business. All new providers should take an inventory their first year in business, and experienced providers should review their inventory each year.

To conduct an inventory, record all the items that you are using in your business, room by room. Include any home improvements that were made before and after your business began. Estimate the fair market value of each item at the time you began using it in your business. Next, determine the depreciation of each item as a business expense.

Gather and keep records that support your business deductions for these items. You can do this with receipts or photographs of the property. To claim depreciation, you must have written evidence. When filling out **Form 4562**, always answer yes to the questions on lines 24a and 24b that ask whether you have evidence to support your claim and whether the evidence is written. *Failure to answer these questions could trigger an audit.*

Need Inventory Help?
The *Family Child Care Inventory-Keeper* includes a series of forms that make it easy to inventory your property and claim depreciation. The *Inventory-Keeper* includes detailed room-by-room listings of household items and charts for your home and for home and land improvements, as well as instructions on how to estimate the fair market value of depreciable items.

Determining Your Depreciation

The depreciation rules can be difficult to understand because there are so many of them. To simplify things, the depreciation process is broken down here into four steps. You must go through these four steps for each item that you are depreciating.

Step One: What Is the Business Amount of the Item?
The first step is to determine the business amount of the property that you are depreciating. Start with the lower of (a) the cost of the property or (b) its fair market value at the time you first used it for business. If you bought the item (new or used) last year, use its actual cost. Multiply the value of the item by your Time-Space percentage or an actual business-use percentage (as described in chapter 1). The result is the business amount (or business basis) of the item you are depreciating.

EXAMPLE
You bought a refrigerator in 2014 for $1,000. In 2015, you started a child care business in your home. When you began using the refrigerator for your business, you calculated that it was worth $600. You use $600 as its value because that's lower than its original cost. If your 2015 Time-Space percentage is 35%, the business amount of this item would be $600 x 35% = $210. If the refrigerator wore out and you discarded it in 2015, you could claim all $210 as an expense; otherwise, you must depreciate this amount.

If Your Time-Space or Business-Use Percentage Changes
If your Time-Space or business-use percentage changes in any year after you have begun depreciating an item, it will affect the amount of business deduction that you can claim. In the following example, a $600 washer is depreciated using seven-year straight-line depreciation. Watch what happens as the Time-Space percentage (T/S%) changes:

2015	$600	x	29%	(T/S%) =	174	x 7.14%	= $12.42
2016	$600	x	30%	(T/S%) =	180	x 14.29%	= $25.72
2017	$600	x	31%	(T/S%) =	186	x 14.29%	= $26.58
2018	$600	x	32%	(T/S%) =	192	x 14.28%	= $27.42

Step Two: How Long Must You Depreciate the Item?

The next step is to determine the number of years over which the property must be depreciated. You must put all your depreciable items into one of the categories listed on page 77. The category that an item falls into determines the number of years over which it must be depreciated. Once you begin depreciating an item, you must stick to the number of years on this chart, even if the rules change in later years.

EXAMPLE

The refrigerator in the above example falls into the category of other personal property. This means that its $70 business amount (see how to calculate this in the previous example) will have to be depreciated over seven years.

Step Three: What Depreciation Method Can You Use?

The third step is to determine which depreciation method to use. In some cases, you will have a choice between the straight-line method and the accelerated method, which is also called the 150% or 200% declining balance method. (For a summary of these methods, see the depreciation tables at the end of this chapter.)

- Under the straight-line method, you claim an equal amount of depreciation each year. Generally, you can't use this method unless you choose it the first year you use the property for business.

- Under the accelerated depreciation method, you claim more depreciation in the first few years and less in later years. Although the accelerated method is usually more beneficial, you may not want to use it if doing so would cause a loss for your business this year or large fluctuations in your deductions from year to year.

EXAMPLE

You decide to use the 200% declining balance depreciation method for your refrigerator, which entitles you to deduct 28.58% of the $210 business amount in the first year. Using this method, the amount of depreciation that you could claim in the first year would be $210 x 28.58% = $60. (See below to determine if you must use the Half-Year Convention rule.)

Once you choose a depreciation method for an item, you must continue using that method for the life of that item; you can't change methods. Also, you must use the same method for all the items in each category that you start depreciating in the same year. For example, if you use straight-line depreciation for a freezer you bought last year, you must use that method for all other personal property that you bought or first used for business last year. You can use another method for a land improvement (such as a fence) that you purchased in that year. (This rule doesn't apply to the Section 179 rule; you can use Section 179 for one furniture item and still use accelerated or straight-line depreciation for other furniture items that you bought that year.)

Each year you can choose again for the items that you buy and start depreciating that year. So for last year's purchases, you could use accelerated depreciation for other personal property and straight-line depreciation for land improvements, but this year you can make a different choice for your new purchases in those categories.

Step Four: Do Any Special Rules Apply?

The final step is to determine if there are any special depreciation rules that apply to the item. There are five special depreciation rules—three conventions, the 50% bonus depreciation rule, and Section 179. Section 179 allows you to deduct the entire cost of some depreciable items in the first year, and the three convention rules are applied to items in the first year they are used for business. These rules—the Half-Year Convention, the Mid-Month Convention, and the Mid-Quarter Convention—may affect the first-year depreciation that you can take in certain circumstances.

THE 50% BONUS DEPRECIATION RULE

Providers who bought new items in 2015 may be eligible to use the 50% bonus depreciation rule. With this rule, providers can deduct 50% of the business portion of the new item in 2015 with the remaining 50% being depreciated. This special depreciation rule will create a much higher business deduction for providers this year.

Property that is eligible for this special rule includes computers (used more than 50% for business), office equipment, furniture and appliances, play equipment, fences and driveway, and cares. The purchase of a home and any used items do not qualify. It appears that the rule may apply to home improvements ("any improvement to an interior portion of a building") but not to an addition (deck, new room, new garage). The item must be purchased new in calendar year 2015 and used in your business in 2015. Providers should claim this 50% bonus depreciation because of the additional tax benefit that they will gain in 2015. This rule was also in effect for 2012–2014.

Here's an example of how this rule works. You bought new outdoor play equipment in March 2015 for $3,000 and your Time-Space percentage for the year is 40%.

- Calculate the business portion of the play equipment: $3,000 x 40% = $1,200

- Enter the amount you can claim on Form 4562, line 14, using the 50% bonus depreciation rule: $1,200 x 50% = $600

- Calculate the remaining amount that will be depreciated: $1,200 - $600 = $600

- Enter the amount that can be depreciated in 2015 on Form 4562, line 19c, using the seven-year accelerated depreciation rule (the 200% declining balance method): $600 x 14.29% = $85.74

- The total amount of depreciation you can claim in 2015: $600 + $85.74 = $685.74

If you elect not to use this rule, you can depreciate the outdoor play equipment over seven years and deduct $171.48 ($1,200 x 14.29%) in 2015.

If you go out of business before the end of the normal depreciation period for each item, you will not have to pay back (recapture) the amount you claimed under the 50% bonus depreciation rule.

If you used the outdoor play equipment more than 50% of the time in your business, you could apply the Section 179 rule and deduct the entire business portion in 2015. If you use the Section 179 rule (see page 84), you will have to recapture some of the depreciation you claimed if you go out of business before the end of the depreciation period for that item.

Note: Although you can use this rule to reduce your federal taxes, you will need to check with your state tax department to know whether or not your state is following the federal rule. In other words, your state may require you to add part of the deduct ($1,200 in the above example) back into your income to determine your state tax liability.

THE HALF-YEAR CONVENTION

Since the items you're depreciating were bought at various times during the year, the IRS won't allow you to claim a full year's worth of depreciation the first year you use an item in your business. Instead, for all items except home improvements and home depreciation, you must apply the Half-Year Convention rule in the first year of depreciation.

This rule says that no matter when you purchased the item or put it into business use, it will be treated as if it were put into business use in the middle of the year. This means that you only get one-half of the normal depreciation deduction in the first year. The other half of that year's deduction is picked up at the end of the depreciation period. In other words, if you are using seven-year straight-line depreciation rules, you will claim half of the normal depreciation in the first year, then six years of full depreciation, and then another half year. This means that you must actually depreciate the item over eight calendar years.

EXAMPLE

The example of the refrigerator from page 79 will be used to illustrate this. Since the refrigerator falls in the category of other personal property, you must apply the Half-Year Convention in the first year you use it for business. The full amount of depreciation that you could normally claim for the first year would be $20. To apply the Half-Year Convention, multiply this amount by 50%. Thus, the depreciation that you can claim this year would be $10 ($20 x 50% = $10).

In the depreciation tables at the end of this chapter, the Half-Year Convention rules are already built into the percentages listed.

THE MID-MONTH CONVENTION

To depreciate your home and home improvements, you must apply the Mid-Month Convention rule instead of the Half-Year Convention rule. Under this rule, the deduction for the first year is based on the month that you first used the home or home improvement in the business, and it doesn't matter when during the month. The rule treats every item as if it was first put into business use in the middle of the first month that it was used for business. The percentages for each month are listed in the depreciation table for home and home improvements.

THE MID-QUARTER CONVENTION

This rule applies if you purchased over 40% of your capital expenditures during the last quarter of last year, which might happen, for example, if you started your business during that quarter. If you didn't purchase over 40% of your capital expenditures during the last quarter of the year, this rule doesn't apply to you. There are some expenses that you don't have to include in your capital expenditures in determining if you must apply the Mid-Quarter Convention rule:

- property that you purchase and sell in the same tax year

- the purchase of a home

- home improvements (you still have to include land improvements)

- deductions for personal property that you claim under Section 179 rules

When you apply the Mid-Quarter Convention in computing your depreciation, it imposes limits on the amount of depreciation that you can claim this year for the items you purchased in each quarter of the year. The depreciation limits for the items you purchased in each quarter are as follows:

First quarter	(January, February, March)	87.5%
Second quarter	(April, May, June)	62.5%
Third quarter	(July, August, September)	37.5%
Fourth quarter	(October, November, December)	12.5%

If this convention applies to you, you will only be able to deduct 87.5% of what you would otherwise be entitled to for the items that you purchased in the first quarter of the year. And you will only be able to deduct 12.5% of the depreciation that you would otherwise be entitled to for the items that you purchased in the last quarter of the year.

EXAMPLE

You purchased a $2,800 swing set in November last year and a $3,000 jungle gym in February last year, and these are your only capital expenditures in this tax year. Your Time-Space percentage is 25%. If you choose to apply seven-year straight-line depreciation to these items, you would get the following results:

$2,800 swing set	x 25%	=	$700	x 7.14%	= $49.98
$3,000 jungle gym	x 25%	=	$750	x 7.14%	= $53.55

Since you purchased more than 40% of your capital expenditures during the last quarter of last year, however, you must apply the Mid-Quarter Convention. Under the straight-line depreciation rules, 7.14% represents only one half of the first year of depreciation. This means that you must multiply by two before applying the limitations:

$2,800 swing set purchased in fourth quarter:	$49.95 x 2 x 12.5% = $12.50
$3,000 jungle gym purchased in first quarter:	$53.55 x 2 x 87.5% = $93.71
Total	$106.21

In the second year of depreciation for these items (and beyond), you will be able to claim the full amount of your normal depreciation:

$2,800 swing set	x 25%	=	$700	x 14.29%	= $100.03
$3,000 sofa	x 25%	=	$750	x 14.29%	= $121.47
Total					$221.50

Is all this work worth it? In our example, the first year doesn't look like much. However, in subsequent years, the numbers will add up. If the Mid-Quarter Convention drives you crazy, you might consider forfeiting the depreciation on your capital expenditures for the first year and begin by claiming the second year of depreciation. In this example, you would lose $106.21 this tax season, but you would be able to claim $221.50 next tax season.

These calculations get far more complicated if you use accelerated depreciation instead of straight-line depreciation, because in every subsequent depreciation year you have to readjust the amount of the item being depreciated by the depreciation you claimed in the first year. Because of this, you may want to always choose straight-line depreciation whenever you use the Mid-Quarter Convention rule.

Section 179

Section 179 is a special rule that allows you to claim up to $25,000 (2015 rule) of your new or used capital expenditures in the year they are incurred. This rule does not apply to home improvements, land improvements, or home depreciation. To be eligible to apply it to an item, you must meet all four of these conditions:

1. You must use the rule that applies to the year that you first used the item in your business. This means you can't use Section 179 on your tax return for any item that you used in your business before last year. But you can claim Section 179 if you amend your taxes for earlier years (see Changing Your Election of Section 179 on page 85).

2. The expenses you claim under Section 179 can't result in a loss on your tax return for this year. (But you can carry forward any unused Section 179 deductions to the next tax year.) If you file jointly, Section 179 expenses can't create a loss on the combined taxable income of both spouses. In other words, any wage income that your spouse reports on your joint **Form 1040** can offset Section 179 losses from your business. If your **Schedule C** shows $5,000 in losses and your spouse reports more than $5,000 in wages on **Form 1040**, you can claim those losses. However, if your spouse has self-employment income, this cannot offset your Section 179 losses. If you file separately, your spouse's tax return doesn't play any role in these limits.

3. You must be using the item more than 50% of the time for your business. Most child care providers use their Time-Space percentage to calculate their personal property depreciation. It's unusual to have a Time-Space percentage greater than 50%, so few providers can use Section 179 for these items.

4. You may not use Section 179 for an item that you purchased from a related party, such as a spouse, child, parent, grandparent, or grandchild (siblings—that is, brothers and sisters—are not covered by this restriction). You can't use Section 179 if you acquired the property as a gift or inheritance.

Note: Your state may or may not recognize the Section 179 rule. If not, you may be required to add back to your income (for state income tax purposes) the amount of extra depreciation you claimed because of this rule.

Put Your Section 179 Expenses on the Right Form

To take advantage of the Section 179 rule, you must claim the expense on **Form 4562**, Part I, not on **Schedule C**. So if you purchased an item that cost over $200 this year, used it mostly for business, and want to claim the entire deduction this year, be sure to put it on the correct form.

The Consequences of Using Section 179

There are some potentially negative consequences of using Section 179 that you should take into consideration before you decide to use this method:

1. If you go out of business before the end of the normal depreciation period for the item, you will have to pay back (recapture) some of the depreciation you claimed and file **Form 4797** (see chapter 11) to report it as income. The sooner you go out of business, the more income you will have to report. Before using Section 179, consider whether you plan to be in business at the end of the normal depreciation period

for that item (five years for a personal computer or a car; seven years for other personal property). If you shut down your business for several months and then start up again, your Section 179 deductions will not be affected.

2. Recapturing some of the depreciation you claimed also comes into play if you sell an item before the end of its normal depreciation period. If this is the case, you must also fill out **Form 4797** (see chapter 11). If you sell the item for a gain, you have to report the gain as income. If you sell it for a loss while you are still in business, you can deduct that loss on your **Form 1040**.

3. You will also have to recapture some of the depreciation you claimed if your business-use percentage of a Section 179 item falls to 50% or less in a later year. To avoid this, only apply Section 179 to items that you will be using more than 50% of the time for business over their entire lives.

Note: Should you use the Section 179 rule or the 50% bonus depreciation rule? If you qualify for the Section 179 rule and won't run afoul of the possible negative consequences, use this rule instead of the 50% bonus depreciation rule. Be careful not to submit to the temptation of using Section 179 unless you're sure that you meet the conditions described above and are fully aware of the possible negative consequences in later years. If you use a tax preparer, don't let your preparer use Section 179 unless you both understand all these rules.

Section 179 after the First Year

Once you use Section 179 to claim the business deduction for an item, you can't claim any further deductions for that item in future years. In other words, you won't record anything on **Form 4562** for this item in any future years. However, if your business use falls below 50%, you will need to recapture some of the depreciation you claimed. See chapter 11 for details.

Changing Your Election of Section 179

The IRS allows you to choose or revoke your choice of the Section 179 rule by amending your tax return for the tax years 2012 through 2014. Once you amend your return to elect or revoke the Section 179 rule, this change cannot be reversed without the consent of the IRS. If you did not take advantage of the Section 179 rule between 2012 and 2014, you may want to consider amending your tax return to get a refund. Here's an example of how this rule might benefit you. Let's say that you bought a computer in 2012 for $2,000 and used it 80% of the time in your business. You depreciate the computer over five years and claim $320 in depreciation deductions ($2,000 x 80% business use x 20% first-year accelerated depreciation = $320).

If you amend your tax return and elect to use the Section 179 rule, you can claim $1,280 as a deduction on your 2012 amended tax return ($2,000 x 80% = $1,600 – $320 = $1,280). This will mean a tax refund of about $384 (30% tax bracket) or $512 (40% tax bracket). If you use this rule, it will eliminate any depreciation deduction for this item on your 2015 tax return.

Depreciation Tip

Don't subtract the first year's depreciation deduction from the cost of the property before calculating the depreciation for the second year. Use the original cost to calculate your depreciation each year.

Calculating Depreciation by Category

The rest of this chapter will review each of the categories of depreciable items in more detail, explaining the specific rules and options that apply to each one. The examples will show the straight-line method, an accelerated method, and Section 179 (where applicable) but will always show the straight-line method first. Straight-line depreciation is the easiest to use, and there are many pitfalls and restrictions involved in using Section 179.

You may prefer to use accelerated rules rather than the straight-line rules. If you depreciate an item under the accelerated rules and go out of business before the end of the recovery period, you won't have to recapture (pay back) any of the depreciation you've claimed. If you sell an item you've used for your business, however, there may be some tax consequences, and if you were using accelerated rules, you'd be more likely to owe tax at this point than if you'd been using straight-line rules.

Check the Tables for More Information

As you read the following examples, refer to the tables at the end of this chapter. These tables list the percentages that you can deduct each year under each of the depreciation methods described on the following pages.

Keep Written Records of All Your Business Deductions

Remember that you need to keep written records to support all the business deductions you claim, in the form of receipts, canceled checks, or other records.

Personal Computer/Office Equipment

Under a new IRS regulation, you can deduct in one year office equipment that individually costs less than $2,500! This category of depreciation includes personal computers and office equipment, including printers, fax machines, copiers, scanners, and electric typewriters. We'll use a computer as an example. You can use your Time-Space percentage or an actual business-use percentage to depreciate the items in this category. If you use an actual business-use percentage, track how much time you use each item for your business (children's games, business record keeping, and so on) and how much time you use it for personal purposes. Divide the number of hours of business use by the total number of hours you use the item. For example, if you use your computer three hours a week for business and nine hours a week for personal purposes, your business-use percentage would be 25% (3 ÷ [3 + 9]).

In this category, your options for depreciation methods are based on your business-use percentage. If it is 50% or less, you must depreciate the item over five years. If it is higher, you can choose from three depreciation periods as described below, after an explanation about a change in recommendations for depreciating listed property.

50% Bonus Depreciation Rule

In the first example below, we will not use the 50% bonus depreciation rule because the computer was not used more than 50% for business. In the second example, we will use the new rule because the computer was used 70% for business.

What Is Listed Property?

Clearly, a cell phone and a vehicle weighing less than 6,000 pounds would both be listed property and should be depreciated on **Form 4562**, Part V. See page 88 for an example of how to fill out Part V. The IRS Regulation Section 1.280F-6 says, "Exception for computers. The term 'listed property' shall not include any computer (including peripheral equipment) used exclusively at a regular business establishment. For purposes of the preceding sentence, a portion of a dwelling unit shall be treated as a regular business establishment if (and only if) the requirements of section 280A(c)(1) are met with respect to that portion."

Family child care providers don't meet the requirements under Tax Code section 280A(c)(1) because it allows taxpayers to claim expenses for their home only if they use part of the home exclusively in their business. Family child care providers have their own rule under section 280A(c)(4), which allows them to claim expenses for their home if they're using rooms on a regular basis. But technically that doesn't meet the requirements under section 280A(c)(1), so a provider's computer should be listed property.

The one exception is that a provider who has an exclusive-use room and uses a computer in that room would be able to claim that the computer was not listed property because it meets the above exception. However, providers who use their computer in a regularly used room in their home do not meet this exception and must claim their computer as listed property.

Claiming a computer as listed property means providers must keep track of business use based on the hours the computer is used for business purposes. The IRS **Child Care Provider Audit Technique Guide** indicates that auditors may be stricter about demanding logs showing the business use of computers. As a practical matter most providers do not keep such logs and instead use their Time percentage. This could be challenged in an audit. You may use the 50% bonus depreciation rule for office equipment purchased new in 2015 regardless of how often it is used in your business. However, you can only use this rule for a computer if it is used more than 50% for your business. You must keep careful records to show this computer use. Such a record might be a log that tracks business and personal use for several months.

Business Use Equal to or Less Than 50%

If your business-use percentage is 50% or less, use the five-year straight-line depreciation rule. See the tables at the end of this chapter for the percentages that you can deduct each year. If you bought a $2,000 computer last year and your business-use percentage was 25%, the amount you can claim as a business expense would be $50:

FIVE-YEAR STRAIGHT-LINE

$3,000 computer x 25% business use   = $750 business basis
$750 x 10% (1st-year depreciation)   = $75

Enter this amount on **Form 4562**, Part V, line 27. column (h).

Business Use Greater Than 50%

If your business-use percentage is more than 50%, you have four choices—you can use the five-year straight-line method, the five-year 200% declining balance method, the 50% bonus depreciation rule, or Section 179. (To use Section 179 you must have bought the computer in 2014.) If your business-use percentage is 70%, this is what these three calculations would look like (refer to the tables at the end of this chapter for more information).

FIVE-YEAR STRAIGHT-LINE

$3,000 computer x 70% business use   = $2,100
$2,100 x 10%   = $210

Enter this amount on **Form 4562**, Part V, line 26, column (h).

FIVE-YEAR 200% DECLINING BALANCE

$3,000 computer x 70% business use   = $2,100
$2,100 x 20%   = $420

Enter this amount on **Form 4562**, Part V, line 26, column (h).

50% BONUS DEPRECIATION

$3,000 computer x 70% business use   = $2,100
$2,100 x 50%   = $1,050
$2,100 - 1,050   = $1,050
$1,050 x 20% (5-year 200% declining balance)   = $210

Enter this amount on **Form 4562**, Part V, line 26, column (h)

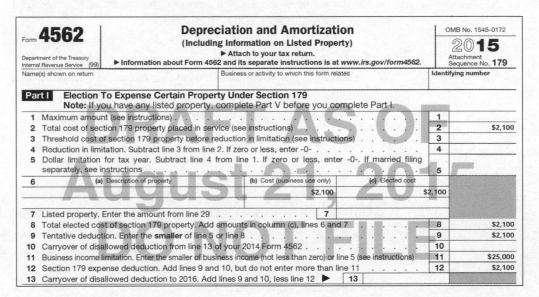

SECTION 179

$3,000 computer x 70% business use = $2,100

Using this method, you can claim the entire business-use percentage of the expense. If you go out of business within five years, however, you will have to pay back some of it. Enter $2,100 on **Form 4562**, Part I, line 2.

After filling out Part I, line 2, notice that there is a limitation amount for line 1 ($250,000) and a business income limitation on line 11 (see the IRS instructions for **Form 4562**). Your business income is your earned income—your net profit from line 31 of **Schedule C**, plus the wages that you (or your spouse) report on line 7 of **Form 1040**. Because of these limitations, you can't take more than the lesser of $250,000 or your earned income as a Section 179 deduction.

If your business income is $25,000, you will enter $25,000 on line 11, since this is the lesser of the two amounts (see example). If this is the case, you will have no problem claiming the full $2,100 for your computer this year, since it is far less than the lower of the two limitations.

Computer Software

If you purchased computer software last year and used it more than 50% in your business, you may use the Section 179 rule to deduct the cost in one year, whether or not the software was purchased as part of the computer. If you used the software 50% or less in your business, you must depreciate it over 36 months, using straight-line rules.

Note: If the software has a life of less than one year (as in the case of tax preparation software), you can claim the entire expense that year on **Schedule C**, line 18.

Other Personal Property

Under a new IRS regulation, you can deduct in one year personal property that individually costs less than $2,500! This category of depreciation includes all personal property other than computers and computer software. It includes large play equipment, furniture, appliances, TVs, VCRs, DVD players, lawn and garden equipment, household tools, and other household capital expenditures.

The 50% bonus depreciation rule can be used for new items purchased in 2015. Normally, you would have to depreciate these items over seven years. In the first set of examples on the next page let's assume that the items being depreciated are used, now new. This means we cannot use the 50% bonus depreciation rule for these items. In the second set of examples, let's assume the same items were purchased new, which means we can use the 50% bonus depreciation rule.

In this category, your options for depreciation rules are based on whether your Time-Space or business-use percentage is more or less than 50%. Assume a Time-Space percentage of 30% for the items in this example, except for a swing set, which will use an actual business-use percentage of 50%. Make a list of all the personal property items you want to depreciate, as shown here:

Item	Date Put in Service	Cost		Business-Use %		Business Basis
Swing set	1/15	$4,000	x	50%	=	$2,00.00

Time-Space or Business-Use Percentage Equal to or Less than 50%

If your Time-Space or business-use percentage is 50% or less, you have two depreciation options: seven-year straight-line or seven-year 200% declining balance.

SEVEN-YEAR STRAIGHT-LINE

To use this method, you would prepare a supporting schedule such as the following, based on the list of items that you made above.

2015 Tax Return
Supporting Schedule for Form 4562, Part III, line 19c
Polly Jones
Social Security #474-66-1234

Item	Date Put in Service	Method	Cost	Business-Use %	Business Basis	Table % Year 1	Deduction 2015
Swing set	1/15	7 YR/SL	$4,000	50%	$2,000.00	7.14%	$142.80
Total			$4,000		$2,000.00		$142.80

Using this method, the amount you can claim as a depreciation expense this year is $142.80. Enter this amount on **Form 4562**, Part III, line 19c, column (g). In column (e), enter "HY" for the Half-Year Convention (see page 82). If you're depreciating more than three items, include your supporting schedule with your tax return.

Part III MACRS Depreciation (Do not include listed property.) (See instructions.)						
Section A						
17 MACRS deductions for assets placed in service in tax years beginning before 2015					**17**	
18 If you are electing to group any assets placed in service during the tax year into one or more general asset accounts, check here . . . . ▶ ☐						
Section B—Assets Placed in Service During 2015 Tax Year Using the General Depreciation System						
(a) Classification of property	**(b)** Month and year placed in service	**(c)** Basis for depreciation (business/investment use only—see instructions)	**(d)** Recovery period	**(e)** Convention	**(f)** Method	**(g)** Depreciation deduction
19a 3-year property						
b 5-year property						
c 7-year property		$2,000	7 YEAR	HY	S/L	$143
d 10-year property						
e 15-year property						
f 20-year property						
g 25-year property			25 yrs.		S/L	
h Residential rental property			27.5 yrs.	MM	S/L	
			27.5 yrs.	MM	S/L	
i Nonresidential real property			39 yrs.	MM	S/L	
				MM	S/L	

SEVEN-YEAR 200% DECLINING BALANCE

To use this method, you would prepare a supporting schedule, such as the following, based on the list of items you made previously.

2015 Tax Return
Supporting Schedule for Form 4562, Part III, line 19c
Polly Jones
Social Security #474-66-1234

Item	Date Put in Service	Method	Cost	Business-Use %	Business Basis	Table % Year 1	Deduction 2014
Swing set	1/14	7YR/200% DB	$4,000	50%	$2,000.00	14.29%	$285.80
Total			$4,000		$2,000.00		$285.80

Using this method, the amount you can claim as a depreciation expense this year is $285.80. Enter this amount on **Form 4562**, Part III, line 19c, column (g). Enter "HY" in column (e). If you're depreciating more than three items, include a supporting schedule.

Part III MACRS Depreciation (Do not include listed property.) (See instructions.)						
Section A						
17 MACRS deductions for assets placed in service in tax years beginning before 2015					**17**	
18 If you are electing to group any assets placed in service during the tax year into one or more general asset accounts, check here . . . . ▶ ☐						
Section B—Assets Placed in Service During 2015 Tax Year Using the General Depreciation System						
(a) Classification of property	**(b)** Month and year placed in service	**(c)** Basis for depreciation (business/investment use only—see instructions)	**(d)** Recovery period	**(e)** Convention	**(f)** Method	**(g)** Depreciation deduction
19a 3-year property						
b 5-year property						
c 7-year property		$2,000	7 YEAR	HY	200%	$286
d 10-year property						
e 15-year property						
f 20-year property						
g 25-year property			25 yrs.		S/L	
h Residential rental property			27.5 yrs.	MM	S/L	
			27.5 yrs.	MM	S/L	
i Nonresidential real property			39 yrs.	MM	S/L	
				MM	S/L	

Time-Space or Business-Use Percentage Greater than 50%

In this category, you have three options: the seven-year straight-line method, the seven-year 200% declining balance method, the 50% bonus depreciation rule, or Section 179. If you purchased the item before 2015, you cannot use the Section 179 rule. In the examples below, we will assume that the items were purchased new in 2015. (Although a business-use percentage above 50% is quite possible, few child care providers will have a Time-Space percentage over 50%. That would mean that you would be regularly using 100% of the rooms in your home for business and caring for children or conducting business activities in your home over 12 hours a day, 7 days a week, 52 weeks a year.)

You need to attach a supporting schedule to your tax return if you are depreciating more than one item. Let's say that you purchased three items in 2015—a new sofa, a new stroller, and a new swing set. You decide to use your Time-Space percentage (55%) for the sofa and actual business-use percentages for the stroller (100%) and the swing set (75%).

SEVEN-YEAR STRAIGHT-LINE

2015 Tax Return
Supporting Schedule for Form 4562, Part III, line 19c
Polly Jones
Social Security #474-66-1234

Item	Method	Cost	Business-Use %	Business Basis	Table % Year 1	Deduction 2015
Swing set	7 YR/SL	$4,000 x	75%	= $3,000 x	7.14%	=$214.20
Total		$4,000		$3,000		$214.20

Enter $214 on **Form 4562**, Part III, line 19c, column (g).

SEVEN-YEAR 200% DECLINING BALANCE

2015 Tax Return
Supporting Schedule for Form 4562, Part II, line 14
Polly Jones
Social Security #474-66-1234

Deduction Item	Method	Cost	Business-Use %	Business Basis	Table % Year 1	Deduction 2015
Swing set	7 YR/200% DB	$4,000 x	75%	= $3,000 x	14.29% =	$428.70
Total		$4,000		$3,000		$428.70

Enter $429 on **Form 4562**, Part III, line 19c, column (g).

Part II	Special Depreciation Allowance and Other Depreciation (**Do not** include listed property.) (See instructions.)						
14	Special depreciation allowance for qualified property (other than listed property) placed in service during the tax year (see instructions)					**14**	
15	Property subject to section 168(f)(1) election					**15**	
16	Other depreciation (including ACRS)					**16**	

Part III	MACRS Depreciation (**Do not** include listed property.) (See instructions.)						

Section A

17	MACRS deductions for assets placed in service in tax years beginning before 2015					**17**	
18	If you are electing to group any assets placed in service during the tax year into one or more general asset accounts, check here . . . . ▶ ☐						

Section B—Assets Placed in Service During 2015 Tax Year Using the General Depreciation System

(a) Classification of property	(b) Month and year placed in service	(c) Basis for depreciation (business/investment use only—see instructions)	(d) Recovery period	(e) Convention	(f) Method	(g) Depreciation deduction
19a 3-year property						
b 5-year property						
c 7-year property		$3,000	7 YEAR	HY	200% DB	$429
d 10-year property						
e 15-year property						
f 20-year property						
g 25-year property			25 yrs.		S/L	
h Residential rental property			27.5 yrs.	MM	S/L	
			27.5 yrs.	MM	S/L	
i Nonresidential real property			39 yrs.	MM	S/L	
				MM	S/L	

50% BONUS DEPRECIATION

2015 Tax Return
Supporting Schedule for Form 4562, Part II, line 14
Polly Jones
Social Security #474-66-1234

Deduction Item	Method	Cost	Business-Use %	Business Basis	Deduction Line 14	Deduction Line 19c
Swing set	50% Bonus	$4,000	x 75%	= $3,000	$1,500	= $214.29
Total		$4,000		$3,000		$214.29

Enter $214 on **Form 4562**, Part III, line 19c, column (g).

SECTION 179

2015 Tax Return
Supporting Schedule for Form 4562, Part I
Polly Jones
Social Security #474-66-1234

Item	Method	Cost	Business Use %	Business Basis	Deduction 2015
Swing set	Section 179	$4,000	x 75%	= $3,000	$3,000
Total		$4,000		$3,000	$3,000

Using this method, the amount that you can claim as a depreciation expense this year is $2,170. Enter this amount on **Form 4562**, Part I.

Which Rule Should You Use?

It only makes sense to use the seven-year straight-line method of depreciation if you don't want to worry about your deductions rising and falling over the years. Because getting a deduction this year is worth more than getting a deduction in a later year, the 200% declining balance method delivers a greater financial benefit than the straight-line method. The 50% bonus depreciation rule beats out both of these methods because it gets a higher deduction in the first year.

Personal Property Expenses Before Last Year

If you were in business before last year, enter your depreciation deductions for the items first used in your business before last year on **Form 4562** as follows:

- Enter computer depreciation on **Form 4562**, line 17.

- Enter other personal property depreciation on **Form 4562**, line 17.

You do not have to attach a supporting schedule to your tax return after the first year you begin depreciating an item. Just enter the proper amount of depreciation for the items from earlier years onto the lines noted above.

> **Warning: Choose Wisely!**
>
> Remember that once you begin depreciating an item using one of the methods described in this chapter, you must continue using that method for the entire life of the item, even if the depreciation rules change in later years.

Home Improvements

A home improvement is something that is attached to your home and adds to its value or substantially prolongs its useful life. Home improvements include room additions, new windows, a new roof, a new garage, new siding, an outdoor deck, or a remodeled kitchen or bath. However, see page 74 for the new definition of what is a repair and what is an improvement. If you made home improvements since you began using your home for business, you must depreciate these improvements separately from your home depreciation.

You may depreciate a home improvement expense even if you are renting your home or apartment. The only requirement is that you must be the person who paid for the improvement. If you have paid for the home improvement in lieu of rent payments, you should claim the cost of the home improvement as rent and deduct it all in the current year. Enter this amount on **Form 8829**, line 18. All home improvements made last year must be depreciated over 39 years. It appears that you can now use the 50% bonus depreciation rule on some home improvements (see page 81). However, we will not use this rule in the example below.

Home improvements are depreciated with the same method used for the home itself, the 39-year straight-line method. To calculate the depreciation deduction for a home improvement, first multiply the cost of the improvement by your Time-Space percentage to get the business basis of the improvement. (When your Time-Space percentage changes, the total that you can depreciate will also change.) Multiply the business basis by the percentage for the month you completed the improvement (as listed in the depreciation tables at the end of this chapter).

If you completed a $3,000 kitchen remodeling project in April of last year, your depreciation calculation might look something like this:

$3,000	Total cost of kitchen remodeling
x 25%	Time-Space percentage
$ 750	
x 1.819%	Depreciation percentage for April
$13.64	Amount you can deduct

The amount you can claim as a depreciation expense this year for your kitchen remodeling project is $13.64. Enter this amount on **Form 4562**, Part III, line 19i, column (g). After the first year of depreciation, you will use 2.564% each year to calculate your deduction.

Part III	**MACRS Depreciation (Do not** include listed property.) (See instructions.)						
			Section A				
17	MACRS deductions for assets placed in service in tax years beginning before 2014					**17**	
18	If you are electing to group any assets placed in service during the tax year into one or more general asset accounts, check here . . . . ▶ ☐						
	Section B—Assets Placed in Service During 2014 Tax Year Using the General Depreciation System						
(a) Classification of property	**(b)** Month and year placed in service	**(c)** Basis for depreciation (business/investment use only—see instructions)	**(d)** Recovery period	**(e)** Convention	**(f)** Method	**(g)** Depreciation deduction	
19a 3-year property							
b 5-year property							
c 7-year property							
d 10-year property							
e 15-year property							
f 20-year property							
g 25-year property			25 yrs.		S/L		
h Residential rental property			27.5 yrs.	MM	S/L		
			27.5 yrs.	MM	S/L		
i Nonresidential real property	KITCHEN	$750	39 yrs.	MM	S/L		$14
				MM	S/L		

You can use your actual business-use percentage instead of your Time-Space percentage in calculating your home improvement depreciation. It may make sense to do this if your business-use percentage is much higher than your Time-Space percentage. If you do use your business-use percentage, you'll need written evidence to support it. It probably isn't possible to claim a higher business-use percentage for home improvements that are an integral part of the structure of your home, such as a new roof, new windows, or new siding.

Depreciating Unfinished Home Improvement Projects

If you started a home improvement project last year but won't finish it until this year, you can depreciate part of the project this tax season if you were able to start using the improvement by the end of last year. Here are your options:

- Wait to take any depreciation on the project until it is finished. If you started a project in 2015 and didn't use the improvement at all that year, start depreciating the project in 2016 in the month the project is finished.

- Treat the unfinished home improvement as two projects. If you began using part of the improvement in December of last year, you can depreciate your expenses for the project starting that month. Depreciate your expenses for this year starting the month the project is finished.

Home Improvement Savings Are Small

Since home improvements must be depreciated over 39 years, the amount you will be able to claim in any one year will be relatively small. Some providers spend thousands of dollars fixing up their homes for their businesses under the mistaken belief that they will be able to write off much of the cost in the first year. As they soon discover, spending money on home improvements is not a good way to create deductions for your business.

In the previous example, a $3,000 remodeling expense resulted in a $13.64 deduction in the first year. If you are in the 15% income tax bracket, this would be a federal tax savings of only $3.68 (15% income tax plus 12% net Social Security tax rate). Your state income taxes will also produce a small tax savings. If you make a home improvement, it's always good to take the depreciation deduction, no matter how small, because it will run for many years. But remember that large home improvement expenses for your business will not translate into significant tax savings.

The Mid-Quarter Convention rule (see page 82) doesn't apply to home improvements. You can't take Section 179 for home improvements, because they aren't considered tangible personal property. If you make home improvements that are necessary to become licensed or regulated or to maintain your license, however, you may be able to depreciate 100% of the cost.

Depreciating Carpeting and Vinyl Flooring

Wall-to-wall carpeting that can be removed without restoring or resurfacing the floor and vinyl flooring that is removable without damaging the floor are considered personal property rather than home improvements. This is good news, because it means that these expenses can be depreciated under the seven-year term for personal property, rather than the 39-year term for home improvements. Replacing wood or ceramic tile flooring in one room would be considered a repair. Replacing a "substantial portion" of the floors in your home would be considered a home improvement.

If you have completed a remodeling project, you can break out the cost of the carpeting and vinyl flooring and depreciate them over the shorter period. If you began depreciating these items under the 39-year rule, you can switch over to the seven-year rules and start claiming the higher depreciation deductions. For example, if you began depreciating your carpet in 2013 under the 39-year rule, you can claim the third year's depreciation in 2015 by using the seven-year rules. To claim your unclaimed depreciation from earlier years, you can either amend your tax return or file **Form 3115** (see chapters 9 and 10).

If you do depreciate carpeting or vinyl flooring under the 39-year rule as part of your home, that flooring will almost certainly wear out before the end of the depreciation period. You're entitled to claim all the remaining depreciation in the year that you replace the flooring, as long as you're still in business.

Home Improvements before Last Year

Use Part III of **Form 4562** only for improvements that you paid for last year. If you made a home improvement before last year and before you began using your home for business, determine whether the cost of the improvement or its fair market value at the time your home was first used for your business is the lesser amount. (Since most home improvements increase in value along with the home, the lower number will usually be the original cost.) Add this amount to the cost of your home, and depreciate it as part of your home depreciation.

If you made a home improvement before last year but after you began using your home for your business, enter the depreciation for that improvement on **Form 8829**, following the instructions given in chapter 2. Calculate the depreciation deduction separately from your home and add that amount to **Form 8829**, line 41. The home improvements you make after you begin using your home for business aren't depreciated with your home because the depreciation periods end on different dates. If you are using tax preparation software and it won't allow you to enter your home improvement on line 41, enter it on line 21 (other expenses), column (b).

Land Improvements

Land improvements include installing a fence around your property or a patio, paving your driveway, adding a cement walkway, or installing a well. If the total cost of your land improvement was the lesser of $10,000 or 2% of the unadjusted basis of your home, you can deduct it in one year, rather than depreciating it. See page 75. To depreciate land improvements that you made last year, use either the 15-year straight-line or the 15-year 150% declining balance method. As with home improvements, you can't take a Section 179 expense for land improvements because they are not considered tangible personal property.

You can use the 50% bonus depreciation rule on a land improvement such as a fence or driveway. In the example below, we will use the 50% bonus depreciation rule because we assume that your fence was purchased new in 2015.

To calculate the depreciation deduction for a land improvement, first multiply its cost by your Time-Space percentage to get the business basis of the improvement. (When your Time-Space percentage changes, the total that you can depreciate will also change.) If you purchased a fence in 2015 for $11,000, your depreciation calculation might look something like this:

> Cost of fence $11,000 x 30% Time-Space percentage = $3,300
> $3,300 x 50% bonus depreciation = $1,650
> Enter this on **Form 4562**, Part II, line 14.
>
> $3,300 - $1,650 = $1,650 x 5% (first year using 15-year 150% declining balance method) = $82.50
> Enter this on **Form 4562**, Part III, line 19c, column (g).

Part II	Special Depreciation Allowance and Other Depreciation (Do not include listed property.) (See instructions.)						

14	Special depreciation allowance for qualified property (other than listed property) placed in service during the tax year (see instructions)					14	$1,650
15	Property subject to section 168(f)(1) election					15	
16	Other depreciation (including ACRS)					16	

Part III	MACRS Depreciation (Do not include listed property.) (See instructions.)

Section A

17	MACRS deductions for assets placed in service in tax years beginning before 2015	17	
18	If you are electing to group any assets placed in service during the tax year into one or more general asset accounts, check here . . . . ▶ ☐		

Section B—Assets Placed in Service During 2015 Tax Year Using the General Depreciation System

(a) Classification of property	(b) Month and year placed in service	(c) Basis for depreciation (business/investment use only—see instructions)	(d) Recovery period	(e) Convention	(f) Method	(g) Depreciation deduction
19a 3-year property						
b 5-year property						
c 7-year property						
d 10-year property						
e 15-year property		$3,300	15 YEAR	HY	150% DB	$82.50
f 20-year property						
g 25-year property			25 yrs.		S/L	
h Residential rental property			27.5 yrs.	MM	S/L	
			27.5 yrs.	MM	S/L	
i Nonresidential real property			39 yrs.	MM	S/L	
				MM	S/L	

Again, you may want to use your actual business-use percentage instead of your Time-Space percentage in calculating the depreciation for land improvements. This may make sense for a fence that you install for your business if you have no young children of your own or if you can show that it is mostly for your business. As noted above, you must be able to support this business-use claim.

Landscaping Is Not a Land Improvement

Landscaping includes trees, shrubbery, sod, plantings, grading, and landscape architect's fees. If the total cost of the landscaping items, plus home improvements, plus home repairs is the lesser of $10,000 or 2% of the unadjusted basis of your home, you can deduct it in one year as a repair on **Form 8829**, line 19. If it costs more than this, and is located immediately adjacent to your home, and would be destroyed if your home was moved or replaced, then it should be treated as a home improvement and depreciated over 39 years. Landscaping that costs more than $500, is installed away from your home, and would not be harmed if your home was moved or replaced is considered part of the land and cannot be depreciated at all.

Land Improvements before Last Year

Use Part II of **Form 4562** only for the land improvements you paid for last year. If you made a land improvement before you began your business, determine whether the cost of the improvement or its fair market value at the time it was first used in your business is the lesser amount. (Since many land improvements increase in value along with the home, the original cost will often be the lower number.) Add this amount to the cost of your home when determining the depreciation deduction for your home.

If you made a land improvement before last year but after you began using your home for your business, enter the depreciation for that land improvement on **Form 8829**. (Follow the instructions under Home Improvements.) Calculate your depreciation deduction and add that amount to **Form 8829**, line 41.

Home Depreciation

You can't take a business deduction for your mortgage payments; instead, depreciate your home using the rules described below. It's always financially beneficial to depreciate your home. There are two important reasons to depreciate your home. First, it will reduce your taxable income while you're in business. Second, any higher taxes that you may have to pay later because you used your home in your business will be the same whether or not you claimed the depreciation you were entitled to. (The rules about the tax consequences when you sell your home don't change the fact that you are still better off claiming all the home depreciation you're entitled to; see chapter 12.)

If you own a mobile home that is fastened to the land and connected to local utilities, use the home depreciation rules described in this section. If your mobile home wears out within 39 years, you can deduct all the unused depreciation in the final year.

Most taxpayers must show that they use part of their home regularly and exclusively for business purposes to qualify to deduct depreciation for their home. Family child care providers are exempt from this requirement. You only need to show that you use part of your home regularly for your business. If that is the case, you can claim part of the value of your home as a depreciation expense each year you are in business.

If you're married and your name isn't on the deed of the home, you can still claim home depreciation for your business. If you aren't married and your companion owns the home, you can't claim home depreciation (see the *Record-Keeping Guide*).

Note: You cannot use the 50% bonus depreciation rule for the purchase of a home.

If You Rent Your Home

If you rent your home instead of own it, deduct your Time-Space percentage of your rent instead of depreciation. To do this, enter your total rent payments on **Form 8829**, line 18, column (b) (see chapter 2).

If You Started Claiming Home Depreciation before Last Year

If you claimed depreciation on your home before last year, enter your depreciation by filling out **Form 8829**, lines 36–41. Don't claim this deduction on **Form 4562**.

If you or your spouse claimed home depreciation in earlier years for another business, continue depreciating your home under the rules for that business. Once your child care business begins, start a separate depreciation calculation for your home for this business. In other words, use two different depreciation schedules to depreciate your home for the two different businesses.

If You Started Claiming Home Depreciation Last Year

If you first began using your home for your business last year, you must enter information on **Form 4562**, Part III, line 19i. Enter the month you started using your home for business in column (b). Enter the business basis of your home in column (c). To calculate the business basis of your home, follow these steps:

STEP ONE

Record the purchase price of your home. If you hired a contractor or built part of the home yourself, only record the amount of money that you actually spent to build your home; don't include the value of your labor.

If you first used your home for business in 2015 and the fair market value of your home in 2015 (including any home improvements you made before your business began) is less than your original purchase price, use the home's fair market value instead of the purchase price.

Note: Because of sharply declining home values across the country, it is much more likely that providers who started their business in the past year will own a home that is worth less than the purchase price. Therefore, new providers should look closely at the fair market value of their home when their business began because this value may be the one to use in determining home depreciation. If the fair market value of your home declines after you begin using it for business, don't reduce its value in calculating your home depreciation in later years.

Special Case

If you lived in and sold a home before May 6, 1997, and took advantage of a rollover rule that allowed you to postpone paying taxes on your gain on the sale of that home, you must subtract that gain from the purchase price of your current home. In other words, if you sold a home before May 6, 1997, and made a profit of $20,000, and the purchase price of your current home was $100,000, you would use $80,000 as the adjusted price of your home for depreciation purposes. If you sold your previous home after May 6, 1997, you don't have to make any adjustment in the purchase price of your new home.

STEP TWO

Add to the above amount the value of any home improvements that you made before you first used your home for business. These improvements might include remodeling expenses, a new roof, room additions, siding, or a new deck. Don't include repairs or maintenance expenses, such as painting, wallpapering, or fixing a broken window.

STEP THREE

Subtract from the above the value of the land (land is not depreciable) to get the adjusted basis of your home. If you don't know the value of the land when you bought the house, use the relationship between the value of your land and home today to calculate the value of your land when you bought your house. Check your property tax statement, or call your county assessor's office for an estimate of the value of your land today.

EXAMPLE

You bought your home in 2010 for $100,000. According to your property tax statement, it's worth $120,000 now. Your county assessor says that the land is worth $12,000 today, and $12,000 ÷ $120,000 = 10%. Therefore the value of your land in 2008 was roughly 10% of the purchase price of your home, or $10,000 ($100,000 x 10% = $10,000). Keep a copy of your tax assessment report for your records.

If you buy more land or are given land and pay for surveying, you can't claim these expenses as business deductions. (For more information, see the *Record-Keeping Guide*.)

STEP FOUR

Multiply the adjusted basis of your home by your Time-Space percentage to get the business basis of your home—the amount you can depreciate. Enter this number in column (c) of **Form 4562**, Part III, line 19i. Here are the calculations:

Step One:	$100,000	purchase price of home in 2010
Step Two:	+ $3,800	new roof in 2011
	$103,800	
Step Three:	−$10,000	value of land in 2010
	$93,800	adjusted basis of home
Step Four:	x 30%	Time-Space percentage
	$28,140	business basis of home

The next step is to determine the percentage of the business basis of your home that you can deduct in the first year of business. This depends on the month you began your business last year; see the depreciation tables at the end of this chapter.

Let's use our example to calculate your first year's home depreciation deduction. If you went into business in January 2014, you would use 2.461%:

$28,140	business basis of home
x 2.461%	began business in January
$692.53	home depreciation deduction

Enter the amount you calculate here in line 19i, column (g). After the first year of depreciation, you will use 2.564% each year to calculate your deduction.

Part III MACRS Depreciation (Do not include listed property.) (See instructions.)

Section A

17 MACRS deductions for assets placed in service in tax years beginning before 2015 . . . . | 17 |

18 If you are electing to group any assets placed in service during the tax year into one or more general asset accounts, check here . . . . ▶ ☐

Section B—Assets Placed in Service During 2015 Tax Year Using the General Depreciation System

(a) Classification of property	(b) Month and year placed in service	(c) Basis for depreciation (business/investment use only—see instructions)	(d) Recovery period	(e) Convention	(f) Method	(g) Depreciation deduction
19a 3-year property						
b 5-year property						
c 7-year property						
d 10-year property						
e 15-year property						
f 20-year property						
g 25-year property			25 yrs.		S/L	
h Residential rental property			27.5 yrs.	MM	S/L	
			27.5 yrs.	MM	S/L	
i Nonresidential real property	1/15	$28,140	39 yrs.	MM	S/L	$693
				MM	S/L	

If you first began using your home for your business last year, fill out Part III of **Form 4562**, as described above. Enter the depreciation deduction ($692.53 in our example) on **Form 4562**, line 22. Don't carry this deduction forward to **Schedule C**, line 13. You will claim your home depreciation on **Form 8829**.

In our example, let's say that you had $250 of personal property depreciation to claim on **Form 4562** as well as $692.53 of home depreciation. You would enter $942.53 on **Form 4562**, line 22 ($250 + $692.53). You would carry forward $250 to **Schedule C**, line 13, and claim $692.53 on **Form 8829**, line 41.

Vehicle Depreciation

You can use either the standard mileage rate method or the actual vehicle expenses method to deduct the vehicle expenses for your business (see chapter 5 and the *Record-Keeping Guide* for information on claiming other expenses for your vehicle). No matter which method you use to claim vehicle expenses, if you used more than one vehicle in your business during the year, report your business miles on **Form 4562** (lines 30–36), not on **Schedule C** (see Vehicle Expenses in chapter 5). If you choose the actual vehicle expenses method, you may take a depreciation deduction on your vehicle. Vehicles are subject to the Mid-Quarter Convention rule (see page 82).

To calculate the depreciation on your vehicle, fill out **Form 4562**, Part V, Section A. (If you began depreciating your vehicle in an earlier year, you must continue depreciating it under the rules that were in effect when you began to depreciate it.)

Caution

If you decide to use the actual vehicle expenses method in the first year you use a vehicle in your business, you'll be locked into this method for the life of that vehicle; you can't switch back to the standard mileage rate method in later years. This means that you'll have to keep detailed records of all your vehicle expenses for every year you use the vehicle in your business.

To depreciate your vehicle, you must first determine if it weighs more or less than 6,000 pounds gross vehicle weight. Look for this information on the inside front door panel of your vehicle. (Vehicles that weigh more than 6,000 pounds include the Dodge Durango SUV, the Ford Econoline Van E150, the GMC Savana Van 1500, and the Chevrolet Express Van 1500.) Next, figure out if the vehicle was used more or less than 50% for your business. Once you have these two facts, follow the instructions below that apply to your situation.

The depreciation you claim for your vehicle cannot create a loss for your business. This may be an issue if your vehicle weighs more than 6,000 pounds and you are using it more than 50% in your business.

Note: If you bought a new car in 2015 and you use it at least 50% of the miles in your business, you may use the 50% bonus depreciation rule. If you use this rule, your depreciation limit for 2015 will be raised by $8,000. This will enable you to claim a much higher depreciation deduction for 2015 and may make it more worth your while to use the actual vehicle expense method, rather than the standard milarge rate method.

If the Vehicle Weighs Less Than Six Thousand Pounds

IF YOU USED THE VEHICLE 50% OR LESS FOR BUSINESS

Use five-year straight-line depreciation. Your depreciation deduction will be subject to limitations each year, based on the first year the vehicle was used for business. The first-year depreciation limit for a passenger vehicle purchased in 2015 is $3,160. The limit is the same if you purchased a vehicle before 2015 and 2015 is the first year you are using it for your business. For all passenger vehicles purchased in 2015, the depreciation limit for 2016 is $5,100, for 2017 is $3,050, and $1,875 each year thereafter.

The first-year depreciation limit for a truck or van purchased in 2015 is $3,460. The limit is the same if you purchased a van or truck before 2015 and 2015 is the first year you are using it for your business. For all trucks and vans purchased in 2015, the depreciation limit for 2016 is $5,500, for 2017 is $3,350, and $1,975 for each year thereafter. These limits will remain in effect for all passenger vehicles, trucks, and vans that are first put into business use in 2015. In these cases, report the first-year depreciation on **Form 4562**, Part II, line 14.

You must reduce these limitations by your business-use percentage of the vehicle. In other words, if you use the vehicle 35% of the time for your business, your depreciation limitation in 2015 would be $1,106 ($3,160 x 35% = $1,106).

To calculate the depreciation deduction for a vehicle, multiply the purchase price by the business-use percentage and then multiply the result by 10% (for the first year of five-year straight-line depreciation). See the depreciation tables at the end of this chapter.

If you purchased a used Mazda Protegé for $15,000 and used it 35% of the time for your business, your first-year depreciation calculation would be

$15,000 x 35% = $5,250 x 10% = $525

Since this is less than the $3,160 limit, you can claim the full $525 as depreciation. See how this is entered on **Form 4562**, Part V, line 27—the S/L in column (g) means straight-line. Enter "HY" for the Half-Year Convention (see page 83).

IF YOU USED THE VEHICLE MORE THAN 50% FOR BUSINESS

In this example, we will assume you purchased a new car in 2015. The year you bought the car, you can choose to use five-year straight-line depreciation, five-year 200% declining balance depreciation, the 50% bonus depreciation rule, or Section 179. If you use five-year straight-line depreciation or the 200% declining balance method, the depreciation deduction limitations are the same as given above.

Let's say that you purchased a new $25,000 car on September 10, 2015, and used it 70% of the time in your business for the rest of the year. If you use the Section 179 rule, the first-year deduction amount limitation is $3,160, for a new or used car. The amount of your car cost that can be depreciated is $17,500 ($25,000 x 70% = $17,500), but you would be entitled to put only $3,160 on **Form 4562**, Part I.

If you used the five-year straight line method:

$25,000 x 70% = $17,500
$17,500 x 10% (first year amout) = $1,750

Claim this amount on **Form 4562,** line 26, column (h).

If you used the five-year 200% declining balance method:

$15,000 x 70% = $17,500
$17,500 x 20% (first year amout) = $3,500

Since this is above the limit of $3,160, you could claim $3,160 on **Form 4562**, line 26, column (h).

Depreciation and Vehicle Expenses

In addition to depreciation, you can claim actual vehicle expenses on **Schedule C**, line 13 (see Vehicle Expenses in chapter 5). If you depreciate a vehicle that you first started using in business last year, you can't use the standard mileage rate to claim expenses for it in later years. If you use Section 179 and go out of business, or use the vehicle 50% or less within five years, you'll have to file **Form 4797** to recapture some of the depreciation you claimed (see chapter 11).

If the Vehicle Weighs More Than Six Thousand Pounds

IF YOU USED THE VEHICLE 50% OR LESS FOR BUSINESS
Use five-year straight-line depreciation. There is a difference in where you enter the depreciation deduction for a vehicle that weighs more than 6,000 pounds. If the vehicle is used 50% or less for business, enter the deduction on **Form 4562**, Part III, line 19b, instead of line 27. Using the figures given in the example on page 103, you would enter $525 on line 19b, column (g).

IF YOU USED THE VEHICLE MORE THAN 50% FOR BUSINESS
In this situation you have several choices. You can use the five-year straight-line method, the 200% declining balance method, the 50% bonus depreciation rule, or Section 179. If you choose the Section 179 rule, you can deduct up to $25,000 in depreciation deductions in the first year. If you purchase a $25,000 new vehicle and use it 70% for business, you could deduct $17,500 ($25,000 x 70% = $17,500). Because the vehicle weighed more than 6,000 pounds, it is not subject to the yearly limitations described earlier. Claim this amount on **Form 4562**, Part I, line 2.

If You Sold Your Vehicle Last Year

If you've been depreciating your vehicle before last year and you sold it last year, use the following options to determine how much depreciation to claim.

If you placed your vehicle in business use between January 1 and September 30 of the first year you used it in your business, you can deduct one half of the regular depreciation amount.

If you placed your vehicle in business use between October 1 and December 31 of the first year you used it in your business, multiply the full-year depreciation amount by the following percentages, based on the month you sold the vehicle:

January–March	12.5%
April–June	37.5%
July–September	62.5%
October–December	87.5%

(For a description of the tax consequences of selling a vehicle, see chapter 11.)

Depreciation after the First Five Years

Vehicles are five-year property, and they must be depreciated using the five-year depreciation rules. If you can't depreciate all of the cost of a vehicle within that period because of the annual limitations, you can continue claiming depreciation (up to $1,875 per year) after that until your depreciation is fully deducted. Under the Half-Year Convention (see page 82), five-year property is actually depreciated over six years.

If you use the vehicle less than 100% of the time during any of the first six years of depreciation, you must do an additional calculation to determine how much depreciation you can claim after the six-year period is up. First, add up the limitations for each year (for example, $3,160 + $5,100 + $3,050 + $1,875 + $1,875 + $1,875 = $16,935). Next, subtract this total from the cost of the business portion of the vehicle. If the vehicle cost $40,000 and you use it 60% of the time in your business, the result would be $7,065:

$40,000 x 60% = $24,000 – $16,935 = $7,065

After year six, you can depreciate the remaining $7,065 over the next two years (up to the $1,875 limit each year), even if your actual depreciation deductions in the first six years didn't equal $16,935. This has the net effect of reducing your depreciation deductions in later years if you use your vehicle less than 100% of the time for business.

Congratulations!

You have entered your depreciation expenses on either **Form 4562** or **Form 8829**. Now enter the total of all your depreciation deductions on **Schedule C**, line 13.

Next, take a deep breath. The most difficult part of doing your taxes is done! Nothing else you'll do on your tax forms will be as complicated as what you have just completed. Your next step will be completing **Schedule C**.

Start-Up Costs: A Special Rule

To the IRS, your business begins when you're ready to enroll children and are advertising that fact to the public. Whether you are licensed or have any children in your care at that point is not important. Here's an example: In February, you are ready to care for your first child and put up a sign at your church announcing your business. In March, you apply for your license, in April you get your license, and in May, you enroll your first child. In this case, the IRS would say that your business began in February. On the other hand, if you get your license in June and aren't ready to care for your first child until August, then the IRS would say that your business began in August.

There are two types of expenses that you are likely to incur before your business begins:

- Items that you would normally depreciate: home improvements, land improvements, furniture, appliances, and other items that originally cost more than $2,500 and that last longer than a year. For these items, simply begin depreciating them in the year you start your business under the rules described in this chapter.

- Items that originally cost less than $2,500 that you would normally be able to deduct in one year. For example, child care workshop fees, smoke detectors, fire department inspection fees, advertising flyers, games, CDs, dishes, pots and pans, and hundreds of other household items.

You can deduct $5,000 worth of the items in the second category in the year your business begins. So, if you bought $3,000 worth of toys and supplies in November and December 2013 in anticipation of starting your business in 2015, and your business did begin last year, then you can deduct that $3,000. If you used these items 100% of the time for your business, you can deduct the full amount. If they were used both in your business and your family, then apply your Time-Space percentage to the cost of the items. Claim start-up expenses of less than $2,500 per item on **Schedule C**, Part V, and write "I.R.C. Sec. 195 Start-Up Expenditures" on one of the blank lines.

Be sure to save the receipts for all the items you bought before your business began. If you spent more than $5,000 on such items before your business began, then you must amortize the remaining amount over 180 months (15 years) using **Form 4562**, Part VI.

Special Cases for Depreciation

If You've Gone In and Out of Business

What if you started depreciating an item, went out of business, and then started up your business again? When you start up again, determine whether the fair market value of the item at that time or the adjusted basis of the item is the lesser amount. The adjusted basis is the cost of the item minus the amount of depreciation you claimed (or were entitled to claim) while you were in business. Then begin depreciating the item as Year 1 for this new amount.

EXAMPLE

In Year 1, you bought a $200 stroller for your own children. You started using the stroller in your business in Year 2; its fair market value at that time was $180. From Year 2 through Year 4, you used the stroller 100% in your business and claimed $64.29 in depreciation (seven-year straight-line depreciation). You stopped doing child care in Year 5 and Year 6.

In Year 7, you started up your business again. At that time, the fair market value of the stroller was $50. The adjusted basis is the original cost ($200) less the depreciation you have claimed ($64.29), or $135.71. Since the fair market value is lower than the adjusted basis of the item, use $50 to begin depreciating in Year 7. In Year 7, you will start depreciating $50 using seven-year straight-line rules for Year 1 and continue for another seven years of depreciation.

If You Haven't Been Taking All Your Depreciation

What if you discover that you didn't take all the depreciation you were entitled to in a previous year? What if you haven't been taking any depreciation at all on your home or some other item? In these cases, you have three options:

1. You can file amended tax returns for 2012, 2013, and 2014 and claim the depreciation you were entitled to for those years. You will get a refund plus interest. (You can only amend your return three years back.)

2. If you didn't deduct the full amount of depreciation that you were entitled to and the error goes back more than three years, you should file **Form 3115** to recapture all the unclaimed depreciation that you are entitled to. (For instructions on filing **Form 3115**, see chapter 10.) To use **Form 3115**, you must have failed to claim the full amount of your depreciation for at least two consecutive years.

3. You can decide not to take advantage of **Form 3115** and just claim the depreciation you would be entitled to this year if you had depreciated the previous years correctly. To do this, calculate the amount of depreciation you are entitled to under the rules that were in effect when the depreciation period began. If you bought the item for your business in 2009, for example, you would claim depreciation based on the fourth year of the seven-year depreciation tables. If you choose this option, you would forget about your unclaimed depreciation from earlier years.

If You Incurred Expenses to Meet Local Regulations

In some parts of the country, the local regulations require you to purchase safety equipment (such as smoke detectors or fire extinguishers) or make home improvements (such as enlarging a basement window or installing a fence) in order to operate a family child care business. These expenses aren't automatically 100% deductible. What matters is how you use the item, not why you bought it.

*   In the case of smoke detectors and fire extinguishers, you can deduct only your Time-Space or business-use percentage of the cost. If these items are in an exclusive-use room, however, you can deduct 100% of the cost.

*   If you enlarge a basement window in order to become licensed and you use that area of the basement 100% for your business, you can depreciate the total cost as a home improvement. If you use that area of the basement for both business and personal purposes, you must apply your Time-Space or business-use percentage to the cost before you depreciate it.

If an Item Wears Out during the Depreciation Period

If an item wears out before its depreciation period ends, you're normally entitled to claim all the remaining depreciation as a business deduction in the year it wears out (start-up costs are an exception to this rule). For instructions on how to claim this amount, see chapter 11. If you buy a new item to replace the old one, you will start a new depreciation period for the new item.

Obtain a Copy of Your Depreciation Schedule

When your tax preparer depreciates items for your business he or she will prepare a depreciation schedule showing each item, cost, depreciation method, and convention. It's important to ask your tax preparer for a copy of this schedule each year. This can be extremely useful for you in preparing future tax returns whether you do them yourself or use a new tax preparer.

For more information about the tax issues discussed in this chapter, refer to the related topics in the other chapters of this book and the Redleaf Press *Family Child Care Record-Keeping Guide*.

2015 Depreciation Tables

	3-Year Straight-Line (computer software)	5-Year Straight-Line (computers, office equipment, and vehicles)	5-Year 200% Declining Balance (computers, office equipment, and vehicles)
Year 1	16.67%	10%	20%
Year 2	33.33%	20%	32%
Year 3	33.33%	20%	19.20%
Year 4	16.67%	20%	11.52%
Year 5		20%	11.52%
Year 6		10%	5.76%
Section 179?	Maybe	No	Yes

	7-Year Straight-Line (furniture and appliances)	7-Year 200% Declining Balance (furniture and appliances)
Year 1	7.14%	14.29%
Year 2	14.29%	24.49%
Year 3	14.29%	17.49%
Year 4	14.28%	12.49%
Year 5	14.29%	8.93%
Year 6	14.28%	8.92%
Year 7	14.29%	8.93%
Year 8	7.14%	4.46%
Section 179?	Maybe	Yes

	15-Year Straight-Line (land improvements)	15-Year 150% Declining Balance (land improvements)	39-Year Straight-Line (home and home improvements after May 13, 1993)	
			For the first year of depreciation, use this table:	*After the first year of depreciation, use:*
Year 1	3.33%	5.00%		
Year 2	6.67%	9.50%		
Year 3	6.67%	8.55%		
Year 4	6.67%	7.70%	January 2.461%	2.564%
Year 5	6.67%	6.93%	February 2.247%	
Year 6	6.67%	6.23%	March 2.033%	
Year 7	6.67%	5.90%	April 1.819%	
Year 8	6.66%	5.90%	May 1.605%	
Year 9	6.67%	5.91%	June 1.391%	
Year 10	6.66%	5.90%	July 1.177%	
Year 11	6.67%	5.91%	August 0.963%	
Year 12	6.66%	5.90%	September 0.749%	
Year 13	6.67%	5.91%	October 0.535%	
Year 14	6.66%	5.90%	November 0.321%	
Year 15	6.67%	5.91%	December 0.107%	
Year 16	3.33%	2.95%		
Section 179?	Maybe	Maybe	Section 179? No	No

CHAPTER 4

Reporting Your Food Program Income and Food Expenses

The first part of this chapter explains how to report your income from the Child and Adult Care Food Program (CACFP). The Food Program is a federal program that reimburses family child care providers for serving nutritious food. The second part of this chapter explains how to claim your food expenses. It's important to claim these expenses properly, because food is the single biggest business deduction that most family child care providers have. The standard meal allowance rates for 2015 are $1.31 for breakfast, $2.47 for lunch or supper, and $0.73 for snack.

Reporting Your Income from the Food Program

All family child care providers who meet their state regulation standards are eligible to participate in the CACFP. All family child care providers should participate in the Food Program because it offers a major source of income. (For a full discussion of the benefits of the Food Program, see the *Record-Keeping Guide*.)

Reimbursement Rates

The Food Program's reimbursement rates are raised on July 1 every year. If you have a low income, live in a low-income area, or serve low-income children, you will be eligible for the Tier I reimbursement rates. If you don't have at least one of these qualifications, you will get the Tier II reimbursement rates.

For your family to be considered low income in 2015 you must meet the following income eligibility guidelines (July 1, 2015–June 30, 2016):

Annual Income	Family of one	Family of two	Each additional person
All states except Alaska and Hawaii	$21,775	$29,471	$7,696
Alaska	$27,232	$36,852	$9,620
Hawaii	$25,068	$33,911	$8,843

FOOD PROGRAM RATES (PER SERVING)

	Tier I Regular Rate		Tier II Reduced Rate	
	Jan–June	July–Dec	Jan–June	July–Dec
Breakfast	$1.31	$1.32	$0.48	$0.48
Lunch/Supper	$2.47	$2.48	$1.49	$1.50
Snack	$0.73	$0.74	$0.20	$0.20
Total	$4.51	$4.54	$2.17	$2.18

If you live in Alaska and Hawaii, the reimbursement rates are higher:

Alaska

Breakfast	$2.09	$2.11	$0.74	$0.75
Lunch/Supper	$4.00	$4.02	$2.41	$2.43
Snack	$1.19	$1.20	$0.33	$0.33
Total	$7.28	$7.33	$3.48	$3.51

Hawaii

Breakfast	$1.53	$1.54	$0.55	$0.55
Lunch/Supper	$2.88	$2.90	$1.74	$1.78
Snack	$0.86	$0.86	$0.23	$0.24
Total	$5.27	$5.30	$2.52	$2.54

As of July 1, 2015, the Tier I reimbursement per child equaled $1,180 per year for serving a daily breakfast, lunch, and snack. The Tier II reimbursement equaled $567 per year.

Reporting CACFP Reimbursements

I recommend that you enter your Food Program reimbursements on **Schedule C**, line 6, and write "CACFP Income" next to this number. This will clearly show the IRS that you are reporting this income. Some providers prefer to include these reimbursements in the parent fees they report on line 1; however, the IRS is always on the alert for unreported income in the child care field. If you combine your Food Program reimbursements with your parent fees, they won't be as identifiable. The IRS may wonder if you have reported all this income properly and might audit your return to find out.

SCHEDULE C (Form 1040)

Department of the Treasury
Internal Revenue Service (99)

Profit or Loss From Business
(Sole Proprietorship)

▶ Information about Schedule C and its separate instructions is at *www.irs.gov/schedulec.*
▶ Attach to Form 1040, 1040NR, or 1041; partnerships generally must file Form 1065.

OMB No. 1545-0074

2015

Attachment
Sequence No. **09**

Name of proprietor
SANDY JAMES

Social security number (SSN)
123-45-6789

A   Principal business or profession, including product or service (see instructions)
FAMILY CHILD CARE

B   Enter code from instructions
▶ 6 2 4 4 1 0

C   Business name. If no separate business name, leave blank.

D   Employer ID number (EIN), (see instr.)

E   Business address (including suite or room no.) ▶ **687 HOOVER ROAD**

City, town or post office, state, and ZIP code   **HUDSON, OH 42383**

F   Accounting method: (1) ☑ Cash   (2) ☐ Accrual   (3) ☐ Other (specify) ▶

G   Did you "materially participate" in the operation of this business during 2015? If "No," see instructions for limit on losses   ☑ Yes ☐ No

H   If you started or acquired this business during 2015, check here   ▶ ☐

I   Did you make any payments in 2015 that would require you to file Form(s) 1099? (see instructions)   ☐ Yes ☐ No

J   If "Yes," did you or will you file required Forms 1099?   ☐ Yes ☐ No

Part I   Income

1	Gross receipts or sales. See instructions for line 1 and check the box if this income was reported to you on Form W-2 and the "Statutory employee" box on that form was checked ▶ ☐	1	
2	Returns and allowances	2	
3	Subtract line 2 from line 1	3	
4	Cost of goods sold (from line 42)	4	
5	**Gross profit.** Subtract line 4 from line 3	5	
6	Other income, including federal and state gasoline or fuel tax credit or refund (see instructions)	6	$4,250
7	**Gross income.** Add lines 5 and 6 ▶	7	

Form 1099

If you have received **Form 1099 Miscellaneous Income** from your Food Program sponsor, be sure to put the amount listed on it on line 6 and identify it as "1099 Income" instead of "CACFP Income." The IRS computers can check whether all **Form 1099** income was properly reported by those who received this form. You want to make sure that anyone who looks at your **Schedule C** can see that you have reported all of your **Form 1099** income.

Reimbursements for Your Own Children

If you received reimbursements from the Food Program for your own children last year, this income is not taxable; however, most Food Program sponsors don't tell you how much of your monthly reimbursement is for your own children. To calculate how much you were reimbursed for your own children, you can use the worksheets in the Tax Organizer (see pages 42–43). Once you've calculated the total reimbursement for your own children, subtract it from your total reimbursements for the year and enter the result on line 6 of **Schedule C**. Show how you got this total in the space next to line 6 ("$5,000 CACFP, $750 own child").

The IRS can find out the total amount you received from the Food Program and is likely to look for this number on your **Schedule C**. By showing how you got the amount entered there, you'll explain why line 6 doesn't match your total reimbursement amount.

If in a previous year you reported the reimbursements for your own child as income and claimed the same amount as a food expense, then the two amounts almost canceled each other out, and no damage was done. If you reported the reimbursements for your own child as income but didn't claim your food expenses for that child, you should file an amended tax return to get a refund, plus interest (see chapter 9).

Reimbursements for a Foster Child

If you have a foster child and you receive Food Program reimbursements for that child, treat these reimbursements the same way you would for your own children. You're receiving them because your family is income-eligible. Therefore, these reimbursements are not taxable income, and the food you serve to a foster child is not a deductible business expense.

Food Stamps

If you receive food stamps, don't report them as income on **Schedule C**, because they are not taxable income. This means that the food you purchase with food stamps can't be deducted as a business expense either. If you receive food stamps, be sure to save records that show how much you received in food stamps.

If One of Your Employees Receives a Check from the Food Program

Some family child care providers operate their business from more than one location and hire employees to care for the children in one or both locations. In this situation, the Food Program will probably issue some of the reimbursement checks to your employee, and your employee should turn over the checks to you. Here's how to handle this transaction on your tax forms:

If your Food Program sponsor sends a **Form 1099** to the employee, the employee should send a **Form 1099** back to you. If the sponsor doesn't use this form, the employee shouldn't do so either. In either case, the employee should show the reimbursement as income on her own **Schedule C** and report the same amount as an expense under line 27 (other expenses). If she does this, she won't owe any tax on this income. You should show the reimbursements as income on your **Schedule C**, line 6 (other income).

Don't Assume That Food Expenses Equal Food Program Reimbursements
Instead of keeping careful food records, some providers just assume that their food expenses equal their Food Program reimbursements, so they report neither of these amounts on their tax return on the assumption that they will "wash out." For example, a provider who received $3,000 from the Food Program would assume that she spent $3,000 on food and not report either number on her **Schedule C**. This is a bad practice.

If you are a Tier I provider, you can justify your deduction by using the standard meal allowance rule and show the IRS your monthly Food Program claim forms to defend your position. If you served extra meals and snacks that weren't reimbursed by the Food Program, then your food deduction will be too low. You can easily claim a higher food deduction by tracking the nonreimbursed meals that you serve.

If you are a Tier II provider who evens out her food income and expenses, you are probably cheating yourself out of hundreds of dollars. If you use the standard meal allowance rule, you will always be able to claim food deductions that are at least twice as much as your Food Program income, because you will be claiming food expenses based on the Tier I rate, while reporting income based on the lower Tier II rate. It makes no sense not to claim this extra deduction.

Why Should You Report Your Food Reimbursements This Way?

The instructions in **Publication 587** tell you to report only your net income or expense for food reimbursements. This means that if you received $3,000 in reimbursements and spent $3,500 on business food, you would report no income and a $500 food expense. I recommend that you always show your taxable reimbursement on line 6 and all deductible food expenses on line 27 of **Schedule C**. The tax result is the same with both methods, but showing only the net income or expense is likely to increase your chance of being audited. Many providers spend far more on food than they receive from the Food Program, and showing a large food expense on **Schedule C** without any reimbursement income will draw attention from the IRS, especially for a Tier II provider.

For example, let's say that you are a Tier II provider who has received $2,000 in reimbursements and spent $5,000 on food. If you follow the IRS instructions, you would report $0 income and $3,000 in food expenses. In this case the IRS may assume that you didn't report your Food Program reimbursements and will audit you to find out if you did. All the IRS agents I have consulted recommend that you show your taxable Food Program reimbursements and all your business food deductions on **Schedule C**.

IRS Child Care Provider Audit Technique Guide on Food Expenses
The guide clearly rejects the netting method described in **Publication 587** saying, "The netting method is not a preferred method since an Examiner will always be looking for the food reimbursement amounts." The guide says that the recommended method is to report Food Program reimbursements as income and report all food expenses as expenses on **Schedule C**.

Determining the Cost of Your Food

You now have two choices for how to claim your food expenses: use the IRS standard meal allowance rule or estimate your actual cost of business food. See the *Record-Keeping Guide* for a complete discussion of these two choices.

Using the Standard Meal Allowance Rule
The IRS meal allowance rule allows you to calculate your food expenses by multiplying the meals and snacks you serve to the children in your care by the Tier I Food Program reimbursement rates in effect at the beginning of the calendar year. The rates for calendar year 2015 are $1.31 for breakfast, $2.47 for lunch or supper, and $0.73 for snacks. (The rates are higher in Alaska and Hawaii; see page 111.) If you use these rates, you won't have to save any of your business or personal food receipts.

You can use the meal allowance for up to one breakfast, one lunch, one supper, and three snacks per child per day. (The Food Program rules haven't changed; they still only reimburse up to three servings a day.) You must actually serve a meal in order to count it.

All family child care providers are eligible to use this rule, including those who aren't licensed or registered, those who receive the lower Tier II reimbursement rate, those who aren't on the Food Program, and those who are operating illegally. You can use the meal allowance one year and estimate your actual cost of food the next year. If you spend less on food than the standard meal allowance, you can still use it.

You can't use the meal allowance rate if you provide care in a building that isn't your home, and you may not count a meal if the child's parent has supplied the food. You also can't count any meals that you serve to your own child. (Food Program reimbursements for your own children aren't taxable income.)

You can count meals that you serve to employees as an actual food cost separate from the meal allowance rate (you must save the receipts). If you hire your child to work for you, you can deduct the actual cost of the food served to your child if that child is eating in the middle of his workday. You can deduct any food that you serve as part of an activity (rather than a meal or snack) as a separate activity expense rather than a food expense. For example, you can deduct the cost of a cake that you serve at a birthday party or the ingredients for a gingerbread house. Nonfood meal preparation supplies, such as containers, paper products, and utensils, continue to be deductible.

To use the standard meal allowance rule, you must maintain the following records: the name of each child, the dates and hours that child was in your care, and the number of breakfasts, lunches, suppers, and snacks served. The IRS provides a meal and snack log that you can use to track this information. In addition, the *Redleaf Calendar-Keeper* has two pages of charts that meet IRS requirements, and those are included in Part I of this book.

Estimating Your Actual Cost of Food

If you are trying to decide whether to use the standard meal allowance rule or your actual cost of food, you may want to estimate the actual cost of the food you serve based on several weeks of menus and compare it with the standard meal allowance rate. It's important to keep in mind that if you choose to estimate your actual cost of food rather than using the standard meal allowance, you will have to keep receipts for all the business and personal food that you purchase.

There are many ways to estimate your actual food expenses (the *Record-Keeping Guide* describes several). Usually the simplest and most accurate method is to estimate your average cost per meal per child, and then multiply this by the total number of meals that you served.

Reporting Your Food Expenses

It's best to claim your deduction for food expenses on one of the blank lines in **Schedule C**, Part V, Other Expenses, although you can also put it elsewhere on this form. Wherever you choose to put it, be sure to identify it clearly as "Food," rather than including it under a general heading, such as "Other," because the IRS will be looking for it. If you're a Tier II provider who spends thousands of dollars more for food than you're reimbursed by the Food Program, you should identify yourself as such by writing "Food (Tier II Provider)" next to your food deduction, rather than simply "Food."

Since large individual expense amounts on **Schedule C** can trigger an audit, don't include any nonfood items in your food expenses. Remove items such as paper products and kitchen supplies from your food receipts and claim them on a different line, such as line 22 (supplies). The food expenses you list on Part V are carried over to line 27 (other expenses) on the front page of **Schedule C**.

If you serve meals to your employees, you can deduct 100% of the cost of the food, and your employees don't have to report these meals as income. You can either include this cost with your other food expenses or list it separately as "Employee meals" on one of the blank lines in Part V. Don't enter employee meals on line 24b, because this deduction is reduced by 50%. (If you are reporting "Employee meals," make sure that you have filed all the proper payroll forms for these employees [see chapter 8].)

Part V **Other Expenses.** List below business expenses not included on lines 8–26 or line 30.	
FOOD	$5,540
or NOT ON FOOD PROGRAM	$5,540
or FOOD (TIER II PROVIDER)	$5,540
EMPLOYEE MEALS	$600

Summary of Food Income and Expenses

Here's a summary of the rules about which food expenses you can deduct as a business expense and how to treat your income from the Food Program and food stamps:

	Report as Taxable Income?	Deduct as a Food Expense?
FOOD INCOME		
Food Program reimbursements for children in your care	Yes	
Food Program reimbursements for your own child	No	
Food Program reimbursements for your foster child	No	
Food stamps for your own family	No	
FOOD EXPENSES		
Food eaten by the children in your care		Yes
Food eaten by you during business hours at home		No
Food eaten by your own child during business hours		No
Lunch leftovers eaten by your family		No
Nonreimbursed meals eaten by the children in your care		Yes
Noncreditable food (ice cream, potato chips, and so on) eaten by the children in your care		Yes
Food eaten by a paid employee during business hours		Yes
Food eaten by foster children		No

> **For more information about the tax issues discussed in this chapter, refer to the related topics in the other chapters of this book and the Redleaf Press *Family Child Care Record-Keeping Guide*.**

CHAPTER 5

Reporting Your Business Income and Expenses: Schedule C

This chapter explains how to fill out **Schedule C Profit or Loss from Business**. On this form you'll report both your business income and your business expenses. You'll find more information about how to calculate and report specific kinds of business income and expenses, such as depreciation, in other chapters of this book. This chapter will take you step-by-step through **Schedule C**. (A copy of **Schedule C** is included in the tax forms at the back of this book.)

If you and your husband work side by side caring for children, you may want to consider filing two **Schedule Cs**. You can then split the income and expenses between the two of you. This may be an option if you want your husband to show more income to increase his Social Security benefits. Before taking this step, consult with a Social Security expert to see the long-term impact on Social Security benefits for both of you. Before reading about how to fill out each line of **Schedule C**, some general issues about how to enter your income and expenses on this form will be addressed.

Reporting Income (Part I of Schedule C)

Part I of **Schedule C** is where you will enter all your income. In addition to parent fees, you must report as income any payments you received from county social service agencies for care you provide to low-income parents. Report all of this income on **Schedule C**, line 1b. If you received reimbursements from the Food Program, see chapter 4 for instructions on how to report this income.

IRS Child Care Provider Audit Technique Guide on Reporting Income
The guide makes it clear that the IRS will look very closely to make sure a provider is reporting all her income. They may examine a provider's contract and policies to see if she got paid additional amounts for late pickup, overnight care, transportation, diaper fees, holding fees, and so on. Providers should keep careful records showing the source of all deposits into checking and savings accounts (both business and personal). If you did not receive the full amount from a parent, as stated in your contract, make a note of the reason. For example, if your contract says that your fee is $150 a week, the IRS would assume you received $7,800 a year from the parent ($150 x 52 weeks). Reasons why you may not have received this full amount could include unpaid vacation or

sick time, part-time care, forgiving payments for a laid off parent, or debt from a parent who left child care. Without records showing deposits of parent payments, you may have trouble showing why you earned less than the full amount.

Cash Payments

If you receive any cash payments, you should record them in a cash journal. Enter the dates you provided child care, the child's and parent's names, the amount, and the date of payment. The IRS is always looking for signs of unreported income, and a cash journal will help your case if you need to show that you didn't earn any more money than you reported. Here's a sample entry from a cash journal:

CASH JOURNAL

Dates of Care	Child/Parent	Amount Pd.	Date Pd.
Jan 3–Jan 7	Jenny/Carol Martinez	$100	Jan 3
Jan 10–Jan 14	Jenny/Carol Martinez	$100	Jan 10

Here's how to report some of the other kinds of business income that you may have received last year.

Grants

If you received grants from a government agency (usually for start-up expenses or home renovations), this money is most likely taxable income. If the granting agency has sent you **Form 1099G Certain Government Payments**, the IRS will be sure to check to see that you have reported this income. Even if you didn't receive **Form 1099G**, you should report the grant as income. Enter your income from grants on **Schedule C**, not on **Form 1040**.

Since you are reporting the grant as income, you will deduct the items that you buy with the grant money according to the usual rules for claiming deductions. For example, if you use the grant money to buy home or land improvements (such as a fence or an egress window), you will have to depreciate that expense over several years (see chapter 3). This will reduce your deductions and increase your taxes in the current year.

The only situation in which you don't have to report a grant as income is if you qualify for it because your family has a low income. If a grant is offered only to low-income families, it may be considered a welfare payment (like food stamps) rather than taxable income. (If you don't know if your grant qualifies, contact the granting agency.) You can't deduct the items that you buy with nontaxable grant money as a business deduction.

Loans

Some loans given to family child care providers for purchasing business equipment are structured so that the loan is forgiven (you don't have to pay it back) if you stay in business for two years. Normally, you don't have to report a loan as income; however, when a business loan is forgiven, you need to report the amount of the loan as income on **Schedule C**, line 6. In the year that you receive the loan, don't report any of the money as income; simply deduct the items that you purchased with the loan money as business expenses.

Gifts from Parents

You must report as business income any cash, gift certificates, or items that you receive from the parents of the children in your care. This is true even if the parent considers the payment to be a gift or a bonus. Report these gifts on **Schedule C**, line 1.

If you use the gift item in your business, you can depreciate it as a business expense. As with any other depreciable item, save the receipt or take a picture of the item and estimate its fair market value when you received it. For example, if a parent gives you a used sofa worth $400, report $400 as income. If you use the sofa in your business, you can claim it as a business expense, using the depreciation rules described in chapter 3.

If a parent gives you a noncash gift as a partial or total payment for child care services, then the item isn't really a gift, and you do have to report it as income. For example, if the parent gives you a $20 scarf as partial payment for child care, you have to report it as income.

Refunds to Parents

Some providers offer a discount to parents who pay for blocks of time in advance. If one of your parents moves away before the end of the paid-up period and you refund some of her money, then subtract the refund from the original payment and report only the net income. If you reported the original payment as income in one year and gave the refund in the next year, the refund becomes a business expense, and you will report it on **Schedule C**, Part V.

Military Housing Allowances

Some family child care providers receive military housing allowances that are called BAQ (Basic Allowance for Quarters) or VHA (Variable Housing Allowance). These housing allowances are not taxable income, so don't report them on **Schedule C**. If you receive a housing allowance but live off-base, see page 70. See the *Record-Keeping Guide* for a full discussion of military housing allowances.

Foster Care Allowances

Some family child care providers receive payments for child or foster care under an arrangement with a charitable organization or governmental agency. These payments don't have to be reported on **Schedule C** if they are received from a foster care placement agency that is licensed or certified by a state or local government or from an agency that is designated by a state or local government to make such payments, because those payments are exempt from federal taxes. Since the payments aren't taxable, you can't deduct any expenses you incur for these children. See the *Record-Keeping Guide* for a full discussion of foster care allowances.

Respite Care Payments

If you receive payments from a government agency for offering respite care for a family, this money is taxable income. (Respite care is usually provided for families that need to be separated from their children on a short-term basis.) Report these payments as income on **Schedule C**, line 1. You can deduct the expenses that you incur in caring for a child in respite care in the same way that you do your expenses for regular child care children.

Interest

If you have earned any interest on a business checking or savings account, don't enter it on **Schedule C**. You must report that type of interest income on **Schedule B**.

Claiming Expenses (Part II of Schedule C)

Part II of **Schedule C** is where you will show all the deductions for your business expenses (sometimes after transferring the information from another tax form). The major expense lines that are listed on **Schedule C** are as follows:

- Line 8: Advertising
- Line 9: Car and truck expenses
- Line 13: Depreciation
- Line 14: Employee benefit programs
- Line 15: Insurance (other than health)
- Line 16: Interest
- Line 17: Legal and professional services
- Line 18: Office expenses
- Line 20: Rent or lease
- Line 21: Repairs and maintenance (of personal property used in the business)
- Line 22: Supplies
- Line 23: Taxes and licenses
- Line 24: Travel, meals, and entertainment
- Line 26: Wages
- Line 27: Other expenses (the total of all the items you've listed on the blank lines in Part V, such as food, toys, household items, cleaning supplies, and activity expenses)

Some of these major line items are covered in more detail in other parts of this book. For example, there's a section on vehicle expenses at the end of this chapter. The topic of depreciation is covered in chapter 3, and issues related to paying wages and hiring employees are covered in chapter 8. If you have any questions about how to calculate the deductions for any of these items, see the relevant part of this book.

If some of your business expenses don't seem to fit on any of the lines on **Schedule C**, bear in mind that it doesn't matter on which line you enter your expenses. The IRS won't penalize you for listing a business expense on one line rather than another. This means that you can make your own decision about what to categorize as supplies or office expenses or any other line on **Schedule C**; however, never use the word *equipment* to describe toys, cribs, or other items that cost less than $500. The IRS will question this because it assumes that all equipment should be depreciated on **Form 4562** rather than deducted on **Schedule C**. (For suggestions on how to categorize your expenses, see the *Record-Keeping Guide*.)

To reduce your chance of an audit, don't lump large expense items together on one line. Instead, use the blank spaces under line 27, other expenses, to list items such as food, cleaning supplies, and activity expenses. If any line on your **Schedule C** is unusually high in comparison with your income, it may trigger an audit. For example, if your income on **Schedule C** is $15,000 and you list $8,000 for cleaning supplies, this will draw attention to your return. If your total expenses are reasonable, and you have just put all your food expenses, kitchen supplies, and children's supplies on line 22, then you don't need to worry. If you're audited, you will need to show the IRS all your records to demonstrate that your expenses are valid.

Calculating the Deductions for Your Business Expenses

You can only deduct the portion of an expense that relates to your business. To calculate how much you can deduct for each business expense, you need to follow the instructions given in chapters 1 through 3 for completing **Form 4562** and Part I of **Form 8829**. If you haven't completed those sections yet, you should do it now. (Calculating the deductions for your business expenses can be a complicated process. If you have any questions about this topic, refer to the *Record-Keeping Guide*, which lists over 1,000 potential business expenses and explains how to deduct them.)

As described in the previous chapters of this book, you will need to divide all your expenses into three categories:

1. 100% personal use (such as jewelry and cigarettes)

2. 100% business use (such as child care food and the toys used only in your business)

3. Shared business and personal use (such as cleaning supplies and lightbulbs)

If an expense is 100% personal use, you can't deduct any of it as a business expense. If it is 100% business use, you can deduct all of it as a business expense. If it has both business and personal uses, you can deduct only part of it as a business expense.

There are two ways to determine the business portion of a shared expense; you can multiply the cost of the item either by your Time-Space percentage (covered in chapter 1) or by the item's actual business-use percentage. For most items, you will use your Time-Space percentage; for some items you may prefer to use an actual business-use percentage, especially if the expense was large and the business-use percentage is significantly higher than your Time-Space percentage.

Determining the Actual Business-Use Percentage

To determine the actual business-use percentage of an item, you need to track how much time you use the item for your business and how much time you use it for personal purposes. Divide the number of hours of business use by the total number of hours that you used the item. For example, if you used an item 3 hours a week for business and 9 hours a week for personal purposes, your business-use percentage would be 25% (3 ÷ [3 + 9]).

You must keep careful notes about how you calculated your business deductions and be able to support them if you are audited. Do your calculations on another sheet of paper, and enter only the business portion of your expenses on **Schedule C**. For example, let's say that you spent a total (business and personal) of $100 for paper towels last year. If your Time-Space percentage is 30%, you can enter $30 on **Schedule C** (probably on line 22). If you determine that 55% of the towels were used for your business, your business-use percentage is 55%, and you can enter $55 instead.

In addition, on line 18 for office expenses, you're claiming the following: books $50 (100% business); business birthday cards $20 (100% business); computer paper $15 (60% actual business use); Internet access fees $250 (50% actual business use); office supplies $100 (40% Time-Space percentage); and magazines $50 (40% Time-Space percentage).

The best way to organize these expenses is to list them by category:

100% Business		**Time-Space Percentage**		**Actual Business-Use Percentage**	
books	$50	office supplies	$100	computer paper $15 x 60% =	$9
birthday cards	$20	magazines	$50	Internet fee $250 x 50% =	$125
Subtotal:	$70	Subtotal:	$150	Subtotal:	$134
			x 40% = $60		

Total Office Expense: $264 ($70 + $60 + $134)

In this example, you would keep this calculation for your files and enter $264 on line 18.

If You Operate Two Home-Based Businesses

If you operate two businesses out of your home, you must file a separate **Schedule C** for each business and report your income and expenses for each business separately. If you earn money on child care–related activities (such as child care training or consulting), enter all your income and expenses for these activities on the same **Schedule C** as your child care business.

Allocate your expenses on a reasonable basis between the two **Schedule C**s. Transfer the net income from both of them to one **Form 1040 Schedule SE**. If you're entitled to claim the home office deduction for your other business, you must also file a separate **Form 8829** for each business. If your other business claims part of your home on **Form 8829**, you won't be able to claim a 100% Space percentage for your child care business.

How to Fill Out Schedule C

On the first few lines of **Schedule C**, enter your name and Social Security number (or employer identification number, if you have one) at the top of the page, and then proceed as follows:

Line A: Enter "Family Child Care."

Line B: Enter your principal business code: 624410 Child Day Care Services.

Line C: If your business has an official name, enter it here. If not, leave the line blank. See your state rules regarding any requirements for having a business name.

Line D: Enter your employer identification number, if you have one.

Line E: Enter your business address.

Line F: Select method (1) Cash. This doesn't mean that you're paid in cash; it means that you report your income when you receive it and your expenses when you incur them. For example, if a parent pays you in January of this year for services provided in December of last year, you will report the payment as income next tax season. If you received a check in December of last year that you don't deposit until January of this year, you count it as income for this tax season. If you buy something for your business with a credit card, you count it as an expense the month you sign the credit card receipt, not the month you pay your credit card bill. (Once you charge something on your credit card, you are legally obligated to pay the bill.)

Line G: Enter "yes." You are considered to have materially participated in your business if you meet any one of the following tests: (1) you worked more than 500 hours in the year, (2) you were the sole participant in your business (no employees), or (3) you worked more than 100 hours, and no other person worked more time than you.

Line H: If this is the first year that you have filed **Schedule C**, check the box.

Line I: If you hired an independent contractor and paid any person $600 or more, you are required to file **Form 1099**. If this is true for you, check "yes." If not, check "no." See the form's instructions for details. Note: If you hire an assistant to help you care for children, this person is an employee, not an independent contractor; this is true no matter how little you pay the person. See chapter 8 for details.

Line J: If you are required to file **Form 1099**, check "yes." If you check "yes" on line I and fail to check it on line J, your chance of being audited will increase.

Part I: Income

Line 1: Enter all your income from parent fees here, including cash payments. Also enter any payments from social service agencies for care you provided to low-income parents.

Lines 2, 3, and 4: Leave these lines blank.

Line 5: Enter the amount from line 1.

Line 6: Enter any other business income you received, such as CACFP reimbursements, grants, gifts, and loans that have been forgiven.

Line 7: Add lines 5 and 6. This is your gross income.

Part II: Expenses

Line 8: **Advertising**. Enter any advertising expenses, which may include business cards, welcome mats, newspaper ads, keepsakes, and children's T-shirts (for more information, refer to the *Family Child Care Marketing Guide,* which lists over 100 advertising deductions).

Line 9: **Car and truck expenses**. Enter the vehicle expenses you have incurred for business purposes here. For information on how to calculate this amount, see the section on vehicle expenses at the end of this chapter.

Line 10: **Commissions and fees**. Leave blank.

Line 11: **Contract labor**. Enter the amount you paid to independent contractors (see page 155).

Line 12: **Depletion**. Leave blank.

Line 13: **Depreciation**. Enter the amount from **Form 4562**, line 22 (see chapter 3). Make sure that you have not included in this amount any depreciation expenses for your house or home improvements. Instead, claim these expenses on **Form 8829** (see chapter 2).

Line 14: **Employee benefit programs**. Enter the cost of any benefits you provide your employees such as health, life, or disability insurance.

Line 15: **Insurance**. Enter the total of any liability insurance you carry for your business and any workers' compensation insurance you purchase for yourself or your employees. Workers' compensation insurance protects a provider or employee who is injured while working. Insurance coverage can include medical benefits, disability income, rehabilitation expenses, and other costs. Liability and workers' compensation insurance is 100% deductible. Life insurance and disability income insurance for yourself are not deductible. Health insurance premiums for yourself aren't deductible on **Schedule C**, but they may be deductible on **Form 1040** (see chapter 6). Don't deduct your homeowners or renters insurance here; put these on **Form 8829** instead (see chapter 2). For a complete discussion of insurance, see the *Family Child Care Legal and Insurance Guide*.

Line 16: **Interest**. Enter the business portion of any interest you paid on items purchased for your business. For example, in January of last year, you bought some large play equipment on credit for $750. Your Time-Space percentage is 25%. By the end of last year, you paid $75 in interest on this purchase. In this case, you can deduct $18.75 ($75 x 25% = $18.75) as a business interest deduction on line 16.

You can put the business-use percentage of your vehicle loan interest on this line or include it in your vehicle expenses on line 9. Don't enter mortgage interest here; instead, enter it on **Form 8829** (see chapter 2). Report any interest you've earned on your business checking or saving accounts on **Schedule B**.

Loan Payments

You can't deduct the loan payments you make on an item purchased for your business. You can depreciate the item or take a Section 179 deduction, even if you're still making payments on it. You can also deduct the business portion of the interest you're paying on the loan.

Line 17: **Legal and professional services**. Enter the total of any legal and professional services you incurred for your business. This includes any costs you incur if you go to small-claims court over a business matter as well as the tax preparation fees to do your business tax forms (**Form 4562**, **Schedule C**, **Form 8829**, **Schedule SE**, **Form 1040-ES**, **Form 8826**, **Form 3115**, payroll tax forms, and others). Ask your tax preparer how much of the fee is for your business tax forms. (You can deduct the tax preparation fees for your personal tax forms as a miscellaneous itemized personal expense on **Schedule A**.)

Line 18: **Office expenses**. Enter the total of any office expenses you incurred (such as bank charges, books, magazines, desk supplies, receipt books), as well as any education or training expenses for yourself.

Line 19: **Pension and profit-sharing plans**. Enter the cost of any pension or profit-sharing plans you have set up for your employees.

Line 20: **Rent or lease**. Enter your total expenses for renting videotapes, carpet cleaning machines, and other business property. If you rent your home, don't enter that expense here; list it on line 18 of **Form 8829** (see chapter 2).

Line 21: **Repairs and maintenance**. Enter your total expenses for repair or maintenance of your personal property, such as appliance service contracts or repair of broken toys. Enter the costs of repair and maintenance of your home on **Form 8829**, line 19 (see chapter 2).

Line 22: **Supplies**. Enter your total expenses for supplies, such as children's supplies (craft items and games) and kitchen supplies (plastic wrap, garbage bags, and food containers).

Line 23: **Taxes and licenses**. Enter the total you've paid for taxes and licenses. Include any payroll taxes you've paid for the employer portion of Social Security, Medicare, and federal unemployment taxes. Also include any license fees you've paid. The sales taxes you've paid on items bought for your business can either be entered here or be included in the cost of each item. Enter your property taxes on **Form 8829**, line 11 (see chapter 2).

Line 24: **Travel, meals, and entertainment**. On line 24a, enter the total lodging and travel costs (such as airfare, bus fare, train fare, vehicle rental, or mileage) you incurred when traveling away from home overnight for a child care conference or other business activity.

On line 24b, enter your meal costs. You can keep receipts for all your meal expenses, or you can claim a per diem meal rate. For trips to most areas of the United States, that rate is $46 a day for 2015. (See the U.S. General Services Administration website for a list of the per diem rates across the country: www.gsa.gov/perdiem.) You don't need any receipts to claim the standard rate, but you must use only one of these methods for all your trips in the year.

You can deduct only 50% of your meal and entertainment expenses. Multiply the amount of your actual food costs or the per diem rate by 50% and enter the result on line 24b. Don't enter your food expenses for the children in your care on line 24b; enter them in Part V (see chapter 4).

If you go out and eat a meal with another child care provider, you can deduct 50% of the cost of your meal if the discussion during the meal is primarily business-related. You should be fairly conservative in claiming such meals as business deductions. If you deduct a meal with another provider, keep a record of who attended the discussion and what topics were discussed. If you take the parent of a child in your care out for a meal, you can deduct the amount that you paid for your meal and the parent's meal on line 24b.

Line 25: **Utilities**. Don't enter your home utilities (gas, electricity, water, sewer, garbage, and cable television) here; put them on line 20 of **Form 8829**, where they'll be added to the home expenses that you carry over to line 30 of **Schedule C** (see chapter 2).

The utilities expense that remains to be put on line 25 is usually telephone service. You can't claim a business deduction for basic monthly service for the first phone line into your home, even if you only installed the phone as a requirement to be licensed. If your phone bill is charged on a cost-per-minute basis, see line 20 on page 65.

If you install a second phone line and use it exclusively for your business, you can deduct 100% of this expense. If you use a second phone line partly for your business, you can deduct the Time-Space percentage of its cost.

Note: A cell phone is not deductible if it is the first line into your home. If you don't have a landline phone and have only one cell phone line, you cannot deduct any portion of your cell phone use.

You can deduct all other phone-related business expenses, such as long-distance calls, call waiting, an answering machine, and Yellow Pages advertising. If you wish, you can depreciate the cost of buying a phone (as other personal property; see chapter 3).

Schedule C versus Form 8829

Both **Schedule C** and **Form 8829** have lines for utilities, mortgage interest, repairs and maintenance, and insurance, which can give rise to some confusion about where to record certain expenses. The answer is that you should enter all the expenses related to your home on **Form 8829** and only the expenses related to your personal property on **Schedule C**. Here's a guide to which expenses to enter on each form:

Form 8829	Schedule C
Home utilities	Business repairs: toys, lawn mower,
Real estate taxes	furniture, freestanding appliances, etc.
Mortgage interest	Payroll taxes
Renters insurance	Liability insurance
Home repairs: furnace, plumbing,	Insurance on personal property
electrical, built-in appliances, etc.	Interest from home equity loan used
Home maintenance	to purchase nonhome items
Homeowners insurance	
Home depreciation	

If you run your business out of a building other than your home, don't follow this guide; instead, enter all your expenses for the building in which your business is located on **Schedule C**; you won't fill out **Form 8829** at all, since you don't have a home-based business.

Line 26: **Wages**. Enter any gross wages you paid to employees, including each employee's share of Social Security, Medicare, and any state taxes that you have withheld. (For more information about paying employees, see chapter 8.)

Line 27: **Other expenses**. This is the total of the expenses listed on the blank lines in Part V of **Schedule C**. To get this total, go to Part V and list there all your remaining business expense categories, including food, toys, household items, cleaning supplies, and activity expenses (which are all major expenses for most family child care providers). Refer to the *Record-Keeping Guide* for many other kinds of expenses that you might include here. The following are special considerations for toys and gifts:

Toys. The IRS **Child Care Provider Audit Technique Guide** places special emphasis on toy expenses. If a provider is deducting a significant amount for toys, the guide suggests that the auditor investigate whether some of those expenses were really toys for her own children. You should keep receipts for the toys that you purchase for your own children to help prove that your business deduction is reasonable.

Gifts. You can deduct up to $25 per person each year for gifts to the parents of a child in your care. (You must spend the money on gifts to be able to take the deduction.) Any gifts that you give to the children themselves may be a gift or it may be an activity expense. If it's an activity expense, there is no $25 per person limitation. A gift is when you give clothing or a gift card to a child. A gift is also a wrapped present that the child opens at her own home and doesn't bring it back to your home for the other children to play with it. An activity expense is a present you give to the child in your home who then allows the other children to play with it. It's still an activity even if the child then takes the present home and never returns with it. Don't list activity expenses as "gifts," or the IRS will assume that the $25 rule applies to them; instead, list them as activity expenses.

Line 28: Enter the subtotal of your direct business expenses by adding lines 8 through 27.

Line 29: Enter the total of line 28 minus line 7. This represents your tentative profit before subtracting the expenses for the business use of your home that you entered on **Form 8829**. You must complete **Form 8829** before you can continue with **Schedule C** (see chapter 2).

Line 30: A 2013 rule allows providers to choose between two methods when claiming house expenses. The first method is to claim these expenses from **Form 8829** (enter the amount from line 35). The second method (the Simplified Method) requires no receipts and involves using the following formula: $5 x your Time percentage x the number of square feet you use your home for your business (not to exceed 300 square feet). Almost all providers use at least 300 square feet of their home. Here's an example, if your Time percentage was 40%: $5 x 40% x 300 = $600. Thus, this provider would claim $600 on line 30 of **Schedule C**. She would also be entitled to claim 100% of her property tax and mortgage interest on **Schedule A**, if she itemized. Follow the instructions to **Schedule C** to use this method.

Warning: The vast majority of providers will be better off using their house expenses as shown on **Form 8829**, rather than using the Simplified Method. If you use the Simplified Method and later discover that you would have been better off using your **Form 8829** expenses, you cannot amend your tax return to fix this. Therefore, do not use the Simplified Method unless you have compared it to what you could have claimed using **Form 8829**.

Line 31: Subtract line 30 from line 29. This is your net profit or loss from your business. Enter this amount on **Form 1040**, line 12, and **Schedule SE**, line 2.

Line 32: If you have a loss on line 31, check box 32a, All investment is at risk.

Showing a Loss on Schedule C

If you don't show a profit at least three years out of every five, the IRS may look more closely at your tax returns to determine if you're really trying to make a profit. You must be able to show that you're acting in a businesslike manner in a serious effort to make a profit. Most providers won't need to worry about this, but if you only care for children infrequently, you should not try to claim a loss.

The IRS **Child Care Provider Audit Technique Guide** states that it is unusual for a family child care business to show a loss. Although this is an overstatement, if you have a legitimate loss, you should be prepared to defend it with good records.

If you claim regular losses, the IRS may take the position that you could have taken in more children or worked longer hours to make a profit. If it rules that you aren't in business to make a profit, it may reduce your business expenses.

Part III: Cost of Goods Sold

Lines 33–40: Skip this section; it doesn't apply to family child care businesses.

Part IV: Information on Your Vehicle

See the example under the section titled Standard Mileage Rate Method on the following pages for instructions on filling out this section.

Schedule C-EZ versus Schedule C

Small business owners can use the short form **Schedule C-EZ** instead of **Schedule C** if they meet all of the following requirements:

- have earnings of less than $25,000
- have business expenses of $5,000 or less
- have no employees
- don't have a net business loss
- don't claim automobile depreciation, personal property depreciation, land improvements, or major home improvements
- don't claim any expenses for the business use of the home

As a family child care provider, it's to your advantage to claim many of the deductions listed above such as expenses for business use of your home. Therefore, almost every family child care provider will be better off using **Schedule C** instead of **Schedule C-EZ**.

Congratulations!

You have completed the second most time-consuming tax form (according to the IRS). For most of you, the hard work is done. After calculating your Social Security tax on **Schedule SE**, you'll be ready to fill out **Form 1040** and file your return. If you need to fill out any other tax forms that address issues such as the Earned Income Credit, the sale of your home, or education credits, see the relevant chapters of this book. If you deliver child care out of a building that is not your home, enter all of your home expenses on **Schedule C** (mortgage interest, house depreciation, homeowners insurance, property tax, rent, house repairs, and utilities), not on **Form 8829**.

Vehicle Expenses (Line 9)

There are two ways to calculate the vehicle expenses that you deduct on line 9—the standard mileage rate method and the actual vehicle expenses method. Which method is better for you?

- The standard mileage rate method allows you to simply multiply your business miles by a set rate and claim the result as your deduction. In addition, you can claim the business portion of your vehicle loan interest and personal property tax, as well as your expenses for parking and tolls.

- The actual vehicle expenses method allows you to claim the business portion of all the expenses associated with your vehicle (gas, repairs, insurance, and so on). If you use this method, you must keep all your receipts for those expenses.

Traditionally, most providers have chosen the standard mileage rate over the actual vehicle expenses method, since the record keeping is simpler. Because of the increase in gas prices, however, more providers should consider using the actual vehicle expenses method. You can calculate your business deduction using both methods and use the one that offers the higher deduction.

If you are now considering using the actual vehicle expenses method, you should try hard to save all your receipts for vehicle expenses. You may be able to reconstruct some of these records; for example, if you bought gas with a credit card, save the copies of your credit card statements that show this. If you bought gas with cash, divide the miles you have driven by your car's average miles per gallon to calculate how many gallons of gas you have used. Then reconstruct what you spent by multiplying the number of gallons by the average price of gas over that period.

If you used the standard mileage rate method in 2014, you can switch to the actual vehicle expenses method in 2015. If you used the actual vehicle expenses method in the first year that you used your vehicle for your business, you can't switch to the standard mileage rate method in later years. If you used the standard mileage rate in the first year you used your vehicle for your business, you can switch to the actual vehicle expenses method in later years. (After you change to the actual vehicle expenses method, you must use straight-line depreciation on your vehicle; see chapter 3. If you lease a vehicle, you cannot switch methods after the first year, no matter which method you use.)

Whichever method you use, you will need to track all your business miles, even if you use the vehicle 100% for business purposes. To track your business trips, refer to records such as receipts, canceled checks, credit card statements, field trip permission forms, training certificates, and calendar notations, or keep a mileage log. (The *Family Child Care Mileage-Keeper* makes it easy to record your mileage.)

If the Vehicle Isn't Registered in Your Name

If you are married, you can claim business expenses for both your vehicle and your spouse's vehicle, even if your name isn't on the vehicle registration.

If you aren't married and use a vehicle that isn't registered to you, you can't claim vehicle expenses for that vehicle. For example, if you use your boyfriend's vehicle, you can't claim any expenses for it, even if he drives it for your business trips.

If you pay your boyfriend for the use of his vehicle or to make a business trip for you, you can deduct these expenses as rent on **Schedule C**, line 20a, and your boyfriend will have to report this payment as income on line 21 of his **Form 1040**. The same is true if you pay anyone else for the use of a vehicle.

Is the Trip Business or Personal?

To determine the vehicle expenses that you have incurred for your business, you need to decide which trips are deductible and which aren't. If you take a trip that involves both business and personal activities, you may still deduct the entire mileage as a business expense if the trip is primarily for business purposes.

What if you take a trip to the grocery store and buy both business and personal groceries? That can be the hardest kind of trip to judge, and there's no firm rule about whether you can deduct the mileage. The only rule is that if the trip was primarily to buy business groceries, you can deduct it as a business trip. Some factors that might make the trip a business expense include the following:

- You purchased more business than personal groceries.

- You spent more time shopping for business items than for personal items.

- You made other separate personal trips to the grocery store; this trip was for regular business shopping.

IRS Child Care Provider Audit Technique Guide on Car Expenses

The guide says that if there is a business destination and a personal destination in one trip that only the round trip miles to and from the business destination are deductible. For example, if a provider drove 5 miles to point A (business purpose) and then 3 miles to point B (personal purpose) and then 4 miles home she could count 10 miles as business miles (the round-trip miles to and from point A).

The Standard Mileage Rate Method

The standard mileage rate is $0.575 per business mile. In addition to your mileage, you may also deduct the following:

- parking fees and tolls

- bus, subway, and train fares for business trips

- any casualty or theft losses on your vehicle

- the business percentage of the interest payments on your vehicle loan

- the business percentage of the local personal property tax on your vehicle

Some tax preparers and IRS auditors are unaware that you are entitled to claim these last two deductions even when you're using the standard mileage rate. (See IRS **Publication 463** for a clear statement of this rule.)

When you use the standard mileage rate method, you need to keep adequate records of how many miles you have driven your vehicle for business. Here's how to calculate your deduction using the standard mileage rate method:

STEP ONE

Go through your business records for last year and write down the destination of every trip you took for your business. Look through your checkbook receipts and calendar for evidence of business trips. If you took more than one trip to the same destination (grocery store, bank, and so on), count the number of trips to each destination.

STEP TWO

Determine the number of miles to each destination. Try to make a habit of recording your trip mileage as you make trips throughout the year. If you haven't done this, use an Internet mapping service (such as MapQuest or Google Maps) to find the length of the trip (or drive to the destination again and record the mileage).

STEP THREE

Multiply the mileage to and from each destination by the number of trips you took to each destination last year. Add the miles together for all the destinations, and multiply the total by the standard mileage rate, which will give you your business-mileage deduction. Here's an example:

Al's Grocery Store	3 miles	x	48 trips	=	144 miles
First Bank	2 miles	x	60 trips	=	120 miles
Como Park	5 miles	x	12 trips	=	60 miles
Tots Toy Store	4 miles	x	10 trips	=	40 miles
Safeway Grocery Store	5 miles	x	40 trips	=	200 miles
Other trips (list)					266 miles
Total miles					830 miles

830 miles (Jan 1–Dec 31) x $0.575 = $477.25

STEP FOUR

Add to the Step Three total any parking fees, tolls, or bus, subway, or train fares you paid while conducting business activities, and enter the total on **Schedule C**, line 9. Keep records showing how you calculated these amounts. If you drive more than one vehicle, you can claim the business mileage rate for both vehicles. Enter any expenses for renting or leasing a vehicle on **Schedule C**, line 20a.

The advantage of the standard mileage rate method is that you don't have to remember to record your mileage every time you take a business trip. Your check stubs, receipts, or notes on your calendar constitute evidence that a trip was taken. To make your record keeping easier, remember to record the odometer reading on your vehicle on January 1 of each year. Once you have measured the mileage to and from each destination, you can use that mileage number forever.

If you use the standard mileage rate method, you can't deduct the cost of vehicle insurance (even for a separate business policy) or vehicle repairs (even if the damage results from using the vehicle for business). To deduct these expenses, you must use the actual vehicle expenses method. When you use the standard mileage rate method, fill out **Schedule C**, Part IV, only if you don't have any depreciation expenses to show on **Form 4562**. Otherwise, fill out **Form 4562**, Part V, Section B, instead of **Schedule C**, Part IV.

Enter the date that you first began using your vehicle for your business on line 43 of **Schedule C**. Enter the total business miles you drove last year on line 44a. (This may include mileage from more than one vehicle.) Don't enter anything under Commuting on line 44b. Put your personal vehicle miles on line 44c. Answer yes on line 45 if you use your car for personal purposes. Line 46 asks if your family had another vehicle available for personal use. Answer yes to this question unless you don't have a second car. If you have kept records of the business use of your vehicle, answer yes to lines 47a and 47b.

You can use the standard mileage rate method even if you are operating more than one vehicle in your business. This is true whether or not you and your spouse are using each of your vehicles at the same time for business purposes. If you used more than one vehicle in your business during the year, report your business miles on **Form 4562** (lines 30–36), not on **Schedule C**.

Part IV	Information on Your Vehicle. Complete this part **only** if you are claiming car or truck expenses on line 9 and are not required to file Form 4562 for this business. See the instructions for line 13 to find out if you must file Form 4562.

43 When did you place your vehicle in service for business purposes? (month, day, year) ▶ 1 / 1 / 2015

44 Of the total number of miles you drove your vehicle during 2015, enter the number of miles you used your vehicle for:

a Business _____830_____ **b** Commuting (see instructions) _____ **c** Other _____11,000_____

45 Was your vehicle available for personal use during off-duty hours? . . . . ☑ Yes ☐ No

46 Do you (or your spouse) have another vehicle available for personal use?. . . . . ☑ Yes ☐ No

47a Do you have evidence to support your deduction? . . . . ☑ Yes ☐ No

b If "Yes," is the evidence written? . . . . ☑ Yes ☐ No

Selling a Vehicle Used in Your Business

To report the sale of a vehicle used in your business, fill out **Form 4797 Sales of Business Property** (see chapter 11). If you sell a vehicle after using the standard mileage rate method for business expenses, you must reduce the business basis of the vehicle by a certain amount for every mile you drove for business purposes. This amount varies according to the year the vehicle was used. For 2015, it's $0.24 per mile. This means that if you drove your vehicle 10,000 business miles last year, your gain from selling it will be raised by $2,400 (10,000 miles x $0.24).

The Actual Vehicle Expenses Method

Under this method you can deduct the business portion of the following:

- gasoline, oil, antifreeze, and windshield wiper fluid
- tires, repairs, tune-ups, car washes, and waxes
- vehicle insurance, vehicle loan interest payments, and lease payments
- vehicle depreciation
- garage rent
- personal property tax on the vehicle and vehicle license fees
- membership in automobile clubs
- casualty or theft losses on the vehicle
- other actual vehicle expenses

In addition, you can still deduct your parking fees, tolls, and bus, subway, and train fares, as you can under the standard mileage rate method. Here's how to calculate your deduction using the actual vehicle expenses method:

STEP ONE

First, calculate the actual business-use percentage for each vehicle by dividing the number of business miles you drove the vehicle that year by the total miles you drove it that year. For example, if you drove your vehicle 12,875 miles, and 1,875 of those miles were for your business, your business use would be 15% (1,875 ÷ 12,875 = 15%).

STEP TWO

List all your actual expenses for all the vehicle expenses listed above (gasoline, oil, antifreeze, and so on). Make sure you have records for all the expenses that you claim. Add up your vehicle expenses, and multiply the total by your business-use percentage. In the example below, the vehicle expenses total $1,550, and the vehicle deduction is $432.50.

Gasoline	$175.00	
Oil	$20.00	
Repairs	$205.00	
Insurance	$700.00	
Taxes and license	$100.00	
Vehicle loan interest	$350.00	
	$1,550.00 x 15% =	$232.50
Additional business vehicle insurance ($200 x 100%)		$200.00
Vehicle deduction		$432.50

STEP THREE

Add to the total from step two any parking fees, tolls, or bus, subway, or train fares that you paid while conducting business activities, and enter the total on **Schedule C**, line 9. Keep the records showing how you calculated these amounts. Enter any expenses for renting or leasing a vehicle on **Schedule C**, line 20a (rent or lease of vehicle).

STEP FOUR

In addition to claiming your actual expenses, this method allows you to take a depreciation deduction for your vehicle. Claim this depreciation on **Form 4562**, Part V, Section B, not on **Schedule C**, Part IV. You will transfer the depreciation expense on **Form 4562** to **Schedule C**, line 13 (see chapter 3 for instructions on how to depreciate your vehicle).

Leasing versus Owning

For a leased vehicle, you can choose between the standard mileage rate method and the actual vehicle expenses method, even if you used the actual vehicle expenses method for the vehicle in earlier years. If your vehicle lease is actually a purchase contract and you want to claim the cost of the purchase contract by depreciating your vehicle, you must use the actual vehicle expenses method.

To use the standard mileage rate method for a leased vehicle, follow the rules described in this chapter. This method doesn't allow you to claim any portion of the cost of the lease. Once you start using the standard mileage rate method for a leased vehicle, you must continue to use it for the remainder of the lease term.

To use the actual vehicle expenses method for a leased vehicle, follow the rules described in this chapter. Calculate your business-use percentage, and apply it against your actual expenses (lease payments, gasoline, insurance, and any other expenses).

If the fair market value of a vehicle you leased in 2015 is more than $18,500 ($19,000 for a truck or van), you must include as income on **Schedule C**, line 6, a small amount for each year that you lease the vehicle (see IRS **Publication 463 Travel, Entertainment, Gift, and Car Expenses** for tables).

In general, you're better off purchasing a vehicle than leasing it. The benefits of leasing are that you get to drive a newer (and usually more expensive) vehicle than if you own one; however, leasing is usually more expensive than buying, and at the end of the lease period you must return the vehicle.

Should You and Your Spouse File Two Schedule Cs?

If you and your husband work side-by-side caring for children, you have the option of each of you filing your own **Schedule C** and splitting the income and expenses.

Why would you do this? Because by doing so, your husband could show a profit that could help him earn higher Social Security benefits. IRS rules allow a married couple in this situation to split the profit, pay Social Security taxes under both their names, and thus spread the future Social Security benefits between the two of them. This can be done without the couple filing as a partnership.

To do this, the husband and wife should each file a separate **Schedule C**. They should split the income and expenses on these two forms and each pay Social Security taxes under their own names. This will not increase the total Social Security taxes they will pay. The two should split the income and expenses according to the amount of work they perform for the business. A husband who works two hours a week doing the record keeping should not claim 50% of the income and expenses.

Warning

The reason to file two **Schedule Cs** for one business is to allow the husband to contribute more to his Social Security account and, later, earn higher benefits. However, before you take this action, I strongly recommend that you find out the long-term impact on the Social Security benefits for both you and your husband.

Social Security rules are complex. You qualify to receive Social Security benefits by working for at least 10 years and earning enough income each of those years. If your husband also works, you can both receive Social Security benefits. If your husband dies, you can receive some of his benefits. Depending on how much you and your husband have earned over the years, it may be more beneficial to have future earnings credited to your husband.

To find out what will be the impact of crediting the profit from your business to you alone or to split it between you and your husband, use the Social Security Retirement Estimator at www.socialsecurity.gov. Talk to someone at your local Social Security office if either of you are within five years of retiring. They can answer your questions to help you make the best decision.

Other Considerations

You can only file two separate **Schedule Cs** if you are married under state law (including same sex couples) and filing jointly. Unmarried couples cannot do this. You cannot do this if you are a Limited Liability Company (LLC) or a corporation.

If you do this, parents can still pay you, and, therefore, your husband does not need to obtain his own EIN. You don't have to put your husband's name on your child care license or contract. There doesn't have to be any change in how you operate your program. You can stop filing two separate **Schedule Cs** in future years if you want to.

For more information about the tax issues discussed in this chapter, refer to the related topics in the other chapters of this book and the Redleaf Press *Family Child Care Record-Keeping Guide*.

CHAPTER 6

Completing Your Tax Return

This chapter explains how to fill out the remaining tax forms that most family child care providers are likely to need to complete their tax returns. It covers the following:

- **Schedule SE**, which you use to show how much self-employment tax you owe
- **Schedule EIC**, which you use to claim the Earned Income Credit
- **Form 8863**, which you use to claim education credits
- **Form 1040**, to which you transfer the amounts from your business tax forms to finish your individual tax return
- **Form 1040-ES**, which you use to estimate your quarterly taxes for the next tax year

You may also need to fill out other tax forms, especially if you are affected by one of the special situations described in Part III; however, the forms covered in this chapter represent the remaining forms that most family child care providers will need to file for a normal tax year.

Filing an Extension

If you need more time to file your tax return, you can file for an extension. This may be helpful if you need more time to calculate your depreciation, sort your records, or deal with a family emergency; however, filing for an extension doesn't give you more time to pay your taxes. Your taxes are due on April 15. If at that time you aren't sure how much you'll owe, pay what you estimate you'll owe. If you underestimate this amount, you will owe interest on the taxes that you didn't pay on April 15.

You may file for an automatic extension of your tax return until October 15. The old rules allowed an automatic extension of four months and a second extension of two more months only after IRS approval. The new rules allow you to automatically extend the deadline for filing your tax return by six months. (There is no further extension after this.)

To get this extension, file **Form 4868 Application for Automatic Extension of Time to File U.S. Individual Income Tax Return**.

Self-Employment Tax: Schedule SE

This section explains how to fill out **Schedule SE Self-Employment Tax**. This form shows how much Social Security tax, if any, you owe for operating your business. Before you can complete it, you will have to fill out **Form 4562**, **Schedule C**, and **Form 8829**. A blank copy of **Schedule SE** is included in the tax forms in Part V of this book.

Self-employment tax is the tax that entitles you to Social Security benefits. If you have a net profit of $400 or more on **Schedule C**, line 31, you must pay this self-employment tax. If you're self-employed and have more than one business, you must pay this tax if you have a combined net profit of $400 or more for all your businesses.

If your spouse is self-employed, you owe self-employment tax only if the $400 threshold is met by each of your businesses. For example, if your net self-employment income is $300 and your spouse's net self-employment income is $20,000, then you don't have to pay self-employment tax and fill out **Schedule SE**, but your spouse does. (It doesn't matter if you're filing jointly or separately.)

Your Social Security benefits are based partly on the Social Security taxes you pay. To receive Social Security benefits, you or your spouse must pay into the Social Security fund. If you haven't worked much outside the home, you can make sure that you'll qualify for Social Security by paying self-employment tax.

Plan for Retirement

When you claim all your allowable deductions, you reduce your taxable income and Social Security taxes, which may result in lower Social Security benefits when you retire. To offset this, save money for retirement by investing in IRAs or other investment plans.

How to Fill Out Schedule SE

Since almost all child care providers can use the short version of the **Schedule SE** form, this chapter will describe only the short form. (See the note at the end of this section.)

Line 1: Leave blank.

Line 2: Enter your net profit from **Schedule C**, line 31.

Line 3: Enter the amount from line 2.

Line 4: Enter the total of line 3 multiplied by 92.35% (0.9235). If this amount is less than $400 or if you have a net loss from **Schedule C**, don't fill out the rest of **Schedule SE**.

Line 5: Enter the total of line 4 multiplied by 15.3% (0.153). This represents your self-employment tax. Enter this amount on **Form 1040**, line 56. If line 4 is more than $117,000 see the instructions.

Line 6: Multiply line 5 by 50% and enter the result on **Form 1040**, line 27.

You can deduct more than half of your self-employment tax from your income on **Form 1040**, line 27, as an adjustment to your income. For example, if your self-employment tax is $1,000, put this amount on **Form 1040**, line 56, and enter $575.10 (57.51% of $1,000) on **Form 1040**, line 27. This reduces your taxable income by $575.10. If you are in the 25% tax bracket, it would reduce your taxes by $144 ($575.10 x 25%).

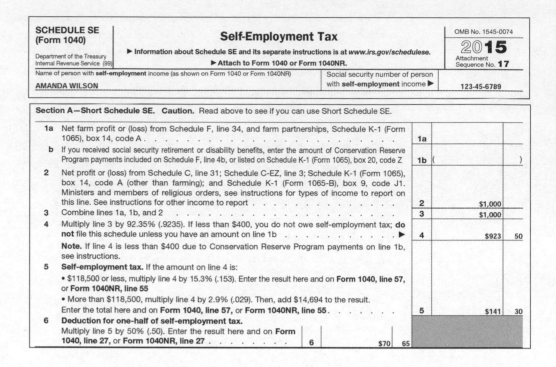

Long Form Schedule SE

In a few circumstances, you may have to fill out the **Long Schedule SE**. You must use this form if your spouse is a minister, if you earned more than $117,000 (including net self-employment income), or if you received tips that weren't reported to your employer and are subject to Social Security or Medicare tax.

Education Credits: Form 8863

If you or any members of your family attend a postsecondary school, even for just one class, you may be able to take advantage of the Lifetime Learning Credit or the American Opportunity Credit. Postsecondary schools include community colleges, vocational education schools, colleges, universities, and any U.S. institution eligible to participate in the Department of Education student aid program. You can't claim both of these credits for the same student in the same year.

The Lifetime Learning Credit

The Lifetime Learning Credit is for those who take a class at a postsecondary school, such as a class to obtain a Child Development Associate (CDA) credential. (The class does not have to be about family child care to be eligible for the credit.) The tax credit is 20% of up to $10,000 of tuition and related expenses incurred during last year. Unrelated expenses include books, meals, lodging, student activities, athletics, transportation, insurance, and personal living expenses.

To be eligible for this credit, your adjusted gross income must be less than $130,000 (if you're married and filing jointly) or $65,000 (if you're single). The credit is phased out when your adjusted gross income is between $110,000 and $130,000 (married filing jointly) or between $55,000 and $65,000 (single). There is a $2,000 maximum credit per family (you, your spouse, and your child). You don't need to be enrolled for any minimum amount of time or be trying to earn a degree.

American Opportunity Credit (Formerly the Hope Credit)

This credit covers the first four years of postsecondary education and is a refundable maximum tax credit of $2,500. To be eligible, your adjusted gross income must be less than $180,000 (married filing jointly) or $90,000 (all others). Education expenses that are eligible for this credit include tuition, fees, and course materials (books, supplies, and equipment). Students must be enrolled at least half-time.

To claim these credits, fill out **Form 8863 Education Credits**. Enter the amount of your credit from this form onto **Form 1040**, line 49.

Caution about Education Credits

You should use these tax credits for courses that aren't related to family child care or for classes that are taken by other members of your family. If you're taking workshops or classes that are related to your business at a postsecondary school, it's better to claim your education costs as a direct business expense on **Schedule C** rather than using these tax credits.

For example, if you spend $100 on a child care workshop, claim it as a business deduction on **Schedule C**; if you are in the 15% bracket, you would save about $30 (15% income tax and 15% Social Security tax). If you are in the 25% bracket, you would save about $40 (25% income tax and 15% Social Security tax). On the other hand, if you used the Lifetime Learning Credit, your savings would be only $20 ($100 x 20% credit = $20).

You can't use the Lifetime Learning Credit for the $20 and claim the other $80 as a business deduction.

The Earned Income Credit: Schedule EIC

This section covers how to claim the Earned Income Credit using **Schedule EIC Earned Income Credit**. The Earned Income Credit is designed to help low-income families reduce their taxes. You don't have to spend any money on child care for your own children to be eligible for this credit. When you claim this credit, you will subtract the credit from the taxes you owe. Read the **Form 1040** instructions to determine if you are eligible for this credit. Here are the income eligibility limits and maximum benefits for 2014:

Family Type	Maximum Income		Maximum Benefit
	Single or Head of Household	Married Filing Jointly	
Families with 1 child	$39,131	$44.651	$3,359
Families with 2 children	$44,454	$49.974	$5,548
Families with 3 or more children	$47,774	$53.267	$6,242
Workers (25–64) without children	$14,820	$20,330	$503

Eligibility for the Earned Income Credit is based on your family's adjusted gross income, which is the amount on your **Form 1040**, line 66a. This amount includes your net income from **Schedule C**, line 31, any earned income from **Form 1040**, line 7, and any money you received from a military housing allowance. You no longer need to add to this any nontaxable employee compensation, such as contributions to 401(k) retirement plans.

A child must meet all three of the following criteria to be eligible for this credit:

1. The child must be your son, daughter, adopted child, grandchild, stepchild, or eligible foster child. A brother, sister, stepbrother, or stepsister (or the child or grandchild of your brother, sister, stepbrother, or stepsister) may also be a qualifying child if you care for this individual as you would for your own child. A foster child is a child you care for as if she were your own child.

2. The child must be either under age 19 at the end of last year, under age 24 and a full-time student, or any age and permanently and totally disabled.

3. The child must have lived with you for more than six months last year (unless the child was born last year). If a foster child, he or she must have lived with you for more than half the year.

You can file under any filing status except married filing a separate return. You must provide a correct Social Security number for each child, as well as for yourself and your spouse. You can apply for a Social Security number by filing **Form SS-5** with your local Social Security Administration office. It takes about two weeks to receive a number. If you don't have the number by April 15 you can request an automatic extension (**Form 4868**) to October 15, but you must still pay your taxes by April 15. Or you can file your taxes without **Schedule EIC** and file an amended return (**Form 1040X**) after you receive the Social Security number.

How to Fill Out Schedule EIC

If you meet the above qualifications, you can either figure out the credit yourself or have the IRS do it for you. If you have a qualifying child and you want the IRS to figure out your credit, complete and attach **Schedule EIC** to your tax return. Proceed as follows:

- Instead of calculating the amount for line 66a on **Form 1040**, simply write "EIC" in that space. Don't fill in lines 74, 75, 76a, and 78 on **Form 1040** (your total payments, overpayment, refund, or amount you owe).

- If you want to figure the credit yourself, use worksheet B in the instructions for **Form 1040** to determine your credit. Enter the credit amount on **Form 1040**, line 66a. Don't attach the worksheet to your return, but do keep it with your tax records. If you have a qualifying child, you must fill out **Schedule EIC** and file it with **Form 1040**.

Fraudulent Claims for the Earned Income Credit

Some taxpayers discover that if they lower some of their expenses on **Form 8829** or **Schedule C**, they will be eligible for a higher EIC that would offset the taxes on their higher business profit. However, the IRS does not allow this. You may not adjust your expenses to claim a higher EIC.

If you make a fraudulent or reckless claim for the Earned Income Credit, you won't be entitled to receive it for either two years (if the IRS finds that you intentionally disregarded the rules) or ten years (if the IRS finds that you made a fraudulent claim).

IRS COMPLIANCE FORM TO PREVENT FRAUD

To reduce fraud, the IRS has begun a pilot program that uses **Form 8836 Qualifying Children Residency Statement** to certify that a child lived with a parent for more than half the year. This proof involves the signature of a child care provider, clergy, employer, health-care provider, landlord, school official, social service agency official, Indian tribal official, or community-based organization official who can certify where the child lived.

Although you can sign a parent's form, if you claim the EIC for your own child, you can't ask a parent of one of the children in your care to sign your form, since they aren't authorized to do so.

Other Tax Credits

Child Care Tax Credit

You may be eligible to claim the child care tax credit for expenses associated with paying someone to care for your own child while you are working. This can be the case when you attend a training workshop or conference and have someone watch your child. It can also apply if you send your child to a preschool program while you are caring for child care children. To qualify for this tax credit, you must meet these tests:

- Your child must be age 12 or younger.

- The care must be provided while you are working. If you are married, you spouse must also be working during the time the care is provided.

- You cannot pay your spouse, the parent of the child, someone you can claim as a dependent, or your own child who is under age 19.

- Your child must have lived with you for more than half of the year.

The maximum amount of child care expenses you can claim for one child is $3,000 ($6,000 for two or more). The tax credit can be up to 35%, depending on your adjusted gross income.

For more information, see IRS **Publication 503 Child and Dependent Care Expenses**, and IRS **Form 2441 Child and Dependent Care Expenses**.

Saver's Credit

If you are a low-income taxpayer, you may be eligible to receive a tax credit for any contributions you have made to an IRA—a 401(k), traditional IRA, Roth IRA, Simplified Employee Pension (SEP), or SIMPLE IRA. This credit is in addition to the tax deductibility of the IRA contribution. If you are married filing jointly, your adjusted gross income must be less than $61,000 to qualify for this credit. If you are single, the income limit is $30,500. The tax credit ranges from 10% to 50% of an IRA contribution up to $2,000. To claim this credit, fill out **Form 8880 Credit for Qualified Retirement Savings Contribution**, and then put the credit amount on **Form 1040**, line 51. See page 26 for more information.

If you made a contribution to an IRA between 2012 and 2014 and did not claim this credit, you can still file an amended tax return (see chapter 9) this year and get a refund.

Completing Your Tax Return: Form 1040

This section explains how to enter the information from your child care tax forms onto your **Form 1040**. (There's a blank copy of **Form 1040** in Part V of this book.) You must fill out **Form 1040** rather than short **Form 1040A** or **1040EZ** because you are reporting income (or loss) from **Schedule C**. You must complete all your business tax forms before you can fill out **Form 1040**. The earlier chapters in this book have covered the business forms that you need to file along with **Form 1040**. Work carefully and make sure that you transfer the numbers accurately from one form to another, as follows:

- Enter your depreciation expenses from **Form 4562** on **Schedule C**, line 13.

- Enter your home expenses from **Form 8829** on **Schedule C**, line 30.

- Enter your net profit (if any) from **Schedule C** on **Schedule SE**, line 2.

Once you have completed these business forms and your other personal tax forms (such as **Schedule A**, if you itemize), you're ready to begin filling out **Form 1040**:

- Enter your net profit (or loss) from **Schedule C**, line 31, on **Form 1040**, line 12.

- Enter your self-employment tax, if any, from **Schedule SE**, line 5, on **Form 1040**, line 57.

- Enter half of your self-employment tax on **Form 1040**, line 27.

- If you aren't eligible to receive health insurance through an employer (usually your spouse's employer) and you buy health insurance for yourself, you can claim 100% of the insurance premium on **Form 1040**, line 29. You may claim this deduction even if the health insurance is purchased in your name. You aren't eligible for this deduction if you qualify for insurance through your spouse's employer and choose not to purchase it. You also aren't eligible if you receive payments under COBRA. If you're eligible to claim this health insurance deduction, it can't exceed your net income on **Schedule C**, line 31.

- If you are eligible for the Earned Income Credit, enter the credit amount from the EIC worksheet on **Form 1040**, line 66a.

- If you made any contributions to a SIMPLE, Simplified Employee Pension (SEP), or Keogh retirement plan, enter the amounts on **Form 1040**, line 28.

Child Tax Credits

If you have dependents (including children, grandchildren, stepchildren, or foster children) who were under age 17 at the end of last year, you're entitled to up to a $1,000 tax credit for each child if your adjusted gross income is less than

- $55,000 for married persons filing separately,

- $75,000 for single and head of household, or

- $110,000 for married filing jointly.

If you earn more than this, your credit will be reduced by $50 for each $1,000, or fraction thereof, above the limit. This credit is refundable (meaning it is payable to you even when you owe no taxes) up to 10% of your earned income over $10,500. So if your earned income (**Schedule C**, line 31) is $12,500, then $200 of the credit is refundable ($2,000 x 10%).

This credit goes with the parent who claims the dependency exemption for the child. (Be sure to check the box in column 4 on line 6c of **Form 1040**.) To get this credit, you must enter the name and Social Security number of each qualifying child on **Form 1040**. To claim the credit, fill out the Child Tax Credit worksheet in the instructions to **Form 1040** and enter the credit amount on line 52.

If you have three or more children, you may be eligible for the Additional Child Tax Credit. This credit is for those who couldn't take full advantage of the Child Tax Credit. Use **Form 8812 Additional Child Tax Credit** to calculate this credit, and enter the credit amount on line 67.

Filing Quarterly Taxes: Form 1040-ES

As a family child care provider, you're self-employed and don't have any income taxes withheld from your earnings, unlike most wage-earning taxpayers. The IRS doesn't want to wait until the end of the year to get all the taxes you'll owe for 2015. If after subtracting all your withholding payments and estimated tax payments, you expect to owe $1,000 or more in federal taxes (federal income tax plus self-employment tax) this year, you may be subject to estimated quarterly tax payments. Many family child care providers aren't aware that they should be paying their taxes quarterly.

Estimated tax payments are due four times a year, on April 15, June 15, September 15, and January 15 of the next year. If you're reading this in early 2016, you may still be able to make the January 15 estimated tax payment for 2015, and you have time to plan ahead for next tax season. You may be able to avoid paying quarterly estimated taxes (see below), but if you can't avoid it, bear in mind that you can now pay these taxes with a credit card. (You may also have to pay quarterly estimated taxes to your state or locality; check your local laws.)

Avoiding the Quarterly Requirement

You don't have to pay any estimated taxes if you meet at least one of the following conditions:

- You estimate that you will receive a tax refund for the year on your individual, joint, or separate return.

- You estimate that you will owe less than $1,000 in taxes (after subtracting any withholding) by the end of the year.

- You estimate that the total tax payments that you or your spouse (if filing jointly) will make during the year will be at least 90% of your total tax bill for the year. Example: your husband has $6,400 in taxes withheld from his paycheck during 2014. You work only in your family child care business. You estimate that your total tax bill this year will be $7,000. Since $6,400 in withholding is 91% of your total tax bill, you won't have to pay estimated tax. If your husband had less than $6,300 in taxes withheld, you would have to pay some estimated tax.

- You had no income tax liability in the previous year.

- You estimate that the income tax that will be withheld from you and your spouse in 2016 will be equal to or greater than your total tax liability for 2015. If your 2015 adjusted gross income was more than $150,000 ($75,000 if married filing separately), you would have to pay the smaller of 90% of your expected tax for 2016 or 110% of the tax shown on your 2015 return to avoid an estimated tax penalty.

Another way to avoid worrying about estimated tax is to have your spouse file a new **Form W-4** to withhold more taxes to cover any taxes that are due because of your business earnings. For more information, see IRS **Publication 505**.

How to Fill Out Form 1040-ES

To find out if you will need to pay quarterly estimated tax this year, use the worksheet and payment vouchers on **Form 1040-ES**. The worksheet takes you through the calculations to determine how much tax you will owe by the end of 2015 after subtracting any withholding payments.

If you find that you need to make estimated tax payments, you will divide by four the total tax you will owe for the year after any withholding payments and pay this amount on April 15. For example, if you're single, have no other job besides your family child care business, and estimate that you will owe $4,000 in taxes by the end of this year, you will pay $1,000 ($4,000 ÷ 4) on April 15. In this case, you will have no withholding payments, because you do not earn a paycheck from an employer.

If your income or expenses rise or fall dramatically during the year, you can adjust your declared estimated tax and quarterly payments accordingly. There's a penalty for not paying enough estimated tax.

```
Form 1040-ES    2015 Estimated Tax          Payment  1
Department of the Treasury                   Voucher     OMB No. 1545-0074
Internal Revenue Service

File only if you are making a payment of estimated tax by check or money order. Mail this    Calendar year—Due April 15, 2015
voucher with your check or money order payable to "United States Treasury." Write your       Amount of estimated tax you are paying
social security number and "2015 Form 1040-ES" on your check or money order. Do not send      by check or        Dollars    | Cents
cash. Enclose, but do not staple or attach, your payment with this voucher.                   money order.        $1,000    |

Your first name and initial              Your last name         Your social security number
FRAN                                     ALLEN                  183-62-4512

If joint payment, complete for spouse

Spouse's first name and initial          Spouse's last name     Spouse's social security number

Address (number, street, and apt. no.)
28 PLAZA DRIVE

City, state, and ZIP code. (If a foreign address, enter city, also complete spaces below.)
BERKELEY, CA 94126

Foreign country name          Foreign province/county          Foreign postal code

For Privacy Act and Paperwork Reduction Act Notice, see instructions.              Form 1040-ES (2015)
```

The name you enter on this form must be shown exactly as it appears on your **Form 1040**. If your spouse's name is listed first on your **Form 1040**, list your spouse first on **Form 1040-ES**. If you separated from your spouse or were divorced last year, consult a tax professional before completing this form.

Example of Estimated Tax Calculations

Let's look at an example to determine whether you must make estimated tax payments. Assume it is January 2015. You care for four children and earn $600 a week.

STEP ONE: ESTIMATE YOUR INCOME

$600 week x 52 weeks = $31,200
Food Program reimbursement: $4,000
Total estimated income: $35,200

STEP TWO: ESTIMATE YOUR EXPENSES

If you provided child care in 2015, revise your 2016 number to take into account any expected changes for 2016. If you have only been providing child care for a short time, calculate your average weekly expenses. Don't forget to include depreciation for your house and personal property. A rough rule of thumb might be to estimate that your expenses will be about 40% of your parent income.

Estimated expenses: $12,480

STEP THREE: ESTIMATE YOUR SOCIAL SECURITY TAXES

$22,720 net income x 92.35% x 13.3% = $2,790 (See **Form 1040SE** for details.)

STEP FOUR: ESTIMATE YOUR INCOME TAX

Your federal income tax rate is determined by your family status and income. The tax brackets for 2015 are listed below. If you income is higher than the table below, there are higher tax brackets of 33%, 35%, and 39.6%.

Tax Brackets

Filing Status	10%	15%	25%	28%
Single	$0–$9,225	$9,226–$37,450	$37,451–$90,750	$90,751–$189,300
Head of household	$0–$13,150	$13,151–$50,200	$50,201–$129,850	$129,851–$209,850
Married filing jointly	$0–$18,450	$18,451–$74,900	$74,901–$151,200	$151,201–$230,450
Married filing separately	$0–$9,225	$9,226–$37,450	$37,451–$75,600	$75,601–$115,225

If you're single:

$22,720	Taxable income
$923	The first $9,225 is taxed at 10%
+$2,024	The remaining $13,495 is taxed at 15%
$2,947	Estimated income taxes due

STEP FIVE: TOTAL YOUR ESTIMATED TAXES

$2,947	Estimated income taxes
+$2,790	Estimated Social Security tax
$5,737	Estimated total taxes due

If you're single and have no withholding payments to apply toward your taxes, you'll have to pay estimated taxes; however, your estimated tax payment will be less than shown above, because you can subtract the standard deduction and personal exemptions from your income.

If you're married, you must make sure that your business income is offset by your spouse's withholding. If in our example none of your taxes are offset by the standard deduction or personal exemption, then by April 15 you should pay one-fourth of the taxes that you will owe this year, which would be $5,737 x 0.25 = $1,434.25.

If your estimates change later in the year, you can adjust your estimated tax payments. If you pay too much, you'll get a refund at the end of the year. See the estimated tax worksheet in **Form 1040-ES**. If you're making estimated tax payments by filing **Form 1040-ES**, don't claim these payments as an expense on **Schedule C**. These payments represent your advanced tax deposits; you'll report them on **Form 1040**, line 62.

Filing Your Tax Return Electronically or via the Internet

An increasing number of taxpayers are filing their tax returns electronically with the IRS e-file system. You can bring your completed tax return to an authorized IRS e-file provider or have a tax preparer prepare your tax return and have it electronically filed. To find an authorized IRS e-file provider, go to www.irs.gov. You can also purchase software and e-file your own tax return with your computer and an Internet connection. For more information, go to www.irs.gov.

Paying Your Taxes Online

You can now pay all your federal taxes via a secure website, www.eftps.gov. Until now the Electronic Federal Tax Payment System (EFTPS) was only available via telephone or special software. Now you can pay directly via the Internet, including your quarterly **Form 1040-ES** estimated tax payments. You must use the EFTPS system to pay any payroll taxes you may owe when you hire employees. See chapter 8 for details. On the EFTPS website, you can also review your tax payment history and print out a confirmation of your payment. To use this site to pay online, you need to enroll first, and the enrollments take two to four weeks to process. For enrollment information, go to www.eftps.gov or call 800-945-8400.

Save Your Records

You should save all of the records you used to complete your tax return for at least three years after you file your return. (Your state laws may require you to save your federal tax records for longer than three years, so check with your state department of revenue.) If you file your federal tax return on March 1, you will need to save your tax records until March 1, 2019. Many family child care providers save their records for an extra year.

You must save records associated with items that you are depreciating for as long as you are depreciating the item plus three years. So if you bought a washer and dryer last year and filed your taxes on March 1, you would save the receipt until March 1, 2027 (eight years of depreciation, plus three years).

When you go out of business, you need only to keep records of the items you are depreciating for three more years. We recommend that you keep copies of your tax returns for as long as you live.

For more information about the tax issues discussed in this chapter, refer to the related topics in the other chapters of this book and the Redleaf Press *Family Child Care Record-Keeping Guide*.

This concludes the Tax Workbook section of this book.
The next chapter is a Tax Return Checklist that you can use to
ensure that you haven't made any common errors or forgotten
anything important while doing your taxes.

CHAPTER 7

Catching Your Errors:
The Tax Return Checklist

The following checklist is designed to help you identify the most common mistakes before you send in your tax return. Review this list after you fill out all your tax forms.

Form 8829

❏ Is line 1 on **Form 8829** less than line 2? If it is, this means that you didn't use all the rooms in your home on a regular basis for your business. Is this correct? Remember that you can claim all the rooms that you use regularly for business purposes, including storage rooms and bedrooms used for naps. If you didn't use some areas of your home regularly for business, be sure that you have included all possible areas on line 2 and line 1, including your porch, shed, detached garage, or deck. See chapter 1.

❏ Is line 7 on **Form 8829** at least 30%? This is your Time-Space percentage. If you work ten hours a day, five days a week, and use all the rooms in your home regularly, your Time-Space percentage will be 30%. Many providers work longer hours or have exclusive-use rooms, which will increase this percentage. Make sure that you have recorded all your hours on line 4. See chapter 1.

❏ Did you enter most of your **Form 8829** expenses in column (b)? Only expenses that are 100% business should go in column (a). See instructions for line 8 in chapter 2.

❏ Did you claim 100% of your property tax and mortgage interest on **Schedule A** and also claim the Time-Space percentage of these items on **Form 8829**? This is incorrect. Make sure that you have only claimed the personal portion of these expenses on **Schedule A**. See chapter 2.

❏ Did you claim insurance, repairs, and utilities (including cable television) on both **Schedule C** and **Form 8829**? Don't count these expenses twice. See instructions for **Form 8829**, line 15, in chapter 2.

❏ Did you claim depreciation deductions for your home on line 41? All family child care providers should depreciate their home. See chapter 2.

Form 4562

❏ Did you purchase household furniture, appliances, or equipment that was used more than 50% in your business? If so, you can use the Section 179 rule in Part I.

❏ If you began depreciating items before last year and haven't fully depreciated them yet, enter the depreciation deduction for these items on line 17. See chapter 3.

❑ Did you claim depreciation for your furniture and appliances on line 19c of **Form 4562**? If you started your business last year or bought any of these items last year, you should have a deduction on this line. See chapter 3.

❑ Did you check "yes" next to the boxes on **Form 4562**, lines 24a and 24b? If you didn't, it could trigger an audit. See chapter 3.

❑ You are entitled to claim depreciation deductions for furniture and appliances that you purchased before you went into business. You should conduct an inventory of all these items and estimate their value at the time your business began. See chapter 3. If you didn't claim depreciation deductions for earlier tax years, you may be able to use **Form 3115 Application for Change in Accounting Method** to recapture previously unclaimed depreciation. See chapter 10.

Schedule C

❑ If you have an employer identification number, did you use this number on your **Schedule C** and **Schedule SE** forms? Did you use your Social Security number on all your other tax forms? See page 6.

❑ If you're making payments on your vehicle, did you claim the business portion of your loan interest on **Schedule C**, line 9, even if you used the standard mileage rate method? Many providers forget this deduction. See chapter 5.

❑ Did you claim the business portion of any credit card interest on line 16b of **Schedule C**? Don't forget to do so. Purchases on credit might include such items as a TV, a DVD player, a sofa, and appliances. See chapter 5.

❑ Don't claim the cost of any food served to the children in your care on line 24b of **Schedule C**. Instead, claim all the food eaten by these children (including restaurant meals) on Part V of **Schedule C**. See chapter 5. (For the same reason, don't claim entertainment expenses for the children in your care on line 24b. Claim them on the blank lines in Part V.)

❑ If you hired someone to care for the children in your care, even if only for a day or two, did you file the proper payroll forms for this person? Almost anyone you pay to work in your business is an employee. If you enter anything on line 26 of **Schedule C**, the IRS will check to see if you filed the proper payroll tax forms. See chapter 8.

❑ If you're on the Tier II reimbursement rate for the Food Program, is the food deduction you listed in **Schedule C**, Part V, substantially greater than the reimbursement amount you listed on **Schedule C**, line 6? It should be. See chapter 4.

❑ Did you check the expense categories on **Schedule C** to see if any one expense line is significantly larger than the others? With the exception of your food expenses, you don't want to dump a lot of expenses into one category such as supplies. Use the blank lines on line 27 to break out some of your expenses. See chapter 5.

❑ Line 30 allows you to choose between claiming your house expenses from **Form 8829** here or to use the new Simplified Method. The directions for how to determine your house deductions using the Simplified Method can be found in the instructions to **Schedule C**. It's highly unlikely that you will benefit by using the Simplified Method as compared to claiming your **Form 8829** expenses. Therefore, enter your **Form 8829** expenses on line 30, unless you are sure that the Simplified Method works better for you.

❑ Do you have a loss on line 31 of **Schedule C**? It's okay to show a loss once or twice every five years, but if it's more often than this, you may attract the attention of the IRS. If you show a large loss, you may want to discuss it with your tax preparer before reporting it.

Schedule SE

❑ If you had a profit of more than $400 on **Schedule C**, line 31, you must fill out this form and pay Social Security taxes.

Form 4797

❑ If you sold or traded in your vehicle last year and used the standard mileage rate method, did you check to see if you have a loss as a result of the sale or trade-in? Any business loss can be deducted on **Form 4797**. See chapter 11.

Form 1040

❑ Did you enter your profit from **Schedule C**, line 31, on line 12 of **Form 1040**?

❑ Did you claim one-half of your self-employment tax on **Form 1040**, line 27? Don't forget this deduction. See chapter 6.

❑ Your health insurance deduction on line 29 can't exceed your net business income (**Schedule C**, line 31). If it does, reduce your health insurance deduction until it equals the amount on **Schedule C**, line 31.

❑ If you have children of your own who were under the age of 17 at the end of last year, did you claim the Child Tax Credit on **Form 1040**, line 52? If so, did you also check the box in column 4 on line 6c? See chapter 6.

❑ Did you enter the correct Social Security numbers for your spouse and your dependents on **Form 1040**?

❑ If you're married filing jointly, did both of you sign your **Form 1040**?

❑ Did you double-check the taxes you owe according to the tax tables in the IRS instruction book?

❑ Did you recheck the math on all your forms?

End-of-Year Record-Keeping Checklist

❑ Gather all your records together, and store them with your tax return.

❑ Record the odometer readings for all your vehicles on January 1, 2016.

❑ Collect receipts from all the parents indicating how much they paid you for the year. Have each parent sign your copy.

❑ Save all your canceled checks, from personal as well as business checking accounts.

❑ Ask your tax preparer for copies of all the backup worksheets or forms used to prepare your tax return.

❑ Organize your expense receipts by category (utilities, food, toys) rather than by month. If you're audited, this will make it easier to present your records to the IRS.

❑ Put all your tax records in a sealed plastic storage box (to protect them from water damage), and put the box in a safe place. Save the records for at least three years after the filing date.

PART III

Tax Instructions for Special Situations

CHAPTER 8

Hiring Employees and Paying Payroll Taxes

This chapter explains how to withhold and pay taxes for your employees. Although the rules are complicated, the consequences of not following them can be serious. This chapter covers only federal tax rules about employees; if you have employees, you'll need to find out if your state has other rules regarding state and local income taxes, state unemployment taxes, and/or workers' compensation insurance.

There are two types of workers—independent contractors and employees—and there are two types of employees—those who are family members and those who are not. First we will discuss the difference between an independent contractor and an employee, and then we will explain how to withhold and pay taxes for the two types of employees.

Domestic Workers versus Employees

Don't confuse the kinds of employees discussed in this chapter with household employees—domestic workers, such as nannies or house cleaners who work in the home. The people who work for your family child care business are not household employees.

Parents who hire a nanny to care for their children don't need to pay Social Security taxes if they pay $1,900 or less per year or hire someone under the age of 18. This rule does not apply to family child care employees, because they are considered to be hired by your business rather than as household employees.

Employee or Independent Contractor?

If you pay anyone else to work with the children in your care, you need to understand that in almost every case the IRS will consider those workers to be your employees rather than independent contractors—and this fact has major tax implications.

When you hire an independent contractor, you don't withhold any taxes; you simply deduct what you pay the person as a miscellaneous expense. When you hire an employee, you must withhold Social Security tax and income tax and pay federal unemployment and Social Security tax. You'll probably also have to withhold state taxes.

It doesn't matter if the person works for only a few hours. A person who works for you 20 hours every week is your employee, and so is a person whom you hire once as a substitute while you go to the doctor. The main reason why someone you hire to care for children is considered your employee is because you have the right to direct and control the work of this person.

Independent Contractors

There are two circumstances in which the IRS might consider a family child care worker to be an independent contractor. The following situations are the exceptions to the general rule that everyone you pay to help with the children in your care is your employee:

1. A person who comes into your home on special occasions to perform specific services is not usually considered an employee. Someone who cleans your home for your business, occasionally repairs your toys, or presents a special magic show or activities program for the children in your care is not an employee. Since these people aren't working under your control and direction, they can be considered independent contractors.

2. A person who is in the business of providing backup child care or who serves as an employee to several other child care providers *may* be considered an independent contractor. To have a chance of being considered an independent contractor, a worker should meet the following conditions:

   - She should advertise to the public that she's available to provide substitute or part-time child care.

   - She should have her own federal (and state, if required) employer identification number and report her income on **Schedule C**.

   - She should work under a business name ("Sally's Substitute Service") that's registered with the state. She may also need a business license (check your state law).

   - She should provide a business contract for you to sign that states her rates and the fact that she's self-employed and in the business of providing substitute child care to the public.

Even if a worker meets all of the above qualifications, there's no guarantee that the IRS will consider her to be an independent contractor. However, it's far more likely to occur if she meets these qualifications than if she doesn't.

For a full discussion of the issue of employees versus independent contractors, refer to the *Record-Keeping Guide*.

A Word to the Wise

Despite the above facts, many family child care providers don't consider their workers to be employees. If the IRS rules that you have employees, you'll be responsible for back Social Security taxes, interest, and penalties. You may also owe state and local taxes, interest, and penalties.

The most likely triggers for an IRS challenge are the following situations:

- One of your workers files an unemployment claim and lists you as a previous employer.

- One of your workers is injured on the job and files a workers' compensation claim. (Your state is likely to turn your name over to the IRS and penalize you for not having workers' compensation insurance.)

- You list a deduction for an employee on **Schedule C**, line 26.

- You file **Form 1099 Miscellaneous Income** for a worker (this form reports payments to an independent contractor). This often triggers an IRS investigation to determine if the payee is actually an independent contractor.

Although it may be tempting to avoid treating your workers as employees to avoid filing withholding forms and paying payroll taxes, you need to take your legal responsibilities seriously. I know how frustrated many family child care providers feel about trying to comply with the legal requirements; however, there are ways to satisfy them at a relatively low cost, such as the following (for more information, see the *Record-Keeping Guide*):

- You can hire a payroll service company to set up a payroll system, withhold the proper amount of taxes, and file the required forms, at a relatively low cost. Payroll service companies include, but are not limited to, Advantage Payroll Services (877-777-9567), ADP (800-225-5237), NuView (800-244-7654), and Paychex (800-322-7292). Look under Bookkeeping Services in the Yellow Pages. We do not recommend any particular company.

- You can use an employee leasing company instead of hiring your own employees. The advantage of this approach is that the leasing company will handle all the payroll and tax paperwork. Its disadvantage is that you won't be able to choose your own workers. Look under Employee Leasing Companies in the Yellow Pages. We do not recommend any particular company.

Note: If you have not treated your assistants as your employees in the past three years, there is some good news. The IRS will not audit you for your mistakes in past years if you apply for the Voluntary Classification Settlement Program. To be eligible, you must pay about 1% of the wages paid to your assistants for the past year; for $1,000 in wages paid, you'll owe $10.68. Apply for this program at least 60 days before the end of any tax quarter and use IRS **Form 8952 Application for Voluntary Classification Settlement Program**. The IRS will not share this information with your state department of revenue. For more information, go to http://tinyurl.com/m9qm5rj.

Reporting Payments to Independent Contractors

If you pay any individual independent contractor $600 or more during the year, you must fill out **Form 1099 Miscellaneous Income**, give a copy to the independent contractor by January 31 of the following year, and file the form with the IRS by February 28.

The purpose of **Form 1099** is to inform the IRS of payments that you make to independent contractors who are responsible for reporting that income to the IRS. If you don't file this form properly, you will be subject to a $50 penalty, but you won't be penalized if the independent contractor fails to report the income. If you didn't pay any independent contractors $600 or more during the year, you don't need to submit any records to the IRS.

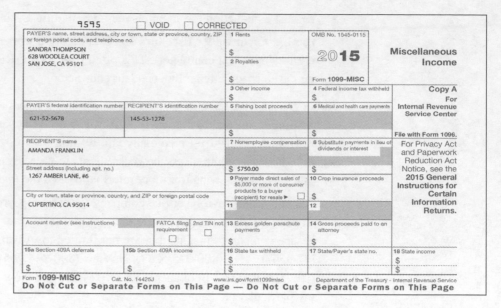

To report payments to independent contractors on your **Schedule C**, enter the total that you paid to independent contractors on line 11. *Don't enter anything on Schedule C, line 26, Wages* (unless you do have an employee). If you do, the IRS will assume that you have an employee and will check to see if you have withheld the proper amount of payroll taxes.

Employee Liability

Hiring an employee brings new risks and responsibilities. Before you start the hiring process, there are several things that you need to check:

- Ask your licensor if there are any state regulations about the qualifications of your employees, if your state requires background checks of new employees, and if it requires you to buy workers' compensation insurance for employees.

- Find out if there are any deed restrictions, homeowners association covenants, or zoning laws that restrict your right to hire.

- Find out if your business liability insurance policy will cover you for any allegations of child abuse against your employees and for any medical expenses that are caused by the actions of your employees.

For a detailed discussion of the risks of having employees and how to reduce them, see the *Family Child Care Legal and Insurance Guide*.

Hiring Employees

When you hire someone, you must fill out the following forms and file them with the IRS: **Form SS-4**, **Form I-9**, and **Form W-4**. During the year you must file **Form 941**, and at the end of the year you must file **Form 940**, **Form W-2**, and **Form W-3**. You can avoid filing the quarterly **Form 941** (by filing a **Form 944**) if you pay less than $4,000 in total wages for the year. See this chapter for details.

All employers are also required to file a report with their state whenever they hire or rehire an employee (including their own children), usually within 15 to 30 days of hiring the employee. This usually involves filling out a simple form and usually doesn't cost anything. Submit this form to your state, not the IRS. Check with your state for further details.

When you hire someone, you must save all your employment records for four years after filing your tax return.

The Federal Minimum Wage

In 2015 the federal minimum wage was $7.25 per hour. The federal minimum wage applies only to a provider who hires more than one employee. It does not apply to a provider who hires her spouse or her own children.

Although you may not be required to pay a federal minimum wage to your employee, your state law may require you to pay a state minimum wage. If you are required to pay a federal minimum wage (because you have more than one employee) and your state minimum wage is higher than the federal rate, you must pay the higher state minimum wage. If the state or federal minimum wage law does apply to you and you pay someone to work more than 40 hours a week, you must pay that person overtime (one-and-a-half times the regular rate, or $10.88 per hour). You can pay a new employee who is younger than 20 years old $4.25 per hour for the first 90 days.

Even though you may not be required to pay a federal or state minimum wage, you can pay your employees these wage rates or higher. If you hire your own children, you may want to pay them the minimum wage to increase your business deductions.

Child Labor Laws

You may not hire anyone under age 14 who is not a family member. (Check with your state department of labor to see if your state laws restrict your ability to hire your own child under age 14.) If you hire someone under age 16 who is not a family member, there are restrictions on how many hours the person may work. Employees who are 14 and 15 years old may only work outside of school hours, no more than 3 hours on a school day and 8 hours on a nonschool day. They can only work 18 hours during a school week and 40 hours during a nonschool week.

Hiring Your Spouse or Children

Although the rules about hiring family members to work in your business are somewhat different from those for hiring nonfamily employees, you must still treat any family member you hire as an employee and fill out **Form SS-4**, **Form I-9**, **Form W-4**, **Form 941** (or possibly **Form 944**), and **Form 940**.

The IRS may also question the business expenses that you deduct for family employees. To protect yourself, you will need to keep good records that show specifically what work was done, how long it took, and how much you paid the employee for it.

Treat these financial transactions in a businesslike manner. For example, don't deposit the money that you pay to your spouse in a joint checking account; it will look as if you're simply paying yourself.

Your spouse or children must report the wages you pay them on their own **Form 1040**. For more information about the tax and financial benefits (and pitfalls) of hiring your spouse or children, see the *Record-Keeping Guide*.

Hiring Your Spouse

If you hire your spouse to work for your business, you must file the same tax forms as you would for any other employee, with one exception. The wages that you pay to a spouse are not subject to federal unemployment taxes; however, you must still fill out **Form 940**. Your spouse's wages are subject to federal income tax withholding and Social Security and Medicare withholding. You must file **Form 941** (or possibly **Form 944**), **Form W-2**, and **Form W-3**. Your spouse must report all money earned by working in your business as wages and pay taxes on it.

Because your spouse will probably pay the same taxes that you would have if you had kept the money yourself, there's only a slight payroll tax advantage involved. The advantage is that you can deduct as a business expense the 7.65% you withhold as an employer for Social Security and Medicare taxes.

Hiring Your Own Children

There are two potential financial benefits to hiring your own children. First, the wages you pay to a child under age 18 aren't subject to Social Security, Medicare, or federal unemployment taxes. Second, a child who earns less than $6,300 doesn't have to file a tax return. A child who has interest income also doesn't have to file a tax return as long as the interest is $300 or less and the total earned income and interest is less than $6,300.

Between ages 18 and 21, children are subject to Social Security and Medicare withholding, but their wages are not subject to federal unemployment taxes. This means that there is little financial incentive to hire them rather than nonfamily employees. Wages paid to children over 21 are subject to federal unemployment taxes.

If you hire your own child, you will need to file all the usual federal tax forms: **Form W-4**, **Form 941**, **Form W-2**, and **Form W-3**. Your child can claim an exemption from income tax withholding if he or she doesn't anticipate owing any federal taxes. In this case, the child wouldn't need to file **Form 1040**, although if he or she also worked for another employer who did withhold taxes, the child could file **Form 1040** to get a refund.

Federal law allows parents to hire their own children under or over the age of 14. In some states, you can't hire your own children who are younger than age 14. Check your state and local laws for any other restrictions on hiring your own children. As with hiring your spouse, it's important to keep good records and treat the work in a proper, businesslike fashion. This means that the child must be doing work for your business and the wages you pay must be distinguished from the child's allowance. See the *Record-Keeping Guide* for more information. Here are some tips to follow:

- Prepare a job description that details the responsibilities of the job: play with the children, clean up before and after the children, prepare meals for the children, clean toys, record keeping, and so on. Do not include personal activities such as shopping, mowing the lawn, and running family errands.

- Prepare a written agreement between you and your family member that describes the employment arrangement: days and hours of work, pay, and so on. Both parties should sign this agreement.

- Keep a daily record of when the work is done. If the work is done at the same time every day, simply record the days and hours worked: Monday 9:00 a.m.–10:00 a.m., Tuesday 9:00 a.m.–10:00 a.m., Wednesday 9:00 a.m.–10:00 a.m., and so on.

- Write out a receipt for each payment, get the family member to sign it, and keep a copy: "Payment of $25 cash for 5 hours of work January 3–7." It is not necessary to pay by check; you can pay with cash. Make this payment out of a separate business account if you have one.

- Payments to family members must be reasonable. If you have a $15,000 business profit, it is unreasonable to pay your own children $6,000 in wages. Payment of $20 per hour to your 15-year-old is also unreasonable. The test of what is reasonable is probably how much you would be willing to pay someone who is not a family member.

- If you also give your child an allowance, keep a record of when you gave this allowance and how much it was.

Labor Law Posters

If you hire employees, you are required to post posters in your home explaining the rights of employees concerning minimum wage and workplace safety. You can put these posters in a back room, as long as it's accessible to employees. You can get these posters for free from the U.S. Department of Labor (http://www.dol.gov/dol/topic/youthlabor/Postingrequirements.htm). This site also gives links to your state department of labor where there may be additional posters you must post. There are companies out there charging employers fees for these posters. Don't be fooled; you can get them free.

Applying for an EIN

Before you can report your employment taxes, you must apply for an employer identification number (EIN). To get an EIN go to the IRS website at www.irs.gov. Enter "Online EIN" in the search box and answer the questions that appear on the screen. If you expect to pay less than $4,000 in total wages for the year, you may be eligible to file the annual **Form 944** rather than the quarterly **Form 941** (see this chapter for further information).

You can also get your EIN by filling out **Form SS-4** (available on the IRS website). Call the IRS Business and Specialty Tax Line (800-829-4933) for help in filling out this form.

If your employee doesn't have a Social Security number, she can apply for one by filling out **Form SS-5 Application for a Social Security Card**, which she can find at the nearest Social Security office.

Don't be fooled into paying anyone to receive your EIN. Some companies (EIN Filing Service, for one) charge a fee to help you get your EIN. Stay away from such "services."

Form I-9 Eligibility of the Employee

Every employer must verify that a new employee is a U.S. citizen or is eligible to work in the United States legally. To prove this, the employee must show evidence (such as a birth certificate, Social Security card, or passport) to the employer. Both parties must fill out and sign **Form I-9**.

The employer must keep **Form I-9** for three years after the date of hire or one year after the employment is terminated, whichever is later.

Form **SS-4** (Rev. January 2010) Department of the Treasury Internal Revenue Service	**Application for Employer Identification Number** (For use by employers, corporations, partnerships, trusts, estates, churches, government agencies, Indian tribal entities, certain individuals, and others.) ► See separate instructions for each line. ► Keep a copy for your records.	OMB No. 1545-0003 EIN

1	Legal name of entity (or individual) for whom the EIN is being requested **SONJA OLSON**	
2	Trade name of business (if different from name on line 1) **FAMILY CHILD CARE**	**3** Executor, administrator, trustee, "care of" name
4a	Mailing address (room, apt., suite no. and street, or P.O. box) **421 PORTLAND AVENUE**	**5a** Street address (if different) (Do not enter a P.O. box.)
4b	City, state, and ZIP code (if foreign, see instructions) **BOISE, ID 83701**	**5b** City, state, and ZIP code (if foreign, see instructions)
6	County and state where principal business is located **SMITH COUNTY, ID**	
7a	Name of responsible party	**7b** SSN, ITIN, or EIN

8a Is this application for a limited liability company (LLC) (or a foreign equivalent)? . . . . ☐ Yes ☑ No

8b If 8a is "Yes," enter the number of LLC members . . . . ►

8c If 8a is "Yes," was the LLC organized in the United States? . . . . ☐ Yes ☐ No

9a **Type of entity** (check only one box). **Caution.** If 8a is "Yes," see the instructions for the correct box to check.

☑ Sole proprietor (SSN) _465_ : _12_ : _7748_
☐ Partnership
☐ Corporation (enter form number to be filed) ►_____
☐ Personal service corporation
☐ Church or church-controlled organization
☐ Other nonprofit organization (specify) ►_____
☐ Other (specify) ►

☐ Estate (SSN of decedent) _____
☐ Plan administrator (TIN) _____
☐ Trust (TIN of grantor) _____
☐ National Guard   ☐ State/local government
☐ Farmers' cooperative ☐ Federal government/military
☐ REMIC   ☐ Indian tribal governments/enterprises
Group Exemption Number (GEN) if any ►

9b If a corporation, name the state or foreign country (if applicable) where incorporated | State | Foreign country

10 **Reason for applying** (check only one box)

☐ Started new business (specify type) ► _____
_____
☑ Hired employees (Check the box and see line 13.)
☐ Compliance with IRS withholding regulations
☐ Other (specify) ►

☐ Banking purpose (specify purpose) ►_____
☐ Changed type of organization (specify new type) ►_____
☐ Purchased going business
☐ Created a trust (specify type) ►_____
☐ Created a pension plan (specify type) ►_____

11 Date business started or acquired (month, day, year). See instructions.
1/1/2015

12 Closing month of accounting year

13 Highest number of employees expected in the next 12 months (enter -0- if none).
If no employees expected, skip line 14.

Agricultural	Household	Other

14 If you expect your employment tax liability to be $1,000 or less in a full calendar year **and** want to file Form 944 annually instead of Forms 941 quarterly, check here. (Your employment tax liability generally will be $1,000 or less if you expect to pay $4,000 or less in total wages.) If you do not check this box, you must file Form 941 for every quarter. ☐

15 First date wages or annuities were paid (month, day, year). **Note.** If applicant is a withholding agent, enter date income will first be paid to nonresident alien (month, day, year) . . . . ►   **1/1/2015**

16 Check **one** box that best describes the principal activity of your business.
☐ Construction ☐ Rental & leasing ☐ Transportation & warehousing
☐ Real estate ☐ Manufacturing ☐ Finance & insurance
☐ Health care & social assistance ☐ Wholesale-agent/broker
☐ Accommodation & food service ☐ Wholesale-other ☐ Retail
☑ Other (specify) **FAMILY CHILD CARE**

17 Indicate principal line of merchandise sold, specific construction work done, products produced, or services provided.

18 Has the applicant entity shown on line 1 ever applied for and received an EIN? ☐ Yes ☑ No
If "Yes," write previous EIN here ►

Third Party Designee	Complete this section **only** if you want to authorize the named individual to receive the entity's EIN and answer questions about the completion of this form.	
	Designee's name	Designee's telephone number (include area code) ( )
	Address and ZIP code	Designee's fax number (include area code) ( )

Under penalties of perjury, I declare that I have examined this application, and to the best of my knowledge and belief, it is true, correct, and complete.

Name and title (type or print clearly) ► **SONJA OLSON**

Applicant's telephone number (include area code)
(**418**)   **222-7261**

Signature ► *Sonja Olson*   Date ► 1/5/2016

Applicant's fax number (include area code)
(   )

For Privacy Act and Paperwork Reduction Act Notice, see separate instructions.   Cat. No. 16055N   Form **SS-4** (Rev. 1-2010)

Type or print clearly.

Employment Eligibility Verification

Department of Homeland Security
U.S. Citizenship and Immigration Services

USCIS
Form I-9
OMB No. 1615-0047
Expires 03/31/2016

▶**START HERE.** Read instructions carefully before completing this form. The instructions must be available during completion of this form.
ANTI-DISCRIMINATION NOTICE: It is illegal to discriminate against work-authorized individuals. Employers **CANNOT** specify which document(s) they will accept from an employee. The refusal to hire an individual because the documentation presented has a future expiration date may also constitute illegal discrimination.

Section 1. Employee Information and Attestation *(Employees must complete and sign Section 1 of Form I-9 no later than the **first day of employment**, but not before accepting a job offer.)*

Last Name (*Family Name*)	First Name (*Given Name*)	Middle Initial	Other Names Used (*if any*)
MULLEN	LELAND	P	

Address (*Street Number and Name*)	Apt. Number	City or Town	State	Zip Code
2340 STILLWATER AVENUE	6	MAPLEWOOD	ME	01629

Date of Birth (*mm/dd/yyyy*)	U.S. Social Security Number	E-mail Address	Telephone Number
08/23/1960	4 6 6 - 2 2 - 5 8 5 8		

I am aware that federal law provides for imprisonment and/or fines for false statements or use of false documents in connection with the completion of this form.

I attest, under penalty of perjury, that I am (check one of the following):

[X] A citizen of the United States

Signature of Employee: *Leland Mullen*	Date (*mm/dd/yyyy*): 02/07/2015

Section 2. Employer or Authorized Representative Review and Verification

(Employers or their authorized representative must complete and sign Section 2 within 3 business days of the employee's first day of employment. You must physically examine one document from List A OR examine a combination of one document from List B and one document from List C as listed on the "Lists of Acceptable Documents" on the next page of this form. For each document you review, record the following information: document title, issuing authority, document number, and expiration date, if any.)

Employee Last Name, First Name and Middle Initial from Section 1:

List A	OR	List B	AND	List C
Identity and Employment Authorization		**Identity**		**Employment Authorization**
Document Title: PASSPORT		Document Title:		Document Title:
Issuing Authority: USA		Issuing Authority:		Issuing Authority:
Document Number: 54321		Document Number:		Document Number:
Expiration Date (*if any)(mm/dd/yyyy*): 09/04/2016		Expiration Date (*if any)(mm/dd/yyyy*):		Expiration Date (*if any)(mm/dd/yyyy*):

Certification

I attest, under penalty of perjury, that (1) I have examined the document(s) presented by the above-named employee, (2) the above-listed document(s) appear to be genuine and to relate to the employee named, and (3) to the best of my knowledge the employee is authorized to work in the United States.

The employee's first day of employment (*mm/dd/yyyy*): 02/07/2015 *(See instructions for exemptions.)*

Signature of Employer or Authorized Representative *Daniel Gorski*	Date (*mm/dd/yyyy*) 02/07/2015	Title of Employer or Authorized Representative
Last Name (*Family Name*) GORSKI	First Name (*Given Name*) DANIEL	Employer's Business or Organization Name

Employer's Business or Organization Address (*Street Number and Name*) 1591 CLARENCE STREET	City or Town MORRIS	State ME	Zip Code 01620

The Rules of Tax Withholding

There are different requirements for withholding and paying payroll taxes for different types of employees. The federal payroll taxes that are subject to withholding include the following:

- federal income tax
- Social Security/Medicare taxes
- federal unemployment taxes

You need to fill out and file different forms for each of the above kinds of taxes, and you may also need to pay or withhold state and local taxes. Here's a chart that summarizes the employer's responsibilities for federal payroll taxes:

	Must withhold federal income taxes	Must withhold and pay Social Security/ Medicare taxes	Must pay federal unemployment taxes***
Nonfamily employee*	Yes**	Yes	Yes
Spouse	Yes	Yes	No
Provider's own child 18 or over	Yes**	Yes	No
Provider's own child under 18	Yes**	No	No
Independent contractor	No	No	No

For the purposes of payroll taxes, siblings, nieces or nephews, and other relatives with whom you don't have a parent-child relationship aren't considered to be family members, and you must withhold payroll taxes for them just as you would for a nonfamily employee. For example, if you hire your 16-year-old granddaughter, you must withhold Social Security and Medicare taxes from her wages.

IF YOU PAY SMALL AMOUNTS

If you pay a nonfamily member a small amount of money during the year, you still have to treat the person as an employee. If the total paid is small, you may not have to pay any unemployment taxes, but you'll still have to withhold Social Security and Medicare taxes and file the appropriate payroll forms. The minimum requirements for withholding are as follows:

- If you pay any amount, you must withhold Social Security and Medicare taxes.
- If you pay less than $1,500 in a calendar quarter, you don't have to pay any federal unemployment taxes.
- If the employee doesn't expect to owe any taxes, you don't have to withhold federal income taxes.

Federal Income Tax Withholding

To calculate how much federal income tax you must withhold, have the employee fill out **Form W-4**. Ask the employee to fill it out when she starts work. If your employee doesn't return a completed **Form W-4** to you, withhold taxes as if the employee were

---

*A nonfamily employee is anyone except your spouse and your own children.
**Only if the employee requests that you do so.
***This assumes that the employer pays any employee $1,500 or more in any calendar quarter or that an employee worked for some part of a day in any 20 different weeks of the year. Unemployment tax is due for provider's own child age 21 or over.

single with no withholding allowances. You won't generally file **Form W-4** with the IRS; instead, you'll keep it with your records to determine how much tax to withhold.

There are a number of ways to figure income tax withholding; they're listed in **Circular E**. You must withhold income taxes for each payroll period. The payroll period is the period of service for which you usually pay wages (for example, once a week, once every two weeks). The amount you need to withhold will depend upon the amount of wages, the number of withholding allowances, and if the employee is married or single.

Form **W-4**	**Employee's Withholding Allowance Certificate**	OMB No. 1545-0074
Department of the Treasury Internal Revenue Service	▶ Whether you are entitled to claim a certain number of allowances or exemption from withholding is subject to review by the IRS. Your employer may be required to send a copy of this form to the IRS.	20**15**

1 Your first name and middle initial	Last name	2 Your social security number
MANUEL	RUIZ	416-22-5757

Home address (number and street or rural route)
168 E. CURTIS STREET

3 ☑ Single ☐ Married ☐ Married, but withhold at higher Single rate.
Note. If married, but legally separated, or spouse is a nonresident alien, check the "Single" box.

City or town, state, and ZIP code
ST. PETERSBURG, FL 81623

4 If your last name differs from that shown on your social security card, check here. You must call 1-800-772-1213 for a replacement card. ▶ ☐

5	Total number of allowances you are claiming (from line **H** above **or** from the applicable worksheet on page 2)	5	1
6	Additional amount, if any, you want withheld from each paycheck	6 $	

7 I claim exemption from withholding for 2015, and I certify that I meet **both** of the following conditions for exemption.
• Last year I had a right to a refund of **all** federal income tax withheld because I had **no** tax liability, **and**
• This year I expect a refund of **all** federal income tax withheld because I expect to have **no** tax liability.
If you meet both conditions, write "Exempt" here . . . . ▶ | 7 |

Under penalties of perjury, I declare that I have examined this certificate and, to the best of my knowledge and belief, it is true, correct, and complete.

Employee's signature
(This form is not valid unless you sign it.) ▶ *Manuel Ruiz*   Date ▶ 3/4/2015

8 Employer's name and address (Employer: Complete lines 8 and 10 only if sending to the IRS.)	9 Office code (optional)	10 Employer identification number (EIN)

For Privacy Act and Paperwork Reduction Act Notice, see page 2.   Cat. No. 10220Q   Form **W-4** (2015)

MAKING FEDERAL INCOME TAX DEPOSITS

The deadline for depositing the income taxes you've withheld depends on how much these taxes amount to. If you withhold $500 or more in income taxes, Social Security, and Medicare taxes in a three-month period, you should deposit the taxes monthly by the fifteenth day of the following month. If the total you withhold is less than $500 for a three-month period, you can deposit the taxes by the end of the month following that quarter. Your federal tax deposit must be made electronically using the Electronic Federal Tax Payment System (EFTPS). If you do not want to use the EFTPS, you can arrange for your tax professional, bank, or payroll service to make deposits on your behalf. The EFTPS is a free service. To enroll in the EFTPS, visit www.eftps.gov or call 800-555-4477. For more information, see IRS **Publication 966 Electronic Federal Tax Payment System: A Guide to Getting Started**.

Social Security and Medicare Withholding

You must also withhold and pay Social Security and Medicare taxes. For wages paid last year, the Social Security tax rate is 6.2% for you as an employer and 6.2% for the employee. The rate for Medicare is 1.45% for you as an employer and 1.45% for the employee. In other words, you must withhold a total of 7.65% of the gross wages you pay an employee. As the employer, you must pay 7.65% into the Social Security and Medicare fund. Refer to **Circular E** for the tables that show how much tax to withhold.

MAKING SOCIAL SECURITY AND MEDICARE DEPOSITS

If you owe less than $2,500 in taxes for federal income tax, Social Security, and Medicare withholding (employer and employee share) in any calendar quarter, you must deposit the money by the end of the month following the calendar quarter (by April 30, July 31,

October 31, and January 31). If you owe more than $2,500 in a quarter, you must file monthly. You must pay these taxes electronically using the EFTPS (www.eftps.gov).

Continue to file **Form 941** as long as you have an employee, even if you don't owe any payroll taxes, because it proves that you have an employee. Without this form, the IRS may assume that you don't have an employee and may not allow you to take employee expenses as a business deduction. If you temporarily stop hiring an employee, continue filing **Form 941** even if you have no taxes to report. When you stop paying wages, file a final return.

Form 944

You can avoid filing **Form 941** if you owe less than $1,000 in payroll taxes for the year. (The IRS created **Form 944 Employer's Annual Federal Tax Return** in response to my request to reduce the paperwork for taxpayers who pay small amounts to their employees.) Payroll taxes include Social Security and Medicare taxes (15.3%) and withheld federal income taxes (10% or 15% or 25% or 28% or more). You can use **Form 944** if you pay less than about $4,000 in wages to all your employees during a year. This option is something to consider as you look forward to 2015. If you use **Form 944**, you must use the Electronic Federal Tax Payment System (EFTPS) to pay your payroll taxes.

You may have already been notified by the IRS to file **Form 944**. If not, and you wish to use **Form 944**, you must contact the IRS to request permission. Call the IRS at 800-829-4933 by April 1, 2015, or send a written request postmarked by March 15, 2015. See the instructions to **Form 944** for the mailing address.

If you are a new employer as of 2015, you can indicate that you want to file **Form 944** when you apply for an employer identification number (see page 159). For more information, visit www.irs.gov/form944.

Federal Unemployment Tax (FUTA)

If you paid an employee $1,500 or more in any calendar quarter or had any employee who worked for some part of a day in any 20 different weeks during the year, you must pay federal unemployment tax (FUTA). The unemployment tax is based on the first $7,000 of wages paid during the year to each employee. This rate assumes that you have paid state payroll or unemployment taxes on time. If not, you will owe unemployment taxes at a rate of .6%. In 18 states you will have to pay a higher FUTA tax rate. See http://tinyurl.com/kxfzmo7. You do not have to pay a FUTA tax on wages over $7,000 for each employee. (In some states, you may be entitled to a reduction in your federal unemployment tax because of your state unemployment tax rules.) The unemployment tax rate is 0.6% for 2014.

You must pay this tax in addition to the wages you pay your employee; you may not withhold or deduct these taxes from the employee's wages.

Making FUTA Deposits

If your total FUTA tax is less than $100 (or $12,500 in wages), pay it when you file your **Form 940**. You need to file this form by January 31 of the following year. If you owe more than $100 in FUTA taxes at the end of any quarter (you can accumulate the tax owed from one quarter to the next), you must make deposits by the end of the month following the quarter. You must pay your FUTA taxes electronically using the EFTPS. If you do not want to use the EFTPS, you can arrange for your tax professional, bank, or payroll service to make deposits on your behalf. The EFTPS is a free service. To enroll in the EFTPS, see www.eftps.gov or call 800-555-4477. For more information, see IRS **Publication 966**.

If You Haven't Filed Any Payroll Forms This Year

If you haven't yet filed the proper payroll forms and it's now early 2015, your best option is to file **Form 941** for the fourth quarter by January 31 and pay all the taxes you owe. You should file **Form 941** as soon as possible, even if you're filing late. The sooner you file, the less interest will accumulate on any taxes you owe. If you miss the January 31 deadline, you can file an amended tax return after April 15 and include the fourth-quarter filing of **Form 941** to cover the year.

Forms W-2 and W-3

In addition to the above forms, you must also file forms **W-2** and **W-3** at the end of the year for all types of employees:

- **Form W-2**

  You must file this form if you have withheld any income, Social Security, or Medicare taxes. It summarizes the wages you've paid and taxes you've withheld for each employee. You must give a copy to each employee as soon as possible after the end of the year, and no later than January 31. An employee who stops working for you during the year may ask you to provide this form within 30 days.

- **Form W-3**

  Use this form to transmit a copy of **Form W-2** to the Social Security Administration. That agency will send the income tax data on **Form W-2** on to the IRS. You must submit **Form W-3** by March 1. Mail **Form W-2** and **Form W-3** to the address indicated on the instructions for **Form W-3**.

Note

If you withheld payroll taxes in 2015 that you did not send to the IRS until January of 2016, you can still claim them as a business deduction in 2015. Payroll taxes that you pay (Social Security/Medicare tax, federal and state unemployment tax) are deductible in the year you pay them. So, if you withheld $200 in Social Security/Medicare taxes for the last quarter of 2015 and sent them in to the IRS along with the employer share of these taxes ($200), you can deduct the withheld taxes in 2015, but you must wait until 2016 to deduct the employer share.

How to Fill Out Payroll Tax Forms

Filling out all the payroll tax forms for an employee can be a real pain in the neck, but the first year is usually the hardest. After that, it becomes easier because the forms are more familiar. And once you've completed all the proper forms, you'll be able to claim the wages and taxes (Social Security, Medicare, and federal and state unemployment taxes) that you paid as a business deduction on **Schedule C**, line 26. Let's look at three examples of filling out employee payroll tax forms—for a nonfamily employee, your own child under age 18, and your spouse. You'll find samples of some of the forms for the first two examples at the end of this chapter. (Check for other state or local rules in your area.)

Example 1: Hiring a Nonfamily Employee

You hire your first employee, Jill, on January 1 of last year. Jill works three days a week, eight hours a day, and you pay her $7.25 per hour. You write her a check at the end of every week. What obligations do you have to withhold and pay taxes to the IRS?

Step One: Employee Eligibility

When you hire Jill, ask her to fill out **Form I-9** to affirm that she isn't an undocumented worker.

Step Two: Employer Identification Number

As soon as you know that you will be hiring an employee, file **Form SS-4** to get an employer identification number. Use this number on all your employer forms.

Step Three: Federal Income Tax Withholding

Jill is single, has no dependents, and declares one withholding allowance on her **Form W-4**, which she filled out the day she started work. Her weekly wages amount to 8 hours x 5 days x $7.25/hour = $290. According to the the wage bracket tables, you need to withhold $8 in income tax. You therefore reduce Jill's weekly paycheck by $8 for income tax withholding.

In the first quarter of the year, Jill will earn $3,770 ($290 per week x 13 weeks). The income tax on this will be $104 ($8 x 13). Since this amount, plus Jill's quarterly Social Security and Medicare taxes, will be less than $2,500 per quarter, you don't have to deposit it with the IRS every month; you can wait and pay it when you file your quarterly **Form 941**.

Step Four: Social Security and Medicare Tax Withholding

To calculate Jill's Social Security and Medicare taxes, multiply her weekly wages by 7.65%: $290 x 7.65% = $22.19. This will further reduce her weekly paycheck by $22.19. Jill's actual take-home pay is now $290 − $8 − $22.19 = $259.81. Each week you must also pay $22.19 ($290 x 7.65%) of your own money into Social Security and Medicare.

Complete **Form 941** by April 30 to cover the first three months of the year. At this time you will owe the IRS $680.81 for Social Security and Medicare taxes:

$576.81	$290 x 13 x 15.3% (7.65% withheld plus 7.65% paid by you)
+$104.00	Income tax withheld ($8 x 13 weeks)
$680.81	Amount you owe the IRS

As long as Jill's hours and wages remain the same, you'll keep paying the IRS $680.81 every quarter. Pay this amount electronically using the EFTPS (www.eftps.gov).

STEP FIVE: FEDERAL UNEMPLOYMENT TAX

Jill earned $15,080 last year ($290 per week x 52 weeks). Since this is more than $1,500, you must pay federal unemployment tax (FUTA) on the first $7,000. At the end of the year, you will fill out **Form 940** and file it by January 31. You will owe $42 on **Form 940**:

$7,000	Jill's wages subject to FUTA tax
x 0.6%	FUTA tax
$42.00	Total FUTA tax

This amount is not withheld from Jill's paycheck; it's paid directly by you. Pay this amount electronically using the EFTPS (www.eftps.gov).

STEP SIX: END-OF-THE-YEAR REPORTING

At the end of the year, fill out **Form W-2** and **Form W-3**. These forms will show

$15,080.00	Wages paid to Jill (**W-2** and **W-3**, lines 1, 3, and 5)
$416.00	Federal income tax withheld ($8 x 52 weeks) (**W-2** and **W-3**, line 2)
$934.96	Social Security tax withheld ($15,080 x 6.2%) (**W-2** and **W-3**, line 4)
$218.66	Medicare tax withheld ($15,080 x 1.45%) (**W-2** and **W-3**, line 6)

SUMMARY

$15,080.00	Jill's yearly wages
– $416.00	Federal income tax withheld
– $1,153.62	Social Security and Medicare tax withheld (7.65%)
$13,510.38	Jill's take-home pay

$1,153.62	Additional Social Security and Medicare taxes you paid (7.65%)
+ $42.00	Federal unemployment tax you paid
$1,195.62	Total taxes you paid for having Jill as an employee

Example 2: Hiring Your Own Child

You have hired your daughter Clarisse, age 16, to clean your home before children arrive in the morning. She works one hour a day, five days a week, and you pay her $5.00 per hour. You keep a record of the work she does and write her a check at the end of every week. You have an employment agreement stating her job description and pay. (See the *Record-Keeping Guide* for a sample.) Clarisse will earn $1,300 a year ($25 a week x 52 weeks). You keep records of your payments to her and make out a receipt each time you pay her. You must file the following IRS forms for this employee:

STEP ONE: EMPLOYEE ELIGIBILITY

Fill out **Form I-9**.

STEP TWO: EMPLOYER IDENTIFICATION NUMBER

File **Form SS-4**.

STEP THREE: FEDERAL INCOME TAX WITHHOLDING

Clarisse must fill out **Form W-4**. She declares no withholding allowance because she is a child and you don't have to withhold income tax on weekly wages of $25.

STEP FOUR: SOCIAL SECURITY AND MEDICARE TAX WITHHOLDING

Since Clarisse is under age 18, you don't have to withhold any Social Security or Medicare taxes for her. File **Form 941**, and check the box on line 4. Continue filing this form quarterly, even though you don't owe any taxes.

Note: Since you paid less than $4,000 in wages to Clarisse, you could use the annual **Form 944** instead of the quarterly **Form 941**. If you have not already been contacted by the IRS and told that you can use **Form 944**, fill out **Form 941**. To find out if you can use **Form 944**, call the IRS at 800-829-4933. See the end of this chapter for a sample of how to fill out **Form 944**.

Forms for Family Employees

If you have hired nonfamily employees or your own children, enter the total wages paid on line 2 of **Form 941**.

I've heard from some providers that the IRS told them it wasn't necessary to file **Forms 941**, **W-2**, and **W-3** when hiring their own children under age 18, since no taxes are due; however, I believe that it's important to file these forms as further evidence that the payments to your children were wages and not an allowance.

STEP FIVE: FEDERAL UNEMPLOYMENT TAX

Since Clarisse is under age 21, you don't owe any federal unemployment taxes. File **Form 940** and claim an exemption for wages on line 4.

STEP SIX: END-OF-THE-YEAR REPORTING

At the end of the year, fill out **Form W-2** and **Form W-3**.

SUMMARY

Wages paid to Clarisse	$1,300
Federal income tax withheld	0
Social Security and Medicare taxes withheld	0
Federal unemployment tax withheld	0

Example 3: Hiring Your Spouse

You've hired your husband, John, to help with your business. He works five hours a week, and you pay him $10 per hour. You keep a record of the work he does and write him a check at the end of every week. John will earn $2,600 a year ($50 a week x 52 weeks).

STEP ONE: EMPLOYEE ELIGIBILITY

Fill out **Form I-9**.

STEP TWO: EMPLOYER IDENTIFICATION NUMBER

File **Form SS-4**.

STEP THREE: FEDERAL INCOME TAX WITHHOLDING

You can avoid withholding federal income tax if John is having enough withheld from the paycheck of another employer. If he does this, you don't have to fill out **Form W-4**.

STEP FOUR: SOCIAL SECURITY AND MEDICARE TAX WITHHOLDING

You must withhold Social Security and Medicare taxes on John's earnings. Multiply his weekly wages by 7.65%: $50 x 7.65% = $3.83. His weekly paycheck is now $46.17. You must pay $3.83 ($50 x 7.65%) of your own money into Social Security and Medicare. Complete **Form 941** by April to cover the first three months of the year. At the end of three months, John will have earned $650 ($50 x 13 weeks = $650). You will owe the IRS $99.45 for Social Security and Medicare taxes ($50 per week x 13 weeks x 15.3% [7.65% from John's paycheck and 7.65% from your pocket] = $99.45). Enter $99.45 on lines 5d, 6e, 10, and 13.

Note: Since you paid your husband less than $4,000 in wages, you can use the annual **Form 944** (see below) instead of the quarterly **Form 941** as long as you received permission to do so from the IRS. Call the IRS at 800-829-4933 to receive permission.

STEP FIVE: FEDERAL UNEMPLOYMENT TAX

You must pay the federal unemployment tax:

$15.60   ($2,600 x 0.6%)
$15.60   Total federal unemployment tax due

File **Form 940** by January 31. Check with your state to see if any state unemployment taxes are due or if workers' compensation insurance is required.

STEP SIX: END-OF-THE-YEAR REPORTING

At the end of the year, fill out **Forms W-2** and **W-3**. You will show $322.40 in Social Security taxes withheld on line 4 ($2,600 x 12.4%) and $75.40 in Medicare taxes withheld on line 6 ($2,600 x 2.9%).

Example 4: Hiring a Part-Time Employee

You may be able to avoid filing the quarterly **Form 941** and instead use **Form 944** if you paid less than $4,000 in total wages last year. To be able to file **Form 944** for your taxes, you either must have been notified by the IRS or must call the IRS to receive permission. *Do not file **Form 944** unless you have IRS approval.*

Let's say you paid Ophelia Lopez $1,000 to provide substitute care for 50 hours last year. You should have withheld 7.65% of her pay ($76.50) when you paid her. Use **Form 944V** to make your payment. See pages 178 to 179 for how **Form 944** and **Form 944V** should be filled out. The deadline to file these forms is January 31. In this example, you would still file forms **I-9**, **W-2**, and **W-3**, but not **Form 941** or **Form 940** (because the amount paid was less than $1,500 in any calendar quarter).

Note: Most states still require you to file quarterly state payroll taxes (state unemployment) even when you file **Form 944**.

For more information about the tax issues discussed in this chapter, refer to the related topics in the other chapters of this book and the Redleaf Press *Family Child Care Record-Keeping Guide.*

For Employee Jill

Form **941 for 2015:** Employer's QUARTERLY Federal Tax Return

(Rev. January 2015)   Department of the Treasury — Internal Revenue Service

950114

OMB No. 1545-0029

Employer identification number (EIN)   9 2 — 1 2 3 4 5 6 7

Name (not your trade name)   SONJA OLSON

Trade name (if any)

Address   421 PORTLAND AVENUE

Number   Street   Suite or room number

BOISE   ID   83701

City   State   ZIP code

Foreign country name   Foreign province/county   Foreign postal code

Report for this Quarter of 2015
(Check one.)

[X] 1: January, February, March

[ ] 2: April, May, June

[ ] 3: July, August, September

[ ] 4: October, November, December

Instructions and prior year forms are available at *www.irs.gov/form941.*

Read the separate instructions before you complete Form 941. Type or print within the boxes.

Part 1:   Answer these questions for this quarter.

1   Number of employees who received wages, tips, or other compensation for the pay period including: *Mar. 12* (Quarter 1), *June 12* (Quarter 2), *Sept. 12* (Quarter 3), or *Dec. 12* (Quarter 4)   **1**   1

2   Wages, tips, and other compensation   **2** $3,770 . 00

3   Federal income tax withheld from wages, tips, and other compensation   **3** $104 . 00

4   If no wages, tips, and other compensation are subject to social security or Medicare tax   [ ] Check and go to line 6.

		Column 1		Column 2
5a	Taxable social security wages	$3,770 . 00	× .124 =	$467 . 48
5b	Taxable social security tips	.	× .124 =	.
5c	Taxable Medicare wages & tips	.	× .029 =	.
5d	Taxable wages & tips subject to Additional Medicare Tax withholding	$3,770 . 00	× .009 =	$109 . 33

5e   Add Column 2 from lines 5a, 5b, 5c, and 5d   **5e**   567 . 81

5f   Section 3121(q) Notice and Demand—Tax due on unreported tips (see instructions)   **5f**   .

6   Total taxes before adjustments. Add lines 3, 5e, and 5f   **6**   680 . 81

7   Current quarter's adjustment for fractions of cents   **7**   .

8   Current quarter's adjustment for sick pay   **8**   .

9   Current quarter's adjustments for tips and group-term life insurance   **9**   .

10   Total taxes after adjustments. Combine lines 6 through 9   **10**   680 . 81

11   Total deposits for this quarter, including overpayment applied from a prior quarter and overpayments applied from Form 941-X, 941-X (PR), 944-X, 944-X (PR), or 944-X (SP) filed in the current quarter   **11**   .

12   Balance due. If line 10 is more than line 11, enter the difference and see instructions   **12**   681 . 81

13   Overpayment. If line 11 is more than line 10, enter the difference   .   Check one: [ ] Apply to next return. [ ] Send a refund.

▶ **You MUST complete both pages of Form 941 and SIGN it.**   Next ▶

For Privacy Act and Paperwork Reduction Act Notice, see the back of the Payment Voucher.   Cat. No. 17001Z   Form **941** (Rev. 1-2015)

950214

Name *(not your trade name)*	Employer identification number (EIN)
SONJA OLSON	92-1234567

Part 2:   Tell us about your deposit schedule and tax liability for this quarter.

If you are unsure about whether you are a monthly schedule depositor or a semiweekly schedule depositor, see Pub. 15 (Circular E), section 11.

14   Check one: ☐ Line 10 on this return is less than $2,500 or line 10 on the return for the prior quarter was less than $2,500, and you did not incur a $100,000 next-day deposit obligation during the current quarter. If line 10 for the prior quarter was less than $2,500 but line 10 on this return is $100,000 or more, you must provide a record of your federal tax liability. If you are a monthly schedule depositor, complete the deposit schedule below; if you are a semiweekly schedule depositor, attach Schedule B (Form 941). Go to Part 3.

☐ **You were a monthly schedule depositor for the entire quarter.** Enter your tax liability for each month and total liability for the quarter, then go to Part 3.

Tax liability:	Month 1	.
	Month 2	.
	Month 3	.
Total liability for quarter		.	Total must equal line 10.

☐ **You were a semiweekly schedule depositor for any part of this quarter.** Complete Schedule B (Form 941), Report of Tax Liability for Semiweekly Schedule Depositors, and attach it to Form 941.

Part 3:   Tell us about your business. If a question does NOT apply to your business, leave it blank.

15   If your business has closed or you stopped paying wages . . . . ☐ Check here, and

enter the final date you paid wages ⬚ / / ⬚ .

16   If you are a seasonal employer and you do not have to file a return for every quarter of the year . . ☐ Check here.

Part 4:   May we speak with your third-party designee?

Do you want to allow an employee, a paid tax preparer, or another person to discuss this return with the IRS? See the instructions for details.

☐ Yes.   Designee's name and phone number ⬚ ⬚

Select a 5-digit Personal Identification Number (PIN) to use when talking to the IRS. ☐ ☐ ☐ ☐ ☐

☐ No.

Part 5:   Sign here. You MUST complete both pages of Form 941 and SIGN it.

Under penalties of perjury, I declare that I have examined this return, including accompanying schedules and statements, and to the best of my knowledge and belief, it is true, correct, and complete. Declaration of preparer (other than taxpayer) is based on all information of which preparer has any knowledge.

X	Sign your name here	*Sonja Olson*	Print your name here	SONJA OLSON
			Print your title here	OWNER
	Date	4 / 11 / 15	Best daytime phone	612-222-2222

Paid Preparer Use Only

Check if you are self-employed . . . ☐

Preparer's name		PTIN	
Preparer's signature		Date	/ /
Firm's name (or yours if self-employed)		EIN	
Address		Phone	
City		State	ZIP code	

Form **941** (Rev. 1-2015)

Form **940 for 2015:** **Employer's Annual Federal Unemployment (FUTA) Tax Return**

Department of the Treasury — Internal Revenue Service

850113

OMB No. 1545-0028

Employer identification number (EIN) 9 2 – 1 2 3 4 5 6 7

Name *(not your trade name)* SONJA OLSON

Trade name *(if any)*

Address 421 PORTLAND AVENUE
Number   Street   Suite or room number

BOISE   City   ID   State   83701   ZIP code

Foreign country name   Foreign province/county   Foreign postal code

Type of Return
(Check all that apply.)

- [ ] **a.** Amended
- [ ] **b.** Successor employer
- [ ] **c.** No payments to employees in 2015
- [ ] **d.** Final: Business closed or stopped paying wages

Instructions and prior-year forms are available at *www.irs.gov/form940.*

Read the separate instructions before you complete this form. Please type or print within the boxes.

Part 1: Tell us about your return. If any line does NOT apply, leave it blank. See instructions before completing Part 1.

1a If you had to pay state unemployment tax in one state only, enter the state abbreviation . **1a**

1b If you had to pay state unemployment tax in more than one state, you are a multi-state employer . . . . **1b** [ ] Check here. Complete Schedule A (Form 940).

2 If you paid wages in a state that is subject to CREDIT REDUCTION . . . . **2** [ ] Check here. Complete Schedule A (Form 940).

Part 2: Determine your FUTA tax before adjustments. If any line does NOT apply, leave it blank.

3 Total payments to all employees . . . . **3** $15,080 .

4 Payments exempt from FUTA tax **4**

Check all that apply: **4a** [ ] Fringe benefits   **4c** [ ] Retirement/Pension   **4e** [ ] Other
4b [ ] Group-term life insurance   **4d** [ ] Dependent care

5 Total of payments made to each employee in excess of $7,000 . . . . **5** $8,080 .

6 Subtotal (line 4 + line 5 = line 6) . . . . **6** $8,080 .

7 Total taxable FUTA wages (line 3 – line 6 = line 7) (see instructions) . . . . **7** $7,000 .

8 FUTA tax before adjustments (line 7 x .006 = line 8) . . . . . . **8** $42 .

Part 3: Determine your adjustments. If any line does NOT apply, leave it blank.

9 If ALL of the taxable FUTA wages you paid were excluded from state unemployment tax, multiply line 7 by .054 (line 7 × .054 = line 9). Go to line 12 . . . . . . **9**

10 If SOME of the taxable FUTA wages you paid were excluded from state unemployment tax, OR you paid ANY state unemployment tax late (after the due date for filing Form 940), complete the worksheet in the instructions. Enter the amount from line 7 of the worksheet . . **10** .

11 If credit reduction applies, enter the total from Schedule A (Form 940) . . . . . **11** .

Part 4: Determine your FUTA tax and balance due or overpayment. If any line does NOT apply, leave it blank.

12 Total FUTA tax after adjustments (lines 8 + 9 + 10 + 11 = line 12) . . . . . **12** $42 .

13 FUTA tax deposited for the year, including any overpayment applied from a prior year . **13** .

14 Balance due (If line 12 is more than line 13, enter the excess on line 14.)
- If line 14 is more than $500, you must deposit your tax.
- If line 14 is $500 or less, you may pay with this return. (see instructions) . . . . . **14** $42 .

15 Overpayment (If line 13 is more than line 12, enter the excess on line 15 and check a box below.) . . . . **15** .

▶ You **MUST** complete both pages of this form and **SIGN** it.

Check one: [ ] Apply to next return. [ ] Send a refund.

Next ▶

850212

Name *(not your trade name)*	Employer identification number (EIN)
SONJA OLSON	92-1234567

Part 5: **Report your FUTA tax liability by quarter only if line 12 is more than $500. If not, go to Part 6.**

16 Report the amount of your FUTA tax liability for each quarter; do **NOT** enter the amount you deposited. If you had no liability for a quarter, leave the line blank.

16a **1st quarter** (January 1 – March 31) . . . . 16a | | . |

16b **2nd quarter** (April 1 – June 30) . . . . 16b | | . |

16c **3rd quarter** (July 1 – September 30) . . . . 16c | | . |

16d **4th quarter** (October 1 – December 31) . . . . . . 16d | | . |

17 **Total tax liability for the year** (lines 16a + 16b + 16c + 16d = line 17) **17** | | . | **Total must equal line 12.**

Part 6: **May we speak with your third-party designee?**

Do you want to allow an employee, a paid tax preparer, or another person to discuss this return with the IRS? See the instructions for details.

☐ **Yes.** Designee's name and phone number

Select a 5-digit Personal Identification Number (PIN) to use when talking to IRS

☐ **No.**

Part 7: **Sign here. You MUST complete both pages of this form and SIGN it.**

Under penalties of perjury, I declare that I have examined this return, including accompanying schedules and statements, and to the best of my knowledge and belief, it is true, correct, and complete, and that no part of any payment made to a state unemployment fund claimed as a credit was, or is to be, deducted from the payments made to employees. Declaration of preparer (other than taxpayer) is based on all information of which preparer has any knowledge.

X **Sign your name here**   *Sonja Olson*

Print your name here   SONJA OLSON

Print your title here   OWNER

Date   4 / 11 / 15

Best daytime phone   622-222-2222

Form **940-V**	**Payment Voucher**	OMB No. 1545-0028
Department of the Treasury Internal Revenue Service	▶ **Don't staple or attach this voucher to your payment.**	20**15**

1 Enter your employer identification number (EIN).	2 **Enter the amount of your payment.** ▶ Make your check or money order payable to **"United States Treasury"**	Dollars	Cents
92-1234567		$42	

3 Enter your business name (individual name if sole proprietor).

SONJA OLSON

Enter your address.

421 PORTLAND AVENUE

Enter your city, state, and ZIP code or your city, foreign country name, foreign province/county, and foreign postal code.

BOISE, ID 83701

22222	**a** Employee's social security number	OMB No. 1545-0008		
b Employer identification number (EIN) 92-1234567			**1** Wages, tips, other compensation $15,080	**2** Federal income tax withheld $416
c Employer's name, address, and ZIP code SONJA OLSON 421 PORTLAND AVENUE BOISE, ID 83701			**3** Social security wages $15,080	**4** Social security tax withheld $934.96
			5 Medicare wages and tips $15,080	**6** Medicare tax withheld $218.66
			7 Social security tips	**8** Allocated tips
d Control number		**9**		**10** Dependent care benefits
e Employee's first name and initial Last name Suff. JILL BROWN 1428 OLIVE STREET BOISE, ID 83701		**11** Nonqualified plans		**12a**
		13 Statutory employee ☐ Retirement plan ☐ Third-party sick pay ☐		**12b**
		14 Other		**12c**
				12d
f Employee's address and ZIP code				

15 State Employer's state ID number	**16** State wages, tips, etc.	**17** State income tax	**18** Local wages, tips, etc.	**19** Local income tax	**20** Locality name

Form **W-2** Wage and Tax Statement   **2015**   Department of the Treasury—Internal Revenue Service

---

DO NOT STAPLE

33333	**a** Control number	For Official Use Only ▶ OMB No. 1545-0008	

b Kind of Payer (Check one)	941 ☒ Military ☐ 943 ☐ 944 ☐ CT-1 ☐ Hshld. emp. ☐ Medicare govt. emp. ☐	Kind of Employer (Check one)	None apply ☒ 501c non-govt. ☐ State/local non-501c ☐ State/local 501c ☐ Federal govt. ☐	Third-party sick pay (Check if applicable) ☐

c Total number of Forms W-2	**d** Establishment number	**1** Wages, tips, other compensation $15,080	**2** Federal income tax withheld $416
e Employer identification number (EIN) 92-1234567		**3** Social security wages $15,080	**4** Social security tax withheld $934.96
f Employer's name SONJA OLSON		**5** Medicare wages and tips $15,080	**6** Medicare tax withheld $218.66
421 PORTLAND AVENUE BOISE, ID 83701		**7** Social security tips	**8** Allocated tips
		9	**10** Dependent care benefits
		11 Nonqualified plans	**12a** Deferred compensation
g Employer's address and ZIP code			
h Other EIN used this year		**13** For third-party sick pay use only	**12b**
15 State Employer's state ID number		**14** Income tax withheld by payer of third-party sick pay	
16 State wages, tips, etc.	**17** State income tax	**18** Local wages, tips, etc.	**19** Local income tax
Employer's contact person		Employer's telephone number	For Official Use Only
Employer's fax number		Employer's email address	

Under penalties of perjury, I declare that I have examined this return and accompanying documents and, to the best of my knowledge and belief, they are true, correct, and complete.

Signature ▶ *Sonja Olson*   Title ▶ OWNER   Date ▶ 01/01/2016

For Employee Clarisse

Form **941 for 2015:** **Employer's QUARTERLY Federal Tax Return**
(Rev. January 2015)   Department of the Treasury — Internal Revenue Service

950114

OMB No. 1545-0029

Employer identification number (EIN) 9 2 – 1 2 3 4 5 6 7

Name (not your trade name) SONJA OLSON

Trade name (if any)

Address 421 PORTLAND AVENUE
Number   Street   Suite or room number

BOISE   ID   83701
City   State   ZIP code

Foreign country name   Foreign province/county   Foreign postal code

Report for this Quarter of 2015
(Check one.)

[X] **1:** January, February, March

[ ] **2:** April, May, June

[ ] **3:** July, August, September

[ ] **4:** October, November, December

Instructions and prior year forms are available at *www.irs.gov/form941.*

Read the separate instructions before you complete Form 941. Type or print within the boxes.

Part 1:   Answer these questions for this quarter.

1	Number of employees who received wages, tips, or other compensation for the pay period including: *Mar. 12 (Quarter 1), June 12 (Quarter 2), Sept. 12 (Quarter 3),* or *Dec. 12 (Quarter 4)* **1**	1
2	Wages, tips, and other compensation **2**	$325 .
3	Federal income tax withheld from wages, tips, and other compensation **3**	.
4	If no wages, tips, and other compensation are subject to social security or Medicare tax [ ] Check and go to line 6.	

		Column 1		Column 2	
5a	Taxable social security wages . .	.	× .124 =	.	
5b	Taxable social security tips . . .	.	× .124 =	.	
5c	Taxable Medicare wages & tips. .	.	× .029 =	.	
5d	Taxable wages & tips subject to Additional Medicare Tax withholding	.	× .009 =	.	

5e	Add Column 2 from lines 5a, 5b, 5c, and 5d **5e**	$0 .
5f	Section 3121(q) Notice and Demand—Tax due on unreported tips (see instructions) **5f**	.
6	Total taxes before adjustments. Add lines 3, 5e, and 5f **6**	$0 .
7	Current quarter's adjustment for fractions of cents **7**	.
8	Current quarter's adjustment for sick pay **8**	.
9	Current quarter's adjustments for tips and group-term life insurance **9**	.
10	Total taxes after adjustments. Combine lines 6 through 9 **10**	$0 .
11	Total deposits for this quarter, including overpayment applied from a prior quarter and overpayments applied from Form 941-X, 941-X (PR), 944-X, 944-X (PR), or 944-X (SP) filed in the current quarter **11**	.
12	Balance due. If line 10 is more than line 11, enter the difference and see instructions **12**	$0 .
13	Overpayment. If line 11 is more than line 10, enter the difference . Check one: [ ] Apply to next return. [ ] Send a refund.	

► You MUST complete both pages of Form 941 and SIGN it.

Next ►

For Privacy Act and Paperwork Reduction Act Notice, see the back of the Payment Voucher.   Cat. No. 17001Z   Form **941** (Rev. 1-2015)

950214

Name (not your trade name)	Employer identification number (EIN)
SONJA OLSON	92-1234567

Part 2:   Tell us about your deposit schedule and tax liability for this quarter.

If you are unsure about whether you are a monthly schedule depositor or a semiweekly schedule depositor, see Pub. 15 (Circular E), section 11.

14   Check one: ☐   Line 10 on this return is less than $2,500 or line 10 on the return for the prior quarter was less than $2,500, and you did not incur a $100,000 next-day deposit obligation during the current quarter. If line 10 for the prior quarter was less than $2,500 but line 10 on this return is $100,000 or more, you must provide a record of your federal tax liability. If you are a monthly schedule depositor, complete the deposit schedule below; if you are a semiweekly schedule depositor, attach Schedule B (Form 941). Go to Part 3.

☐   **You were a monthly schedule depositor for the entire quarter.** Enter your tax liability for each month and total liability for the quarter, then go to Part 3.

Tax liability: Month 1   [.   ]

Month 2   [.   ]

Month 3   [.   ]

Total liability for quarter   [.   ]   **Total must equal line 10.**

☐   **You were a semiweekly schedule depositor for any part of this quarter.** Complete Schedule B (Form 941), Report of Tax Liability for Semiweekly Schedule Depositors, and attach it to Form 941.

Part 3:   Tell us about your business. If a question does NOT apply to your business, leave it blank.

15   If your business has closed or you stopped paying wages . . . . ☐ Check here, and

enter the final date you paid wages   [/   /   ] .

16   If you are a seasonal employer and you do not have to file a return for every quarter of the year   .   .   ☐ Check here.

Part 4:   May we speak with your third-party designee?

Do you want to allow an employee, a paid tax preparer, or another person to discuss this return with the IRS? See the instructions for details.

☐ Yes.   Designee's name and phone number   [   ]   [   ]

Select a 5-digit Personal Identification Number (PIN) to use when talking to the IRS.   [ ] [ ] [ ] [ ] [ ]

☐ No.

Part 5:   Sign here. You MUST complete both pages of Form 941 and SIGN it.

Under penalties of perjury, I declare that I have examined this return, including accompanying schedules and statements, and to the best of my knowledge and belief, it is true, correct, and complete. Declaration of preparer (other than taxpayer) is based on all information of which preparer has any knowledge.

X   Sign your name here   *Sonja Olson*

Print your name here   SONJA OLSON

Print your title here   OWNER

Date   4 / 11 / 15

Best daytime phone   622-222-2222

Paid Preparer Use Only   Check if you are self-employed . . . ☐

Preparer's name		PTIN	
Preparer's signature		Date	/ /
Firm's name (or yours if self-employed)		EIN	
Address		Phone	
City	State	ZIP code	

Form **941** (Rev. 1-2015)

22222	**a** Employee's social security number	OMB No. 1545-0008		
b Employer identification number (EIN) 92-1234567		**1** Wages, tips, other compensation $1.300	**2** Federal income tax withheld	
c Employer's name, address, and ZIP code SONJA OLSON 421 PORTLAND AVENUE BOISE, ID 83701		**3** Social security wages	**4** Social security tax withheld	
		5 Medicare wages and tips	**6** Medicare tax withheld	
		7 Social security tips	**8** Allocated tips	
d Control number		**9**	**10** Dependent care benefits	
e Employee's first name and initial Last name Suff. CLARISSE OLSON 421 PORTLAND AVENUE BOISE, ID 83701		**11** Nonqualified plans	**12a** code	
		13 Statutory employee ☐ Retirement plan ☐ Third-party sick pay ☐	**12b** code	
		14 Other	**12c** code	
			12d code	
f Employee's address and ZIP code				

15 State	Employer's state ID number	**16** State wages, tips, etc.	**17** State income tax	**18** Local wages, tips, etc.	**19** Local income tax	**20** Locality name

Form **W-2** Wage and Tax Statement   **2015**   Department of the Treasury—Internal Revenue Service

---

DO NOT STAPLE

33333	**a** Control number	**For Official Use Only ▶** OMB No. 1545-0008		

b Kind of Payer (Check one)	941 [X] Military ☐ 943 ☐ 944 ☐ CT-1 ☐ Hshld. emp. ☐ Medicare govt. emp. ☐	**Kind of Employer** (Check one)	None apply [X] 501c non-govt. ☐ State/local non-501c ☐ State/local 501c ☐ Federal govt. ☐	Third-party sick pay (Check if applicable) ☐
c Total number of Forms W-2	**d** Establishment number	**1** Wages, tips, other compensation $1,300	**2** Federal income tax withheld	
e Employer identification number (EIN) 92-1234567		**3** Social security wages	**4** Social security tax withheld	
f Employer's name SONJA OLSON 421 PORTLAND AVENUE BOISE, ID 83701		**5** Medicare wages and tips	**6** Medicare tax withheld	
		7 Social security tips	**8** Allocated tips	
		9	**10** Dependent care benefits	
g Employer's address and ZIP code		**11** Nonqualified plans	**12a** Deferred compensation	
h Other EIN used this year		**13** For third-party sick pay use only	**12b**	
15 State Employer's state ID number		**14** Income tax withheld by payer of third-party sick pay		
16 State wages, tips, etc.	**17** State income tax	**18** Local wages, tips, etc.	**19** Local income tax	
Employer's contact person		Employer's telephone number	For Official Use Only	
Employer's fax number		Employer's email address		

Under penalties of perjury, I declare that I have examined this return and accompanying documents and, to the best of my knowledge and belief, they are true, correct, and complete.

Signature ▶ *Sonja Olson*   Title ▶ OWNER   Date ▶ 01/01/2016

For Employee Ophelia

Form **944 for 2015:** **Employer's ANNUAL Federal Tax Return**

Department of the Treasury — Internal Revenue Service

OMB No. 1545-2007

Employer identification number (EIN) 4 1 — 1 2 3 4 5 6 7

Name (not your trade name) **SUSAN PROVIDER**

Trade name (if any)

Address **1470 ASHLAND AVENUE**

Number   Street   Suite or room number

SAINT PAUL   **MN**   **55105**

City   State   ZIP code

Foreign country name   Foreign province/county   Foreign postal code

Who Must File Form 944

You must file annual Form 944 instead of filing quarterly Forms 941 **only if the IRS notified you in writing.**
Instructions and prior-year forms are available at *www.irs.gov/form944*.

Read the separate instructions before you complete Form 944. Type or print within the boxes.

Part 1: Answer these questions for this year. Employers in American Samoa, Guam, the Commonwealth of the Northern Mariana Islands, the U.S. Virgin Islands, and Puerto Rico can skip lines 1 and 2.

1	Wages, tips, and other compensation	1	$1,000 ·
2	Federal income tax withheld from wages, tips, and other compensation	2	·
3	If no wages, tips, and other compensation are subject to social security or Medicare tax	3 ☐	Check and go to line 5.

4 Taxable social security and Medicare wages and tips:

	Column 1		Column 2
4a Taxable social security wages	$1,000 ·	× .124 =	$124 ·
4b Taxable social security tips	·	× .124 =	·
4c Taxable Medicare wages & tips	$1,000 ·	× .029 =	$29 ·
4d Taxable wages & tips subject to Additional Medicare Tax withholding	·	× .009 =	·

	4e Add Column 2 from lines 4a, 4b, 4c, and 4d	4e	$153 ·
5	Total taxes before adjustments. Add lines 2 and 4e	5	$153 ·
6	Current year's adjustments (see instructions)	6	·
7	Total taxes after adjustments. Combine lines 5 and 6	7	$153 ·
8	Total deposits for this year, including overpayment applied from a prior year and overpayments applied from Form 944-X, 944-X (PR), 944-X (SP), 941-X, or 941-X (PR) . .	8	·
9a	Reserved		
9b	Reserved		
10	Reserved		
11	**Balance due.** If line 7 is more than line 8, enter the difference and see instructions . .	11	$153 ·
12	**Overpayment.** If line 8 is more than line 7, enter the difference [·] Check one: ☐ Apply to next return. ☐ Send a refund.		

▶ You MUST complete both pages of Form 944 and SIGN it.

Next ▶

For Privacy Act and Paperwork Reduction Act Notice, see the back of the Payment Voucher.

Cat. No. 39316N   Form **944** (2015)

Name *(not your trade name)*	Employer identification number (EIN)
SUSAN PROVIDER	41-1234567

Part 2: Tell us about your deposit schedule and tax liability for this year.

13 Check one: [X] **Line 7 is less than $2,500. Go to Part 3.**

☐ Line 7 is $2,500 or more. Enter your tax liability for each month. If you are a semiweekly depositor or you accumulate $100,000 or more of liability on any day during a deposit period, you must complete Form 945-A instead of the boxes below.

	Jan.		Apr.		Jul.		Oct.
13a	.	13d	.	13g	.	13j	.
	Feb.		May		Aug.		Nov.
13b	.	13e	.	13h	.	13k	.
	Mar.		Jun.		Sep.		Dec.
13c	.	13f	.	13i	.	13l	.

Total liability for year. Add lines 13a through 13l. Total must equal line 7.   **13m** [.]

Part 3: Tell us about your business. If question 14 does NOT apply to your business, leave it blank.

14 If your business has closed or you stopped paying wages...

☐ Check here and enter the final date you paid wages. [ ]

Part 4: May we speak with your third-party designee?

Do you want to allow an employee, a paid tax preparer, or another person to discuss this return with the IRS? See the instructions for details.

☐ Yes. Designee's name and phone number [ ] [ ]

Select a 5-digit Personal Identification Number (PIN) to use when talking to IRS. [ ] [ ] [ ] [ ] [ ]

☐ No.

Part 5: Sign Here. You MUST complete both pages of Form 944 and SIGN it.

Under penalties of perjury, I declare that I have examined this return, including accompanying schedules and statements, and to the best of my knowledge and belief, it is true, correct, and complete. Declaration of preparer (other than taxpayer) is based on all information of which preparer has any knowledge.

X Sign your name here   *Susan Provider*

Print your name here SUSAN PROVIDER

Print your title here OWNER

Date 4/11/2015

Best daytime phone 612-221-1111

Paid Preparer Use Only   Check if you are self-employed ☐

Preparer's name		PTIN	
Preparer's signature		Date	
Firm's name (or yours if self-employed)		EIN	
Address		Phone	
City		State		ZIP code	

CHAPTER 9

Amending Your Tax Return:
Form 1040X

If you discover that you made a mistake on your tax returns in an earlier year, either by not claiming all your business income or by not deducting all your business expenses, you may be able to do something about it.

You can't e-file an amended return. Don't amend your return if you realize later you made a math error. The IRS will correct math errors when processing your original return. If you didn't include a required form or schedule, the IRS will send you a request for the missing item. If you are waiting for a refund from your original return, don't file your amended return until after you receive the refund. You may cash the refund check from your original return. Amended returns take up to 12 weeks to process.

You can amend your tax return by filing **Form 1040X** within three years of the date you filed the original return or two years from the time you paid the taxes on your original return, whichever is later. If you filed your return before April 15, it will be treated as if you had filed it on April 15. If you obtained an extension, you can count from the date you actually filed. This means that most people have until April 15 to file an amended return for the years 2014, 2013, and 2012. After April 15, it will be too late for most providers to file an amended return for 2012.

Don't be shy about filing an amended return. The IRS doesn't audit them any more often than original returns. If you think you may have missed some business deductions, check the list of more than a thousand deductions in the *Record-Keeping Guide*. If you find that you were entitled to deductions that you didn't claim and you have adequate records to back this up, don't hesitate to file an amended return.

You must file a separate **Form 1040X** for each annual tax return that you are amending. If you're entitled to a refund and your original return also showed a refund, you'll get another refund check, in addition to interest on the amount owed to you.

If you're claiming unclaimed depreciation on your amended tax return, you must use accelerated depreciation rules (see chapter 3). You can only use straight-line rules if you did so in the first year you began using the property in your business. The IRS allows you to elect to use the Section 179 rule when amending your 2013 or 2014 tax return. See chapter 3.

When you file **Form 1040X**, you must send with it copies of any tax forms for the year that is affected by the amended **Form 1040X**. (Don't send copies of your original tax forms, just amended versions of the forms that show changes.) A change on **Schedule C** will affect **Schedule SE** and **Form 1040**. A change in your Time-Space percentage will affect **Form 4562**, **Form 8829**, and **Schedule A**. For more information, see the instructions for **Form 1040X**, which also tell you where to mail your amended return. You can track the status of your amended return three weeks after you file by going online at www.irs.gov/Filing/Individuals/Amended-Returns-%28Form-1040-X%29 /Wheres-My-Amended-Return-1 or by phone at 866-464-2050.

Amending your federal tax return will probably mean that you must also amend your state tax return. Check with your state for information on amending your state return.

How Much Will It Be Worth?

Here's how to estimate how much you might save by amending your federal tax return:

- If you're in the 15% federal tax bracket for 2015 (if married filing jointly, making less than $74,900):

    15% + 12% (net self-employment tax) = 27%.

    You'll get a refund of about $0.27 on every additional dollar of deductions you claim on your amended return.

- If you're in the 25% federal tax bracket for 2015 (if married filing jointly, making between $74,901 and $151,200):

    25% + 12% (net self-employment tax) = 37%.

    You'll get a refund of about $0.37 on every additional dollar of deductions you claim on your amended return.

Example of an Amended Return

Here is an example of how to amend your tax return, based on the sample tax return shown in appendix A.

Example

Sandy James filed her tax return (see appendix A) on April 15. In September, she realizes that although she uses a 400–square-foot room exclusively for business, she didn't claim that on her last tax return. Here's her new Time-Space percentage:

Percentage for exclusive-use room: 400 ÷ 2,200 = 18%
Time-Space percentage for rest of home: 1,800 ÷ 2,200 = 81.8% x 39% Time percentage = 32%
Revised Time-Space percentage: 18% + 32% = 50%

Now Sandy must redo all the forms she filled out last tax season that are affected by this change:

- **Form 8829**
  Line 7 will now be 50%. Adjust the expenses on this form using this 50% Time-Space percentage. Line 35 will now be $6,885.

- **Form 4562**
  Recalculate the furniture, dining room set, and land improvement using the 50% Time-Space percentage. Line 22 will now be $2,5448.

- **Schedule C**
  Line 13 will now be $2,448.

Line 16b will now be $50.

Line 21 will now be $15.

Line 22 will now be $450.

Line 28 will now be $15,332.

Line 29 will now be $24,828.

Line 30 from **Form 8829** will now be $6,885.

Line 31 will now be $17,973, a reduction of net profit of $1,003

- **Schedule SE**

  Line 5 will now be $2,535.

- **Schedule A**

  Since Sandy took the standard deduction, she won't file **Schedule A**.

See the sample **Form 1040X** to see how Sandy saved $274 in federal taxes by amending her return.

Because Sandy's business profit is lower, she is able to reduce her Social Security taxes as well as her federal income taxes. Do not fill out lines 23–31 unless you are changing the number of your exemptions.

For more information about the tax issues discussed in this chapter, refer to the related topics in the other chapters of this book and the Redleaf Press *Family Child Care Record-Keeping Guide*.

Form **1040X** (Rev. December 2015)	Department of the Treasury—Internal Revenue Service **Amended U.S. Individual Income Tax Return** ▶ Information about Form 1040X and its separate instructions is at *www.irs.gov/form1040x*.		OMB No. 1545-0074

This return is for calendar year ☑ 2015 ☐ 2014 ☐ 2013 ☐ 2012

Other year. Enter one: calendar year   **or** fiscal year (month and year ended):

Your first name and initial	Last name	Your social security number
SANDY	JAMES	1 2 3 4 5 6 7 8 9
If a joint return, spouse's first name and initial	Last name	Spouse's social security number
BILL	JAMES	9 8 7 6 5 4 3 2 1

Current home address (number and street). If you have a P.O. box, see instructions.   Apt. no.   Your phone number

687 HOOVER STREET   212-541-7742

City, town or post office, state, and ZIP code. If you have a foreign address, also complete spaces below (see instructions).

HUDSON, OH 43287

Foreign country name	Foreign province/state/county	Foreign postal code

Amended return filing status. You must check one box even if you are not changing your filing status. **Caution:** In general, you cannot change your filing status from joint to separate returns after the due date.

☐ Single
☑ Married filing jointly
☐ Married filing separately
☐ Head of household (If the qualifying person is a child but not your dependent, see instructions.)
☐ Qualifying widow(er)

Full-year coverage.
If all members of your household have full-year minimal essential health care coverage, check "Yes." Otherwise, check "No." (See instructions.)

☑ Yes   ☐ No

Use Part III on the back to explain any changes

			A. Original amount or as previously adjusted (see instructions)	B. Net change—amount of increase or (decrease)—explain in Part III	C. Correct amount
Income and Deductions					
1	Adjusted gross income. If net operating loss (NOL) carryback is included, check here ▶☐	1	$57,588	($913)	$56,675
2	Itemized deductions or standard deduction	2	$12,600		$12,600
3	Subtract line 2 from line 1	3	$44,988	($913)	$44,075
4	Exemptions. **If changing, complete Part I on page 2 and enter the amount from line 29**	4	$12,000		$12,000
5	Taxable income. Subtract line 4 from line 3	5	$32,988	($913)	$32,075
Tax Liability					
6	Tax. Enter method(s) used to figure tax (see instructions):	6	$4,024	($135)	$3,889
7	Credits. If general business credit carryback is included, check here ▶☐	7	$1,000		$1,000
8	Subtract line 7 from line 6. If the result is zero or less, enter -0-	8	$3,024	($135)	$2,889
9	Health care: individual responsibility (see instructions)	9			
10	Other taxes	10	$2,674	($139)	$2,535
11	Total tax. Add lines 8, 9, and 10	11	$5,698	($274)	$5,424
Payments					
12	Federal income tax withheld and excess social security and tier 1 RRTA tax withheld (**if changing**, see instructions)	12	$5,800		$5,800
13	Estimated tax payments, including amount applied from prior year's return	13			
14	Earned income credit (EIC)	14			
15	Refundable credits from: ☐ Schedule 8812 Form(s) ☐ 2439 ☐ 4136 ☐ 8801 ☐ 8863 ☐ 8885 ☐ 8962 or ☐ other (specify): _____	15			
16	Total amount paid with request for extension of time to file, tax paid with original return, and additional tax paid after return was filed	16			$5,800
17	Total payments. Add lines 12 through 16	17			$5,800
Refund or Amount You Owe					
18	Overpayment, if any, as shown on original return or as previously adjusted by the IRS	18			
19	Subtract line 18 from line 17 (If less than zero, see instructions)	19			$5,800
20	**Amount you owe.** If line 11, column C, is more than line 19, enter the difference	20			
21	If line 11, column C, is less than line 19, enter the difference. This is the amount **overpaid** on this return	21			$376
22	Amount of line 21 you want **refunded to you**	22			$376
23	Amount of line 21 you want **applied to your** (enter year): _____ estimated tax .	23			

Complete and sign this form on Page 2.

For Paperwork Reduction Act Notice, see instructions.   Cat. No. 11360L   Form **1040X** (Rev. 12-2015)

Form 1040X (Rev. 12-2015)   Page **2**

Part I   Exemptions

Complete this part **only** if you are increasing or decreasing the number of exemptions (personal and dependents) claimed on line 6d of the return you are amending.

See *Form 1040 or Form 1040A instructions* and *Form 1040X instructions.*

		A. Original number of exemptions or amount reported or as previously adjusted	B. Net change	C. Correct number or amount
24	Yourself and spouse. **Caution:** If someone can claim you as a dependent, you cannot claim an exemption for yourself	24		
25	Your dependent children who lived with you	25		
26	Your dependent children who did not live with you due to divorce or separation	26		
27	Other dependents	27		
28	Total number of exemptions. Add lines 24 through 27	28		
29	Multiply the number of exemptions claimed on line 28 by the exemption amount shown in the instructions for line 29 for the year you are amending. Enter the result here and on line 4 on page 1 of this form. .	29		

30   List **ALL** dependents (children and others) claimed on this amended return. If more than 4 dependents, see instructions.

(a) First name Last name	**(b)** Dependent's social security number	**(c)** Dependent's relationship to you	**(d)** Check box if qualifying child for child tax credit (see instructions)
			☐
			☐
			☐
			☐

Part II   Presidential Election Campaign Fund

Checking below will not increase your tax or reduce your refund.

☐   Check here if you did not previously want $3 to go to the fund, but now do.

☐   Check here if this is a joint return and your spouse did not previously want $3 to go to the fund, but now does.

Part III   Explanation of changes. In the space provided below, tell us why you are filing Form 1040X.

▶ Attach any supporting documents and new or changed forms and schedules.

I DID NOT PREVIOUSLY INCLUDE A 400 SQUARE FOOT ROOM THAT IS USED EXCLUSIVELY FOR MY BUSINESS.

Sign Here
Remember to keep a copy of this form for your records.

Under penalties of perjury, I declare that I have filed an original return and that I have examined this amended return, including accompanying schedules and statements, and to the best of my knowledge and belief, this amended return is true, correct, and complete. Declaration of preparer (other than taxpayer) is based on all information about which the preparer has any knowledge.

▶ *Sandy James*	9/30/2016	▶ *Bill James*	9/30/2016
Your signature	Date	Spouse's signature. If a joint return, **both** must sign.	Date

Paid Preparer Use Only

▶

Preparer's signature	Date	Firm's name (or yours if self-employed)	
Print/type preparer's name		Firm's address and ZIP code	
	☐ Check if self-employed		
PTIN		Phone number	EIN

For forms and publications, visit IRS.gov.   Form **1040X** (Rev. 12-2015)

CHAPTER 10

Recovering Your Unclaimed Depreciation: Form 3115

This chapter explains how to use **Form 3115 Application for Change in Accounting Method** to take advantage of any depreciation deductions that you may have overlooked in previous years. Several IRS rulings (specifically, Revenue Procedure 2011-14) state that you can use **Form 3115** to deduct all the depreciation that you haven't claimed for items that you've used in your business (with some restrictions; see below). Before these rulings, the only way you could deduct unclaimed depreciation without incurring a fee was to file an amended tax return—and you can only do that for the last three years.

If you have any unclaimed depreciation from earlier years, you can use **Form 3115** to deduct it on your tax return. (Note that you can't file **Form 3115** electronically.) Since family child care providers are entitled to depreciate a wide range of small and large household items, it's easy to overlook depreciation opportunities, yet by claiming them now, you could reap hundreds of dollars of deductions on this year's tax return.

For example, let's say that you started your business in 2006, and in 2007 you bought a sofa for $800; however, you've never claimed any depreciation for it. If your Time-Space percentage for 2007–2015 was 40%, you would have been entitled to depreciate $320 of the cost of the sofa ($800 x 40%), using seven-year accelerated depreciation (see chapter 3). Since you didn't claim any of this depreciation, you can use **Form 3115** to claim the entire $320 on your tax return. (You'll find a completed sample of **Form 3115** at the end of this chapter.)

For information about what kinds of property you can depreciate, see chapter 3 of this book (and refer to the *Record-Keeping Guide* for a comprehensive list). Here's a sampling of the items that family child care providers can typically depreciate:

- the home
- home appliances, such as a washer, dryer, freezer, stove, or refrigerator
- fences, outdoor play equipment, lawn mowers, snowblowers
- furniture, such as beds, chairs, or sofas
- televisions, DVD players, computers, home entertainment systems
- home improvements, such as remodeling or a new furnace

You can deduct unclaimed depreciation for property that you never previously depreciated and for property that you only partly depreciated. For example, let's say that you remodeled your basement in January 2009 but didn't start claiming depreciation until 2015 because you weren't aware that you could depreciate this expense. You would continue to claim the depreciation on your tax return (as year 7 under the 39-year home improvement rules).

If you used the wrong depreciation method in earlier years, you can't use **Form 3115** to correct it. Let's say that you began depreciating a carpet over 39 years, and you realized several years later that you could have depreciated it over seven years. You can't use **Form 3115** to correct this error. You can only amend your tax return for the last three years and start claiming the proper depreciation amount in 2015.

Let's say that you started depreciating the carpet in 2011 over 39 years and discovered your error in 2015. It's too late to amend your 2011 tax return, but you can amend your 2012, 2013, and 2014 tax returns and claim the extra depreciation that you were entitled to, using the seven-year 200% declining balance method. In 2015, you would continue depreciating the carpet under the seven-year method by using the fifth-year percentage (8.93%) as shown on the depreciation tables in chapter 3.

Requirements for Using Form 3115

To be eligible to deduct your previously unclaimed depreciation by filing **Form 3115**, you must meet the following requirements:

1. You must still be in business.
If you go out of business for a year or two and then start up again, you can't use **Form 3115** to recapture any depreciation for the years before you closed your business. You also can't use **Form 3115** if you closed your child care business and used your home for some other business (such as renting out rooms).

2. You must own the property that you are deducting.
You must own the property in question at the start of the year in which you deduct the unclaimed depreciation. For example, let's say that you began your business in 2010 and have never claimed any depreciation on your home. You decide to file **Form 3115** with your tax return to claim your home depreciation for the years 2010 to 2014. To be eligible to do this, you must still own the home and be in business on January 1, 2014.

If you sell the home before January 1, 2015, you can't claim any deductions on **Form 3115** for 2010–2014. If you sell the home during 2015, you can still deduct your home depreciation for the years 2010–2014 by filing **Form 3115** with your tax return. If you had sold the home in 2014, the only way you'd be able to claim the unclaimed depreciation would be to file an amended return for the years 2012–2014. (You can only file an amended return up to three years after filing the original return.)

3. You must be using the property that you're deducting in your business.
You must have been using the item in your business on January 1, 2015. For example, if you used a sewing machine in your business from 2010 to 2013 but haven't used it since then, you can't use **Form 3115** to claim the unclaimed depreciation for it now.

You *can* use **Form 3115** for items that you continue to use in your business after their depreciation life is over. For example, if you've been using a sofa in your business for more than seven years (its depreciation period), you can still use **Form 3115**, as long as you've used it for your business in the current year.

4. You must file Form 3115 by the tax deadline (including any extensions) for the year in which you are deducting your previously unclaimed depreciation.

To claim your past year's depreciation on your current tax return, you must file **Form 3115** no later than the due date of that tax return. In other words, to deduct previously unclaimed depreciation on your tax return, you must file **Form 3115** by April 15. If you file for an extension on your tax return, you could file **Form 3115** as late as October 15 and still claim the deductions on your tax return.

There is one way you could claim the deductions using **Form 3115** if you haven't filed it with your original tax return. You can amend your tax return up to October 15 using **Form 1040X**, attach **Form 3115** to your amended return, and file **Form 3115** before sending in your amended return. Write on the top of your amended return "Filed Pursuant to IRS Tax Code Section 301.9100-2."

There's no time limit for your right to claim your depreciation from previous years. You can do it anytime you discover that you haven't claimed earlier depreciation. If you file your tax return on April 15 and don't file **Form 3115** by that date, you can always claim the depreciation on your next tax return, as long as you're still in business, still own the property, and continue to use it in your business.

5. You can't claim an expense that you've already deducted.

You can't reclaim depreciation if you have already deducted the property under Section 179 (see chapter 3). For example, if you bought a computer in 2010 and deducted the entire business-use portion of its cost that year, you can't use **Form 3115**, because you've already claimed all the expense that you're entitled to deduct for that computer. You also can't use **Form 3115** to go back and use Section 179 on property that you purchased in earlier years. You can only use Section 179 in the year you purchase the property.

6. You must not have depreciated the item for at least two years before using Form 3115.

To take advantage of filing **Form 3115**, you must not have claimed depreciation on the items you are recapturing for at least two years immediately preceding the year you use **Form 3115**. In other words, if you didn't claim depreciation on your furniture and appliances from 2009 to 2013, but you did claim depreciation on them in 2014, you can't use **Form 3115**. Also, if you amended your tax return for 2012 and 2013 to recapture depreciation, you can't use **Form 3115**.

7. You must use the proper depreciation method.

You can't use **Form 3115** to change the depreciation rules on an item that you've already started depreciating. For example, if you began depreciating a swing set in 2005 under straight-line rules, you can't use **Form 3115** to switch to accelerated depreciation and claim higher deductions for the earlier years.

Unless you've already started depreciating the item under straight-line rules, you must generally use accelerated depreciation rules on **Form 3115** to calculate your unclaimed depreciation for previous years. This is because you can't generally use straight-line depreciation for an item unless you chose this method in the first year you used the item in your business. If you didn't have the option of using straight-line depreciation in the first year you used the item, you must abide by the rules that were in effect at that time. Here are the rules you must use when claiming depreciation on **Form 3115**:

- Home (nonresidential real property): 39-year (or 31.5-year) straight-line

- Home improvements (nonresidential real property): 39-year (or 31.5-year) straight-line

- Land improvements (asset class 00.3): 15-year 150% declining balance

- Computers (asset class 00.12 information systems): if used 50% or less in business, 5-year straight-line; if used more than 50% in business, 5-year 200% declining balance

- Other personal property (asset class 00.11 office furniture, entertainment/recreation items, fixtures, and equipment): 7-year 200% declining balance

- Cars (asset class 00.22): 5-year 200% declining balance

Check Your State Rules

If you claim **Form 3115** depreciation deductions on your federal tax return, check to see if your state tax rules will permit you to include these deductions when calculating your state tax return. Some states don't allow you to transfer these deductions to your state tax return.

Unclaimed Depreciation and Losses on Schedule C

Although depreciation of personal property can always be used to claim a loss for your business, depreciation of a home or home improvement is not allowed to create a loss on **Schedule C**. You can carry forward those depreciation expenses to another year. (For a detailed explanation of how to depreciate property, see chapter 3.)

For example, let's say that you didn't claim any home depreciation for the years 2005–2010, and this year you're using **Form 3115** to claim that depreciation. You discover that the home depreciation deductions that you're claiming for 2005–2007 would have created a loss for your business if you had claimed them in those years; however, you would have been able to carry those deductions forward to 2008–2009, because your business made enough profit to cover the deductions in the later years. In a case like this, you would be able to claim all the home depreciation from 2005 to 2009 on this year's tax return.

If the deductions on your **Form 3115** create a loss for your business, you can't deduct the part of the depreciation for home or home improvements that creates a loss on your **Schedule C**. If you still have a loss after taking out all the depreciation for home and home improvements, that's fine; you can show that loss. You can also carry forward the unallowed portion of your home or home improvement depreciation from 2014 **Form 3115** to line 30 of 2015 **Form 8829**. (Enter "Section 481(a) Adjustment" on this line.)

You must also follow the usual instructions on **Form 8829** about deduction limitations. You may have to carry forward some of your deductions to your **Form 8829** for next tax season.

Claiming Depreciation on Vehicles

You can only use **Form 3115** to claim depreciation on your vehicle if you used the actual vehicle expenses method of claiming car expenses in earlier years or if you never claimed any car expenses. You can't claim past depreciation on your car if you used the standard mileage rate method. In calculating how much vehicle depreciation you can take, you must apply the yearly limitations on vehicle depreciation.

Will Filing Form 3115 Increase My Chances of Being Audited?

Your chances of being audited at all are very slim, and it's unlikely that you will be audited just because you file **Form 3115**—so don't base your decision about whether to claim depreciation on this. (If all your records are in order, you have nothing to worry about anyway.) If you don't claim all the depreciation you're entitled to, you're paying more taxes than you should.

What If You Don't Have the Receipts Anymore?

You need to calculate depreciation based on the lower of the cost of an item or its fair market value at the time you started using it for business (see chapter 3). But what if you don't know the cost of the item? Let's say that you've been using your freezer in your business since 2007, but you've never depreciated it and didn't save the receipt when you bought it because you didn't know it was deductible. What can you do?

Start by looking for other records you may have that show how much you paid for the item, such as a credit card statement, repair service contract, canceled check, or statement from the store where you purchased the item. If you can't find any of those kinds of records, estimate the value of the property when you began using it. Look up newspaper ads for used freezers from that year or visit a thrift store to get an idea of the fair market value of a used freezer.

See if you have any old family photos that show that you owned the item in 2006 or earlier. If your estimated fair market value of the item in 2007 is reasonable, you should be okay. Don't be aggressive by inflating the value of your item. The IRS should accept a reasonable estimate of its value, as long as you have some kind of evidence that you owned the item from 2007 to 2015.

Maximize Your Reclaimed Depreciation

Previously unclaimed depreciation could be one of your biggest deductions this year. Here are some ways to ensure that you'll be able to claim all the depreciation that you're entitled to:

- Recapture the biggest unclaimed depreciation first. This will probably be your home or home improvements. Don't worry that this will increase your taxes when you sell your home. The tax consequences of selling your home will be the same regardless of whether or not you've claimed all the depreciation you're entitled to (see chapter 12). The IRS rules state that all allowable depreciation must be treated as if it had been claimed, so any property that you haven't depreciated will be treated as if it had been depreciated. Therefore, you will have to pay the same amount later, and you should claim your depreciation today.

- Save all your receipts for home purchases, home improvements, furniture, appliances, and outdoor play equipment. To document items that you bought in earlier years, dig out the receipts, canceled checks, or credit card statements. (It's easy to track these purchases and improvements if you use the *Inventory-Keeper*, which provides a room-by-room listing of depreciable items.)

- Don't throw away any household property that you have used in earlier years for your business and are still using in your business. Remember, you can only claim depreciation on an item this year if you still own it as of January 1 of last year.

How important is it to deduct your unclaimed depreciation? Here's an example. Let's say that you've never depreciated the following property:

- Your home, which has a business basis of $30,000 ($100,000 adjusted basis x 30% Time-Space percentage)

- Your major appliances (washer, dryer, freezer, refrigerator, stove, microwave oven), which have a business basis of $1,000

- Your furniture (sofa, chairs, tables, bed, lawn mower), which has a business basis of $1,000

Applying 39-year straight-line rules to the house and 7-year 200% declining balance rules to the appliances and furniture, you would be entitled to a business deduction of about $1,019 for each year that you've used these items in your business. This would translate into a tax savings of $275 per year if you're in the 15% tax bracket (15% federal income tax and 12% net Social Security tax) and $377 if you're in the 25% tax bracket (25% federal income tax and 12% net Social Security tax). In addition, there may be state income tax savings. As you can see, your tax savings will rise quickly for every year that you haven't claimed the depreciation for this property.

Although **Form 3115** isn't the simplest tax form to fill out, you have a lot to gain by filing it. Even if you have to pay a tax preparer to do it for you, it may be well worth the extra cost. If you've been reluctant to claim all the depreciation you're entitled to, you should seriously consider filing this form; it can mean a substantial one-time business deduction.

How to Fill Out Form 3115

To start filling out **Form 3115**, write "Automatic method change under Rev. Proc. 2011-14" above the title. If you're filing jointly, enter the names and Social Security numbers of both spouses in the same order they appear on your **Form 1040**. If you have an employer identification number (see page 6), enter it here instead of your Social Security number. The principal business activity code number is 62441. Enter "1/1/15" as the date when the change begins. Enter "12/31/15" as the date when the change ends.

Check the box to indicate the applicant:
> Check Individual (unless you are incorporated).

Check the appropriate box to indicate the type of accounting method change being requested:
> Check Depreciation or Amortization.

Part I

Line 1:   Enter "107" for the change number. Enter "recapture depreciation" under the description.

Line 2:   Check the No column.

Part II

Lines 3–11:   Check the No column.

Lines 12–13:   Attach a statement to the form to answer these questions. (See example shown later in this chapter.)

Line 14:   Check the Yes column.

Lines 15–16:   Check the No column.

Lines 17:   Leave blank.

Part III

Lines 18–23:   Check the No column.

Part IV

Line 24:   Check the No column.

Line 25:   Enter the net change in depreciation that you are claiming. (See example shown later in this chapter.)

Line 26:   Check the Yes column if you are claiming less than $25,000 in net depreciation deduction.

Line 27:   Check the No column.

Schedule A, B, C, and D of Form 3115

Family child care providers do not have to complete these sections on pages 4–7 of **Form 3115**.

Schedule E (not shown)

Lines 1–3:   Check the No column.

Line 4a: This question has already been answered.

Lines 4b–4c: Check the No column.

Lines 5–7:   These questions have already been answered.

Transfer Your Unclaimed Depreciation to Schedule C

Enter the amount from **Form 3115**, Part IV, line 25, on one of the blank lines of **Schedule C**, Part V. Title that entry "Section 481(a) Adjustment." Include this amount in the total that you enter on **Schedule C**, line 27 (other expenses).

Professional Help Is Recommended

The IRS rulings that allow you to claim previously unclaimed depreciation on **Form 3115** are relatively new, and they may require clarification. If you file **Form 3115**, you should consult a tax preparer to help you with it. If you aren't using a tax preparer, it would be worth it to hire one just to do (or review) your **Form 3115**.

Remember, there's no deadline for filing **Form 3115**. If you don't file it this year, you can do it next year, as long as you're still in business and still own the property you want to depreciate.

Two Examples of How to Fill Out Form 3115

The following examples show you how to fill out the remaining lines on **Form 3115**. In the first example, the depreciation period is over; in the second, it is still in progress.

EXAMPLE 1

This example is shown on the forms and the attachment at the end of this chapter.

Karin Roth has been in business since 2007, and her Time-Space percentage each year has been 35%. In 2007, she bought a washer for $400 and a dryer for $300. She has never claimed any depreciation for these items. To claim it on her tax return, she'll have to file **Form 3115** by April 15 (unless she takes an extension). To answer questions 12, 13, and 25, Karin will write an attachment to **Form 3115** (see example at end of chapter). To calculate the proper amount of her depreciation, Karin will consult chapter 3. As her attachment shows, she was entitled to deduct $245 in depreciation over eight years. Because the eight-year recovery period has expired, she can claim all $245 as a deduction this year.

Karin will enter "–$245" on **Form 3115**, Part IV, line 25. Then she will enter $245 on one of the blank lines of her **Schedule C**, Part V, and write "Section 481(a) Adjustment" on that line.

EXAMPLE 2

In this case, Karin bought the washer and dryer in 2010, and her Time-Space percentages for the years 2011–2014 are as follows: 35%; 38%; 35%; 40%. Karin will fill out **Form 3115** in the same way, and her depreciation calculation will look like this:

2011: $700 x 35% = $245 x 14.29% = $35.01
2012: $700 x 38% = $266 x 24.49% = $65.14
2013: $700 x 35% = $245 x 17.49% = $42.85
2014: $700 x 40% = $280 x 12.49% = $34.97
Total depreciation allowed 2011–2014: $177.97

In this case, Karin will enter "–$178" on **Form 3115**, Part IV, line 25, and will claim this amount on her **Schedule C**, Part V. Karin is also entitled to claim $25.00 as the fifth year of depreciation on the washer and dryer for last year:

2014: $700 x 40% = $280 x 8.93% = $25

Karin will enter this $25.00 on line 1 of her **Form 4562**. Since there is still one more year of depreciation left, she will also be entitled to claim the sixth year of depreciation on the washer and dryer on her **Form 4562** next tax season:

2015: $700 x 40% = $280 x 8.92% = $24.98

Next year, she will enter this $25 on line 17 of her **Form 4562**. (Although no attachment is shown for this example, Karin would complete **Form 3115** and the attachment in exactly the same way as example 1, except for her entry for question 25.)

How to File Form 3115

In the past, if you wanted to deduct previously unclaimed depreciation, you had to pay a hefty fee and get the consent of the commissioner of the IRS to change your accounting method. Now there is no fee for filing **Form 3115** and you can get automatic consent, if you proceed as follows:

1. Fill out **Form 3115**. Be sure to write "Automatic method change under Rev. Proc. 2011-14" above the title. Attach the original of **Form 3115** with your tax return.

2. Mail a copy of **Form 3115** by the filing deadline (April 15 or your extension deadline) to:

   Commissioner of Internal Revenue
   Automatic Rulings Branch
   PO Box 7604
   Ben Franklin Station
   Washington, DC 20044

   Since you won't receive any acknowledgment that the IRS has received the form, send it by certified mail with a return receipt request in case you have to prove that it was delivered. If your **Form 3115** isn't postmarked by the deadline, the IRS will deny the deductions on your tax return. (You could file again next year and claim the deductions.) If for any reason the IRS does not consent to your **Form 3115**, it will notify you.

3. Attach a list of your previously unclaimed or underclaimed property to **Form 3115**, as shown at the end of this chapter. Be sure to include your name and Social Security number and indicate that this is an attachment to **Form 3115**.

A Note to Tax Professionals
The two types of unclaimed depreciation are **Schedule C** operating expenses depreciation (furniture, appliances, and other personal property) and **Form 8829** operating expenses depreciation (home and home improvements).

Calculate how much of each type of depreciation the provider was entitled to deduct for each unclaimed year. Check to see whether claiming this depreciation would have created a loss on **Form 8829** for each year in question. Higher **Schedule C** depreciation deductions may affect the provider's ability to claim some of the deductions on **Form 8829**.

After taking this into account, check to see if the provider is allowed to deduct all unclaimed depreciation on **Form 8829** each year. If so, the provider won't need to recalculate **Form 8829** each year. If not, she will need to recalculate the allowed deductions on **Form 8829** and carry forward any unallowed deductions to the next year's **Form 8829**. There may be a number of years of carry-forward deductions. The provider should keep copies of the recalculated **Form 8829**s as backup supporting statements.

Although **Form 8829** was introduced in 1991, the earlier rules were the same about the limitation on claiming home expenses that create a business loss. Consider the potential complexity of these calculations before agreeing to file **Form 3115**.

For more information about the tax issues discussed in this chapter, refer to the related topics in the other chapters of this book and the Redleaf Press *Family Child Care Record-Keeping Guide.*

Form **3115**	**Application for Change in Accounting Method**	OMB No. 1545-0152

Form **3115**
(Rev. December 2009)
Department of the Treasury
Internal Revenue Service

Application for Change in Accounting Method

OMB No. 1545-0152

Name of filer (name of parent corporation if a consolidated group) (see instructions)

HANK AND KARIN ROTH

Identification number (see instructions)

468-78-9123

Principal business activity code number (see instructions)

62441

Number, street, and room or suite no. If a P.O. box, see the instructions.

466 WOBBLY LANE

City or town, state, and ZIP code

DULUTH, MN 55671

Tax year of change begins (MM/DD/YYYY)   **1/1/2015**

Tax year of change ends (MM/DD/YYYY)   **12/31/2015**

Name of contact person (see instructions)

Name of applicant(s) (if different than filer) and identification number(s) (see instructions)

Contact person's telephone number

If the applicant is a member of a consolidated group, check this box . . . . ▶ ☐

If **Form 2848,** Power of Attorney and Declaration of Representative, is attached (see instructions for when Form 2848 is required), check this box . . . . ▶ ☐

Check the box to indicate the type of applicant.

- ☑ Individual
- ☐ Corporation
- ☐ Controlled foreign corporation (Sec. 957)
- ☐ 10/50 corporation (Sec. 904(d)(2)(E))
- ☐ Qualified personal service corporation (Sec. 448(d)(2))
- ☐ Exempt organization. Enter Code section ▶

- ☐ Cooperative (Sec. 1381)
- ☐ Partnership
- ☐ S corporation
- ☐ Insurance co. (Sec. 816(a))
- ☐ Insurance co. (Sec. 831)
- ☐ Other (specify) ▶

Check the appropriate box to indicate the type of accounting method change being requested. (see instructions)

- ☑ Depreciation or Amortization
- ☐ Financial Products and/or Financial Activities of Financial Institutions
- ☐ Other (specify) ▶

Caution. *To be eligible for approval of the requested change in method of accounting, the taxpayer must provide all information that is relevant to the taxpayer or to the taxpayer's requested change in method of accounting. This includes all information requested on this Form 3115 (including its instructions), as well as any other information that is not specifically requested.*
The taxpayer must attach all applicable supplemental statements requested throughout this form.

Part I	Information For Automatic Change Request		Yes	No
1	Enter the applicable designated automatic accounting method change number for the requested automatic change. Enter only one designated automatic accounting method change number, except as provided for in guidance published by the IRS. If the requested change has no designated automatic accounting method change number, check "Other," and provide both a description of the change and citation of the IRS guidance providing the automatic change. See instructions.			
	▶ (a) Change No. ___107___ (b) Other ☐ Description ▶ **RECAPTURE DEPRECIATION**			
2	Do any of the scope limitations described in section 4.02 of Rev. Proc. 2008-52 cause automatic consent to be unavailable for the applicant's requested change? If "Yes," attach an explanation.			✓

Note. *Complete Part II below and then Part IV, and also Schedules A through E of this form (if applicable).*

Part II	Information For All Requests		Yes	No
3	Did or will the applicant cease to engage in the trade or business to which the requested change relates, or terminate its existence, in the tax year of change (see instructions)? . . . . If "Yes," the applicant is not eligible to make the change under automatic change request procedures.			✓
4a	Does the applicant (or any present or former consolidated group in which the applicant was a member during the applicable tax year(s)) have any Federal income tax return(s) under examination (see instructions)? . . . . . If "No," go to line 5.			✓
b	Is the method of accounting the applicant is requesting to change an issue (with respect to either the applicant or any present or former consolidated group in which the applicant was a member during the applicable tax year(s)) either (i) under consideration or (ii) placed in suspense (see instructions)?			✓

Signature *(see instructions)*

Under penalties of perjury, I declare that I have examined this application, including accompanying schedules and statements, and to the best of my knowledge and belief, the application contains all the relevant facts relating to the application, and it is true, correct, and complete. Declaration of preparer (other than applicant) is based on all information of which preparer has any knowledge.

Filer

Preparer (other than filer/applicant)

Hank Roth Karin Roth   1/10/2016

Signature and date

Signature of individual preparing the application and date

HANK ROTH   **KARIN ROTH**

Name and title (print or type)

Name of individual preparing the application (print or type)

Name of firm preparing the application

For Privacy Act and Paperwork Reduction Act Notice, see the instructions.   Cat. No. 19280E   Form **3115** (Rev. 12-2009)

Form 3115 (Rev. 12-2009)   Page **2**

Part II	Information For All Requests (continued)	Yes	No

4c Is the method of accounting the applicant is requesting to change an issue pending (with respect to either the applicant or any present or former consolidated group in which the applicant was a member during the applicable tax year(s)) for any tax year under examination (see instructions)? . . . . | | ✓

d Is the request to change the method of accounting being filed under the procedures requiring that the operating division director consent to the filing of the request (see instructions)? . . . . | | ✓

If "Yes," attach the consent statement from the director.

e Is the request to change the method of accounting being filed under the 90-day or 120-day window period? . . | | ✓

If "Yes," check the box for the applicable window period and attach the required statement (see instructions).

☐ 90 day   ☐ 120 day: Date examination ended ▶ _____

f If you answered "Yes" to line 4a, enter the name and telephone number of the examining agent and the tax year(s) under examination.

Name ▶ _____   Telephone number ▶ _____   Tax year(s) ▶ _____

g Has a copy of this Form 3115 been provided to the examining agent identified on line 4f? . . . . | | ✓

5a Does the applicant (or any present or former consolidated group in which the applicant was a member during the applicable tax year(s)) have any Federal income tax return(s) before Appeals and/or a Federal court? . . . . | | ✓

If "Yes," enter the name of the (check the box)   ☐ Appeals officer and/or   ☐ counsel for the government, telephone number, and the tax year(s) before Appeals and/or a Federal court.

Name ▶ _____   Telephone number ▶ _____   Tax year(s) ▶ _____

b Has a copy of this Form 3115 been provided to the Appeals officer and/or counsel for the government identified on line 5a? . . . . | | ✓

c Is the method of accounting the applicant is requesting to change an issue under consideration by Appeals and/or a Federal court (for either the applicant or any present or former consolidated group in which the applicant was a member for the tax year(s) the applicant was a member) (see instructions)? . . . . | | ✓

If "Yes," attach an explanation.

6 If the applicant answered "Yes" to line 4a and/or 5a with respect to any present or former consolidated group, attach a statement that provides each parent corporation's **(a)** name, **(b)** identification number, **(c)** address, and **(d)** tax year(s) during which the applicant was a member that is under examination, before an Appeals office, and/or before a Federal court.

7 If, for federal income tax purposes, the applicant is either an entity (including a limited liability company) treated as a partnership or an S corporation, is it requesting a change from a method of accounting that is an issue under consideration in an examination, before Appeals, or before a Federal court, with respect to a Federal income tax return of a partner, member, or shareholder of that entity? . . . . | | ✓

If "Yes," the applicant is **not** eligible to make the change.

8a Does the applicable revenue procedure (advance consent or automatic consent) state that the applicant does not receive audit protection for the requested change (see instructions)? . . . . | | ✓

b If "Yes," attach an explanation.

9a Has the applicant, its predecessor, or a related party requested or made (under either an automatic change procedure or a procedure requiring advance consent) a change in method of accounting within the past 5 years (including the year of the requested change)? . . . . | | ✓

b If "Yes," for each trade or business, attach a description of each requested change in method of accounting (including the tax year of change) and state whether the applicant received consent.

c If any application was withdrawn, not perfected, or denied, or if a Consent Agreement granting a change was not signed and returned to the IRS, or the change was not made or not made in the requested year of change, attach an explanation.

10a Does the applicant, its predecessor, or a related party currently have pending any request (including any concurrently filed request) for a private letter ruling, change in method of accounting, or technical advice? . . . | | ✓

b If "Yes," for each request attach a statement providing the name(s) of the taxpayer, identification number(s), the type of request (private letter ruling, change in method of accounting, or technical advice), and the specific issue(s) in the request(s).

11 Is the applicant requesting to change its **overall** method of accounting? . . . . | | ✓

If "Yes," check the appropriate boxes below to indicate the applicant's present and proposed methods of accounting. Also, complete Schedule A on page 4 of this form.

| **Present method:** | ☐ Cash | ☐ Accrual | ☐ Hybrid (attach description) |
| **Proposed method:** | ☐ Cash | ☐ Accrual | ☐ Hybrid (attach description) |

Form **3115** (Rev. 12-2009)

Form 3115 (Rev. 12-2009)   Page **3**

Part II	Information For All Requests (continued)	Yes	No

12 If the applicant is either (i) **not** changing its overall method of accounting, or (ii) is changing its overall method of accounting and also changing to a special method of accounting for one or more items, attach a detailed and complete description for each of the following:

a The item(s) being changed.

b The applicant's present method for the item(s) being changed.

c The applicant's proposed method for the item(s) being changed.

d The applicant's present overall method of accounting (cash, accrual, or hybrid).

13 Attach a detailed and complete description of the applicant's trade(s) or business(es), and the principal business activity code for each. If the applicant has more than one trade or business as defined in Regulations section 1.446-1(d), describe: whether each trade or business is accounted for separately; the goods and services provided by each trade or business and any other types of activities engaged in that generate gross income; the overall method of accounting for each trade or business; and which trade or business is requesting to change its accounting method as part of this application or a separate application.

14 Will the proposed method of accounting be used for the applicant's books and records and financial statements? For insurance companies, see the instructions . . . .   ✓

If "No," attach an explanation.

15a Has the applicant engaged, or will it engage, in a transaction to which section 381(a) applies (e.g., a reorganization, merger, or liquidation) during the proposed tax year of change determined without regard to any potential closing of the year under section 381(b)(1)? . . . .   ✓

b If "Yes," for the items of income and expense that are the subject of this application, attach a statement identifying the methods of accounting used by the parties to the section 381(a) transaction immediately before the date of distribution or transfer and the method(s) that would be required by section 381(c)(4) or (c)(5) absent consent to the change(s) requested in this application.

16 Does the applicant request a conference with the IRS National Office if the IRS proposes an adverse response?   ✓

17 If the applicant is changing to either the overall cash method, an overall accrual method, or is changing its method of accounting for any property subject to section 263A, any long-term contract subject to section 460, or inventories subject to section 474, enter the applicant's gross receipts for the 3 tax years preceding the tax year of change.

1st preceding year ended: mo. yr.	2nd preceding year ended: mo. yr.	3rd preceding year ended: mo. yr.
$	$	$

Part III	Information For Advance Consent Request	Yes	No

18 Is the applicant's requested change described in any revenue procedure, revenue ruling, notice, regulation, or other published guidance as an automatic change request? . . . .   ✓

If "Yes," attach an explanation describing why the applicant is submitting its request under advance consent request procedures.

19 Attach a full explanation of the legal basis supporting the proposed method for the item being changed. Include a detailed and complete description of the facts that explains how the law specifically applies to the applicant's situation and that demonstrates that the applicant is authorized to use the proposed method. Include all authority (statutes, regulations, published rulings, court cases, etc.) supporting the proposed method. Also, include either a discussion of the contrary authorities or a statement that no contrary authority exists.

20 Attach a copy of all documents related to the proposed change (see instructions).

21 Attach a statement of the applicant's reasons for the proposed change.

22 If the applicant is a member of a consolidated group for the year of change, do all other members of the consolidated group use the proposed method of accounting for the item being changed? . . . .   ✓

If "No," attach an explanation.

23a Enter the amount of **user fee** attached to this application (see instructions). ▶ $ _____

b If the applicant qualifies for a reduced user fee, attach the required information or certification (see instructions).

Part IV	Section 481(a) Adjustment	Yes	No

24 Does the applicable revenue procedure, revenue ruling, notice, regulation, or other published guidance require the applicant to implement the requested change in method of accounting on a cut-off basis rather than a section 481(a) adjustment? . . .   ✓

If "Yes," do not complete lines 25, 26, and 27 below.

25 Enter the section 481(a) adjustment. Indicate whether the adjustment is an increase (+) or a decrease (-) in income. ▶ $ _____ -$245 Attach a summary of the computation and an explanation of the methodology used to determine the section 481(a) adjustment. If it is based on more than one component, show the computation for each component. If more than one applicant is applying for the method change on the same application, attach a list of the name, identification number, principal business activity code (see instructions), and the amount of the section 481(a) adjustment attributable to each applicant.

Form **3115** (Rev. 12-2009)

Attachment to Form 3115 for Tax Year 2015

Hank and Karin Roth

SS #123-45-6789, 987-65-4321

Answers to Questions:

12a) Applicant is deducting unclaimed depreciation for a washer bought for $400 in 2007 and a dryer bought for $300 in the same year.

12b) Present method: Applicant has previously not depreciated this property.

12c) Proposed method: Applicant is depreciating this property under the 7-year MACRS 200% declining balance method under Section 168.

12d) Overall method of accounting: Cash basis.

13)   The applicant is a family child care provider. She takes care of children in her home. The business activity code is 62441.

25)   Depreciation Calculation

Washer (asset class 00.11): $400

Dryer (asset class 00.11): $300

Total: $700

The Time-Space percentage was 35% for all the years of depreciation.

2007: $700 x 35% = $245 x 14.29%   = $35.01

2008: $700 x 35% = $245 x 24.49%   = $60.00

2009: $700 x 35% = $245 x 17.49%   = $42.85

2010: $700 x 35% = $245 x 12.49%   = $30.60

2011: $700 x 35% = $245 x 8.93%   = $21.88

2012: $700 x 35% = $245 x 8.92%   = $21.85

2013: $700 x 35% = $245 x 8.93%   = $21.88

2014: $700 x 35% = $245 x 4.46%   = $10.93

Total depreciation allowed 2007–2014 = $245.00

CHAPTER 11

Selling Your Business Property:
Form 4797

If you sold items that you used for your business this year, you may be able to claim some additional tax deductions by filing **Form 4797 Sales of Business Property** with your income tax forms. You should fill out **Form 4797** if you experienced any of the following situations last year:

- An item you're depreciating wears out before the end of its depreciation period.

- You sell your car.

- You sell your home or land.

- You sell property that was used in your business while you were still in business.

- Your business use drops to 50% or less for an item that you depreciated under Section 179 or accelerated rules, and you must recapture (pay back) some of the depreciation that you've claimed.

To illustrate these situations, we'll look at ten examples. Examples 1 and 2 show how to handle an item that wears out before the end of its depreciation period. Examples 3 through 6 deal with selling items that you're using in your business. Examples 7 through 9 show how to handle the sale of a vehicle, and example 10 explains how to recapture depreciation. Report the net gain or loss for all the sales (except for the car) that you show on **Form 4797** and on **Form 8829**, line 8.

Selling Your Home
The IRS rules issued in December 2002 have greatly simplified the tax consequences of selling your home. Most family child care providers will now be able to avoid paying any taxes on the profit made by selling a home but will still have to pay taxes on the home depreciation that has been claimed since May 6, 1997. For more information, see chapter 12.

An Item Wears Out during the Depreciation Period

Example 1

You've been providing child care since 2009. In January 2010, you install a new deck for $2,000. In March 2015, the deck is rotted out, and you demolish it. Later that year, you build a new deck and start depreciating it (see chapter 3 for instructions). You were depreciating the first deck over 39 years as a home improvement. Your Time-Space percentages have been as follows: 2010: 30%; 2011: 28%; 2012: 27%; 2013: 31%; 2014: 32%; 2015: 33%. Your depreciation deductions for 2010–2014 were as follows:

> 2010: $2,000 x 30% = $600 x 2.461% = $14.77
> 2011: $2,000 x 28% = $560 x 2.564% = $14.36
> 2012: $2,000 x 27% = $540 x 2.564% = $13.85
> 2013: $2,000 x 31% = $620 x 2.564% = $15.90
> 2014: $2,000 x 32% = $640 x 2.564% = $16.41
>
> Total claimed so far: $75.29

For 2015, you must first calculate the amount of depreciation you're entitled to for the last year you used the old deck in your business (2015):

> $2,000 x 33% = $660 x 2.564% = $16.92

Under the Half-Year Convention rules (see chapter 3), you can claim only half the normal depreciation for 2015 (you last used the deck in March 2015). Therefore, enter $8.46 ($16.92 x 50% = $8.46) on **Form 4562**, line 17, as your depreciation for 2014.

So far you've claimed a total of $83.75 for the old deck ($75.29 for 2010–2014 and $8.46 for 2015). Since the deck has now worn out, you're also entitled to claim the rest of the depreciation for the deck this year. The remaining depreciation that you haven't yet claimed amounts to $576.25 ($2,000 x 33% Time-Space percentage for 2015 = $660 – $83.75).

You'll claim this $576.25 as a loss on Part I of **Form 4797** because the deck was used in business for more than one year. (See example form at the end of chapter 11.) It is a loss because you weren't able to claim all the depreciation before the deck wore out. You'll carry over the total of this amount and any other amounts you enter here to **Form 1040**, line 14, where it will reduce your taxable income and thus your taxes.

If you are no longer in business when the deck wears out, you won't be able to claim this remaining depreciation; you can only claim a business loss if you're still in business.

Example 2

In 2012, you bought a microwave oven for $300 and started using it in your business. In 2015, the oven breaks down; you discard it and buy a new one. Your Time-Space percentages have been as follows: 2012: 35%; 2013: 38%; 2014: 37%; 2015: 36%. You've been depreciating the oven under seven-year 200% declining balance rules. Your depreciation deductions for 2012–2014 were as follows:

> 2012: $300 x 35% = $105 x 14.29% = $15.00
> 2013: $300 x 38% = $114 x 24.49% = $27.92
> 2014: $300 x 37% = $111 x 17.49% = $19.41
>
> Total claimed so far: $62.33

In 2015, the business basis of the microwave oven is $108 ($300 x 36% Time-Space percentage), so you can claim $6.74 in depreciation ($108 x 12.49% x 50%) on **Form 4562**, line 17. You can claim the remaining depreciation, $38.93 ($108 – $62.33 – $6.74), as a loss on Part I of **Form 4797**. You'll carry over this loss (and any other amounts in this section) to **Form 1040**, line 14. (This example is not shown on the forms at the end of this chapter.)

You Sell an Item You've Used for Business

There are special rules you must follow when you sell items that you've used in your business, and the reporting procedures differ depending on whether you have a gain or a loss on the sale. To determine that, follow these steps:

1. If you bought the item while you were in business, start with its original cost. If you bought it before you went into business, use the lesser of its original cost or its fair market value when you began using it for business. (This will usually be the item's fair market value.) This is the basis of the item.

2. Determine the total depreciation that you were entitled to claim on the item while using it for your business, using straight-line depreciation rules. Determine the total depreciation that you actually claimed for the item. Use the larger of these two amounts for the next step.

3. Subtract the item's total depreciation (step 2) from the item's basis (step 1). You must subtract all the depreciation that you could have claimed, even if you didn't claim it all. The result is the item's adjusted basis.

4. Subtract the adjusted basis (step 3) from the price you got for the item when you sold it. The result is your gain or loss on the sale.

IF YOU'RE NO LONGER IN BUSINESS

If you sell an item after you're no longer in business (or no longer using the item in your business), use the above calculations to determine if you have a gain or a loss, adjusting the basis of the item by any depreciation that you were entitled to claim. If you have a gain, enter it on **Schedule D** and **Form 1040** but not on **Form 4797**. If you have a loss, there are no further forms to fill out. Since you're no longer using the item in your business, you can't claim a deduction for a business loss.

IF THE ITEM WAS ORIGINALLY A GIFT

If someone gave you the item as a gift or as payment for child care services, use the donor's basis to determine your gain or loss for the item. The donor's basis is the lesser of the donor's adjusted basis (usually the original cost) of the item or its fair market value when it was given to you.

• If someone bought a $1,000 swing set in 2012 and gave it to you in that same year, you would use $1,000 as its basis and follow the calculations above.

• If someone bought a $1,000 swing set in 2008 and gave it to you in 2012, its 2012 fair market value would be less than $1,000. If you estimate it to be worth $600 in 2012, you would use $600 as your basis instead of the $1,000 purchase price.

Example 3: Item Used 100% for Business and Sold at a Gain

You started your business in 2010. In 2013 you buy a swing set to use 100% for your business. You're still in business on May 1, 2015, when you sell the swing set for $900.

$1,000   purchase price of swing set (2012)
– $475   depreciation claimed 2013–2015 (7-year 200% declining balance)

2013: $1,000 x 14.29%	= $142.90
2014: $1,000 x 24.49%	=$244.90
2015: $1,000 x 17.49% x 50%	=$87.45
Total:	$475.25

$525   adjusted basis of swing set

$900   sale price of swing set in 2015
– $525   adjusted basis
$375   gain

Report this gain on **Form 4797**, Part I, and carry it over to **Schedule D**, line 10 (see end-of-chapter example), along with any other amounts you've reported in this section. The amounts on line 8 will be totaled on line 17 and carried over to **Form 1040**, line 13, where they will increase your taxable income. Since this is not a business gain, you won't owe any additional Social Security tax on it.

Charitable Contributions

If you give an item to a charitable organization, either while you're in business or after you've closed your business, your deduction for it would be the lower of the fair market value of the item at the time you donated it or the adjusted basis of the item. Since a self-employed person can't claim a business deduction for a charitable contribution, report the donation on **Schedule A**, line 16.

For example, if you had given the swing set in example 3 to a charity on May 1, 2015, you could claim a charitable deduction of $525 ($1,000 – $475 depreciation = $525 adjusted basis) if its fair market value at that time was more than $525. If it was worth $500 at that time, you would deduct $500.

If you give an item away but *not* to a charitable organization before it's fully depreciated, you can't take any more depreciation deductions for that item.

Example 4: Item Used 40% for Business and Sold at a Gain

How would example 3 change if your own children also used the swing set and your Time-Space percentage was 40% each year?

$400   business basis of swing set ($1,000 purchase price x 40% Time-Space percentage)
– $190   depreciation claimed 2013–2015 (7-year 200% declining balance)

2013: $400 x 14.29%	= $57.16	
2014: $400 x 24.49%	= $97.96	
2015: $400 x 17.49% x 50%	= $34.98	(only a half year of depreciation because it was sold during the year)
Total:	$190.10	

$210   adjusted business basis of swing set

$360   business basis of swing set sale ($900 x 40%)
– $210   adjusted business basis
$150   gain

You'll report this gain on **Form 4797**, Part I, and **Form 8949**, Part II, and then transfer the gain to **Schedule D** (see example at end of chapter) and **Form 1040**. Since you've also used the swing set for personal use, there may also be personal tax consequences:

$600	personal basis of swing set ($1,000 purchase price x 60% personal use)
$540	personal basis of swing set sale ($900 x 60%)
$540	personal basis of sale
– $600	personal basis of purchase
($60)	personal loss

Since you can't deduct a personal loss, in this case you won't fill out any other forms; however, if you had a personal gain on the sale, you'd report it as income on **Schedule D**.

Example 5: Item Used 100% for Business and Sold at a Loss

How would Example 3 change if you sold the swing set in 2015 for $500?

$500	sale price of swing set in 2015
– $525	adjusted basis
($25)	loss

In this case, you would deduct the $25 loss as a business expense on **Form 4797**, Part I. (This example is not shown on the forms at the end of this chapter.)

Example 6: Item Used 40% for Business and Sold at a Loss

How would Example 3 change if you sold the swing set for $400, your own children used the swing set, and your Time-Space percentage was 40% each year?

$160	business basis of sale price ($400 x 40%)
– $190	adjusted business basis
($30)	business loss

Enter this $30 as a loss on **Form 4797**, Part I (see example at end of chapter). If your total gains and losses on **Form 4797** result in a loss, enter that amount onto **Form 1040**, line 14.

What If You Sell an Item at a Garage Sale?

The tax impact of selling an item at a garage sale is the same as in examples 3 through 6. You must take depreciation into account and calculate an adjusted basis for the item:

- If you never used the item sold in your business, report any gain you made on the sale on **Schedule D** and **Form 1040**. If you have a loss on the sale, don't report it on any tax form.

- If you're in business and you sell an item used in your business, report the business gain or loss on **Form 4797** and any personal gain on **Schedule D**.

- If you're no longer in business and you sell an item used in your business for a profit, report it as a gain on **Schedule D**. If you have a loss on the sale, don't report it on any tax form.

Because of the low prices at garage sales, it's unlikely that you'll have any gains to report on **Form 4797**, **Schedule D**, and **Form 1040**. You may, however, have business losses that you can claim on **Form 4797** and **Form 1040**. Although you're entitled to claim these losses, many child care providers probably wouldn't do so, and there's no penalty for not claiming them.

You Sell a Vehicle You've Used for Business

Calculating a gain or loss on the sale of a vehicle is a little more complicated than it is for other items; however, it's good to follow the special rules about selling a vehicle because often they'll allow you to claim a business loss and save taxes. The procedure you'll follow will depend on which method you've used to deduct your vehicle expenses.

ACTUAL VEHICLE EXPENSES METHOD

If you used the actual vehicle expenses method to claim your vehicle expenses, you have claimed a depreciation deduction. When the vehicle is sold, you will take your depreciation deductions into account as shown in the previous examples.

STANDARD MILEAGE RATE METHOD

If you used the standard mileage rate method to claim your vehicle expenses, you must do a special calculation to determine how much depreciation to apply to the sale. Each year you use the standard mileage rate method, part of the deduction is considered to be depreciation. Here are the depreciation amounts for the last several years:

2015	$0.24 per mile
2014	$0.22 per mile
2013	$0.23 per mile
2012	$0.23 per mile
2011	$0.22 per mile
2010	$0.23 per mile
2008–2009	$0.21 per mile
2007	$0.19 per mile
2004–2006	$0.17 per mile
2003	$0.16 per mile
2001–2002	$0.15 per mile
2000	$0.14 per mile
1994–1999	$0.12 per mile

Multiply your business miles for each year you used your vehicle in business by the appropriate depreciation amount. Add these results together to get the total depreciation you will use to determine the adjusted basis of your vehicle.

Example 7: Sale of a Vehicle without a Trade-In (Standard Mileage Rate)

In 2010, you buy a $15,000 vehicle and use it for business. You drive it 1,500 business miles in 2010, 1,400 miles in 2011, 1,700 miles in 2012, 1,452 miles in 2013, 1,130 miles in 2014, and 830 miles in 2015. You sell the vehicle in September 2015 for $4,000.

You use the standard mileage rate method every year, and your average business-use percentage this tax season is 20%. Here's how you would calculate your gain or loss on the sale:

Depreciation per year

1,500 miles in 2010 x $0.23 =	$345
1,400 miles in 2011 x $0.22 =	$308
1,700 miles in 2012 x $0.23 =	$391
1,452 miles in 2013 x $0.23 =	$334
1,130 miles in 2014 x $0.22 =	$249
830 miles in 2015 x $0.24 =	$199
Total:	$1,826

$3,000	business basis of vehicle ($15,000 purchase price x 20% business use)
– $1,826	depreciation claimed as part of standard mileage rate method
$1,174	adjusted business basis
$800	business basis of vehicle sold ($4,000 x 20% business use)
– $1,174	adjusted business basis
($374)	business loss

You can deduct this loss as a business expense on **Form 4797**, Part I. Enter –$374 on lines 11, 18a, and 18b and transfer –$374 to **Form 1040**, line 14.

Example 8: Sale of a Vehicle without a Trade-In (Actual Vehicle Expenses)

If you had used the actual vehicle expenses method instead, you'd use the depreciation that you could have claimed over the years (even if you didn't actually claim it). This example is otherwise like example 7 except that you're depreciating the vehicle based on 20% business use. After six years of use, you would have claimed the full amount of depreciation ($15,000 purchase price x 20% = $3,000).

$3,000	business basis of vehicle
– $3,000	depreciation claimed under actual vehicle expenses method
0	adjusted basis
$800	business basis of vehicle sold
– 0	adjusted basis
$800	business gain

You would report this gain as shown in example 3.

Selling a Vehicle with a Trade-In

If you trade your vehicle for another vehicle, you won't have a taxable gain or loss, because this transaction is considered to be a like-kind exchange. If you used the standard mileage rate method on your traded-in vehicle and the same method on your new vehicle, there is no tax consequence at the time of the trade-in. If you eventually sell your new vehicle without trading it in, you should follow the procedure in example 7.

If you used the standard mileage rate method on your traded-in vehicle and the actual vehicle expenses method (or Section 179) on your new vehicle, then you would base the depreciation for the new vehicle on the actual cash you paid for it, without reference to the amount you received for the trade-in. In other words, if your new vehicle cost $30,000 and you paid $22,000 in cash in addition to the $8,000 you received for the trade-in value of the old vehicle, you would base your depreciation deduction on $22,000.

If you use the actual vehicle expenses method on both your traded-in vehicle and your new vehicle, follow this procedure to determine the depreciation amount on the new car: Take the original price of the old car and subtract it from depreciation amount you claimed for the years you used it in your business. Then add the amount you paid for the new car. For example, if you paid $28,000 for the old car, claimed $3,449 in depreciation for the old car, and paid $10,000 (plus the traded-in old car) for the new car, the adjusted basis for depreciating the new car is $34,551 ($28,000 – $3,449 + $10,000).

Example 9: Sale of a Vehicle with a Trade-In

You originally purchased a car for $28,000, and for the last three years you have been using the actual vehicle expenses method to deduct your expenses for that vehicle. Your business-use percentage for all three years was 20%. In 2015, you bought a new car for

$10,000 ($10,000 cash plus the trade-in value for your old car). Here's how you would claim your depreciation deduction for 2015:

> Traded-in car: $28,000 x 20% business use = $5,600
> x 20% (4th year straight-line depreciation) = $1,120

Since the depreciation deduction limitation is $335 ($1,675 x 20% = $335), you can only claim $335. The depreciation basis for the new car is $34,551 (see above).

> New car: $34,551 x 20% business use = $6,910
> x 10% (1st year straight-line depreciation) = $691

Since the depreciation deduction limitation is $632 ($3,160 x 20% = $632), you can only claim $632 this year.

> Total depreciation claimed: $967 ($335 + $632)
> Enter $967 on **Form 4562**, line 27.

IRS **Notice 2002-4** doesn't clarify how to calculate the depreciation on the traded-in vehicle if your business-use percentage fluctuated during the years you used it in your business. I assume that you should use an average business-use percentage for the years you used it in your business and continue using this average percentage for the remaining depreciation period.

You Have to Recapture Some Depreciation

For a description of the many circumstances under which you might have to recapture depreciation, see chapter 3. This example is one of the most common scenarios: you used Section 179 to deduct the entire business portion of an item in the year you bought it, and then your business-use percentage dropped to 50% or below before the end of the item's depreciation period. In this case, you'll have to recapture some of the depreciation you've claimed by filling out Part IV of **Form 4797**.

Example 10: Business Use Drops below 50% after Using Section 179

In 2013, you used Section 179 to deduct a $1,000 set of children's furniture. Since you expected to use it 100% for business purposes, you deducted the entire $1,000 in 2013. In 2015, your own children began using the furniture 60% of the time. Since your business-use percentage dropped below 50% in 2014, you must recapture some of the Section 179 deduction you claimed by filling out lines 33–35 of **Form 4797** as follows:

Line 33: Enter "$1,000."

Line 34: Enter the amount of depreciation you would have been entitled to claim each year through 2015, under straight-line rules, if you had not used Section 179.

> 2013: $1,000 x 100% business use = $1,000 x 7.14% = $71.40
> 2014: $1,000 x 100% business use = $1,000 x 14.29% = $142.90
> 2015: $1,000 x 40% business use = $400 x 14.29%   = <u>$57.16</u>
> Total: $271.46

Line 35: Subtract line 34 from line 33:

> $1,000 – $271.46 = $728.54

Part IV	Recapture Amounts Under Sections 179 and 280F(b)(2) When Business Use Drops to 50% or Less (see instructions)		(a) Section 179	(b) Section 280F(b)(2)
33	Section 179 expense deduction or depreciation allowable in prior years.	33	$1,000	
34	Recomputed depreciation (see instructions)	34	$271	
35	Recapture amount. Subtract line 34 from line 33. See the instructions for where to report . .	35	$729	

Form **4797** (2015)

Also enter $729 on **Schedule C**, line 6 (other income). You'll have to pay Social Security tax and income tax on this amount. You could still claim the $57.16 as a depreciation deduction for 2014 on **Form 4562**.

If you went out of business by the end of 2015, you'd report the $729 as income on **Schedule C** and wouldn't be able to take any further depreciation deductions on the furniture.

If you remain in business, you'd report the $729 as income but would now be able to claim depreciation on the furniture in 2016 and beyond. (2016 would be the fourth year of depreciation; you'd be able to deduct $57.12 [$1,000 x 40% Time-Space percentage = $400 x 14.28% = $57.12]. You'd enter this amount on **Form 4562**, line 17.)

For more information about the tax issues discussed in this chapter, refer to the related topics in the other chapters of this book and the Redleaf Press *Family Child Care Record-Keeping Guide*.

Form **4797**

Department of the Treasury
Internal Revenue Service

Sales of Business Property
(Also Involuntary Conversions and Recapture Amounts
Under Sections 179 and 280F(b)(2))
▶ Attach to your tax return.
▶ Information about Form 4797 and its separate instructions is at *www.irs.gov/form4797.*

OMB No. 1545-0184

20**15**

Attachment
Sequence No. **27**

Name(s) shown on return
LUPE SERANNO

Identifying number
621-33-7454

1 Enter the gross proceeds from sales or exchanges reported to you for 2015 on Form(s) 1099-B or 1099-S (or substitute statement) that you are including on line 2, 10, or 20 (see instructions) . . . . . . | **1** |

Part I | **Sales or Exchanges of Property Used in a Trade or Business and Involuntary Conversions From Other Than Casualty or Theft—Most Property Held More Than 1 Year** (see instructions)

2 (a) Description of property	(b) Date acquired (mo., day, yr.)	(c) Date sold (mo., day, yr.)	(d) Gross sales price	(e) Depreciation allowed or allowable since acquisition	(f) Cost or other basis, plus improvements and expense of sale	(g) Gain or (loss) Subtract (f) from the sum of (d) and (e)
#1 DECK	1/8/2010	3/1/2015	$0	$84	$660	($576)
#3 SWING SET	1/1/2013	5/1/2015	$900	$475	$1,000	$375
#4 SWING SET	1/1/203	5/1/2015	$360	$190	$400	$150
#6 SWING SET	1/1/2013	5/1/2015	$160	$190	$400	($30
#7 VEHICLE	1/1/2010	9/1/2015	$800	$1,174	$3,000	($374)

3 Gain, if any, from Form 4684, line 39 . . . . | **3** |
4 Section 1231 gain from installment sales from Form 6252, line 26 or 37 . . . . | **4** |
5 Section 1231 gain or (loss) from like-kind exchanges from Form 8824 . . . . | **5** |
6 Gain, if any, from line 32, from other than casualty or theft. . . . . | **6** |
7 Combine lines 2 through 6. Enter the gain or (loss) here and on the appropriate line as follows: . . . . . . | **7** |

Form **8949**

Department of the Treasury
Internal Revenue Service

Sales and Other Dispositions of Capital Assets
▶ Information about Form 8949 and its separate instructions is at *www.irs.gov/form8949.*
▶ File with your Schedule D to list your transactions for lines 1b, 2, 3, 8b, 9, and 10 of Schedule D.

OMB No. 1545-0074

20**15**

Attachment
Sequence No. **12A**

Name(s) shown on return

Social security number or taxpayer identification number

Part II | **Long-Term.** Transactions involving capital assets you held more than 1 year are long term. For short-term transactions, see page 1.

Note: You may aggregate all long-term transactions reported on Form(s) 1099-B showing basis was reported to the IRS and for which no adjustments or codes are required. Enter the totals directly on Schedule D, line 8a; you aren't required to report these transactions on Form 8949 (see instructions).

You must check Box D, E, or F below. Check only one box. If more than one box applies for your long-term transactions, complete a separate Form 8949, page 2, for each applicable box. If you have more long-term transactions than will fit on this page for one or more of the boxes, complete as many forms with the same box checked as you need.

- ☐ **(D)** Long-term transactions reported on Form(s) 1099-B showing basis was reported to the IRS (see **Note** above)
- ☐ **(E)** Long-term transactions reported on Form(s) 1099-B showing basis was **not** reported to the IRS
- ☑ **(F)** Long-term transactions not reported to you on Form 1099-B

1 (a) Description of property (Example: 100 sh. XYZ Co.)	(b) Date acquired (Mo., day, yr.)	(c) Date sold or disposed of (Mo., day, yr.)	(d) Proceeds (sales price) (see instructions)	(e) Cost or other basis. See the **Note** below and see *Column (e)* in the separate instructions	Adjustment, if any, to gain or loss. If you enter an amount in column (g), enter a code in column (f). See the separate instructions. (f) Code(s) from instructions	(g) Amount of adjustment	(h) Gain or (loss). Subtract column (e) from column (d) and combine the result with column (g)
#3 SWING SET	1/1/2013	5/1/2015	$900	$1,000		($475)	$375
#4 SWING SET	1/1/2013	5/1/2015	$360	$400		($190)	150

SCHEDULE D (Form 1040)	Capital Gains and Losses	OMB No. 1545-0074
Department of the Treasury Internal Revenue Service (99)	► Attach to Form 1040 or Form 1040NR. ► Information about Schedule D and its separate instructions is at *www.irs.gov/scheduled*. ► Use Form 8949 to list your transactions for lines 1b, 2, 3, 8b, 9, and 10.	2015 Attachment Sequence No. 12

Name(s) shown on return | Your social security number

Part I   Short-Term Capital Gains and Losses—Assets Held One Year or Less

See instructions for how to figure the amounts to enter on the lines below. This form may be easier to complete if you round off cents to whole dollars.	(d) Proceeds (sales price)	(e) Cost (or other basis)	(g) Adjustments to gain or loss from Form(s) 8949, Part I, line 2, column (g)	(h) Gain or (loss) Subtract column (e) from column (d) and combine the result with column (g)
1a Totals for all short-term transactions reported on Form 1099-B for which basis was reported to the IRS and for which you have no adjustments (see instructions). However, if you choose to report all these transactions on Form 8949, leave this line blank and go to line 1b .				
1b Totals for all transactions reported on Form(s) 8949 with **Box A** checked				
2 Totals for all transactions reported on Form(s) 8949 with **Box B** checked				
3 Totals for all transactions reported on Form(s) 8949 with **Box C** checked				

4 Short-term gain from Form 6252 and short-term gain or (loss) from Forms 4684, 6781, and 8824 .	4	
5 Net short-term gain or (loss) from partnerships, S corporations, estates, and trusts from Schedule(s) K-1	5	
6 Short-term capital loss carryover. Enter the amount, if any, from line 8 of your **Capital Loss Carryover Worksheet** in the instructions	6	( )
7 **Net short-term capital gain or (loss).** Combine lines 1a through 6 in column (h). If you have any long-term capital gains or losses, go to Part II below. Otherwise, go to Part III on the back	7	

Part II   Long-Term Capital Gains and Losses—Assets Held More Than One Year

See instructions for how to figure the amounts to enter on the lines below. This form may be easier to complete if you round off cents to whole dollars.	(d) Proceeds (sales price)	(e) Cost (or other basis)	(g) Adjustments to gain or loss from Form(s) 8949, Part II, line 2, column (g)	(h) Gain or (loss) Subtract column (e) from column (d) and combine the result with column (g)
8a Totals for all long-term transactions reported on Form 1099-B for which basis was reported to the IRS and for which you have no adjustments (see instructions). However, if you choose to report all these transactions on Form 8949, leave this line blank and go to line 8b .				
8b Totals for all transactions reported on Form(s) 8949 with **Box D** checked				
9 Totals for all transactions reported on Form(s) 8949 with **Box E** checked				
10 Totals for all transactions reported on Form(s) 8949 with **Box F** checked.	#3 SWINGS $900 #4 SWINGS $360	$1,000 $400	($475) ($190)	$375 $150

11 Gain from Form 4797, Part I; long-term gain from Forms 2439 and 6252; and long-term gain or (loss) from Forms 4684, 6781, and 8824	11	
12 Net long-term gain or (loss) from partnerships, S corporations, estates, and trusts from Schedule(s) K-1	12	
13 Capital gain distributions. See the instructions	13	
14 Long-term capital loss carryover. Enter the amount, if any, from line 13 of your **Capital Loss Carryover Worksheet** in the instructions	14	( )
15 **Net long-term capital gain or (loss).** Combine lines 8a through 14 in column (h). Then go to Part III on the back	15	

For Paperwork Reduction Act Notice, see your tax return instructions.   Cat. No. 11338H   Schedule D (Form 1040) 2015

CHAPTER 12

Selling Your Home:
Form 4797 and Schedule D

In June 2013, the U.S. Supreme Court struck down the Defense of Marriage Act (DOMA) and ended federal discrimination against same-sex couples who are legally married under state law. This means a family child care provider who is legally married to a same-sex partner can take advantage of the ability to depreciate her home, even if the home is in her spouse's name. It also means that the same provider will be taxed on this depreciation when the home is sold.

When you sell your home, you potentially face two taxes. The first tax is on the depreciation you claimed (or were entitled to claim) for all the years you used your home for your business. The second tax is on the profit of the sale of your home. Almost every provider must pay the first tax but can avoid paying the second tax.

The Tax on the Depreciation of Your Home
When you use your home for business, you are entitled to depreciate its value. You always want to depreciate your home because doing so will usually generate a substantial deduction each year.

Here's a very simple example. You purchase your home for $200,000. Each year, your Time-Space percentage is 35%. You run your family child care business for seven years and then stop offering child care. Years later, you sell your home:

$200,000 x 35% = $70,000
Homes are depreciated over 39 years: $70,000 divided by 39 = $1,795
You used your home for your business for 7 years: $1,795 x 7 years = $12,565

Over the seven years, you were entitled to claim $12,565 of business deductions. (See chapter 3 for a discussion of how to depreciate your home.) As a result, when you sell you home, you will owe taxes on $12,565.

The tax rate you will pay on this amount depends on your tax bracket in the year you sell your home. The current tax rates are as follows:

- 10% if you are in the 10% tax bracket
- 15% if you are in the 15% tax bracket
- 25% if you are in the 25% or higher tax bracket (see page 145 for a description of the 2015 tax brackets)

If you sold your home in 2015, and you were in the 15% tax bracket, you would owe $1,885 in taxes ($12,565 x 15% = $1,885).

Important Note!

In the above example, you would owe $1,885 in taxes even if you didn't claim house depreciation for the seven years you were in business; this tax is due if you were entitled to claim house depreciation—even if you didn't! The IRS rules clearly state that if you were entitled to claim house depreciation in any tax year, you will be treated as if you did when you sell your home. You will owe this tax even if you do not offer child care services for many years before you sell your home. The only situation in which you would not be entitled to claim house depreciation (and therefore not have to pay taxes on it when you sell your home) is if you showed a loss in your business in any year. For example, if you showed a business loss for the last two tax years, you wouldn't owe any tax on depreciation for those years.

When you consider the above information, you should realize that you always want to depreciate your home, no matter what! You will owe the same amount in taxes on your home later, even if you didn't depreciate it. Depreciating your home can mean a significant tax deduction each year, so don't let anyone tell you it's not a good idea. If you did not depreciate your home in earlier years, you can amend your tax return (going back up to three years) or use **Form 3115** (see chapter 10) to recapture the depreciation (going back many years). The amount of depreciation subject to tax is the lower of the amount of depreciation claimed or the gain from the sale of the home.

Note: The tax on house depreciation is only due for depreciation claimed—or entitled to be claimed—after May 6, 1997.

The Tax on the Profit on the Sale of Your Home

Normally, when you sell something for a profit, you will owe a tax on this profit. So, if you bought your home for $200,000 and sold it for $275,000, you earned a profit of $75,000 that would be subject to taxes. You can avoid paying taxes on the first $250,000 ($500,000 if you are married) of the profit on the sale of your home, however, under a 2002 rule.

Let's say that you are married and sold your home for $750,000. You would only owe tax on $50,000 (the amount above the $500,000 of profit). This tax would be due in addition to the tax on the depreciation you claimed over the years. Because most providers will not make a profit of $250,000 (or $500,000!) on the sale of their home, you probably won't have to worry about this tax!

To take advantage of this rule you must meet two tests. First, you must be able to show that you owned your home for two of the last five years before you sold it. Second, you must show that you lived in your home (as your main home) for two of the last five years before you sold it. Before 2002, it was more difficult for providers to avoid paying a tax on this profit. Now it doesn't matter if you offered child care up until the day you sold your home or closed your child care business years before you sold your home. You can take advantage of this two-year rule if you claimed that some of the rooms in your home were used exclusively for your business over the years.

Additional Clarifications of the Home Sale Rule

- Any profit on the sale of vacant land that you own and use as part of your principal residence is also excluded from taxes (up to $250,000/$500,000 for both the home and the land), if sold at the same time as the home or within two years before or after that. (Vacant land that is sold by itself is subject to taxes.)

- If you use a building for your business that is a separate dwelling unit from your home, it will be subject to taxes when you sell it unless you can show two years of personal use (no business use) during the last five years.

- The rule doesn't clarify whether a detached garage is considered part of a principal residence and not subject to tax if it is sold. I believe that it should be considered part of the residence because it's part of the definition of the home given in **Publication 587 Business Use of Your Home**. Therefore, if your home meets the two-year personal use test, this will include a detached garage.

- If you set aside an area in your basement for your business, you don't have a separate dwelling unit (even with a separate entrance) unless there's no interior connection between the basement area and the rest of the home.

- If you sell your home at a loss and don't meet the two-year goal, you can deduct the business portion of your loss on **Form 4797**.

- Check with your state to see how it will treat the sale of a home. Although you may be able to exclude your gain from federal taxes, you may not be able to exclude it from state income taxes.

If You Still Don't Meet the Two-Year Test

The IRS has also issued a ruling that provides tax relief in some situations in which you sell a home that you have owned or used for less than two years or have sold a previous home within the past two years. The amount that is eligible under this rule is limited to the percentage of the two years that you fulfilled the requirements. So, if you owned and used a home for one year (half of the two-year requirement), you would be eligible to exclude up to half of the usual amount, or up to $125,000/$250,000.

This rule defines specific situations in which you may be able to exclude part of your gain on the sale of a home from taxes. To be eligible for this reduced exclusion, the primary reason that you are selling your home must be a change in employment, health considerations, or unforeseen circumstances:

- You can meet the change in employment test if your primary reason for selling your home is a change in the location of your business or a change in your spouse's place of employment. If the new place of employment is located at least 50 miles away from your home, the IRS will automatically assume that the primary purpose of the home sale is because of the change in employment.

- You can also take advantage of this rule if the home sale is due to health issues, such as age-related infirmities, a move in order to care for a family member, severe allergies, or emotional problems.

- The third trigger for the reduced exclusion is unforeseen circumstances, which include death, divorce or legal separation, a multiple-birth pregnancy, involuntary conversion of the home, a natural or human-made disaster, loss of a job in which the employee (your spouse) is eligible for unemployment compensation, a change in employment that results in an inability to pay housing costs and basic living expenses, or an act of war or terrorism that results in a casualty to the residence.

This reduced maximum exclusion may make it possible to avoid a tax on a home sale even if you haven't lived in or owned the home for two full years.

When You Would Have to Pay Taxes

Under these rules, there are only three situations in which you would owe a tax on the profit from the sale of a home:

- You operated your business in a building separate from your home and did not use this building for two years of personal use as a primary residence in the last five years of ownership. You would owe a tax on the separate building only.

- Your profit from the sale of the home that exceeds the $250,000/$500,000 exclusion amounts.

- You owned and used your home for less than two years before selling it and weren't able to meet the reduced exclusion exceptions of a change in place of employment, health issues, or unforeseen circumstances.

The Tax Rate

The tax rates on the profit from the sale of a home are listed below.

- 5% if you are in the 15% tax bracket

- 15% if you are in the 25% or higher tax bracket

How To Get a Copy of These Rules

For more information, see IRS **Publication 523 Selling Your Home** at www.irs.gov/pub523.

Home Sale Example

The home in this example was bought on January 1, 2002, and used for business from January 1, 2009, until it was sold on January 1, 2015. The owner's Time-Space percentage was 35% for each year.

Purchase Price ($75,000 home + $9,000 land)	$84,000
Depreciation claimed (2009–2015)	- $3,315
Adjusted basis of the home	$80,685

Sale Price (includes land)	$212,000
Expenses to sell the home	-$12,000
	$200,000
Adjusted basis of the home	-$80,685
Profit on the sale of the home	$119,315
Profit	$116,000
Profit that represents depreciation	$3,315

This provider will owe tax on the depreciation that she claimed (or was entitled to claim) after May 6, 1997 ($3,315). Since she owned and lived in this home for two of the last five years before it was sold, the $116,000 profit is excluded from taxes.

If she moved out of the home on January 1, 2015, and sells it on January 1, 2020, she wouldn't meet the two-year test of living in the home during the last five years before the sale, and therefore she would owe capital gains tax on the $116,000 (if the home was sold for $212,000 in 2020) as well as tax on the $3,315 in depreciation.

How to Calculate Your Depreciation

You must depreciate your home over 39 years if it was first put into business use after May 6, 1993. In the first year of business use, you would claim 2.461% of the adjusted business basis as a business deduction, and each year after that you would claim 2.546% of the adjusted business basis (see chapter 3).

In the example, the business basis of the home for depreciation purposes is $26,250 (35% x the original purchase price of $75,000, without counting the value of the land). This means that the home depreciation for the first year would be $643 ($26,250 x 2.451% = $643). The home depreciation for years two through five would be $2,672 ($26,250 x 2.546% = $668 x 4 years = $2,672). Thus the total depreciation is $3,315.

How to Fill Out the Tax Forms

When you sell your home, you must fill out **Form 8949** and **Schedule D**. We'll use the above example to show how to fill out these forms. First, let's look at a case in which the owner doesn't have to pay the tax on the profit on the sale of the home because she owned and lived in the home for two of the last five years; then we'll look at a case in which she doesn't meet this goal.

IF YOU'VE MET THE TWO-YEAR GOAL

In this case, you only have to pay tax on the depreciation that you claimed (or were entitled to claim) after May 6, 1997 ($3,315 in the example). Since you have met the two-year goal, your profit on the sale ($116,000 in the example) is excluded from taxes up to the exclusion amounts of $250,000 or $500,000. In this situation, you would fill out **Form 8949** and **Schedule D** as shown at the end of this chapter. The amount of $128,000 on **Form 8849**, line 1 (g) comes from adding the profit on the sale of the home ($116,000) to the expenses associated with selling the home ($12,000). Transfer the amount on **Schedule D**, line 16, to **Form 1040**, line 13, and add to it your other income for the year.

Accurately filling out the required tax forms when you sell your home is complicated. First, fill out **Form 8949**. Next, fill out **Schedule D**. Before you can fill out **Schedule D** you must complete the worksheet for unrecaptured section 1250 gains (found in the instructions for **Schedule D**). Enter the depreciation you claimed while you used your home for your business on line 18 of this worksheet ($3,315 in our example) and then transfer this amount to line 19 of **Schedule D**. Finally, transfer the amount from line 16 on **Schedule D** to line 13 on **Form 1040**. Your depreciation amount ($3,315 in our example) will be added to your other ordinary income.

Here is one more complication: The highest tax rate you can pay on your depreciation is 25%. If your family's income is higher than this bracket (more than $151,200 if you are filing jointly, or $90,750 if single) then you should fill out the tax worksheet in the instructions to **Schedule D** before transferring your depreciation to **Form 1040**. If you are in a higher tax bracket, this worksheet will demonstrate how to pay only 25% tax on your depreciation. This worksheet, as well as **Schedule D**, can be extremely difficult to follow. I recommend consulting with a tax professional before filling out these worksheets and **Schedule D** on your own.

IF YOU HAVEN'T MET THE TWO-YEAR GOAL (NOT SHOWN ON THE TAX FORMS AT THE END OF THIS CHAPTER)
In this case, you will owe the tax on your profit ($116,000 in our example) as well as taxes on the depreciation that you claimed (or were entitled to claim) after May 6, 1997. Fill out **Form 8949** and **Schedule D**.

The provider in the example sold her home after May 6, 2007, and she is in the 25% tax bracket, so the tax rate on her profit on the sale would be 15%, or $17,400. She would add to this the tax on her depreciation, $829 ($3,315 x 25% = $829), for a total tax bill of $18,229.

Note: If you sold your home, made a profit of less than $250,000 (or $500,000 if married), and were not entitled to depreciate your home (because you showed business losses for each year you were in business), do not fill out **Form 8949** or **Schedule D**.

Other Points to Consider

The longer you use your home for business after May 6, 1997, the more tax you'll have to pay on depreciation when you sell your home. For example, let's say that the basis of your home is $100,000, you use 39-year depreciation rules, and your Time-Space percentage is 35%. If you sell your home five years after May 6, 1997, you'll owe tax on $4,485. If you sell it ten years after May 6, 1997, you'll owe tax on $8,970. If you sell it fifteen years after May 6, 1997, you'll owe tax on $13,455. (This assumes that your gain on the sale is at least equal to these amounts.)

HOME IMPROVEMENTS
If you've made home improvements while living in your home, you can reduce the profit on the sale of your home. You can increase the basis of the home by the cost of the improvement and then decrease the basis by the amount of depreciation you claimed (or were entitled to claim) on the improvement. The more home improvements you make on your home, the lower your gain will be when you sell your home. This will only be important if the profit of your home is over the $250,000 or $500,000 exclusion limits.

LAND IMPROVEMENTS

If you've been depreciating land improvements using the 150% declining balance method (see chapter 3), you may need to recapture some of that depreciation when you sell your home. The amount that you will have to recapture and pay income tax on is the difference between the depreciation that you claimed using the 150% declining balance method and the depreciation that you would have claimed with the straight-line method. Report this amount on **Form 4797**, Part IV, and then transfer it to **Schedule C**, line 6.

Like-Kind Exchanges

One way to avoid paying the tax on the sale of a home is to conduct a like-kind exchange. If you expect to make a profit on the sale of your home over the limits of $250,000 or $500,000, you may want to consider a like-kind exchange. The Tax Code states that "no gain or loss shall be recognized if property held for productive use in trade or business . . . is exchanged solely for property of a like-kind to be held for productive use in trade or business." This means that you can exchange your old home for a new one and avoid most of the taxes you would otherwise owe, even if you don't meet the two-year test. (Doing a like-kind exchange does allow you to defer paying taxes on depreciation claimed after May 6, 1997, but eventually you will have to pay tax on this depreciation.) To take advantage of the like-kind exchange rules, you have to intend to continue providing child care in your new home.

The best way to do a like-kind exchange is to hire an intermediary to handle the transactions and ensure that all the proper rules are followed. You are allowed 180 days after closing on your old home, but before you've received the money from the sale, to conduct a like-kind exchange. Once you've accepted the money from the sale of your home, you can no longer do a like-kind exchange.

Conducting a like-kind exchange is far more complicated than described here. You should hire a qualified intermediary to handle this complicated transaction. I strongly urge you to talk to a tax professional before you sell your home and use a tax preparer, lawyer, or real estate professional to help you follow the requirements of the law. For more information, see **Form 8824**, **Publication 544**, and the *Record-Keeping Guide*.

Changes in Marital Status

Changes in your marital status can complicate the tax impact of selling your home. If you're planning to marry or divorce, you should consult a tax professional to find out how the home sale rules will apply in your situation.

For more information about the tax issues discussed in this chapter, refer to the related topics in the other chapters of this book and the Redleaf Press *Family Child Care Record-Keeping Guide*.

Form 8949 (2015)   Attachment Sequence No. **12A**   Page **2**

Name(s) shown on return. Name and SSN or taxpayer identification no. not required if shown on other side	Social security number or taxpayer identification number

Before you check Box D, E, or F below, see whether you received any Form(s) 1099-B or substitute statement(s) from your broker. A substitute statement will have the same information as Form 1099-B. Either will show whether your basis (usually your cost) was reported to the IRS by your broker and may even tell you which box to check.

Part II   **Long-Term.** Transactions involving capital assets you held more than 1 year are long term. For short-term transactions, see page 1.

Note: You may aggregate all long-term transactions reported on Form(s) 1099-B showing basis was reported to the IRS and for which no adjustments or codes are required. Enter the totals directly on Schedule D, line 8a; you aren't required to report these transactions on Form 8949 (see instructions).

You **must** check Box D, E, **or** F below. **Check only one box.** If more than one box applies for your long-term transactions, complete a separate Form 8949, page 2, for each applicable box. If you have more long-term transactions than will fit on this page for one or more of the boxes, complete as many forms with the same box checked as you need.

- ☐ **(D)** Long-term transactions reported on Form(s) 1099-B showing basis was reported to the IRS (see **Note** above)
- ☐ **(E)** Long-term transactions reported on Form(s) 1099-B showing basis was **not** reported to the IRS
- ☑ **(F)** Long-term transactions not reported to you on Form 1099-B

1 (a) Description of property (Example: 100 sh. XYZ Co.)	(b) Date acquired (Mo., day, yr.)	(c) Date sold or disposed of (Mo., day, yr.)	(d) Proceeds (sales price) (see instructions)	(e) Cost or other basis. See the **Note** below and see *Column (e)* in the separate instructions	(f) Code(s) from instructions	(g) Amount of adjustment	(h) Gain or (loss). Subtract column (e) from column (d) and combine the result with column (g)
MAIN HOME 12 ELM STREET	1/1/2002	1/1/2015	$212,000	$80,685	EH	($128,000)	$3,315
2 Totals. Add the amounts in columns (d), (e), (g), and (h) (subtract negative amounts). Enter each total here and include on your Schedule D, **line 8b** (if **Box D** above is checked), **line 9** (if **Box E** above is checked), or **line 10** (if **Box F** above is checked) ▶			$212,000	$80,685		($128,000)	$3,315

Note: If you checked Box D above but the basis reported to the IRS was incorrect, enter in column (e) the basis as reported to the IRS, and enter an adjustment in column (g) to correct the basis. See *Column (g)* in the separate instructions for how to figure the amount of the adjustment.

Form **8949** (2015)

SCHEDULE D
(Form 1040)

Department of the Treasury
Internal Revenue Service (99)

Capital Gains and Losses

▶ Attach to Form 1040 or Form 1040NR.
▶ Information about Schedule D and its separate instructions is at *www.irs.gov/scheduled*.
▶ Use Form 8949 to list your transactions for lines 1b, 2, 3, 8b, 9, and 10.

OMB No. 1545-0074

2015

Attachment
Sequence No. **12**

Name(s) shown on return

Your social security number

Part I Short-Term Capital Gains and Losses—Assets Held One Year or Less

See instructions for how to figure the amounts to enter on the lines below. This form may be easier to complete if you round off cents to whole dollars.	**(d)** Proceeds (sales price)	**(e)** Cost (or other basis)	**(g)** Adjustments to gain or loss from Form(s) 8949, Part I, line 2, column (g)	**(h) Gain or (loss)** Subtract column (e) from column (d) and combine the result with column (g)
1a Totals for all short-term transactions reported on Form 1099-B for which basis was reported to the IRS and for which you have no adjustments (see instructions). However, if you choose to report all these transactions on Form 8949, leave this line blank and go to line 1b .				
1b Totals for all transactions reported on Form(s) 8949 with **Box A** checked				
2 Totals for all transactions reported on Form(s) 8949 with **Box B** checked				
3 Totals for all transactions reported on Form(s) 8949 with **Box C** checked				

4 Short-term gain from Form 6252 and short-term gain or (loss) from Forms 4684, 6781, and 8824 .	**4**	
5 Net short-term gain or (loss) from partnerships, S corporations, estates, and trusts from Schedule(s) K-1	**5**	
6 Short-term capital loss carryover. Enter the amount, if any, from line 8 of your **Capital Loss Carryover Worksheet** in the instructions	**6** ( )
7 **Net short-term capital gain or (loss).** Combine lines 1a through 6 in column (h). If you have any long-term capital gains or losses, go to Part II below. Otherwise, go to Part III on the back	**7**	

Part II Long-Term Capital Gains and Losses—Assets Held More Than One Year

See instructions for how to figure the amounts to enter on the lines below. This form may be easier to complete if you round off cents to whole dollars.	**(d)** Proceeds (sales price)	**(e)** Cost (or other basis)	**(g)** Adjustments to gain or loss from Form(s) 8949, Part II, line 2, column (g)	**(h) Gain or (loss)** Subtract column (e) from column (d) and combine the result with column (g)
8a Totals for all long-term transactions reported on Form 1099-B for which basis was reported to the IRS and for which you have no adjustments (see instructions). However, if you choose to report all these transactions on Form 8949, leave this line blank and go to line 8b .				
8b Totals for all transactions reported on Form(s) 8949 with **Box D** checked				
9 Totals for all transactions reported on Form(s) 8949 with **Box E** checked				
10 Totals for all transactions reported on Form(s) 8949 with **Box F** checked.	$212,000	$80,685	($128,000)	$3,315

11 Gain from Form 4797, Part I; long-term gain from Forms 2439 and 6252; and long-term gain or (loss) from Forms 4684, 6781, and 8824	**11**	$3,315
12 Net long-term gain or (loss) from partnerships, S corporations, estates, and trusts from Schedule(s) K-1	**12**	
13 Capital gain distributions. See the instructions	**13**	
14 Long-term capital loss carryover. Enter the amount, if any, from line 13 of your **Capital Loss Carryover Worksheet** in the instructions	**14** ( )
15 **Net long-term capital gain or (loss).** Combine lines 8a through 14 in column (h). Then go to Part III on the back	**15**	$3,315

For Paperwork Reduction Act Notice, see your tax return instructions.   Cat. No. 11338H   **Schedule D (Form 1040) 2015**

Schedule D (Form 1040) 2015   Page **2**

Part III   **Summary**

16 Combine lines 7 and 15 and enter the result **16** $3,315

- If line 16 is a **gain,** enter the amount from line 16 on Form 1040, line 13, or Form 1040NR, line 14. Then go to line 17 below.
- If line 16 is a **loss,** skip lines 17 through 20 below. Then go to line 21. Also be sure to complete line 22.
- If line 16 is **zero,** skip lines 17 through 21 below and enter -0- on Form 1040, line 13, or Form 1040NR, line 14. Then go to line 22.

17 Are lines 15 and 16 **both** gains?
☐ **Yes.** Go to line 18.
☐ **No.** Skip lines 18 through 21, and go to line 22.

18 Enter the amount, if any, from line 7 of the **28% Rate Gain Worksheet** in the instructions . . ▶ **18**

19 Enter the amount, if any, from line 18 of the **Unrecaptured Section 1250 Gain Worksheet** in the instructions . . . . ▶ **19** $3,315

20 Are lines 18 and 19 **both** zero or blank?
☐ **Yes.** Complete the **Qualified Dividends and Capital Gain Tax Worksheet** in the instructions for Form 1040, line 44 (or in the instructions for Form 1040NR, line 42). **Do not** complete lines 21 and 22 below.

☐ **No.** Complete the **Schedule D Tax Worksheet** in the instructions. **Do not** complete lines 21 and 22 below.

21 If line 16 is a loss, enter here and on Form 1040, line 13, or Form 1040NR, line 14, the **smaller** of:

- The loss on line 16 or
- ($3,000), or if married filing separately, ($1,500) } . . . . **21** (   )

Note: When figuring which amount is smaller, treat both amounts as positive numbers.

22 Do you have qualified dividends on Form 1040, line 9b, or Form 1040NR, line 10b?

☐ **Yes.** Complete the **Qualified Dividends and Capital Gain Tax Worksheet** in the instructions for Form 1040, line 44 (or in the instructions for Form 1040NR, line 42).

☐ **No.** Complete the rest of Form 1040 or Form 1040NR.

Schedule D (Form 1040) 2015

CHAPTER 13

Closing Your Child Care Business

From a tax point of view, it's almost as easy to close your child care business as it is to start it. You don't need to notify the IRS of your decision to quit. (Check your state revenue department to see if your state has any special requirements.) If you ended your business in 2014, however, there are some tax issues that you should review carefully, especially in regard to depreciation.

Depreciation Issues

General Depreciation Rule

In general, if you go out of business before you have fully depreciated your property, you stop claiming depreciation and forfeit the ability to claim the remainder of the depreciation. In addition, you don't have to report any of the depreciation you have already claimed as income. This includes any depreciation you claimed using the 50% or 100% bonus depreciation rules. There are two exceptions to this general depreciation rule: Section 179 depreciation and accelerated depreciation on a vehicle (see next page).

The Half-Year Convention

For items you've been depreciating under the Half-Year Convention rules (see chapter 3), you can only claim a half year's worth of the normal depreciation in the year you end your business. The items covered by this convention include personal property, land improvements, and vehicles.

For example, you bought a washer in 2013 for $500 and used it in your business until you closed your business in 2015. Your Time-Space percentage in 2015 is 35%, and you've been using straight-line depreciation. Your depreciation deduction for the washer in 2015 would normally be $25 ($500 x 35% x 14.29% [Year 3 depreciation rate] = $25); however, if you went out of business last year, you can only claim half of this amount, or $12.50.

If you bought these items in 2015 and went out of business in 2015, you would claim the normal amount of depreciation for them, since you only get a half year's worth of depreciation in the first year using the Half-Year Convention rules.

The Mid-Month Convention

For items you've been depreciating under the Mid-Month Convention rules (see chapter 3), you can claim only a prorated part of the normal depreciation in the year you end your business, based on the month you quit. The items covered by this convention include your home and home improvements.

For example, you bought a new roof in 2014 for $6,000 and went out of business in July 2015. Your Time-Space percentage in 2015 is 30%. Your normal depreciation for all of 2015 would be $46.15 ($6,000 x 30% x 2.564%). You are considered to be in business for 6.5 months in 2015, because the month you go out of business counts for half of a month. Thus, multiply $46.15 by 6.5 months and divide by 12 months. The result, $25.00, is your depreciation deduction for 2015.

Section 179

If you used Section 179 rules (see chapter 3) on any personal property items while you were in business, check to see whether the recovery period has run out for each item. This period is five years for computers and vehicles, and seven years for furniture, appliances, TVs, VCRs, DVD players, and large play equipment. If the recovery period is still in effect, you'll have to pay additional taxes to recapture the unused depreciation (see chapter 11).

Recapturing Accelerated Depreciation on a Vehicle

If you use accelerated depreciation (the 200% declining balance method) to depreciate a vehicle that you use more than 50% for business, and your business use of the vehicle falls below 50% during the five-year recovery period, you will have to recapture some of the depreciation that you claimed and report it as income. Use the rules for recapturing depreciation described in chapter 11. You would also need to recapture some depreciation if you had used the 50% or 100% bonus depreciation rules on the vehicle. You do not have to recapture depreciation if you used the 50% or 100% bonus depreciation rules on any other property.

Going Out of Business Checklist

If you closed your business in 2015, here's a checklist of some other business reminders and tax issues that could affect your tax return:

❑ Make sure that you've taken all the depreciation you're entitled to on your home and other property used in your business. If you haven't, use **Form 3115** to take these deductions in 2015 (see chapter 10). They can add up to a large amount, and if you went out of business in 2015, this will be your last chance to claim them.

❑ If you paid employees in 2015 (including your spouse and children), be sure to file **Form 941** or **Form 944** to report wages for Social Security and Medicare taxes for the quarter you quit. Check the box at the top of the form to indicate that you won't be filing any more of these forms. File **Form 940** at the end of the year, as usual. You must file **Form W-2** by the date the next **Form 941** is due and file **Form W-3** one month later (see chapter 8).

❑ If you weren't in business until December 31, adjust the number of hours on **Form 8829**, line 5. For example, if you ended your business on August 31, write in 5,856 hours (the number of hours from January 1 to August 31). Enter on **Form 8829** only expenses that you incurred during this time period. In this case, you would enter only 67% (5,832 hours divided by 8,760 total hours in the year) of your mortgage interest, real estate taxes, and homeowners insurance, and you would enter your actual expenses for utilities, home repairs, and maintenance for these months.

❑ It's a good idea to send a letter to the parents of the children in your care officially informing them of your decision to end your business. Keep a copy of the letter for your files. Take photographs that show you have converted your play areas back to personal use.

❑ If you're planning to sell your home in the next few years, consult a tax professional about how to reduce your tax liability when selling your home.

❑ Since you'll file your final business forms this tax season, you won't need to file **Schedule C**, **Form 4562**, **Form 8829**, or **Schedule SE** for 2015.

❑ If you have any carryover expenses from **Form 8829** in your last year of business, you won't be able to claim them after your business ends.

❑ Notify your state regulatory department, local child care resource and referral agency, Food Program sponsor, and local family child care association that you are going out of business so they can update their records.

❑ If you sell any items you've used in your business *before* you go out of business, you may be entitled to a business deduction or (more rarely) need to report some additional business income. See chapter 11 for details.

❑ Contact your insurance agent to review your policies (homeowners, business liability, and car) to see if you are entitled to a refund.

The IRS does not consider you to have gone out of business if you simply move from one home to another and continue your child care business in your new home. Your business has continued, even if you're operating at a new location. You'll still file one **Schedule C**, **Form 4562**, and **Schedule SE**. You will need to file two **Form 8829**s, showing your Time-Space percentage and expenses for each home separately.

If you go out of business and later decide to start up again, just start claiming your income and expenses as if you were beginning your business for the first time. To claim depreciation for items that you used before, use the lower of the item's fair market value or its adjusted basis at the time you start using it again for your business (see chapter 3).

For more information about the tax issues discussed in this chapter, refer to the related topics in the other chapters of this book and the Redleaf Press *Family Child Care Record-Keeping Guide*.

CHAPTER 14

Dealing with an Audit

Although your chances of being audited are less than 2%, if you are audited, your best defense is to have good records for your business. You should keep documents such as receipts, bills, record books, and menus for at least three years after the date you file your tax return. Keep the records for items that you are depreciating (such as your home, personal property, and business equipment) for the depreciation period plus three years. In other words, if you began depreciating your stove in 2014, you should keep the receipt for eight years (the depreciation period) plus three years, or until the year 2025.

You may wish to bring another person with you to the audit, such as your spouse, a friend, your tax preparer, a certified public accountant, an enrolled agent, an enrolled federal tax accountant, or an attorney. Sometimes it can help to have another person in the room, especially someone who is more objective or familiar with the audit process.

When auditing a family child care business, IRS auditors often target the following five areas of the tax return:

- unreported income
- Time-Space percentage
- food expenses
- shared business and personal expenses
- business mileage

Unreported Income

The first thing the auditor is likely to do is ask you to identify the source of all the deposits to your personal and business bank accounts. You should mark the source of every deposit on the deposit slip, your check register, or your computer software program, even if they are simply transfers from one account to another. Label each business deposit by the parent's name. If you can't account for a deposit, the IRS is likely to assume that it is business income and will tax it.

Time-Space Percentage

The auditor may challenge your Time-Space percentage. You need to have records showing the hours you worked and that the space you are claiming was used on a regular basis for your business. The higher your Time-Space percentage is, the more closely the IRS will examine your records. Don't let the auditor challenge your right to count the hours you spent cooking, cleaning, and planning activities for your business (see chapter 1).

Food Expenses

With the passage of the standard meal allowance rule (see chapter 4), the IRS may be less likely to challenge your food expenses in an audit. The only question is likely to be whether you can prove that you served the number of meals and snacks that you are claiming. The meals reimbursed by the Food Program will appear on your monthly claim forms, but you must keep very careful daily records of all the meals and snacks you serve that aren't reimbursed by the Food Program. If you are claiming food expenses based on the actual cost of food, be sure to keep all your business and personal food receipts.

Shared Business and Personal Expenses

The auditor may try to claim that some of your business expenses are personal, especially items such as household supplies and repairs. To support your case, you can take pictures that show children using the item or get letters from parents.

Business Mileage

Auditors have sometimes held that a provider can't deduct any miles for a trip in which some personal items were purchased; however, this is not what the law says. It says that you may deduct all of the miles for a trip if it is *primarily* for business purposes.

Avoiding an Audit

No one wants to be audited by the IRS. It's a scary prospect that most of us would do just about anything to avoid. Instead of worrying about whether you'll be audited, focus on keeping the proper records for your business. If your records are complete and organized, you have nothing to fear from an audit.

For example, I often hear people say, "I don't claim all my allowable expenses because I'm afraid I'll be audited" or "I used a lower Time-Space percentage than I really had because I didn't want to trigger an audit." It isn't a good idea to think like this. You have little control over *if* you'll be audited; your real concern should be "If I'm audited, do I have the records to back up my deductions?" If the answer is yes, you have little to worry about.

People also ask, "If I claim many deductions that I haven't claimed before, my expenses will be a lot higher than usual. Will the IRS notice and audit my return?" Again, don't worry about this. Just claim the deductions that you're entitled to and keep the records to back them up.

In an audit you can submit records and receipts for expenses that you didn't originally claim on your tax return to offset any deductions the auditor disallows (or even to give you a refund). For example, you could claim a higher Time-Space percentage or a larger business food expense. (If you discover additional deductions after the audit is completed, ask the IRS to reopen your case. If the IRS won't do this, you can file an amended return up to three years after you filed the original return, even after being audited.)

Errors by Your Tax Preparer

You're always responsible for paying the proper taxes, even if your tax preparer has made a mistake on your return. That's why it's important to make sure that you understand what your tax preparer has done. If the mistake was the tax preparer's error, a good tax preparer will pay some, if not all, of the interest that is because of the mistake. (Tax preparers aren't required to pay this, however.) If you knew that what your tax preparer did was wrong, you should pay the penalty. If you didn't know that it was wrong, ask your tax preparer to pay the penalty. (It's best to find out your tax preparer's policy on this issue when you hire the preparer.)

You Have the Right to Appeal

Remember that some auditors aren't familiar with the unique way that the tax rules apply to family child care businesses, so an auditor may not be aware of all the deductions you're entitled to. When this happens, some providers have told the auditor, "Tom Copeland said I could do it in his *Tax Workbook*!" Although I've tried to interpret the tax laws and show you how to apply them in a reasonable manner, in any specific situation they may be subject to various interpretations. If there's a dispute, ask your auditor to justify his or her interpretation with a written reference. (If you need more help, refer to the resources listed on the next page.)

If you don't agree with your auditor's findings, you have a right to ask that the auditor's supervisor review the problem. If you aren't satisfied with the supervisor's decision, you have the right to appeal. Do your best to settle the matter with the auditor and the supervisor first.

Appealing the decision is a relatively simple matter. Tell your auditor that you want to appeal. Better yet, put your request for an appeal in writing. When you appeal, your auditor will write up the facts of your case and pass them on to an appeals officer; however, your auditor (or your auditor's supervisor) may offer to settle your case before sending it to appeal.

Appearing before the appeals officer is an informal affair. Bring your tax preparer (or even better, have your tax preparer appear without you). If you can't resolve the case here, you can appeal to the U.S. Tax Court. There is a $60 filing fee to appeal to the Tax Court (there's no fee for the appeals up to this point). You can choose to go before the "S-Court," which handles disputes that involve only a few thousand dollars. Although you don't need a lawyer to appear before the Tax Court, it's common to hire professional assistance at this level. (For more information on this process, refer to **Publication 556**.)

Get the Help You Need

If you're audited, you don't have to do it alone; get the help you need. We recommend that you hire a tax professional to assist you. To be qualified to represent you before the IRS, this person must be an enrolled agent, a certified public accountant, or an attorney.

- Check my website, www.tomcopelandblog.com, for a wealth of resource materials and a special section on audits. This site has copies of all the IRS rulings and Tax Court cases that involve family child care businesses.

- Get the text of the IRS **Child Care Provider Audit Technique Guide** at my website (www.tomcopelandblog.com) or the IRS website (www.irs.gov/Businesses /Small-Businesses-&-Self-Employed/Child-Care-Provider-Audit-Technique-Guide). Although this guide doesn't have the force of law, it can help you understand what your auditor may be looking for. You can challenge its interpretations, but if you do you should be prepared to cite some other authority for your position. (The statements in the **Child Care Provider Audit Technique Guide** may need to be modified based on new laws, Tax Court cases, IRS Revenue Rulings, and IRS Revenue Procedures that have been released since its publication.)

IRS Taxpayer Advocate Service

If you have one of the following problems or an ongoing issue with the IRS that hasn't been resolved through normal processes, you can call the IRS Taxpayer Advocate Service (877-777-4778, 24 hours a day) for help:

- You're suffering, or are about to suffer, a significant hardship.
- You're facing an immediate threat of adverse action.
- You're about to incur significant costs (including fees for professional representation).
- You haven't received a response or resolution by the date promised.
- You've experienced a delay of more than 30 days to resolve an issue.

For more information about the tax issues discussed in this chapter, refer to the related topics in the other chapters of this book and the Redleaf Press *Family Child Care Record-Keeping Guide*.

PART IV

Appendixes

APPENDIX A

Sample Tax Return

Sandy James began her child care business on January 1, 2012. She has one child of her own, Vanessa, age three, and she cares for six children, ages two through eight. Sandy's husband, Bill, earned $40,000 in 2015 as a construction worker. His **Form W-2** shows that he had $5,800 withheld in federal taxes and $1,200 withheld in state taxes. He paid $4,104 in medical bills in 2015. Sandy's Time-Space percentage is 35%. Let's see how Sandy should fill out her tax forms.

Sandy's first task will be to organize her records by income and expense categories, using the worksheets in the Tax Organizer. Next, she'll place the worksheets next to the proper tax form. A step-by-step process of how she'll fill out her tax forms follows. You can also refer to the copies of her completed forms at the end of this appendix.

In this example, the numbers on the tax forms will be rounded to the nearest dollar, as you should also do on your tax forms. (The deductions in this sample tax return aren't intended to be used as a guideline. Your deductions may be significantly more or less than shown here.)

Form 8829 Expenses for Business Use of Your Home

Lines 1–7: Sandy has a Time-Space percentage of 35%.

Line 8: Sandy carries forward her tentative profit from **Schedule C**, line 29, to this line on **Form 8829**.

Lines 10–14: Sandy enters her deductible mortgage interest ($5,000) and real estate taxes ($3,000) in column (b) because they also have a personal component. She multiplies the total ($8,000) by her Time-Space percentage (35%) from line 7, and enters the result on lines 13 and 14.

Lines 17–25: Homeowners insurance ($1,500) and utilities (gas, electricity, water, sewer, cable TV, and trash hauling = $2,000) go in column (b) because they have a personal component. A $15 replacement of a window broken by a child in her care is a 100% business expense and goes on line 19, column (a). A screen door that cost $85 to repair was damaged by normal wear and tear and goes on line 19, column (b). Sandy multiplies the total of the items in column (b) ($3,585) by her Time-Space percentage (39%) from line 7. She adds to the result ($1,398) the $15 from column (a) and enters the total ($1,243) on line 25.

Lines 29, and 36–41: Sandy skips to Part III to enter her home depreciation (the information she's using to calculate her home depreciation is shown on page 231, under **Form 4562**). Sandy enters "2.564%" on line 40 because that's the percentage for a full year of depreciation for a home that was first used for business in 2012. She enters "$1,303" ($1,283 + $20, see page 231) on line 41 and line 29.

Line 30:   Sandy was unable to claim $125 worth of home depreciation in 2014 because her home expenses exceeded her income. Therefore, she's carrying this expense forward to 2015.

Line 35:   When she finishes this form, Sandy will transfer the amount on line 35 ($5,961) to **Schedule C**, line 30. Then she'll be able to calculate her net profit on **Schedule C**.

Sandy could choose to use the IRS Simplified Method or claim her expenses from **Form 8829** on her **Schedule C**. If she used the Simplified Method, her maximum deduction for house expenses would be $585 (300 square feet x $5 x 39%). Since her actual house expenses ($5,851 – **Form 8829**, line 35) are more than this, she will use her **Form 8829** expenses.

Form 4562 Depreciation and Amortization

COMPUTER

In August 2015, Sandy bought a $2,000 computer and is using it 100% for her business.

$2,000 x 100% = $2,000

Because the computer is used more than 50% of the time in her business, Sandy can use the Section 179 rule and deduct the business portion of the computer in 2015, rather than depreciating it. She will enter $25,000 on lines 1, 3, and 5. This represents the maximum Section 179 deductions you can claim. She will enter $2,000 on line 2 ($2,000 computer x 100%). She will fill out line 26 (as shown) because the computer is listed property. She will enter $2,000 from line 26 onto line 7 as well as on lines 8, 9, and 12. Sandy will enter her business profit from **Schedule C**, line 31, without taking into account her Section 179 deduction ($19,419 - $2,000 = $17,419).

OTHER PERSONAL PROPERTY

In 2012, Sandy began depreciating some appliances and furniture worth $3,300. She owned these items before she went into business and began using them in her business in 2012. In April 2015, she purchased a $3,000 dining room table and chair set. She will use the seven-year 200% declining balance rule. Here's how she'll calculate her depreciation for these expenses:

Furniture/appliances: $3,300 purchased before 2012
$3,300 x 35% (T/S%) = $1,155
$1,155 x 12.49% (7-year 200% DB method, year 4) = $144

Sandy will enter "$144" on line 17.

Dining room set: $3,000
$3,000 x 39% (T/S%) = $1,170
$1,170 x 14.29% (7-year 200% DB method, year 1) = $167
    Enter on line 19c.

Sandy bought a $100 new stroller last year that she used 100% for her business. Use the Section 179 rule and deduct it all on Part I of **Form 4562**.

Stroller: $100 x 100% = $100

Sandy will add "$100" to line 2.

HOME IMPROVEMENT

Sandy installed new paneling in a basement playroom in March 2015 for $1,000. The children in her care are the only ones who use the basement. Here's how she'll calculate her depreciation for this expense:

> $1,000 paneling x 100% business use = $1,000
> $1,000 x 2.033% (39-year work done in March, year 1) = $20

This amount is not entered on **Form 4562**. Instead, it is added onto **Form 8829**, line 41. This will make line 41 now total $1,303.

LAND IMPROVEMENTS

In June of 2013, Sandy bought a fence for her back yard. She will use the 50% bonus depreciation rule. Even though this rule expired in 2014, she can continue to depreciate the amount not claimed in 2013.

> $3,600 x 35% (T/S%) = $1,260 x 50% = $630
>   Bonus depreciation claimed in 2013.

> $630 x 8.55% (15-year 150% DB method, year 3) = $53.87
>   Enter on line 19e.

HOME DEPRECIATION

Sandy purchased her home in 2004 for $150,000 ($15,000 of this was the value of the land). In 2006, she remodeled her kitchen for $8,000. In 2007, she hired a contractor to paint her living room and bedrooms for $750. In 2014, she had $125 worth of home depreciation that she was unable to claim on **Form 8829**. Here's how she'll calculate her depreciation for her home and home improvements:

$150,000	Purchase price of home
+ $8,000	Kitchen improvement done before business began
$158,000	
– $15,000	Land
$143,000	Basis of home
x 35%	Time-Space percentage
$50,050	Business basis of home
x 2.564%	(Because Sandy began depreciating her home after May 13, 1993, she uses 39-year depreciation rules. This is the percentage she uses after the first year.)
$1,283	Home depreciation

Since the painting was a repair, it isn't added to this calculation. Sandy can't claim a business expense for it because it was done before she began her business.

Sandy won't enter the $1,283 on **Form 4562**, line 17. Instead, she'll enter her home depreciation on **Form 8829**, Part III. Notice that the $20 for the home improvement deduction also gets added to this line, for a total of $1,303.

Part V: Sandy will record her vehicle mileage in Part V, Section B.

Schedule C Profit or Loss from Business

PART I INCOME

Sandy earned $38,080 in parent fees last year. Of this amount, she received $80 in January 2016 for care that she provided in December 2015. Another $140 is a bounced check that a parent never honored. Sandy also received $2,300 in reimbursements from the Food Program. Here's how she'll report this income:

Line 1b: $38,080

        – $80   Received

      $38,000

      – $140   Bounced check

      $37,860

Line 6: $2,300

PART II EXPENSES

Line 8:   **Advertising**: Sandy paid $150 for business cards, newspaper ads, and so on.

Line 9:   **Automobile expenses**: The value of Sandy's vehicle on January 1, 2012 (when she first used it for business) was $4,000. She drove the vehicle 14,241 miles in 2015, and 3,546 of those miles were for business trips. Sandy's actual vehicle expenses were

Gas, oil, repairs	$600
Vehicle insurance	$800
Extra vehicle insurance for her business	$200
Vehicle loan interest	$237
Parking for business trips	$15
Vehicle property tax	$150

Here's how Sandy will calculate her deduction for vehicle expenses—first, to decide whether to use the standard mileage rate method or the actual vehicle expenses method, she calculates her vehicle expenses using both methods:

STANDARD MILEAGE RATE METHOD

3,546 business miles (Jan–Dec) x $0.575	=	$2,039
Vehicle loan interest:		
$237 x 24.9% (3,546 ÷ 14,241)	=	$59
Parking		$15
Vehicle property tax:		
$150 x 24.9%	=	$37
Total		$2,150

ACTUAL VEHICLE EXPENSES METHOD

3,546 miles ÷ 14,241 miles = 24.9% business use

Gas, oil, repairs	$600
Vehicle insurance	$800
Vehicle loan interest	$237
Vehicle property tax	$150
Total	$1,787 x 24.99% = $447
Extra vehicle insurance	$200
Parking	$15
Total	$662

Vehicle depreciation (5-year straight-line, year 3):

      $4,000

      x 24.99%

      $1,000 x 20.0% = $200

Total $862

Sandy will use the standard mileage rate method because it gives her a larger deduction ($2,150 vs. $862). She enters "$2,150" on **Schedule C**, line 9. Sandy will not fill out Part IV, because she must fill out **Form 4562**.

If Sandy were to use the actual vehicle expenses method, she would report her $59 loan interest on line 16b and her $37 property tax on line 23.

Line 13: **Depreciation**: Sandy enters "$2,454" from **Form 4562**, line 22. She doesn't include home depreciation or the home improvement ($20), which goes on **Form 8829**.

Line 15: **Insurance**: Sandy paid $410 for business liability insurance premiums.

Line 16b: **Interest**: Sandy paid $100 in interest on her credit card for her dining room furniture.

$100 x 39% Time-Space percentage = $39

Line 17: **Legal and professional services**: Last year Sandy paid a tax preparer to file her tax return. The tax preparer charged her $500 to file her business tax forms and $250 to file her personal tax forms. Sandy will enter "$500" here, and "$250" on **Schedule A**, line 21.

Line 18: **Office expenses**: Sandy purchased the following items last year:

Notebooks, calculator, copies, postage	$84.00
Subscriptions to child care magazines	$40.00
Child care books/calendar (*Tax Workbook,*	
Record-Keeping Guide, and *Minute Menu Kids Pro Software*)	$105.85
Membership fee in local child care association	$15.00
Training workshops	$37.00
Long-distance calls to parents of children in her care	$25.39
Total:	$307.24

Since these expenses were used 100% for her business, she will enter "$307" on line 18. Sandy also spent $300 on her monthly phone bill, but none of this is deductible.

Line 20b: **Rent of business property**: Sandy rented videotapes ($159) for the children in her care. Since these tapes were rented solely for her business, she will enter "$159" on line 20b.

Line 21: **Repairs and maintenance**: Sandy spent $30 on a service contract for her refrigerator and microwave oven.

$30 x 39% Time-Space percentage = $12.00

Line 22: **Supplies**: Sandy purchased the following supplies last year:

Kitchen supplies (soap, scrubbers, napkins)	$50
Can opener	$20
Children's games and toys	$440
Total:	$510

Since these items were also used for personal purposes, she can only claim her Time-Space percentage:

$510 x 39% = $211

This year Sandy also purchased the following:

Arts and crafts supplies	$240
Household supplies (paper towels, toilet paper, etc.)	$150
Total:	$390

Sandy calculated that these items were used 50% in her business ($390 x .50 = $195). This gives her a new total of $406 ($211 + $195), which she enters on line 22.

Line 24: **Travel**: Sandy traveled to a three-day family child care conference in Bloomington, Minnesota, in July and incurred these expenses:

Plane ticket	$675	
Hotel	$520	
Taxis	$40	
Total:	$1,235	Enter on line 24a.

IRS **Publication 1542 Per Diem Rates** lists the amount of meal expenses you can claim for a business trip without having to keep food receipts. The general meal rate is $46 per day, but there are some cities that have a higher rate. Bloomington, Minnesota has a higher rate of $71 per day, so Sandy can claim $213 ($71 x 3 days) with this method. But you can only deduct 50% of meal expenses, so she enters "$107" on line 24b.

Line 27: **Other Expenses**: On the blank lines of Part V, Sandy has entered the following line items:

Food for children in her care	$5,802
Fire extinguisher (required by licensing)	$45
Security locks	$102
Cleaning supplies	$422
Activity expenses	$380
Toys	$600
Total:	$7,351

Sandy will enter "$7,351" on line 27a.

Schedule SE Self-Employment Tax

This form is easy to complete. Sandy transfers her net profit from **Schedule C**, line 31, onto line 2 of this form and follows the directions to calculate her self-employment tax of $2,744. Then she transfers this total to **Form 1040**, line 57.

Schedule A Itemized Deductions

Lines 1–4: **Medical and dental expenses**: Sandy's husband paid $4,104 in medical bills, which he enters on line 1.

Line 5: **State and local income taxes**: Sandy's husband had $1,200 withheld from his wages for state taxes.

Line 6: **Real estate taxes**: Sandy and Bill paid $3,000 in real estate taxes. They deducted $1,050 as a business expense on **Form 8829**, line 10 ($3,000 x 35% Time-Space percentage), and can claim the remaining $1,950 here.

Line 10: **Home mortgage interest**: Sandy and Bill paid $5,000 in mortgage interest. They deducted $1,750 as a business expense on **Form 8829**, line 10 ($5,000 x 35% Time-Space percentage), and can claim the remaining $3,250 here.

Line 16: **Charitable contributions**: Sandy and Bill contributed a total of $1,200 to their church and the United Negro College Fund.

Line 21: Sandy and Bill enter "$100" in tax preparer fees for their 2013 personal tax forms (see previous page).

Line 28: The total of itemized deductions for Sandy and Bill is $7,790. Since this is less than the standard deduction of $12,600 that they can claim on **Form 1040**, they will claim the standard deduction on **Form 1040**, line 40, and not file **Schedule A**.

Line 53: Sandy and Bill are entitled to claim the child tax credit of $1,000.

Schedule EIC Earned Income Credit

Sandy and Bill earned more than the limit of $42,130 in adjusted gross income (**Form 1040**, line 66a), so they aren't eligible for this credit.

Form 1040 U.S. Individual Income Tax Return

Sandy and Bill can now transfer the amounts from their other tax forms to **Form 1040**.

Form **8829**	**Expenses for Business Use of Your Home**	OMB No. 1545-0074
Department of the Treasury Internal Revenue Service (99)	▶ File only with Schedule C (Form 1040). Use a separate Form 8829 for each home you used for business during the year. ▶ Information about Form 8829 and its separate instructions is at *www.irs.gov/form8829*.	**20**15 Attachment Sequence No. **176**

Name(s) of proprietor(s)	Your social security number
SANDY JAMES	123-45-6789

Part I   Part of Your Home Used for Business

1	Area used regularly and exclusively for business, regularly for daycare, or for storage of inventory or product samples (see instructions)	**1**	2,200
2	Total area of home	**2**	2,200
3	Divide line 1 by line 2. Enter the result as a percentage	**3**	100 %

For daycare facilities not used exclusively for business, go to line 4. All others, go to line 7.

4	Multiply days used for daycare during year by hours used per day	**4**	3,399 hr.	
5	Total hours available for use during the year (365 days x 24 hours) (see instructions)	**5**	8,760 hr.	
6	Divide line 4 by line 5. Enter the result as a decimal amount	**6**	.39	
7	Business percentage. For daycare facilities not used exclusively for business, multiply line 6 by line 3 (enter the result as a percentage). All others, enter the amount from line 3 ▶	**7**		39 %

Part II   Figure Your Allowable Deduction

		(a) Direct expenses	(b) Indirect expenses		
8	Enter the amount from Schedule C, line 29, **plus** any gain derived from the business use of your home, **minus** any loss from the trade or business not derived from the business use of your home (see instructions)			**8**	$24,880
	See instructions for columns (a) and (b) before completing lines 9–21.				
9	Casualty losses (see instructions)	**9**			
10	Deductible mortgage interest (see instructions)	**10**	$5,000		
11	Real estate taxes (see instructions)	**11**	$3,000		
12	Add lines 9, 10, and 11	**12**	$8,000		
13	Multiply line 12, column (b) by line 7	**13**	$3,120		
14	Add line 12, column (a) and line 13			**14**	$3,120
15	Subtract line 14 from line 8. If zero or less, enter -0-			**15**	$21,760
16	Excess mortgage interest (see instructions)	**16**			
17	Insurance	**17**	$1,500		
18	Rent	**18**			
19	Repairs and maintenance	**19** $15	$85		
20	Utilities	**20**	$2,000		
21	Other expenses (see instructions)	**21**			
22	Add lines 16 through 21	**22** $15	$3,585		
23	Multiply line 22, column (b) by line 7	**23**	$1,398		
24	Carryover of prior year operating expenses (see instructions)	**24**			
25	Add line 22, column (a), line 23, and line 24			**25**	$1,413
26	Allowable operating expenses. Enter the **smaller** of line 15 or line 25			**26**	$1,413
27	Limit on excess casualty losses and depreciation. Subtract line 26 from line 15			**27**	$20,347
28	Excess casualty losses (see instructions)	**28**			
29	Depreciation of your home from line 41 below	**29**	$1,450		
30	Carryover of prior year excess casualty losses and depreciation (see instructions)	**30**	$125		
31	Add lines 28 through 30			**31**	$1,575
32	Allowable excess casualty losses and depreciation. Enter the **smaller** of line 27 or line 31			**32**	$1,575
33	Add lines 14, 26, and 32			**33**	$6,108
34	Casualty loss portion, if any, from lines 14 and 32. Carry amount to **Form 4684** (see instructions)			**34**	
35	**Allowable expenses for business use of your home.** Subtract line 34 from line 33. Enter here and on Schedule C, line 30. If your home was used for more than one business, see instructions ▶			**35**	$6,108

Part III   Depreciation of Your Home

36	Enter the **smaller** of your home's adjusted basis or its fair market value (see instructions)	**36**	$158,000
37	Value of land included on line 36	**37**	$15,000
38	Basis of building. Subtract line 37 from line 36	**38**	$143,000
39	Business basis of building. Multiply line 38 by line 7	**39**	$55,770
40	Depreciation percentage (see instructions)	**40**	2.564 %
41	Depreciation allowable (see instructions). Multiply line 39 by line 40. Enter here and on line 29 above	**41**	$1,450

Part IV   Carryover of Unallowed Expenses to 2016

42	Operating expenses. Subtract line 26 from line 25. If less than zero, enter -0-	**42**	
43	Excess casualty losses and depreciation. Subtract line 32 from line 31. If less than zero, enter -0-	**43**	

For Paperwork Reduction Act Notice, see your tax return instructions.   Cat. No. 13232M   Form **8829** (2015)

Form **4562**	**Depreciation and Amortization**	OMB No. 1545-0172
Department of the Treasury Internal Revenue Service (99)	**(Including Information on Listed Property)** ▶ Attach to your tax return. ▶ **Information about Form 4562 and its separate instructions is at** *www.irs.gov/form4562.*	20**15** Attachment Sequence No. **179**

Name(s) shown on return	Business or activity to which this form relates	Identifying number
SANDY JAMES	FAMILY CHILD CARE	123-45-6789

Part I   Election To Expense Certain Property Under Section 179
        Note: If you have any listed property, complete Part V before you complete Part I.

1	Maximum amount (see instructions)	1	$25,000
2	Total cost of section 179 property placed in service (see instructions)	2	$2,100
3	Threshold cost of section 179 property before reduction in limitation (see instructions)	3	$25,000
4	Reduction in limitation. Subtract line 3 from line 2. If zero or less, enter -0-	4	0
5	Dollar limitation for tax year. Subtract line 4 from line 1. If zero or less, enter -0-. If married filing separately, see instructions	5	$25,000

6	**(a)** Description of property	**(b)** Cost (business use only)	**(c)** Elected cost

7	Listed property. Enter the amount from line 29 . . . . [7]		
8	Total elected cost of section 179 property. Add amounts in column (c), lines 6 and 7	8	
9	Tentative deduction. Enter the **smaller** of line 5 or line 8	9	
10	Carryover of disallowed deduction from line 13 of your 2014 Form 4562	10	
11	Business income limitation. Enter the smaller of business income (not less than zero) or line 5 (see instructions)	11	
12	Section 179 expense deduction. Add lines 9 and 10, but do not enter more than line 11	12	
13	Carryover of disallowed deduction to 2016. Add lines 9 and 10, less line 12 ▶ [13]		

Note: Do not use Part II or Part III below for listed property. Instead, use Part V.

Part II   Special Depreciation Allowance and Other Depreciation (Do not include listed property.) (See instructions.)

14	Special depreciation allowance for qualified property (other than listed property) placed in service during the tax year (see instructions)	14	
15	Property subject to section 168(f)(1) election	15	
16	Other depreciation (including ACRS)	16	

Part III   MACRS Depreciation (Do not include listed property.) (See instructions.)

Section A

17	MACRS deductions for assets placed in service in tax years beginning before 2015	17	$144
18	If you are electing to group any assets placed in service during the tax year into one or more general asset accounts, check here ▶ ☐		

Section B—Assets Placed in Service During 2015 Tax Year Using the General Depreciation System

(a) Classification of property	**(b)** Month and year placed in service	**(c)** Basis for depreciation (business/investment use only—see instructions)	**(d)** Recovery period	**(e)** Convention	**(f)** Method	**(g)** Depreciation deduction
19a 3-year property						
b 5-year property						
c 7-year property		$1,050	7 YEAR	HY	200% DB	$167
d 10-year property						
e 15-year property		$630	15 YEAR	HY	150% DB	$54
f 20-year property						
g 25-year property			25 yrs.		S/L	
h Residential rental property			27.5 yrs.	MM	S/L	
			27.5 yrs.	MM	S/L	
i Nonresidential real property			39 yrs.	MM	S/L	
				MM	S/L	

Section C—Assets Placed in Service During 2015 Tax Year Using the Alternative Depreciation System

20a Class life					S/L	
b 12-year			12 yrs.		S/L	
c 40-year			40 yrs.	MM	S/L	

Part IV   Summary (See instructions.)

21	Listed property. Enter amount from line 28	21	
22	**Total.** Add amounts from line 12, lines 14 through 17, lines 19 and 20 in column (g), and line 21. Enter here and on the appropriate lines of your return. Partnerships and S corporations—see instructions	22	$2,465
23	For assets shown above and placed in service during the current year, enter the portion of the basis attributable to section 263A costs . . . . . . [23]		

For Paperwork Reduction Act Notice, see separate instructions.	Cat. No. 12906N	Form **4562** (2015)

Form 4562 (2015)   Page **2**

Part V Listed Property (Include automobiles, certain other vehicles, certain aircraft, certain computers, and property used for entertainment, recreation, or amusement.)

Note: For any vehicle for which you are using the standard mileage rate or deducting lease expense, complete **only** 24a, 24b, columns (a) through (c) of Section A, all of Section B, and Section C if applicable.

Section A—Depreciation and Other Information (Caution: See the instructions for limits for passenger automobiles.)

24a Do you have evidence to support the business/investment use claimed? ☐ Yes ☐ No   24b If "Yes," is the evidence written? ☐ Yes ☐ No

(a) Type of property (list vehicles first)	(b) Date placed in service	(c) Business/ investment use percentage	(d) Cost or other basis	(e) Basis for depreciation (business/investment use only)	(f) Recovery period	(g) Method/ Convention	(h) Depreciation deduction	(i) Elected section 179 cost
25 Special depreciation allowance for qualified listed property placed in service during the tax year and used more than 50% in a qualified business use (see instructions) . **25**								
26 Property used more than 50% in a qualified business use:								
COMPUTER		100 %	$2,000		5 YEAR			$2,000
		%						
		%						
27 Property used 50% or less in a qualified business use:								
		%				S/L –		
		%				S/L –		
		%				S/L –		

28 Add amounts in column (h), lines 25 through 27. Enter here and on line 21, page 1 . . . . . **28** $2,000

29 Add amounts in column (i), line 26. Enter here and on line 7, page 1 . . . . **29**

Section B—Information on Use of Vehicles

Complete this section for vehicles used by a sole proprietor, partner, or other "more than 5% owner," or related person. If you provided vehicles to your employees, first answer the questions in Section C to see if you meet an exception to completing this section for those vehicles.

	(a) Vehicle 1		(b) Vehicle 2		(c) Vehicle 3		(d) Vehicle 4		(e) Vehicle 5		(f) Vehicle 6	
30 Total business/investment miles driven during the year (**do not** include commuting miles) .												
31 Total commuting miles driven during the year	3,576											
32 Total other personal (noncommuting) miles driven	10,665											
33 Total miles driven during the year. Add lines 30 through 32	$14,241											
	Yes	No	Yes	No	Yes	No	Yes	No	Yes	No	Yes	No
34 Was the vehicle available for personal use during off-duty hours?	✓											
35 Was the vehicle used primarily by a more than 5% owner or related person? . .	✓											
36 Is another vehicle available for personal use?	✓											

Section C—Questions for Employers Who Provide Vehicles for Use by Their Employees

Answer these questions to determine if you meet an exception to completing Section B for vehicles used by employees who **are not** more than 5% owners or related persons (see instructions).

		Yes	No
37	Do you maintain a written policy statement that prohibits all personal use of vehicles, including commuting, by your employees?		
38	Do you maintain a written policy statement that prohibits personal use of vehicles, except commuting, by your employees? See the instructions for vehicles used by corporate officers, directors, or 1% or more owners . .		
39	Do you treat all use of vehicles by employees as personal use?		
40	Do you provide more than five vehicles to your employees, obtain information from your employees about the use of the vehicles, and retain the information received?		
41	Do you meet the requirements concerning qualified automobile demonstration use? (See instructions.) . .		

Note: If your answer to 37, 38, 39, 40, or 41 is "Yes," do not complete Section B for the covered vehicles.

Part VI Amortization

(a) Description of costs	(b) Date amortization begins	(c) Amortizable amount	(d) Code section	(e) Amortization period or percentage	(f) Amortization for this year
42 Amortization of costs that begins during your 2015 tax year (see instructions):					

43 Amortization of costs that began before your 2015 tax year **43**

44 **Total.** Add amounts in column (f). See the instructions for where to report **44**

Form **4562** (2015)

SCHEDULE C (Form 1040) Department of the Treasury Internal Revenue Service (99)	**Profit or Loss From Business** (Sole Proprietorship) ▶ Information about Schedule C and its separate instructions is at *www.irs.gov/schedulec.* ▶ **Attach to Form 1040, 1040NR, or 1041; partnerships generally must file Form 1065.**

OMB No. 1545-0074

20**15**

Attachment
Sequence No. **09**

Name of proprietor	Social security number (SSN)
SANDY JAMES	123-45-6789

A Principal business or profession, including product or service (see instructions)
FAMILY CHILD CARE

B Enter code from instructions
▶ 6 2 4 4 1 0

C Business name. If no separate business name, leave blank.

D Employer ID number (EIN), (see instr.)

E Business address (including suite or room no.) ▶ 687 HOOVER ROAD
City, town or post office, state, and ZIP code   HUDSON, OH 42383

F Accounting method: (1) ☑ Cash   (2) ☐ Accrual   (3) ☐ Other (specify) ▶ _____

G Did you "materially participate" in the operation of this business during 2015? If "No," see instructions for limit on losses   . ☑ Yes ☐ No

H If you started or acquired this business during 2015, check here . . . . ▶ ☐

I Did you make any payments in 2015 that would require you to file Form(s) 1099? (see instructions) . . . . ☐ Yes ☑ No

J If "Yes," did you or will you file required Forms 1099? . . . . ☐ Yes ☐ No

Part I   Income

1	Gross receipts or sales. See instructions for line 1 and check the box if this income was reported to you on Form W-2 and the "Statutory employee" box on that form was checked . . . . ▶ ☐	1	$37,860
2	Returns and allowances	2	$37,860
3	Subtract line 2 from line 1	3	
4	Cost of goods sold (from line 42)	4	$37,860
5	**Gross profit.** Subtract line 4 from line 3	5	
6	Other income, including federal and state gasoline or fuel tax credit or refund (see instructions)	6	$2,300
7	**Gross income.** Add lines 5 and 6 . . . . ▶	7	$40,160

Part II   Expenses. Enter expenses for business use of your home **only** on line 30.

8	Advertising	8	$150	18	Office expense (see instructions)	18	$307
9	Car and truck expenses (see instructions)	9	$2,150	19	Pension and profit-sharing plans .	19	
10	Commissions and fees .	10		20	Rent or lease (see instructions):		
11	Contract labor (see instructions)	11		a	Vehicles, machinery, and equipment	20a	
12	Depletion	12		b	Other business property . . .	20b	$159
13	Depreciation and section 179 expense deduction (not included in Part III) (see instructions)	13	$2,465	21	Repairs and maintenance . . .	21	$12
				22	Supplies (not included in Part III) .	22	$406
				23	Taxes and licenses	23	
				24	Travel, meals, and entertainment:		
14	Employee benefit programs (other than on line 19) . .	14		a	Travel	24a	$1,235
15	Insurance (other than health)	15	$410	b	Deductible meals and entertainment (see instructions)	24b	$107
16	Interest:			25	Utilities	25	
a	Mortgage (paid to banks, etc.)	16a		26	Wages (less employment credits) .	26	
b	Other	16b	$39	27a	Other expenses (from line 48) . .	27a	$7,351
17	Legal and professional services	17	$500	b	**Reserved for future use** . . .	27b	

28	**Total expenses** before expenses for business use of home. Add lines 8 through 27a . . . . . . ▶	28	$15,274
29	Tentative profit or (loss). Subtract line 28 from line 7	29	$24,886
30	Expenses for business use of your home. Do not report these expenses elsewhere. Attach Form 8829 unless using the simplified method (see instructions). **Simplified method filers only:** enter the total square footage of: (a) your home: _____ and (b) the part of your home used for business: _____ . Use the Simplified Method Worksheet in the instructions to figure the amount to enter on line 30	30	$5,916
31	**Net profit or (loss).** Subtract line 30 from line 29. • If a profit, enter on both **Form 1040, line 12** (or **Form 1040NR, line 13**) and on **Schedule SE, line 2.** (If you checked the box on line 1, see instructions). Estates and trusts, enter on **Form 1041, line 3.** • If a loss, you **must** go to line 32.	31	$18,925
32	If you have a loss, check the box that describes your investment in this activity (see instructions). • If you checked 32a, enter the loss on both **Form 1040, line 12,** (or **Form 1040NR, line 13**) and on **Schedule SE, line 2.** (If you checked the box on line 1, see the line 31 instructions). Estates and trusts, enter on **Form 1041, line 3.** • If you checked 32b, you **must** attach **Form 6198.** Your loss may be limited.	32a ☐ All investment is at risk. 32b ☐ Some investment is not at risk.

For Paperwork Reduction Act Notice, see the separate instructions.   Cat. No. 11334P   Schedule C (Form 1040) 2015

Schedule C (Form 1040) 2015   Page **2**

Part III   Cost of Goods Sold (see instructions)

33   Method(s) used to
      value closing inventory: **a** ☐ Cost   **b** ☐ Lower of cost or market   **c** ☐ Other (attach explanation)

34   Was there any change in determining quantities, costs, or valuations between opening and closing inventory?
      If "Yes," attach explanation . . . .   ☐ Yes   ☐ No

35	Inventory at beginning of year. If different from last year's closing inventory, attach explanation . . .	35	
36	Purchases less cost of items withdrawn for personal use	36	
37	Cost of labor. Do not include any amounts paid to yourself	37	
38	Materials and supplies	38	
39	Other costs	39	
40	Add lines 35 through 39	40	
41	Inventory at end of year	41	
42	**Cost of goods sold.** Subtract line 41 from line 40. Enter the result here and on line 4	42	

Part IV   Information on Your Vehicle. Complete this part **only** if you are claiming car or truck expenses on line 9 and are not required to file Form 4562 for this business. See the instructions for line 13 to find out if you must file Form 4562.

43   When did you place your vehicle in service for business purposes? (month, day, year) ▶ _____ / _____ / _____

44   Of the total number of miles you drove your vehicle during 2015, enter the number of miles you used your vehicle for:

   a Business _____   **b** Commuting (see instructions) _____   **c** Other _____

45   Was your vehicle available for personal use during off-duty hours? . . . .   ☐ Yes   ☐ No

46   Do you (or your spouse) have another vehicle available for personal use? . . . .   ☐ Yes   ☐ No

47a   Do you have evidence to support your deduction? . . . .   ☐ Yes   ☐ No

   b If "Yes," is the evidence written? . . . .   ☐ Yes   ☐ No

Part V   Other Expenses. List below business expenses not included on lines 8–26 or line 30.

TIER II PROVIDER FOOD	$5,802
HOUSEHOLD ITEMS	$147
CLEANING SUPPLIES	$422
ACTIVITY SUPPLIES	$380
TOY	$600
48 **Total other expenses.** Enter here and on line 27a 48	$7,351

Schedule C (Form 1040) 2015

SCHEDULE SE
(Form 1040)

Department of the Treasury
Internal Revenue Service (99)

Self-Employment Tax

▶ Information about Schedule SE and its separate instructions is at *www.irs.gov/schedulese.*
▶ **Attach to Form 1040 or Form 1040NR.**

OMB No. 1545-0074

2015

Attachment
Sequence No. **17**

Name of person with **self-employment** income (as shown on Form 1040 or Form 1040NR)

SANDY JAMES

Social security number of person
with **self-employment** income ▶   123-45-6789

Before you begin: To determine if you must file Schedule SE, see the instructions.

May I Use Short Schedule SE or Must I Use Long Schedule SE?

Note. Use this flowchart **only if** you must file Schedule SE. If unsure, see *Who Must File Schedule SE* in the instructions.

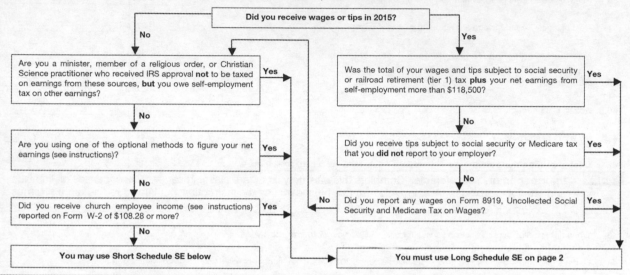

Section A—Short Schedule SE.   Caution.   Read above to see if you can use Short Schedule SE.

1a	Net farm profit or (loss) from Schedule F, line 34, and farm partnerships, Schedule K-1 (Form 1065), box 14, code A	**1a**	
b	If you received social security retirement or disability benefits, enter the amount of Conservation Reserve Program payments included on Schedule F, line 4b, or listed on Schedule K-1 (Form 1065), box 20, code Z	**1b**	( )
2	Net profit or (loss) from Schedule C, line 31; Schedule C-EZ, line 3; Schedule K-1 (Form 1065), box 14, code A (other than farming); and Schedule K-1 (Form 1065-B), box 9, code J1. Ministers and members of religious orders, see instructions for types of income to report on this line. See instructions for other income to report	**2**	$18,925
3	Combine lines 1a, 1b, and 2	**3**	$18,925
4	Multiply line 3 by 92.35% (.9235). If less than $400, you do not owe self-employment tax; **do not** file this schedule unless you have an amount on line 1b . . . . ▶	**4**	$17,477
	Note. If line 4 is less than $400 due to Conservation Reserve Program payments on line 1b, see instructions.		
5	**Self-employment tax.** If the amount on line 4 is: • $118,500 or less, multiply line 4 by 15.3% (.153). Enter the result here and on **Form 1040, line 57, or Form 1040NR, line 55** • More than $118,500, multiply line 4 by 2.9% (.029). Then, add $14,694 to the result. Enter the total here and on **Form 1040, line 57,** or **Form 1040NR, line 55**	**5**	$2,674
6	**Deduction for one-half of self-employment tax.** Multiply line 5 by 50% (.50). Enter the result here and on **Form 1040, line 27,** or **Form 1040NR, line 27** **6** $1,337		

For Paperwork Reduction Act Notice, see your tax return instructions.

Cat. No. 11358Z

Schedule SE (Form 1040) 2015

Form **1040**	Department of the Treasury—Internal Revenue Service (99)				

Form 1040 Department of the Treasury—Internal Revenue Service (99)

U.S. Individual Income Tax Return **2015** OMB No. 1545-0074 | IRS Use Only—Do not write or staple in this space.

For the year Jan. 1–Dec. 31, 2015, or other tax year beginning _____, 2015, ending _____, 20 ___   See separate instructions.

Your first name and initial	Last name	Your social security number
SANDY	JAMES	1 2 3 4 5 6 7 8 9

If a joint return, spouse's first name and initial	Last name	Spouse's social security number
BILL	JAMES	9 8 7 6 5 4 3 2 1

Home address (number and street). If you have a P.O. box, see instructions.   Apt. no.

687 HOOVER STREET

▲ Make sure the SSN(s) above and on line 6c are correct.

City, town or post office, state, and ZIP code. If you have a foreign address, also complete spaces below (see instructions).

HUDSON, OH 42387

Presidential Election Campaign

Check here if you, or your spouse if filing jointly, want $3 to go to this fund. Checking a box below will not change your tax or refund.   ☐ You   ☐ Spouse

Foreign country name	Foreign province/state/county	Foreign postal code

Filing Status

Check only one box.

1. ☐ Single
2. ☑ Married filing jointly (even if only one had income)
3. ☐ Married filing separately. Enter spouse's SSN above and full name here. ▶
4. ☐ Head of household (with qualifying person). (See instructions.) If the qualifying person is a child but not your dependent, enter this child's name here. ▶
5. ☐ Qualifying widow(er) with dependent child

July 29, 2015 — DO NOT FILE

Exemptions

6a ☑ **Yourself.** If someone can claim you as a dependent, **do not** check box 6a . . . . . .
b ☑ **Spouse** . . . .

c **Dependents:**

(1) First name Last name	(2) Dependent's social security number	(3) Dependent's relationship to you	(4) ✓ if child under age 17 qualifying for child tax credit (see instructions)
VANESSA JAMES	1 2 4 6 5 4 4 1 1	DAUGHTER	☑
			☐
			☐
			☐

If more than four dependents, see instructions and check here ▶ ☐

Boxes checked on 6a and 6b	2
No. of children on 6c who: • lived with you	1
• did not live with you due to divorce or separation (see instructions)	
Dependents on 6c not entered above	
Add numbers on lines above ▶	3

d Total number of exemptions claimed

Income

Attach Form(s) W-2 here. Also attach Forms W-2G and 1099-R if tax was withheld.

If you did not get a W-2, see instructions.

7	Wages, salaries, tips, etc. Attach Form(s) W-2	7	$40,000
8a	**Taxable** interest. Attach Schedule B if required	8a	
b	**Tax-exempt** interest. **Do not** include on line 8a . . . 8b		
9a	Ordinary dividends. Attach Schedule B if required	9a	
b	Qualified dividends 9b		
10	Taxable refunds, credits, or offsets of state and local income taxes . . .	10	
11	Alimony received	11	
12	Business income or (loss). Attach Schedule C or C-EZ	12	$18,925
13	Capital gain or (loss). Attach Schedule D if required. If not required, check here ▶ ☐	13	
14	Other gains or (losses). Attach Form 4797	14	
15a	IRA distributions . 15a	b Taxable amount . . .	15b	
16a	Pensions and annuities 16a	b Taxable amount . . .	16b	
17	Rental real estate, royalties, partnerships, S corporations, trusts, etc. Attach Schedule E	17	
18	Farm income or (loss). Attach Schedule F	18	
19	Unemployment compensation	19	
20a	Social security benefits 20a	b Taxable amount . . .	20b	
21	Other income. List type and amount _____	21	
22	Combine the amounts in the far right column for lines 7 through 21. This is your **total income** ▶	22	$58,925

Adjusted Gross Income

23	Reserved 23		
24	Certain business expenses of reservists, performing artists, and fee-basis government officials. Attach Form 2106 or 2106-EZ 24		
25	Health savings account deduction. Attach Form 8889 . 25		
26	Moving expenses. Attach Form 3903 26		
27	Deductible part of self-employment tax. Attach Schedule SE . 27	$1,337	
28	Self-employed SEP, SIMPLE, and qualified plans . . 28		
29	Self-employed health insurance deduction 29		
30	Penalty on early withdrawal of savings 30		
31a	Alimony paid b Recipient's SSN ▶ _____ 31a		
32	IRA deduction 32		
33	Student loan interest deduction 33		
34	Reserved 34		
35	Domestic production activities deduction. Attach Form 8903 35		
36	Add lines 23 through 35	36	$1,337
37	Subtract line 36 from line 22. This is your **adjusted gross income** . . . . ▶	37	$57,588

For Disclosure, Privacy Act, and Paperwork Reduction Act Notice, see separate instructions.   Cat. No. 11320B   Form **1040** (2015)

Form 1040 (2015)   **Page 2**

Tax and Credits

Line	Description	Amount
38	Amount from line 37 (adjusted gross income)	$57,588
39a	Check if: You were born before January 2, 1951, ☐ Blind. Spouse was born before January 2, 1951, ☐ Blind. Total boxes checked ▶ 39a	
b	If your spouse itemizes on a separate return or you were a dual-status alien, check here ▶ 39b ☐	

Standard Deduction for—
- People who check any box on line 39a or 39b **or** who can be claimed as a dependent, see instructions.
- All others:
  Single or Married filing separately, $6,300
  Married filing jointly or Qualifying widow(er), $12,600
  Head of household, $9,250

Line	Description	Amount
40	Itemized deductions (from Schedule A) or your standard deduction (see left margin)	$12,600
41	Subtract line 40 from line 38	$44,988
42	Exemptions. If line 38 is $154,950 or less, multiply $4,000 by the number on line 6d. Otherwise, see instructions	$12,000
43	Taxable income. Subtract line 42 from line 41. If line 42 is more than line 41, enter -0-	$32,988
44	Tax (see instructions). Check if any from: a ☐ Form(s) 8814 b ☐ Form 4972 c ☐	$4,024
45	Alternative minimum tax (see instructions). Attach Form 6251	
46	Excess advance premium tax credit repayment. Attach Form 8962	
47	Add lines 44, 45, and 46 ▶	$4,024
48	Foreign tax credit. Attach Form 1116 if required	
49	Credit for child and dependent care expenses. Attach Form 2441	
50	Education credits from Form 8863, line 19	
51	Retirement savings contributions credit. Attach Form 8880	
52	Child tax credit. Attach Schedule 8812, if required	$1,000
53	Residential energy credit. Attach Form 5695	
54	Other credits from Form: a ☐ 3800 b ☐ 8801 c ☐	
55	Add lines 48 through 54. These are your total credits	$1,000
56	Subtract line 55 from line 47. If line 55 is more than line 47, enter -0- ▶	$3,024

Other Taxes

Line	Description	Amount
57	Self-employment tax. Attach Schedule SE	$2,674
58	Unreported social security and Medicare tax from Form: a ☐ 4137 b ☐ 8919	
59	Additional tax on IRAs, other qualified retirement plans, etc. Attach Form 5329 if required	
60a	Household employment taxes from Schedule H	
b	First-time homebuyer credit repayment. Attach Form 5405 if required	
61	Health care: individual responsibility (see instructions) Full-year coverage ☐	
62	Taxes from: a ☐ Form 8959 b ☐ Form 8960 c ☐ Instructions; enter code(s)	
63	Add lines 56 through 62. This is your total tax ▶	$5,698

Payments

If you have a qualifying child, attach Schedule EIC.

Line	Description	Amount
64	Federal income tax withheld from Forms W-2 and 1099	$5,800
65	2015 estimated tax payments and amount applied from 2014 return	
66a	Earned income credit (EIC)	
b	Nontaxable combat pay election 66b	
67	Additional child tax credit. Attach Schedule 8812	
68	American opportunity credit from Form 8863, line 8	
69	Net premium tax credit. Attach Form 8962	
70	Amount paid with request for extension to file	
71	Excess social security and tier 1 RRTA tax withheld	
72	Credit for federal tax on fuels. Attach Form 4136	
73	Credits from Form: a ☐ 2439 b ☐ Reserved c ☐ 8885 d ☐	
74	Add lines 64, 65, 66a, and 67 through 73. These are your total payments ▶	$5,800

Refund

Line	Description	Amount
75	If line 74 is more than line 63, subtract line 63 from line 74. This is the amount you overpaid	$102
76a	Amount of line 75 you want refunded to you. If Form 8888 is attached, check here ▶ ☐	$102
b	Routing number ▶ c Type: ☐ Checking ☐ Savings	
d	Account number	
77	Amount of line 75 you want applied to your 2016 estimated tax ▶ 77	

Amount You Owe

Line	Description	Amount
78	Amount you owe. Subtract line 74 from line 63. For details on how to pay, see instructions ▶	
79	Estimated tax penalty (see instructions) 79	

Third Party Designee

Do you want to allow another person to discuss this return with the IRS (see instructions)? ☐ **Yes.** Complete below. ☐ **No**

Designee's name ▶   Phone no. ▶   Personal identification number (PIN) ▶

Sign Here

Under penalties of perjury, I declare that I have examined this return and accompanying schedules and statements, and to the best of my knowledge and belief, they are true, correct, and complete. Declaration of preparer (other than taxpayer) is based on all information of which preparer has any knowledge.

Joint return? See instructions. Keep a copy for your records.

Your signature: *Sandy James*   Date: 1/1/2016   Your occupation: FAMILY CHILD CARE   Daytime phone number

Spouse's signature. If a joint return, both must sign: *Bill James*   Date: 1/1/2016   Spouse's occupation: CONSTRUCTION   If the IRS sent you an Identity Protection PIN, enter it here (see inst.)

Paid Preparer Use Only

Print/Type preparer's name   Preparer's signature   Date   Check ☐ if self-employed   PTIN

Firm's name ▶   Firm's EIN ▶

Firm's address ▶   Phone no.

IRS Resources

You can call the IRS Business and Specialty Tax Line at 800-829-4933 with any tax question. This toll-free number for business questions should make it easier for you to get through to an IRS employee who can answer your questions. If you aren't sure if the answer you are given is correct, ask the IRS employee to tell you which IRS publication or part of the Tax Code the answer is based on. If you have a hearing impairment and TDD equipment, you can call 800-829-4059. If you live outside the United States and have a tax question, call your U.S. Embassy. In Puerto Rico, call 787-622-8929.

You can find IRS forms and publications at local IRS offices, banks, libraries, and post offices. You can also call 800-829-3676 to have any IRS form mailed to you. The IRS has its own website (www.irs.gov) from which you can download any IRS form, publication, or instruction book. The site also has other information that may help you with your taxes.

You can also get IRS tax forms by fax. Dial 703-368-9694 from the voice unit of your fax machine and follow the voice prompts. Tax forms must be on plain paper, not thermal paper, to be acceptable for filing. (You can copy the form if necessary.) For help with transmission problems, call the Fed World Help Desk at 703-487-4608.

If you want to report that another taxpayer (an illegal child care provider, for example) is cheating, call the IRS criminal investigation informant hotline at 800-829-0433. Your name will be kept confidential, and you are eligible for a reward if the IRS collects taxes due.

Below is a list of the IRS publications and Tax Court cases that address family child care tax issues. You can find copies at www.tomcopelandblog.com.

Child Care Provider Audit Technique Guide
This guide from the IRS is a must if you are audited. It contains guidance on the many unique tax issues facing child care providers. You can find the guide at www .tomcopelandblog.com.

Publication 587 Business Use of Your Home
Under the section Day-Care Facility, this publication clarifies that providers who have applied for, have been granted, or are exempt from a license, certification, or registration under applicable state law can claim home expenses as shown on **Form 8829**. This publication also discusses how to calculate the Time-Space percentage in filling out **Form 8829**. It includes a discussion of how to claim food expenses and report Food Program income.

Instructions for Form 8829 Expenses for Business Use of Your Home

Under the section Special Computation for Certain Day-Care Facilities, the instructions spell out how to calculate the Time-Space percentage of the home when at least one of the rooms in the home is used exclusively for the business.

IRS Revenue Ruling 92-3

This Revenue Ruling, based on an audit of a family child care provider, clarifies how to calculate the Time-Space percentage. It also defines what "regular use" means.

Tax Court Cases

Robert Neilson and Dorothy Neilson v. Commissioner, 94-1, 1990

In this case, the court ruled that a provider could claim 75 hours a week (including preparation and cleanup time) in determining her Time-Space percentage. The court also allowed the provider to deduct a portion of her lawn care expenses.

Uphus and Walker v. Commissioner
Tax Court Memo 1994-71, February 23, 1994

In these two cases, the court ruled that providers could claim rooms (laundry room, basement storage area, garage, and furnace area) as regularly used for the business even if the children in care never entered the rooms. The use of these rooms by the provider for business purposes was enough to meet the regular-use test.

Hewett v. Commissioner
Tax Court Memo 1996-110

In this case, the court allowed a taxpayer to claim an exclusive-use area for a grand piano that occupied a small recessed section of the living room and had no partition separating it from the rest of the home. The court ruled that it wasn't necessary to have a physical barrier to prove that an area was used exclusively for business.

Scott C. and Patricia A. Simpson v. Commissioner
Tax Court Memo 1997-223, May 12, 1997

In this case, a new provider was not allowed to claim most of her first two years of expenses because they were not related to her business. These expenses included cross-country ski machine, personal food expenses, payments to wineries, and much more. Despite the loss of many deductions, the court did allow her to show a loss of $2,000–3,000 for these two years. The court also acknowledged that cable TV and water were proper business deductions.

Peter and Maureen Speltz v. Commissioner
Tax Court Summary Opinion 2006-25

A provider hired her husband and set up a medical reimbursement plan without paying him a salary. The court ruled that the plan was valid, the husband was a bona fide employee, and the provider was allowed to deduct thousands of dollars in medical expenses.

Jonelle Broady v. Commissioner
Tax Court Summary Opinion 2008-63
An illegal provider was entitled to claim business expenses such as advertising, car expenses, office supplies, repairs and maintenance, and supplies and food. Illegal providers are not entitled to claim expenses associated with the home.

Tax Help on the Internet
Commercial Internet services have special sites on which you can get tax assistance; however, be careful about accepting advice from these sources, because none of the information is guaranteed.

State Tax Information and Forms
If you need state tax information and forms, contact your state tax office.

List of IRS Forms and Publications

Here's a list of the IRS forms and publications that are mentioned in this book:

Form W-5 Earned Income Credit Advance Payment Certificate
Form W-10 Dependent Care Provider's Identification and Certification
Form 1040 U.S. Individual Income Tax Return
Form 1040-ES Estimated Tax for Individuals
Form 1040-SE Self-Employment Tax
Form 1040X Amended U.S. Individual Income Tax Return
Form 3115 Application for Change in Accounting Method
Form 4562 Depreciation and Amortization
Form 4684 Casualties and Thefts
Form 4797 Sales of Business Property
Form 4868 Application for Automatic Extension of Time to File U.S. Individual
    Income Tax Return
Form 5305-SEP Simplified Employee Pension
Form 5695 Residential Energy Credits
Form 8109 Federal Tax Deposit Coupon
Form 8812 Additional Child Tax Credit
Form 8824 Like-Kind Exchange
Form 8829 Expenses for Business Use of Your Home
Form 8863 Education Credits
Form 8880 Credit for Qualified Retirement Savings Contributions
Form 8949 Sales and Other Dispositions of Capital Assets
Publication 463 Travel, Entertainment, Gift, and Car Expenses
Publication 505 Tax Withholding and Estimated Tax
Publication 523 Selling Your Home
Publication 534 Depreciating Property Placed in Service Before 1987
Publication 544 Sales and Other Dispositions of Assets
Publication 556 Examination of Returns, Appeal Rights, and Claims for Refund

Publication 583 Starting a Business and Keeping Records

Publication 587 Business Use of Your Home

Publication 590 Individual Retirement Arrangements

Publication 596 Earned Income Credit

Publication 946 How to Depreciate Property

Publication 1542 Per Diem Rates

Schedule A Itemized Deductions

Schedule B Interest and Dividend Income

Schedule C Profit or Loss from Business

Schedule D Capital Gains and Losses

Schedule EIC Earned Income Credit

Schedule SE Self-Employment Tax

Employee and Payroll Tax Forms

Circular E Employer's Tax Guide

Form I-9 Employment Eligibility Verification

Form SS-4 Application for Employer Identification Number

Form SS-5 Application for a Social Security Card

Form W-2 Wages and Tax Statement

Form W-3 Transmittal of Income and Tax Statements

Form W-4 Employee's Withholding Allowance Certificate

Form W-11 Hiring Incentives to Restore Employment (HIRE) Act Employee Affidavit

Form 940 Employer's Annual Federal Unemployment Tax Return (FUTA)

Form 941 Employer's Quarterly Federal Tax Return

Form 944 Employer's Annual Federal Tax Return

Form 1099 Miscellaneous Income

Form 8861 Welfare-to-Work Credit

Finding and Working with a Tax Professional

Tax Professional Directory

The National Association for Family Child Care (NAFCC) maintains a list of tax professionals around the country who have experience filing tax returns for family child care providers. This list is posted at www.nafcc.org.

Working with a Tax Professional

When hiring or working with a tax professional, follow these guidelines:

- Get referrals from other providers who have a good tax professional.

- Ask the professionals you are considering about their training, experience, and knowledge of the unique tax laws that affect family child care providers (see pages 4–5).

- Always review your tax return before signing it, and ask questions if you don't understand something on your return.

- Never sign a blank tax form or one that has been filled out in pencil.

- Keep a copy of your return for your records.

- Remember that you are ultimately responsible for your tax return even if your tax professional makes an error.

- Watch out for the following warning signs of an unscrupulous tax professional:
  Someone who says that he or she can obtain larger refunds than other preparers.
  Someone who bases his or her fee on a percentage of the amount of the refund.
  Someone who refuses to sign your return or give you a copy for your records.

PART V

Tax Forms

Form **W-10**
(Rev. October 2015)
Department of the Treasury
Internal Revenue Service

Dependent Care Provider's Identification and Certification

▶ Do NOT file Form W-10 with your tax return. Instead, keep it for your records.
▶ Information about Form W-10 and its instructions is at *www.irs.gov/formw10*.

Part I   Dependent Care Provider's Identification (See instructions.)

Please print or type	Name of dependent care provider	Provider's taxpayer identification number
	Address (number, street, and apt. no.)	If the above number is a social security number, check here ▶ . . . . . . ☐
	City, state, and ZIP code	

Certification and Signature of Dependent Care Provider. Under penalties of perjury, I, as the dependent care provider, certify that my name, address, and taxpayer identification number shown above are correct.

Please Sign Here	Dependent care provider's signature	Date

Part II   Name and Address of Person Requesting Part I Information (See instructions.)

Name, street address, apt. no., city, state, and ZIP code of person requesting information

---

For calendar year 2015, I paid $ _____ (amount paid) to

_____ (name of provider) for the care of

_____ (name of child(ren)).

_____   _____
Signature of Parent   Date

_____   _____
Signature of Provider   Date

Form **W-10**
(Rev. October 2015)
Department of the Treasury
Internal Revenue Service

Dependent Care Provider's Identification and Certification

▶ Do NOT file Form W-10 with your tax return. Instead, keep it for your records.
▶ Information about Form W-10 and its instructions is at *www.irs.gov/formw10*.

Part I   Dependent Care Provider's Identification (See instructions.)

Please print or type	Name of dependent care provider	Provider's taxpayer identification number
	Address (number, street, and apt. no.)	If the above number is a social security number, check here ▶ . . . . . . ☐
	City, state, and ZIP code	

Certification and Signature of Dependent Care Provider. Under penalties of perjury, I, as the dependent care provider, certify that my name, address, and taxpayer identification number shown above are correct.

Please Sign Here	Dependent care provider's signature	Date

Part II   Name and Address of Person Requesting Part I Information (See instructions.)

Name, street address, apt. no., city, state, and ZIP code of person requesting information

---

For calendar year 2015, I paid $ _____ (amount paid) to

_____ (name of provider) for the care of

_____ (name of child(ren)).

_____   _____
Signature of Parent   Date

_____   _____
Signature of Provider   Date

Electing the $2,500 Safe Harbor Rule

If you bought items costing $2,500 or less that you want to deduct in 2015, rather than depreciating, attach this statement to your 2015 tax return.

For the year ending December 31, 2015 I am electing the de minimis safe harbor under Treas. Reg. Section 1.263(a)-1(f) for my business expenses of less than $2,500.

_____   _____
Signature   Date

Taxpayer identification number:

Address:

Electing the Small Taxpayer Safe Harbor Rule

If you bought home improvements or a fence, a patio, or a driveway that cost the lesser of $10,000 or 2% of the unadjusted basis of your home, you can deduct them in one year if you attach this statement to your 2015 tax return.

For the year ending December 31, 2015 I am electing the safe harbor election for small taxpayers under Treas. Reg. Section 1.263(a)-3(g) for the following: [list your improvements].

_____   _____
Signature   Date

Taxpayer identification number:

Address:

Form 1040   Department of the Treasury—Internal Revenue Service   (99)

U.S. Individual Income Tax Return   **2015**   OMB No. 1545-0074   IRS Use Only—Do not write or staple in this space.

For the year Jan. 1–Dec. 31, 2015, or other tax year beginning _____ , 2015, ending _____ , 20 ____   See separate instructions.

Your first name and initial _____ Last name _____   Your social security number _____

If a joint return, spouse's first name and initial _____ Last name _____   Spouse's social security number _____

Home address (number and street). If you have a P.O. box, see instructions. _____   Apt. no. _____

▲ Make sure the SSN(s) above and on line 6c are correct.

City, town or post office, state, and ZIP code. If you have a foreign address, also complete spaces below (see instructions). _____

Presidential Election Campaign
Check here if you, or your spouse if filing jointly, want $3 to go to this fund. Checking a box below will not change your tax or refund.   ☐ You   ☐ Spouse

Foreign country name _____   Foreign province/state/county _____   Foreign postal code _____

[Watermark: July 29, 2015 DO NOT FILE]

Filing Status

Check only one box.

1 ☐ Single
2 ☐ Married filing jointly (even if only one had income)
3 ☐ Married filing separately. Enter spouse's SSN above and full name here. ▶
4 ☐ Head of household (with qualifying person). (See instructions.) If the qualifying person is a child but not your dependent, enter this child's name here. ▶
5 ☐ Qualifying widow(er) with dependent child

Exemptions

6a ☐ **Yourself.** If someone can claim you as a dependent, **do not** check box 6a . . . .
b ☐ **Spouse** . . . .

Boxes checked on 6a and 6b _____

c Dependents:

(1) First name Last name	(2) Dependent's social security number	(3) Dependent's relationship to you	(4) ✓ if child under age 17 qualifying for child tax credit (see instructions)
_____	_____	_____	☐
_____	_____	_____	☐
_____	_____	_____	☐
_____	_____	_____	☐

If more than four dependents, see instructions and check here ▶ ☐

No. of children on 6c who:
• lived with you _____
• did not live with you due to divorce or separation (see instructions) _____

Dependents on 6c not entered above _____

Add numbers on lines above ▶ _____

d Total number of exemptions claimed . . . .

Income

Attach Form(s) W-2 here. Also attach Forms W-2G and 1099-R if tax was withheld.

If you did not get a W-2, see instructions.

7	Wages, salaries, tips, etc. Attach Form(s) W-2	7
8a	**Taxable** interest. Attach Schedule B if required	8a
b	**Tax-exempt** interest. **Do not** include on line 8a . . . 8b	
9a	Ordinary dividends. Attach Schedule B if required	9a
b	Qualified dividends 9b	
10	Taxable refunds, credits, or offsets of state and local income taxes	10
11	Alimony received	11
12	Business income or (loss). Attach Schedule C or C-EZ	12
13	Capital gain or (loss). Attach Schedule D if required. If not required, check here ▶ ☐	13
14	Other gains or (losses). Attach Form 4797	14
15a	IRA distributions . 15a _____ b Taxable amount . . .	15b
16a	Pensions and annuities 16a _____ b Taxable amount . . .	16b
17	Rental real estate, royalties, partnerships, S corporations, trusts, etc. Attach Schedule E	17
18	Farm income or (loss). Attach Schedule F	18
19	Unemployment compensation	19
20a	Social security benefits 20a _____ b Taxable amount . . .	20b
21	Other income. List type and amount _____	21
22	Combine the amounts in the far right column for lines 7 through 21. This is your **total income** ▶	22

Adjusted Gross Income

23	Reserved	23	
24	Certain business expenses of reservists, performing artists, and fee-basis government officials. Attach Form 2106 or 2106-EZ	24	
25	Health savings account deduction. Attach Form 8889 .	25	
26	Moving expenses. Attach Form 3903	26	
27	Deductible part of self-employment tax. Attach Schedule SE .	27	
28	Self-employed SEP, SIMPLE, and qualified plans . .	28	
29	Self-employed health insurance deduction	29	
30	Penalty on early withdrawal of savings	30	
31a	Alimony paid b Recipient's SSN ▶ _____	31a	
32	IRA deduction	32	
33	Student loan interest deduction	33	
34	Reserved	34	
35	Domestic production activities deduction. Attach Form 8903	35	
36	Add lines 23 through 35		36
37	Subtract line 36 from line 22. This is your **adjusted gross income** . . . . . ▶		37

For Disclosure, Privacy Act, and Paperwork Reduction Act Notice, see separate instructions.   Cat. No. 11320B   Form **1040** (2015)

Form 1040 (2015)   Page **2**

Tax and Credits	38	Amount from line 37 (adjusted gross income)	38	
	39a	Check if: ☐ **You** were born before January 2, 1951, ☐ Blind. } **Total boxes** ☐ **Spouse** was born before January 2, 1951, ☐ Blind. } checked ▶ 39a		
	b	If your spouse itemizes on a separate return or you were a dual-status alien, check here ▶ 39b ☐		
Standard Deduction for— • People who check any box on line 39a or 39b **or** who can be claimed as a dependent, see instructions. • All others: Single or Married filing separately, $6,300 Married filing jointly or Qualifying widow(er), $12,600 Head of household, $9,250	40	**Itemized deductions** (from Schedule A) **or** your **standard deduction** (see left margin) . .	40	
	41	Subtract line 40 from line 38	41	
	42	**Exemptions.** If line 38 is $154,950 or less, multiply $4,000 by the number on line 6d. Otherwise, see instructions	42	
	43	**Taxable income.** Subtract line 42 from line 41. If line 42 is more than line 41, enter -0-	43	
	44	**Tax** (see instructions). Check if any from: **a** ☐ Form(s) 8814 **b** ☐ Form 4972 **c** ☐	44	
	45	**Alternative minimum tax** (see instructions). Attach Form 6251 . . .	45	
	46	Excess advance premium tax credit repayment. Attach Form 8962 . .	46	
	47	Add lines 44, 45, and 46 . . . . ▶	47	
	48	Foreign tax credit. Attach Form 1116 if required . . .	48		
	49	Credit for child and dependent care expenses. Attach Form 2441	49		
	50	Education credits from Form 8863, line 19 . . .	50		
	51	Retirement savings contributions credit. Attach Form 8880	51		
	52	Child tax credit. Attach Schedule 8812, if required . . .	52		
	53	Residential energy credit. Attach Form 5695	53		
	54	Other credits from Form: **a** ☐ 3800 **b** ☐ 8801 **c** ☐	54		
	55	Add lines 48 through 54. These are your **total credits**	55	
	56	Subtract line 55 from line 47. If line 55 is more than line 47, enter -0- . . . ▶	56	
Other Taxes	57	Self-employment tax. Attach Schedule SE	57	
	58	Unreported social security and Medicare tax from Form: **a** ☐ 4137 **b** ☐ 8919 . .	58	
	59	Additional tax on IRAs, other qualified retirement plans, etc. Attach Form 5329 if required . .	59	
	60a	Household employment taxes from Schedule H	60a	
	b	First-time homebuyer credit repayment. Attach Form 5405 if required	60b	
	61	Health care: individual responsibility (see instructions) Full-year coverage ☐ . .	61	
	62	Taxes from: **a** ☐ Form 8959 **b** ☐ Form 8960 **c** ☐ Instructions; enter code(s)	62	
	63	Add lines 56 through 62. This is your **total tax** . . . . . . ▶	63	
Payments If you have a qualifying child, attach Schedule EIC.	64	Federal income tax withheld from Forms W-2 and 1099 . .	64		
	65	2015 estimated tax payments and amount applied from 2014 return	65		
	66a	**Earned income credit (EIC)**	66a		
	b	Nontaxable combat pay election 66b			
	67	Additional child tax credit. Attach Schedule 8812	67		
	68	American opportunity credit from Form 8863, line 8 . . .	68		
	69	Net premium tax credit. Attach Form 8962	69		
	70	Amount paid with request for extension to file	70		
	71	Excess social security and tier 1 RRTA tax withheld . .	71		
	72	Credit for federal tax on fuels. Attach Form 4136 . . .	72		
	73	Credits from Form: **a** ☐ 2439 **b** ☐ Reserved **c** ☐ 8885 **d** ☐	73		
	74	Add lines 64, 65, 66a, and 67 through 73. These are your **total payments** . . . . ▶	74	
Refund Direct deposit? ▶ See instructions.	75	If line 74 is more than line 63, subtract line 63 from line 74. This is the amount you **overpaid**	75	
	76a	Amount of line 75 you want **refunded to you**. If Form 8888 is attached, check here . ▶ ☐	76a	
	b	Routing number			
		▶ c Type: ☐ Checking ☐ Savings			
	d	Account number			
	77	Amount of line 75 you want **applied to your 2016 estimated tax** ▶	77		
Amount You Owe	78	**Amount you owe.** Subtract line 74 from line 63. For details on how to pay, see instructions ▶	78	
	79	Estimated tax penalty (see instructions)	79		

Third Party Designee	Do you want to allow another person to discuss this return with the IRS (see instructions)? ☐ **Yes.** Complete below. ☐ **No**
	Designee's name ▶	Phone no. ▶	Personal identification number (PIN) ▶ ☐☐☐☐☐

Sign Here Joint return? See instructions. Keep a copy for your records.	Under penalties of perjury, I declare that I have examined this return and accompanying schedules and statements, and to the best of my knowledge and belief, they are true, correct, and complete. Declaration of preparer (other than taxpayer) is based on all information of which preparer has any knowledge.
	Your signature	Date	Your occupation	Daytime phone number
	Spouse's signature. If a joint return, **both** must sign.	Date	Spouse's occupation	If the IRS sent you an Identity Protection PIN, enter it here (see inst.)

Paid Preparer Use Only	Print/Type preparer's name	Preparer's signature	Date	Check ☐ if self-employed	PTIN
	Firm's name ▶			Firm's EIN ▶	
	Firm's address ▶			Phone no.	

www.irs.gov/form1040   Form **1040** (2015)

SCHEDULE C
(Form 1040)

Department of the Treasury
Internal Revenue Service (99)

Profit or Loss From Business
(Sole Proprietorship)

▶ Information about Schedule C and its separate instructions is at *www.irs.gov/schedulec*.

▶ Attach to Form 1040, 1040NR, or 1041; partnerships generally must file Form 1065.

OMB No. 1545-0074

2015

Attachment
Sequence No. 09

Name of proprietor	Social security number (SSN)

A	Principal business or profession, including product or service (see instructions)	**B** Enter code from instructions ▶
C	Business name. If no separate business name, leave blank.	**D** Employer ID number (EIN), (see instr.)

E Business address (including suite or room no.) ▶ _____

 City, town or post office, state, and ZIP code

F Accounting method: **(1)** ☐ Cash **(2)** ☐ Accrual **(3)** ☐ Other (specify) ▶ _____

G Did you "materially participate" in the operation of this business during 2015? If "No," see instructions for limit on losses ☐ Yes ☐ No

H If you started or acquired this business during 2015, check here . . . . ▶ ☐

I Did you make any payments in 2015 that would require you to file Form(s) 1099? (see instructions) . . . . ☐ Yes ☐ No

J If "Yes," did you or will you file required Forms 1099? . . . . ☐ Yes ☐ No

Part I   Income

1	Gross receipts or sales. See instructions for line 1 and check the box if this income was reported to you on Form W-2 and the "Statutory employee" box on that form was checked . . . . ▶ ☐	1
2	Returns and allowances	2
3	Subtract line 2 from line 1	3
4	Cost of goods sold (from line 42)	4
5	**Gross profit.** Subtract line 4 from line 3	5
6	Other income, including federal and state gasoline or fuel tax credit or refund (see instructions) . . .	6
7	**Gross income.** Add lines 5 and 6 . . . . ▶	7

Part II   Expenses. Enter expenses for business use of your home **only** on line 30.

8	Advertising	8	18	Office expense (see instructions)	18
9	Car and truck expenses (see instructions).	9	19	Pension and profit-sharing plans	19
10	Commissions and fees .	10	20	Rent or lease (see instructions):	
11	Contract labor (see instructions)	11	a	Vehicles, machinery, and equipment	20a
12	Depletion	12	b	Other business property . . .	20b
13	Depreciation and section 179 expense deduction (not included in Part III) (see instructions).	13	21	Repairs and maintenance . . .	21
			22	Supplies (not included in Part III) .	22
			23	Taxes and licenses	23
			24	Travel, meals, and entertainment:	
14	Employee benefit programs (other than on line 19) . .	14	a	Travel	24a
15	Insurance (other than health)	15	b	Deductible meals and entertainment (see instructions) .	24b
16	Interest:		25	Utilities	25
a	Mortgage (paid to banks, etc.)	16a	26	Wages (less employment credits) .	26
b	Other	16b	27a	Other expenses (from line 48) . .	27a
17	Legal and professional services	17	b	**Reserved for future use**	27b

28	**Total expenses** before expenses for business use of home. Add lines 8 through 27a . . . . . ▶	28
29	Tentative profit or (loss). Subtract line 28 from line 7	29
30	Expenses for business use of your home. Do not report these expenses elsewhere. Attach Form 8829 unless using the simplified method (see instructions). **Simplified method filers only:** enter the total square footage of: (a) your home: _____ and (b) the part of your home used for business: _____ . Use the Simplified Method Worksheet in the instructions to figure the amount to enter on line 30	30
31	**Net profit or (loss).** Subtract line 30 from line 29. • If a profit, enter on both **Form 1040, line 12** (or **Form 1040NR, line 13**) and on **Schedule SE, line 2**. (If you checked the box on line 1, see instructions). Estates and trusts, enter on **Form 1041, line 3**. • If a loss, you **must** go to line 32.	31
32	If you have a loss, check the box that describes your investment in this activity (see instructions). • If you checked 32a, enter the loss on both **Form 1040, line 12,** (or **Form 1040NR, line 13**) and on **Schedule SE, line 2.** (If you checked the box on line 1, see the line 31 instructions). Estates and trusts, enter on **Form 1041, line 3.** • If you checked 32b, you **must** attach **Form 6198.** Your loss may be limited.	32a ☐ All investment is at risk. 32b ☐ Some investment is not at risk.

For Paperwork Reduction Act Notice, see the separate instructions.   Cat. No. 11334P   Schedule C (Form 1040) 2015

Page **2**

| **Part III** | **Cost of Goods Sold** (see instructions) |

33 Method(s) used to
value closing inventory: **a** ☐ Cost   **b** ☐ Lower of cost or market   **c** ☐ Other (attach explanation)

34 Was there any change in determining quantities, costs, or valuations between opening and closing inventory?
If "Yes," attach explanation . . . . ☐ Yes   ☐ No

35	Inventory at beginning of year. If different from last year's closing inventory, attach explanation . . .	**35**	
36	Purchases less cost of items withdrawn for personal use	**36**	
37	Cost of labor. Do not include any amounts paid to yourself	**37**	
38	Materials and supplies	**38**	
39	Other costs	**39**	
40	Add lines 35 through 39	**40**	
41	Inventory at end of year	**41**	
42	**Cost of goods sold.** Subtract line 41 from line 40. Enter the result here and on line 4	**42**	

| **Part IV** | **Information on Your Vehicle.** Complete this part **only** if you are claiming car or truck expenses on line 9 and are not required to file Form 4562 for this business. See the instructions for line 13 to find out if you must file Form 4562. |

43 When did you place your vehicle in service for business purposes? (month, day, year) ▶ _____ / _____ / _____

44 Of the total number of miles you drove your vehicle during 2015, enter the number of miles you used your vehicle for:

a Business _____   **b** Commuting (see instructions) _____   **c** Other _____

45 Was your vehicle available for personal use during off-duty hours? . . . . ☐ Yes   ☐ No

46 Do you (or your spouse) have another vehicle available for personal use? . . . . ☐ Yes   ☐ No

47a Do you have evidence to support your deduction? . . . . ☐ Yes   ☐ No

b If "Yes," is the evidence written? . . . . ☐ Yes   ☐ No

| **Part V** | **Other Expenses.** List below business expenses not included on lines 8–26 or line 30. |

_____	
_____	
_____	
_____	
_____	
_____	
_____	
_____	

48	**Total other expenses.** Enter here and on line 27a	**48**	

SCHEDULE SE
(Form 1040)

Department of the Treasury
Internal Revenue Service (99)

Self-Employment Tax

▶ Information about Schedule SE and its separate instructions is at *www.irs.gov/schedulese.*

▶ **Attach to Form 1040 or Form 1040NR.**

OMB No. 1545-0074

2015

Attachment
Sequence No. **17**

Name of person with **self-employment** income (as shown on Form 1040 or Form 1040NR)	Social security number of person with **self-employment** income ▶

Before you begin: To determine if you must file Schedule SE, see the instructions.

May I Use Short Schedule SE or Must I Use Long Schedule SE?

Note. Use this flowchart **only if** you must file Schedule SE. If unsure, see *Who Must File Schedule SE* in the instructions.

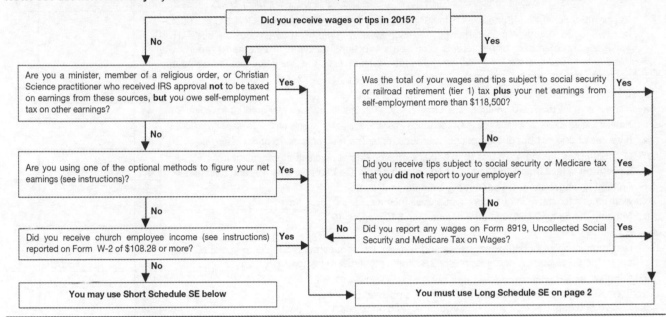

Section A—Short Schedule SE.   Caution. Read above to see if you can use Short Schedule SE.

1a	Net farm profit or (loss) from Schedule F, line 34, and farm partnerships, Schedule K-1 (Form 1065), box 14, code A	**1a**		
b	If you received social security retirement or disability benefits, enter the amount of Conservation Reserve Program payments included on Schedule F, line 4b, or listed on Schedule K-1 (Form 1065), box 20, code Z	**1b**	(	)
2	Net profit or (loss) from Schedule C, line 31; Schedule C-EZ, line 3; Schedule K-1 (Form 1065), box 14, code A (other than farming); and Schedule K-1 (Form 1065-B), box 9, code J1. Ministers and members of religious orders, see instructions for types of income to report on this line. See instructions for other income to report	**2**		
3	Combine lines 1a, 1b, and 2	**3**		
4	Multiply line 3 by 92.35% (.9235). If less than $400, you do not owe self-employment tax; **do not** file this schedule unless you have an amount on line 1b . . . . ▶	**4**		
	Note. If line 4 is less than $400 due to Conservation Reserve Program payments on line 1b, see instructions.			
5	**Self-employment tax.** If the amount on line 4 is:			
	• $118,500 or less, multiply line 4 by 15.3% (.153). Enter the result here and on **Form 1040, line 57, or Form 1040NR, line 55**			
	• More than $118,500, multiply line 4 by 2.9% (.029). Then, add $14,694 to the result. Enter the total here and on **Form 1040, line 57,** or **Form 1040NR, line 55**	**5**		
6	**Deduction for one-half of self-employment tax.** Multiply line 5 by 50% (.50). Enter the result here and on **Form 1040, line 27,** or **Form 1040NR, line 27**	**6**		

For Paperwork Reduction Act Notice, see your tax return instructions.   Cat. No. 11358Z   **Schedule SE (Form 1040) 2015**

Schedule SE (Form 1040) 2015 | Attachment Sequence No. **17** | Page **2**

Name of person with **self-employment** income (as shown on Form 1040 or Form 1040NR)	Social security number of person with **self-employment** income ▶

Section B—Long Schedule SE

Part I   Self-Employment Tax

Note. If your only income subject to self-employment tax is **church employee income,** see instructions. Also see instructions for the definition of church employee income.

A   If you are a minister, member of a religious order, or Christian Science practitioner **and** you filed Form 4361, but you had $400 or more of **other** net earnings from self-employment, check here and continue with Part I . . . . ▶ ☐

1a	Net farm profit or (loss) from Schedule F, line 34, and farm partnerships, Schedule K-1 (Form 1065), box 14, code A. **Note.** Skip lines 1a and 1b if you use the farm optional method (see instructions)	**1a**	
b	If you received social security retirement or disability benefits, enter the amount of Conservation Reserve Program payments included on Schedule F, line 4b, or listed on Schedule K-1 (Form 1065), box 20, code Z	**1b** (	)
2	Net profit or (loss) from Schedule C, line 31; Schedule C-EZ, line 3; Schedule K-1 (Form 1065), box 14, code A (other than farming); and Schedule K-1 (Form 1065-B), box 9, code J1. Ministers and members of religious orders, see instructions for types of income to report on this line. See instructions for other income to report. **Note.** Skip this line if you use the nonfarm optional method (see instructions)	**2**	
3	Combine lines 1a, 1b, and 2	**3**	
4a	If line 3 is more than zero, multiply line 3 by 92.35% (.9235). Otherwise, enter amount from line 3	**4a**	
	Note. If line 4a is less than $400 due to Conservation Reserve Program payments on line 1b, see instructions.		
b	If you elect one or both of the optional methods, enter the total of lines 15 and 17 here . .	**4b**	
c	Combine lines 4a and 4b. If less than $400, **stop;** you do not owe self-employment tax. **Exception.** If less than $400 and you had **church employee income,** enter -0- and continue ▶	**4c**	
5a	Enter your **church employee income** from Form W-2. See instructions for definition of church employee income . . . **5a**		
b	Multiply line 5a by 92.35% (.9235). If less than $100, enter -0-	**5b**	
6	Add lines 4c and 5b	**6**	
7	Maximum amount of combined wages and self-employment earnings subject to social security tax or the 6.2% portion of the 7.65% railroad retirement (tier 1) tax for 2015	**7**	118,500 00
8a	Total social security wages and tips (total of boxes 3 and 7 on Form(s) W-2) and railroad retirement (tier 1) compensation. If $118,500 or more, skip lines 8b through 10, and go to line 11 **8a**		
b	Unreported tips subject to social security tax (from Form 4137, line 10) **8b**		
c	Wages subject to social security tax (from Form 8919, line 10) **8c**		
d	Add lines 8a, 8b, and 8c . . . . ▶	**8d**	
9	Subtract line 8d from line 7. If zero or less, enter -0- here and on line 10 and go to line 11 . ▶	**9**	
10	Multiply the **smaller** of line 6 or line 9 by 12.4% (.124)	**10**	
11	Multiply line 6 by 2.9% (.029)	**11**	
12	**Self-employment tax.** Add lines 10 and 11. Enter here and on **Form 1040, line 57,** or **Form 1040NR, line 55**	**12**	
13	**Deduction for one-half of self-employment tax.** Multiply line 12 by 50% (.50). Enter the result here and on **Form 1040, line 27,** or **Form 1040NR, line 27** **13**		

Part II   Optional Methods To Figure Net Earnings (see instructions)

Farm Optional Method. You may use this method **only** if **(a)** your gross farm income[1] was not more than $7,320, **or (b)** your net farm profits[2] were less than $5,284.

14	Maximum income for optional methods	**14**	4,880 00
15	Enter the **smaller** of: two-thirds (2/3) of gross farm income[1] (not less than zero) **or** $4,880. Also include this amount on line 4b above	**15**	

Nonfarm Optional Method. You may use this method **only** if **(a)** your net nonfarm profits[3] were less than $5,284 and also less than 72.189% of your gross nonfarm income,[4] **and (b)** you had net earnings from self-employment of at least $400 in 2 of the prior 3 years. **Caution.** You may use this method no more than five times.

16	Subtract line 15 from line 14	**16**	
17	Enter the **smaller** of: two-thirds (2/3) of gross nonfarm income[4] (not less than zero) **or** the amount on line 16. Also include this amount on line 4b above	**17**	

[1] From Sch. F, line 9, and Sch. K-1 (Form 1065), box 14, code B.

[2] From Sch. F, line 34, and Sch. K-1 (Form 1065), box 14, code A—minus the amount you would have entered on line 1b had you not used the optional method.

[3] From Sch. C, line 31; Sch. C-EZ, line 3; Sch. K-1 (Form 1065), box 14, code A; and Sch. K-1 (Form 1065-B), box 9, code J1.

[4] From Sch. C, line 7; Sch. C-EZ, line 1; Sch. K-1 (Form 1065), box 14, code C; and Sch. K-1 (Form 1065-B), box 9, code J2.

Schedule SE (Form 1040) 2015

Form **4562**	**Depreciation and Amortization**	OMB No. 1545-0172
Department of the Treasury Internal Revenue Service (99)	**(Including Information on Listed Property)** ▶ Attach to your tax return. ▶ Information about Form 4562 and its separate instructions is at *www.irs.gov/form4562.*	**2015** Attachment Sequence No. **179**

Name(s) shown on return	Business or activity to which this form relates	Identifying number

Part I   Election To Expense Certain Property Under Section 179
Note: If you have any listed property, complete Part V before you complete Part I.

1	Maximum amount (see instructions)	**1**
2	Total cost of section 179 property placed in service (see instructions)	**2**
3	Threshold cost of section 179 property before reduction in limitation (see instructions)	**3**
4	Reduction in limitation. Subtract line 3 from line 2. If zero or less, enter -0-	**4**
5	Dollar limitation for tax year. Subtract line 4 from line 1. If zero or less, enter -0-. If married filing separately, see instructions	**5**

6	(a) Description of property	(b) Cost (business use only)	(c) Elected cost

7	Listed property. Enter the amount from line 29 . . . . **7**	
8	Total elected cost of section 179 property. Add amounts in column (c), lines 6 and 7	**8**
9	Tentative deduction. Enter the **smaller** of line 5 or line 8	**9**
10	Carryover of disallowed deduction from line 13 of your 2014 Form 4562	**10**
11	Business income limitation. Enter the smaller of business income (not less than zero) or line 5 (see instructions)	**11**
12	Section 179 expense deduction. Add lines 9 and 10, but do not enter more than line 11	**12**
13	Carryover of disallowed deduction to 2016. Add lines 9 and 10, less line 12 ▶	**13**

Note: Do not use Part II or Part III below for listed property. Instead, use Part V.

Part II   Special Depreciation Allowance and Other Depreciation (Do not include listed property.**)** (See instructions.)

14	Special depreciation allowance for qualified property (other than listed property) placed in service during the tax year (see instructions)	**14**
15	Property subject to section 168(f)(1) election	**15**
16	Other depreciation (including ACRS)	**16**

Part III   MACRS Depreciation (Do not include listed property.**)** (See instructions.)

Section A

17	MACRS deductions for assets placed in service in tax years beginning before 2015	**17**
18	If you are electing to group any assets placed in service during the tax year into one or more general asset accounts, check here . . . . ▶ ☐	

Section B—Assets Placed in Service During 2015 Tax Year Using the General Depreciation System

(a) Classification of property	(b) Month and year placed in service	(c) Basis for depreciation (business/investment use only—see instructions)	(d) Recovery period	(e) Convention	(f) Method	(g) Depreciation deduction
19a 3-year property						
b 5-year property						
c 7-year property						
d 10-year property						
e 15-year property						
f 20-year property						
g 25-year property			25 yrs.		S/L	
h Residential rental property			27.5 yrs.	MM	S/L	
			27.5 yrs.	MM	S/L	
i Nonresidential real property			39 yrs.	MM	S/L	
				MM	S/L	

Section C—Assets Placed in Service During 2015 Tax Year Using the Alternative Depreciation System

20a Class life					S/L	
b 12-year			12 yrs.		S/L	
c 40-year			40 yrs.	MM	S/L	

Part IV   Summary (See instructions.)

21	Listed property. Enter amount from line 28	**21**
22	**Total.** Add amounts from line 12, lines 14 through 17, lines 19 and 20 in column (g), and line 21. Enter here and on the appropriate lines of your return. Partnerships and S corporations—see instructions	**22**
23	For assets shown above and placed in service during the current year, enter the portion of the basis attributable to section 263A costs **23**	

For Paperwork Reduction Act Notice, see separate instructions.	Cat. No. 12906N	Form **4562** (2015)

Watermark: DRAFT AS OF August 21, 2015 DO NOT FILE

Form 4562 (2015)   Page **2**

Part V   Listed Property (Include automobiles, certain other vehicles, certain aircraft, certain computers, and property used for entertainment, recreation, or amusement.)

Note: For any vehicle for which you are using the standard mileage rate or deducting lease expense, complete **only** 24a, 24b, columns (a) through (c) of Section A, all of Section B, and Section C if applicable.

Section A—Depreciation and Other Information (Caution: See the instructions for limits for passenger automobiles.)

24a Do you have evidence to support the business/investment use claimed? ☐ Yes ☐ No   **24b** If "Yes," is the evidence written? ☐ Yes ☐ No

(a) Type of property (list vehicles first)	(b) Date placed in service	(c) Business/investment use percentage	(d) Cost or other basis	(e) Basis for depreciation (business/investment use only)	(f) Recovery period	(g) Method/Convention	(h) Depreciation deduction	(i) Elected section 179 cost
25 Special depreciation allowance for qualified listed property placed in service during the tax year and used more than 50% in a qualified business use (see instructions) .					**25**			
26 Property used more than 50% in a qualified business use:								
		%						
		%						
		%						
27 Property used 50% or less in a qualified business use:								
		%				S/L –		
		%				S/L –		
		%				S/L –		
28 Add amounts in column (h), lines 25 through 27. Enter here and on line 21, page 1 .						**28**		
29 Add amounts in column (i), line 26. Enter here and on line 7, page 1							**29**	

Section B—Information on Use of Vehicles

Complete this section for vehicles used by a sole proprietor, partner, or other "more than 5% owner," or related person. If you provided vehicles to your employees, first answer the questions in Section C to see if you meet an exception to completing this section for those vehicles.

	(a) Vehicle 1		(b) Vehicle 2		(c) Vehicle 3		(d) Vehicle 4		(e) Vehicle 5		(f) Vehicle 6	
30 Total business/investment miles driven during the year (**do not** include commuting miles) .												
31 Total commuting miles driven during the year												
32 Total other personal (noncommuting) miles driven												
33 Total miles driven during the year. Add lines 30 through 32												
34 Was the vehicle available for personal use during off-duty hours?	Yes	No	Yes	No	Yes	No	Yes	No	Yes	No	Yes	No
35 Was the vehicle used primarily by a more than 5% owner or related person? . .												
36 Is another vehicle available for personal use?												

Section C—Questions for Employers Who Provide Vehicles for Use by Their Employees

Answer these questions to determine if you meet an exception to completing Section B for vehicles used by employees who **are not** more than 5% owners or related persons (see instructions).

		Yes	No
37	Do you maintain a written policy statement that prohibits all personal use of vehicles, including commuting, by your employees?		
38	Do you maintain a written policy statement that prohibits personal use of vehicles, except commuting, by your employees? See the instructions for vehicles used by corporate officers, directors, or 1% or more owners . .		
39	Do you treat all use of vehicles by employees as personal use?		
40	Do you provide more than five vehicles to your employees, obtain information from your employees about the use of the vehicles, and retain the information received?		
41	Do you meet the requirements concerning qualified automobile demonstration use? (See instructions.) . . .		

Note: If your answer to 37, 38, 39, 40, or 41 is "Yes," do not complete Section B for the covered vehicles.

Part VI   Amortization

(a) Description of costs	(b) Date amortization begins	(c) Amortizable amount	(d) Code section	(e) Amortization period or percentage	(f) Amortization for this year
42 Amortization of costs that begins during your 2015 tax year (see instructions):					
43 Amortization of costs that began before your 2015 tax year				**43**	
44 **Total.** Add amounts in column (f). See the instructions for where to report				**44**	

Form **4562** (2015)

Form **8829**

Department of the Treasury
Internal Revenue Service (99)

Expenses for Business Use of Your Home

▶ File only with Schedule C (Form 1040). Use a separate Form 8829 for each
home you used for business during the year.

▶ Information about Form 8829 and its separate instructions is at *www.irs.gov/form8829.*

OMB No. 1545-0074

2015

Attachment
Sequence No. **176**

Name(s) of proprietor(s)

Your social security number

Part I   Part of Your Home Used for Business

1	Area used regularly and exclusively for business, regularly for daycare, or for storage of inventory or product samples (see instructions)	**1**	
2	Total area of home	**2**	
3	Divide line 1 by line 2. Enter the result as a percentage	**3**	%

For daycare facilities not used exclusively for business, go to line 4. All others, go to line 7.

4	Multiply days used for daycare during year by hours used per day	**4**		hr.
5	Total hours available for use during the year (365 days x 24 hours) (see instructions)	**5**	8,760	hr.
6	Divide line 4 by line 5. Enter the result as a decimal amount . . .	**6**	.	
7	Business percentage. For daycare facilities not used exclusively for business, multiply line 6 by line 3 (enter the result as a percentage). All others, enter the amount from line 3 . . . . . ▶	**7**		%

Part II   Figure Your Allowable Deduction

8	Enter the amount from Schedule C, line 29, **plus** any gain derived from the business use of your home, **minus** any loss from the trade or business not derived from the business use of your home (see instructions)		**8**	

See instructions for columns **(a)** and **(b)** before completing lines 9–21.

			(a) Direct expenses	**(b)** Indirect expenses		
9	Casualty losses (see instructions).	**9**				
10	Deductible mortgage interest (see instructions)	**10**				
11	Real estate taxes (see instructions)	**11**				
12	Add lines 9, 10, and 11	**12**				
13	Multiply line 12, column (b) by line 7		**13**			
14	Add line 12, column (a) and line 13				**14**	
15	Subtract line 14 from line 8. If zero or less, enter -0-				**15**	
16	Excess mortgage interest (see instructions) .	**16**				
17	Insurance	**17**				
18	Rent	**18**				
19	Repairs and maintenance	**19**				
20	Utilities	**20**				
21	Other expenses (see instructions).	**21**				
22	Add lines 16 through 21	**22**				
23	Multiply line 22, column (b) by line 7		**23**			
24	Carryover of prior year operating expenses (see instructions) . .		**24**			
25	Add line 22, column (a), line 23, and line 24				**25**	
26	Allowable operating expenses. Enter the **smaller** of line 15 or line 25				**26**	
27	Limit on excess casualty losses and depreciation. Subtract line 26 from line 15				**27**	
28	Excess casualty losses (see instructions)		**28**			
29	Depreciation of your home from line 41 below		**29**			
30	Carryover of prior year excess casualty losses and depreciation (see instructions)		**30**			
31	Add lines 28 through 30				**31**	
32	Allowable excess casualty losses and depreciation. Enter the **smaller** of line 27 or line 31 . .				**32**	
33	Add lines 14, 26, and 32				**33**	
34	Casualty loss portion, if any, from lines 14 and 32. Carry amount to **Form 4684** (see instructions)				**34**	
35	**Allowable expenses for business use of your home.** Subtract line 34 from line 33. Enter here and on Schedule C, line 30. If your home was used for more than one business, see instructions ▶				**35**	

Part III   Depreciation of Your Home

36	Enter the **smaller** of your home's adjusted basis or its fair market value (see instructions) . .	**36**	
37	Value of land included on line 36	**37**	
38	Basis of building. Subtract line 37 from line 36	**38**	
39	Business basis of building. Multiply line 38 by line 7.	**39**	
40	Depreciation percentage (see instructions).	**40**	%
41	Depreciation allowable (see instructions). Multiply line 39 by line 40. Enter here and on line 29 above	**41**	

Part IV   Carryover of Unallowed Expenses to 2016

42	Operating expenses. Subtract line 26 from line 25. If less than zero, enter -0-	**42**	
43	Excess casualty losses and depreciation. Subtract line 32 from line 31. If less than zero, enter -0-	**43**	

For Paperwork Reduction Act Notice, see your tax return instructions.   Cat. No. 13232M   Form **8829** (2015)

Using Redleaf Record-Keeping Tools

This chart shows how the books in the Redleaf business series work together to help you prepare and pay your taxes and communicate with the IRS. If you use these resources throughout the tax year, it will be much easier to complete your tax forms at the end of the year.

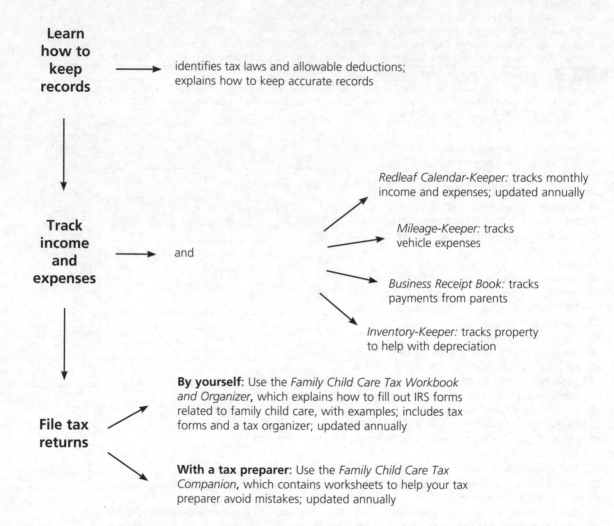

Learn how to keep records → identifies tax laws and allowable deductions; explains how to keep accurate records

Track income and expenses → and →

Redleaf Calendar-Keeper: tracks monthly income and expenses; updated annually

Mileage-Keeper: tracks vehicle expenses

Business Receipt Book: tracks payments from parents

Inventory-Keeper: tracks property to help with depreciation

File tax returns

By yourself: Use the *Family Child Care Tax Workbook and Organizer*, which explains how to fill out IRS forms related to family child care, with examples; includes tax forms and a tax organizer; updated annually

With a tax preparer: Use the *Family Child Care Tax Companion*, which contains worksheets to help your tax preparer avoid mistakes; updated annually